**Abdul Aziz ibn Abdur Rahman ibn Faisal as Saud**
Age: 33                    Kuwait, March 1910

# IBN SAUD
## King by Conquest

By NESTOR SANDER

International Standard Book Number: 1-58736-0179 (hard cover)
Library of Congress Control Number: 00-110018

Published by Hats Off Books™
610 East Delano Street, Suite 104, Tucson, Arizona 85705, U.S.A.
www.hatsoffbooks.com

Book design by Atilla Vékony

Printed in the United States of America

# CONTENTS

# Contents

## PART III: THE MAN (95–121)

# PLATES

# Contents

## MAPS

# SOURCES

## PLATES

DATES NOT ENCLOSED ARE PUBLICATION DATES. DATES IN PARENTHESES INDICATE YEAR PHOTO WAS TAKEN.

RGS =ROYAL GEOGRAPHICAL SOCIETY  MEC=MIDDLE EAST CENTRE, ST. ANTONY'S COLLEGE, OXFORD

Permission to use photographs was obtained from H. St. J. B. Philby's estate (Pl. III, figs. 6–7 A. X); the Middle East Centre, St Antony's College, Oxford (Pl. VII, fig. 22); The Royal Geographical Society (Pl. VI, fig. 15, Pl. VIII, fig. 27, Pl. XI, frontispiece and jacket photo); the Ameen Rihani organization (Pl. XII); Frank Cass (Pl. III, fig. 5, Pl. VI, fig. 16, A. VII); AMIDEAST Pl. VII, fig. 23); Black Star (Pl. IX, fig. 36); Fox (Pl. VII, figs. 21, 24); Imperial War Museum (Plate VII, fig. 21).

# MAPS

# TEXT FIGURES

# TEXT

Many sources gave permission to quote text. The source of most quotations is identified by publication date and author; some provide the page number in the text quoted. Through the author's name the source is identifiable from the bibliography. The entities that have authorized quotations are: H. St. J. B. Philby's Estate, the widow of Daniel van der Meulen, Random House for Jonathan Cape, University of California (Berkeley) Press, The Ameen Rihani Organization, Frank Cass Publishers, HarperCollins Publishers for George Allen and Undwin and Penguin Putnam for E. P. Dutton & Company. Note 10, quotations from from Sir Wilfred Thesiger's 'Arabian Sands,' (1959) was authorized by Curtis Brown, the copyright holder (Copyright © Wilfred Thesiger 1959). I was unable to locate the copyright holder for Gerald de Gaury's works, published by Harrap and Company.

# Foreword

This book adds another to the many recitals of the Ibn Saud saga. But it also attempts to evoke his persona, and to show how it, along with his physical, intellectual, and moral endowments, enabled him to recover his heritage. The undertaking required perusal of the many books, reports, and journals written about him, and examination of his correspondence with peers and other governments. Some of the accounts written by visitors to or members of his court and many of the books and articles by later biographers and commentators infer specific motives from his actions and statements or consider them as indications of traits of character. The validity of these judgments is at best conjectural, in view of the man's high level of intelligence and the complexity of his commitments.

My conclusion is that no completely objective account of Ibn Saud's career or his person exists. Many of these representations are more or less biased because of personal feeling or prejudice. None are truly objective because all human observation is inherently subjective and interpretative. Small wonder that the narratives penned by chroniclers of the acts, words, or writings of Ibn Saud differ so much that the details of many incidents are lost in a dense fog of speculation.

A good example is the great disparity in the accounts of the death of one member of the long-time Saud enemy, the Ar Rashid family. There are at least three radically different versions of the events leading to his demise, which agree only in that it occurred before dawn from gunshot wounds at a site known as Raudhat al Muhanna. Other uncertainties among a host include: Was the Riyadh exploit of January 1902 premeditated by Ibn Saud before his departure from Kuwait, or did he decide to attempt a coup only after the arrival of the troop at Ain Haradh? What were the true reasons for his apparently inopportune withdrawal from the Qasim in the spring of 1905 and his subsequent journey to al Hasa in August? Were the first attacks on the Hejaz in 1924 carefully orchestrated as most authors suggest, or were they haphazard as Philby insists?

Was his long association with the British only a ploy to insure their support and to gain a subsidy? It is clear that his relation with at least two and perhaps several British officials was truly that of friendship and regard. Yet in the First World War he avoided an active role in support of the Allies, and in the Second remained uncommitted until the outcome was clear.

I attempt to point out differences in the published accounts of some of the decisive moments in the life of this man and have assembled a number of the comments about and descriptions of his aspect and character. One thing is certain. All of his actions were intended to safeguard his dynasty against any eventuality. He used every means his superior intellect could devise and exercised all of his well-documented charisma to that end. The state he founded has endured for a century, and is still guided by his offspring, who hold their father and his achievements in deep respect. The religious tenets he espoused are to this day the law of the land.

While collating information from publications about the man and his exploits, I found understandable the diversity in the motivations ascribed his actions and deeds but could not comprehend the reasons for differences in affirmations of fact. For example, until recently Ibn Saud's birth was widely accepted to have been in the year 1880, although two contemporaries who talked with him and later wrote about their experiences, Gertrude Bell and Amin Rihani, indicate without ambiguity that the year was 1876. *(See Note 2; hereafter n._.)* Lacey must be commended for obtaining confirmation of this date. But like other authors he overlooks explicit statements about the age of the Saudi ruler in these earlier publications, although quoting from both of them on other matters.

I found it expedient in recounting the achievements of this remarkable man to discuss the Saudi state during Ibn Saud's lifetime—its nature, growth, and survival in spite of grave difficulties. His masterly handling of foreign relations is reviewed at some length. I relate how the first concessions were acquired and the effects of the discovery of oil in commercial quantities on the economy of this then mainly pastoral state, for without the exploitation of this vast store of energy his sons would not govern today.

The third and last portion of the main text is an attempt to depict the man as his contemporaries saw him and to evaluate his work. It is followed by notes enlarging on or explaining thirty-one items of interest. Three essays to enlighten the general reader and seven brief biographies or sketches of contemporaries important in Ibn Saud's career are appended along with an annotated bibliography. In this work, judgments regarding the man and opinions concerning the writings about him and his contemporaries are my own. *Quantum animis erroris in est.*

# IBN SAUD: KING BY CONQUEST

## INTRODUCTION

On 1 May 1939, after dinner with him in the new mess hall, I gripped briefly the scarred, long-fingered, sinewy hand of the first king of Saudi Arabia: Abdul Aziz ibn Abdur Rahman ibn Faisal ibn Turki as Saud (n. 1). To him it was a gesture of goodwill toward us Americans who had found oil in his land; to me it was a moment of deep respect tinged with deference. By force of arms and consummate statecraft he had won undisputed and absolute sway over 865,000 square miles, a realm four times the size of France. He looked the part. Towering over my six feet, he was every inch the sovereign in dignity and commanding presence. At the moment jovial, he smiled at me, but the furrows on his leathery tan face attested that for forty of his sixty-two years he had waged war and exercised masterly diplomacy to establish and to safeguard his kingdom (n. 2). The black patch over his left eye, full lips, prominent nose and scanty black beard gave him the look of a freebooter, but the deep-set, dark right eye asserted the authority of unlimited power and belied the kindness of his smile.

He was garbed as a paramount shaikh. Most of his dark, long hair was covered by a red- and white-checked head scarf held in place by a two-tiered gold thread and black wool headdress—an emblem of high rank—ornate when compared with the plain black wool circlets worn by his followers. A collarless, shirt-like robe of white cotton was buttoned at the neck and reached the feet shod in open-toed brown leather sandals. Over his shoulders he wore a nut-brown, lightly woven, floor-length camels' hair cloak edged in golden passementerie that lent elegance to the flowing, long-sleeved garment. At his waist hung a heavy dagger of deeply enchased massive gold, the blunt end of its broad silver-encrusted sheath turned at a right angle to the hilt.

Ibn Saud had followed some 200 miles of trails and had crossed barriers of treacherous sand in the journey from Riyadh, his capital, to Jebel Dhahran near the Persian Gulf. He had accepted an invitation to open the valve of a pipeline at Ras Tanura, the newly constructed tanker-loading terminal some 25 miles north of our camp at Dhahran. This symbolic gesture would start the flow of crude oil to fill a tanker making the first direct delivery by sea of 'Arabian Light' from mainland Arabia to Europe.

1

The arrival of the king and his party had been spectacular. On either side of the windshield of his speeding black Chrysler sedan stood a very tall and black Somali soldier, long, vividly red robes flying in the wind *(Plate I, figs. 1 and 2; hereafter Pl._)*. Both were armed with a long sword in a black scabbard, a dagger, a pistol, and a magazine rifle slung over crossed bandoliers. This equipage was followed by some twenty open-bodied trucks filled with shouting, white-robed bodyguards brandishing weapons.

Tents were set up just south of the cluster of buildings of our camp, and soon cauldrons of rice and mutton were boiling to be served on yard-wide, round copper trays *(Pl. II, fig. 3)*. Evening prayer ended, feasting began. Then a dance by long lines of solemn-faced, white-clad retainers who, planted in place and chanting monotonously, rocked from one foot to the other to the monotonous beat of a great drum. From time to time one would step forward, lift his rifle, and fire into the air.

*But that was sixty odd years ago. Now free of other tasks after helping to find crude oil in many countries, I recalled that encounter and decided to learn more about the man. He made such a strong impression that I can still recall every detail of our meeting. I am not alone. All those who have recorded their judgments concerning his aspect, personality and qualities of mind are unanimous in finding him exceptional in all three. And their number is considerable. (See annotated bibliography.) I have consulted many of their writings in preparing this appreciation of a man who founded a kingdom that has existed for nearly a century in a land where no previous régime had endured so long. Like the other studies of his eventful career, mine is chronological in describing the deeds of the warrior intent on recovering his ancestral holdings. It differs in that I choose to discuss his qualities of mind and character apart, and to examine their effect on his governance of a land that had remained essentially unchanged since the time of Abraham.*

Fig. 1. On either side of the windshield of his speeding black Chrysler sedan stood a very tall and black Somali soldier, long, vividly red robes flying in the wind.

Fig. 2. ... armed with a long sword in a black scabbard, a dagger, a pistol, and a magazine rifle.

# THE KING ARRIVES

PLATE II
Figs. 3, 4

Fig. 3. Tents were set up just south of the cluster of buildings of our camp, and soon cauldrons of rice and mutton were boiling, to be served on round, yard-wide copper trays.

Fig. 4. ... solemn-faced, white-clad retainers....

# Part I:

# Conflict and Coalescence

# (1890–1934)

# CONFLICT AND COALESCENCE

## Nadir of the Sauds (1890–1901)

**Proem:** In an impoverished land where nomadic folkways *(n. 10)* under patriarchal leadership had for centuries insured survival, ties of family were paramount. Outsiders were fair game. Under such circumstances alliances between tribes were short-lived, except those based on kinship or long tradition. Ibn Saud was the first of his line to create lasting loyalty or at least enduring respect for his house in families and tribes other than his own, and to require their acceptance of his sovereignty as *al malik*—the king. In large part he accomplished this by using traditional methods of carrot and stick, but with a carrot juicier and a stick often heavier than those of his ancestors. Like them he used religious fanaticism to kindle the ardor of his warriors, but fully aware of the unreliability and fickleness of nomads he induced them to accept a new way of life that made them both steadfast in battle and loyal to him as their leader.

Despite the prowess of his armies, Ibn Saud's realm was never to become as large as the vast empire controlled by his great-great grandfather in the first decade of the nineteenth century. Yet his achievements were truly remarkable.

Starting with nothing but his name he regained the Saudi patrimony and kept it. To accomplish this he overcame a plethora of enemies: the Turkish Empire, neighboring Arab princes, recalcitrant tribes *(see Addendum I, hereafter A. I, etc.)*, some members of his family, and for a time certain factions in the British government. Because of internecine sibling rivalry none of his immediate forbears had been able to do this *(A. II)*.

**Debacle:** In 1890 when our story begins, the fortunes of the As Saud (the family) had declined markedly as the result of a long struggle for supremacy *(n. 3)* between two of Ibn Saud's four paternal uncles—Abdullah ibn Faisal, the titular ruler, and a pretender, Saud ibn Faisal. *(See genealogical chart in A. II.)* Now both were dead. The paramount shaikh of the Shammar tribe *(see tribal map in A. I)*, Mohammed ibn Abdullah ar Rashid, had for years taken advantage of their strife to seize most of the Saudi lands and to suborn the loyalty of the inhabitants. In his own lands he had gained ascendancy over his sibling congeners through a

5

series of brutal murders of both adults and children. Thereafter, a consummate autocrat, he had enlarged his domain both to the north and to the south.

Only now, in the first year of the last decade of the 19th century, did a third brother, Abdur Rahman, take command of the resources in men and property remaining to the Saud family. He began to rebuild sway over the remnants of his domain, although forced to acknowledge Rashidi hegemony.

Mohammed ibn Abdullah ar Rashid decided to eliminate this last obstacle to his autocracy. His military governor, installed in the Saudi capital, Riyadh, requested a meeting with the Sauds to present his good wishes on the occasion of the feast day commemorating Abraham's willingness to sacrifice Ishmael (not Isaac) at God's command. This event is celebrated annually as one of the rites of the Pilgrimage to Mecca, the *Hajj*.

The governor informed Abdur Rahman that his master had asked all the males of the Saud family to be present when he came to visit them on the first day of the fête, the *Id al Adha*, for he carried a message of friendship from his lord, the amir of Haïl. This gesture from a long-time enemy of the family must have aroused suspicion. In any event, Abdur Rahman maintained good relations with certain shaikhs and amirs now nominally under the aegis of ibn Rashid, and from them or from his own agents had word that the governor's true purpose was assassination. Several accounts say that he agreed to receive the emissary and his party in the Great Hall of the Saudi palace. The deputation of at least ten (probably more if extirpation of the family was the plan) entered the hall, but only one, the leader, is said to have escaped death. One sensational account has him too seized and thrown into a well as he sat down to dine with the Saud family. A slaughter took place, but its details are lost.

When ibn Rashid learned of the fate of his mission he hastily assembled a large force and led it to Riyadh. Upon arrival he began a siege and blockade. Unable to overcome the defenses of the town—a mud-brick wall twenty-five feet high and three feet thick—he ordered the palm groves and gardens of the neighboring oases to be destroyed. After forty days of investment the people pleaded with Abdur Rahman to negotiate a truce. They were starving and eager to avoid the destruction of the last of their groves.

Abdur Rahman's older brother, Mohammed, who had aided the legitimate heir Abdullah in his struggle with Saud, headed the negotiators. The thirteen-year-old Abdul Aziz accompanied the party, perhaps as a surety for the good faith of his father, Abdur Rahman. It was his first appearance in affairs of state. The conference was held outside the walled town in ibn Rashid's great tent where ceremonial protocol governed the proceedings.

Discussion between the parties went on for many hours. The agreement reached left Abdur Rahman amir (governor) of Aridh, the central province, but required that he do nothing against ibn Rashid's interests. The mildness of the terms, not the first leniency that ibn Rashid had shown the As Saud, may have had its roots in the fact that one of Abdur Rahman's wives was of ibn Rashid's family. But this surmise appears contrary to ibn Rashid's nature and to the then current attitude toward marriage.

After his return to Haïl, ibn Rashid continued to make demands on the people of the Qasim, the most fertile area of the former Saudi demesne. *(See Loca-*

*tion Maps 1 and 2.*) He appointed new governors to enforce his will in the towns, and imposed new taxes on the tribes. Abdur Rahman learned of these exactions and of the ill-feeling they engendered. So, in an attempt to regain his heritage he conspired to take the field with the malcontents: the 'Anaiza tribe and men from the town of Buraida. In January 1891, before Abdur Rahman's contingent had reached the Qasim these allies attacked ibn Rashid's Shammar tribesmen. For a time they held the upper hand in the skirmishing, but on 21 January ibn Rashid's experienced cavalry won the battle at a site called Mulaida, not far from Buraida. Allied losses in the bloody strife included many of the leaders and six hundred men.

News of the defeat of his allies reached Abdur Rahman when he was well on the way to join them. Victory was no longer possible. If he were caught his head would be forfeited. Posting back to Riyadh he decided to avoid capture by going to the great sea of sand in the far south where ibn Rashid's writ did not reach.

**Hegira:** So, on a cold night early in February a procession of groaning camels and a few horses left Riyadh through one of its nine entryways, the Thamairi gate (*Pl. III, fig. 7*). The plodding beasts carried several servants and Abdur Rahman's numerous family. Abdul Aziz was the fourth child, with two older brothers and a sister, Nura. He was fourteen and probably found the almost furtive flight amusing as he bestrode his *dhalul* (riding camel). After a few days of travel eastward, his father left them. Abdur Rahman wanted to avoid being interrogated or worse by the Turks in al Hasa because seventeen years before he had incited a revolt of local tribes there. Too, because ibn Rashid was nominally a friend and ally of the Turks, he might well have asked them to detain the remaining adult male of the house of Saud capable of inciting resistance to his rule.

The mother and her children continued the 230-mile journey to Bahrain island where Abdul Aziz was treated for an illness now thought to be rheumatic fever. After three months the family left Bahrain and journeyed south to the fringes of a sea of sand, the Rub' al Khali (the Empty Quarter to us; *ar Ramla*, the sands, to its inhabitants). Abdur Rahman escorted them with a guard of Murra, members of a tribe that had never accepted ibn Rashid's domination. For nearly two years the family lived among them. Abdul Aziz immersed himself in the their customs, improving his desert skills. In later life he often used for effect the idiom and accent of the Al Murra, the most adept of the nomadic tribes in coping with the harshest of environments and unsurpassed as trackers of man or beast.

During this time Abdur Rahman returned to Nejd in an attempt to get help in regaining his position of amir. Some accounts report that he fought his way to the walls of Haïl, the Rashidi capital, where his force was badly mauled. More probably it was at or near Riyadh that he met defeat. Then, recognizing the hopelessness of his cause, he returned to his family in the sands and took them north to Qatar, the broad peninsula south of Bahrain island. There he asked the shaikh to approach the small Turkish garrison and arrange an interview for him with their headquarters in Hofuf, an outpost of the mighty Ottoman Empire. Probably to his surprise, these authorities proffered help in recovering his domain, provided that he accept their tutelage. Perhaps the offer was made only because the Sublime Porte considered ibn Rashid's fief too large and his power too great for their peace of mind and would have liked a counterbalance to his sway. The Saudi refugee refused their proposal of armed assistance, but agreed to their offer of asylum in Kuwait for the women of the family, an offer later (early 1895?) extended to the As Saud males.

The prudent Turks also offered Abdur Rahman a small subsidy: sixty Turkish pounds a month. After all, his family was of the élite ruling class and might be useful in the future. The shaikh of Kuwait would recognize the kudos and other possible advantages in harboring such a distinguished fugitive. But the indolent shaikh delayed his acceptance of the family and offered no subvention or other aid, probably because he feared ibn Rashid's ire. The new guests had to put up with his neglect for only a short time after their arrival. On 18 May 1896 he and his brother were murdered by a sibling, Mubarak as Sabah *(A. III, Pl. XI)*, who was to become the friend and mentor of Ibn Saud.

**Refuge:** The exiles settled into what can be described as a plebian existence, broken for Abdur Rahman and Abdul Aziz by forays into the hinterland. Some of them were attempts to regain the fealty of former lieges, some to win loot, for the Turkish subsidy was far from generous. The family's quarters were very ordinary—a flat-roofed, three-room, mud-brick house—in a town not noted for its sanitation or cleanliness. The number of mouths to feed was considerable—four sons and at least as many daughters, along with a few slaves. Later, their number increased to eight sons and sixteen daughters. In spite of his modest means Abdur Rahman saw to it that his sons had a good education. Schooling for Abdul Aziz had begun in Riyadh at the age of seven. His instructor was a *qadi* (judge) who taught him to read and to memorize the Koran. In Kuwait his education continued with strict attention to Wahhabi tenets, the puritan dogma that prohibited some activities common in the Middle East: smoking, drinking alcohol, playing musical instruments, extravagance in dress, and mourning the dead or marking their graves.

Because of his imposing build and strength Abdul Aziz soon won renown as a warrior. He led lucrative raids against the tribes allied with ibn Rashid. This attracted many a poor nomad to follow him. Thus he honed his skills as a leader in battle.

But his stay in Kuwait prepared him for much more than a warrior's career. Kuwait was a major port for the transshipment to the interior of goods from the Far East, India, Europe, and Africa. It was the queen of the pearl fisheries and a market place where the nomads bought necessities and sold their livestock. In the closing years of the nineteenth century all the European powers sent representatives or agents to the Persian Gulf because of the mounting interest in a railway from Turkey or the Levant to the Gulf.

As the son of a man of importance and a protégé of the shaikh, Abdul Aziz was privileged to attend the daily *majlis*, the council and court, where foreign emissaries were received, business was transacted, licenses and permits were granted, and justice rendered. He saw the shaikh's dealings with envoys, merchants, slavers, traders, thieves and murderers, even householders' disputes.

All matters were resolved according to Koranic tenets or to the codes of law sanctioned by ancient custom.

After 1899 the shaikh was protected by Britain. His young friend saw at first hand the posture of the British representatives, straightforward when compared to the devious maneuvers of the Turkish envoys. For many years thereafter Ibn Saud professed full confidence in British fairness and honesty, but after a time he raged privately against what he considered Albion's duplicity. In any event, his lifelong interest in foreign affairs must have begun in Mubarak's council hall. This period of education was to stand Ibn Saud in good stead, but it ended suddenly.

In the spring of 1900 Abdur Rahman led a raid on the Qahtan tribe, ancestral to ar Rashid's Shammar. He had found that conditions in Nejd favored revolt, for Mohammed ibn Abdullah ar Rashid, the consummate autocrat, had died in December 1897. His successor, Abdul Aziz ibn Mitab ar Rashid was equally war-minded, but less skilled in government, often alienating his people through harshness, extortion and duplicity.

In that lack of comprehension, Mubarak saw an opportunity to become paramount shaikh in northern Arabia and Abdur Rahman wanted to regain his former status. Between them they recruited a force of about ten thousand (*n. 5*) from the Ajman, Suhul, Mutair and Murra tribes, along with Muntafiq from the Basra area. Late in January 1901 this army left Kuwait and in mid-February reached the Shauki Valley west of the Dahana sand belts. The people of this agricultural region had been harshly treated by the Rashids and many flocked to Mubarak's standard. Ibn Rashid met the challenge.

On 18 March 1901 battle was joined near the village of Tarafiya, fifteen miles northeast of Buraida. The confederation of tribes and townsmen attacked but was hurled back in great disorder because of defection during the fray by the Muntafiq and Ajman. The survivors fled in all haste back to Kuwait. Losses had been high.

After punishing the rebellious towns in the Qasim whose warriors had fought against him, ibn Rashid's army closed on Kuwait with the intention of taking the town. A large force gathered to oppose the invaders and a British warship, the gunboat *Perseus*, helped to drive them off with a threat of bombardment. This ship and others, not all British, were in the area because of German pretensions to a position in the Middle East, the *Drang nach Osten*, at this time centered on a railroad to Basra or Kuwait from Turkey or the Levant. Russia had a similar project in Persia, planned to run from the Caspian Sea to the Persian Gulf.

Ibn Saud was not with the vanquished army. He had been detached long before the battle to head a small force with the mission of creating a diversion in Nejd. Many nomads joined him as he rode south. After taking some loot from supporters of ibn Rashid he reached Riyadh. With his small force he could not take the fort, but he could isolate it because the town wall, partially destroyed after Abdur Rahman's flight ten years before, had been left in ruins. When he learned of the disaster in the Qasim he at once quit the blockade of nearly four months. But he had seen the state of the defenses of Riyadh, in particular the crumbling wall.

*Was it then that he decided on a plan to recover his heritage?*

# Steps Upward (1902–1912)

After consulting his father and winning the approval and support of Shaikh Mubarak (*Pl. XI*), Ibn Saud decided to act. Was the venture he was to embark on planned only as a razzia, as most authors suggest, or had he already determined to attempt to restore his family to its high estate? He was almost twenty-five years old. Thrice married, he had two living wives and a son, Turki. Surely it was time to free himself and his family from dependence on a meager stipend from the Turks and the uncertain income from raids.

*Would a man of his stock be content to continue only as a leader of forays? If not, concealment of his true purpose was essential, for spies were everywhere. Raiding would serve to dissimulate his intent.*

**Prologue:** In the autumn of 1901 Abdul Aziz left Kuwait with an older half-brother Mohammed (*Pl. XI*), three cousins, four more distant relatives, and about fifty followers from the tribes of eastern Arabia. They were mounted on riding camels, *dhulul*, some ridden double. With Ibn Saud's servant and his bodyguard, both slaves, the troop totaled sixty (*n. 6*). The band was soon joined by nomads eager to share in the plunder and derring-do of the nearly bloodless raids, a form of gainful employment age-old in the desert. For a time the forays were successful, garnering many camels near the village of Majma'a two hundred miles southwest of Kuwait. But the looted tribes and ibn Rashid's supporters began to fight back and Turkish patrols had to be avoided. So, four months after its departure from Kuwait the band of several hundred shrank as prospects of easy booty vanished. Too, Ramadan was near, the month of daylight fasting when raiding usually ceased. Ibn Saud stopped his forays and retreated southward, ignoring a request from his father to return to Kuwait.

*Many accounts say that he was unable to return to Kuwait because he was blocked by ibn Rashid's forces, but the desert is like the sea, except that there are watering places, most of which are generally known and can be denied in time of war. The Turks had few troops and could occupy continuously only one or two wells or oases near the coast. Messengers from ibn Rashid could have insured that the raiders had no access to water in places occupied by his supporters, but it is unlikely that this mighty shaikh would put his soldier-tribesmen on a war-time footing merely to stop a ghazzu.*

**Decision (?):** A messenger from Kuwait found Ibn Saud to warn him that ibn Rashid had asked the Turks to capture him. He and his band were camped in southern al Hasa at a well called Ain Haradh. According to some published accounts this site was his Rubicon, but was it in fact only then that he decided to retake Riyadh? All agree that it was only then that he asked his followers to undertake the perilous mission, but it was only then that he could be sure that no one would return to Kuwait to betray his purpose, for the fate of anyone who chose not to join him might have been uncertain. Among the sixty he could be sure only of his brother, seven other relatives and his two slaves. The loyalty of the rest was doubtful for most were from other tribes. Hence the oath of fealty to him and his cause that he demanded from them, and his pledge of fidelity to them, a pact made much of by some writers.

The party then moved fifty miles farther south to the Jabrin oasis. Only the Murra frequented it, for its ponds are at the northern edge of the Rub' al Khali and in summer its far-flung palm groves were hotbeds of malarial fever. There the now oath-bound sixty passed the first days of the month of Ramadan secure from prying eyes, for the Murra, like many of the tribes of southern Nejd and Asir owed no allegiance to the Rashids.

On 23 December 1901, almost three weeks before the new moon would mark the end of Ramadan, the small troop left its covert and set out for Riyadh, two hundred miles to the northwest. It avoided the usual watering places both for security and because in the cool of winter the camels drank only every ninth day, or with good forage, not at all. Leisurely night marches punctuated by long halts to avoid detection by travelers and Bedu shepherds found them on the evening of 12 January 1902 at the limestone cliffs and steep slopes forming the weathered scarp in front of which lay the deep ravine containing the five wells of Abu Jifan. As the last of these marches began the party saw a pale sliver of new moon and knew that no travelers or even dispatch riders would be at the wells, for no one traveled during the three holidays of the *Id al Fitr*. Nevertheless they scouted the area before couching the camels and spent the next day furbishing their arms and sleeping.

That night, a forty-mile ride brought them in sight of the cluster of villages near Riyadh. The party moved with extreme caution to avoid discovery, but on the morning of the second day, 15 January 1902, all lay concealed in the hills north of the populated area.

At nightfall on that day men and beasts quit their hiding places and stole into the shelter of the very extensive plantations of date palms that lay on all sides of the town. At an outlying grove, Shamsiyah, thirty men, headed by the Ibn Saud's stocky, heavily bearded half-brother, Mohammed, were detailed to guard the couched camels. They were instructed to wait until noon of the following day for news. If none came they should try to escape, for the others of the band would be dead. Desire to share in the attack ran high, but in the narrow streets near the fort a large group would have been conspicuous and the surprise that was the keystone of Ibn Saud's strategy might have been lost.

The twenty-three accompanying Ibn Saud in his approach to the wall included three cousins and several more distant relatives. The party moved silently through the dark shelter of the deserted groves carrying the long trunk of a palm tree. For an hour the men thus burdened stole through long rows of boles and then through the gardens nearer the gates: a maze of sunken paths, wells, irrigation channels and palm-thatched shelters. The cemetery just outside the north wall offered less difficulty—no stone fences and ditches to slow progress. But the approach had taken more than two hours and the sliver of new moon glowed dully in the west.

In front of the ruinous wall was a dry moat half-filled with dirt and debris. After the family's departure a decade before, the twenty-five-foot barrier *(Pl. III, fig. 5)* of sun-dried brick had been left to the weather by ibn Rashid's governors, and in some places was less than half its original height. The guard towers were not manned and all was silent, except for an occasional bark from a troubled dog and the droning whine from the wooden pulleys of the few draw-wells working during the last night of the *Id*. The palm trunk as ladder, and Abdul Aziz and eight of his party were over the crumbling obstacle. The other fifteen rested at its base to await events.

The nine stole warily through narrow dark streets and alleys, past the barred doors and the blank façades of low mud-brick dwellings. Shut-in dogs warned loudly of their hushed passage but the clamor raised no alarm. Their walk was short for the massive stone *Mismak (citadel: fig. 6)* was not far from the north wall *(Fig. 7)*. Silhouetted against the backdrop of the cold blaze of myriad stars in a blue-black heaven, the round towers of the fort rose high above the dark rectangle of its bulk. The open ground around the stronghold was bounded to the west and south by low, flat-roofed houses. The governor's residence, known to be close to the seat of power, must be one of the few two-story homes facing it to the west, but which one? A likely prospect, larger than some of the others, had a heavy door below and a latticed opening on the second floor. This house was less than three hundred feet from the massive iron-studded wooden portal *(Fig. 8)* of the citadel.

*The events that ensued have been recounted many times in print, and Ibn Saud himself told the story often. The published versions vary in detail, even in such basics as the number of participants, and differ even more in their interpretation of intangibles such as the state of mind of the doers. Some suggest that Ibn Saud changed the particulars of his story at will. And why not? He had created a legend.*

*This version is based on probabilities, given the circumstances, the place, the ambience of the high desert in winter, and Ibn Saud's propensity, recorded by several observers, to outbursts of violent anger.*

**Coup:** (16 January 1902) The nine discussed their next move cloaked in the dark obscurity of a narrow street bounded by low, windowless houses. They huddled, heads together, the white vapor of their breath streaming in the chill north wind that fluttered the loose ends of their checkered head cloths and wrapped the skirts of their long white *thobes* tightly against their legs. All were bundled up against the cold and burdened with arms: rifles wrapped in tanned goatskin slung over a shoulder or clutched by the barrel, butt in the dust; swords hitched high, belted daggers partly hidden under quilted vests. One of Ibn Saud's cousins, Abdullah ibn Jiluwi *(Pl. VI, fig. 20)*, short and heavily bearded, leaned on a stout, iron-tipped spear.

'The two-story place with the latticed window must be the one,' ibn Jiluwi said, 'No other house has a window.'

'Probably,' replied Abdul Aziz, 'but we have to be sure. Let's get off the street and ask somebody. If we stay here we might be seen and reported. There could be guards in the towers of the fort, too. There's just enough light for them to spot us if we move around much.... Look! This used to be Juwaisir's place. He sold cows. Maybe he's still here.'

A repeated peremptory but cautious knock was at last answered by the voice of a querulous woman, 'Who is it? What do you want at this hour?'

'It's ibn Mutriff [one of the guards at the citadel known to Ibn Saud]. The amir wants to buy two cows. Let me in to talk it over,' answered Abdul Aziz.

'It's late, nearly midnight. No honorable man would knock at the door of a respectable house now. There are no *Qahab* [sluts] here. Go away!'

'Amir Ajlan will not take that kindly. You know what he's like. Juwaisir will suffer for it. Is he there? Is Juwaisir there?'

With a rasp of wood on iron a bar was lifted from its sockets. The heavy door opened a crack and the dim light inside silhouetted a man's bare head. Ibn Saud wrenched the door wide open. 'Quick, men, in with you!' A rush of bodies at full pelt surged through the doorway. Shouldered roughly aside, the man at the door fell to his knees.

The troop jostled in the dark of the small, close room. 'Build up the fire so we can see!' Abdul Aziz ordered. Shaken by his fall, Juwaisir, old and stooped, staggered to his feet and heaped brushwood on the hearth, which crackled into a roaring blaze.

Peering dazedly at the weapons of the group crowding his dwelling he quavered, 'What do you want? We are poor folk, as you see.... O Master! I saw you on your mare when you had Ajlan cooped up in the fort. Why did you go away?'

'Well, we're back now. You can help us. Where is Ajlan? That's his house, isn't it, the big one opposite the door of the fort?'

The old man bowed as he said that his abode was his Master's. Yes, that was the governor's residence, but he wasn't there. He slept in the fort with his men, some eighty of them. But in the morning just after prayer he visited his wife, although sometimes he rode for a time before going to her. Six guards accompanied him everywhere.

'Can we get to Ajlan's terrace from yours?' Ibn Saud asked.

'Almost, Sir. There is a gap of about four feet, and of course it's higher. But the wall of Sa'ad's house touches his. Next door, you know.'

'Is Sa'ad alone?'

'Only his wife. They are like me—too poor to buy a slave.'

'Thank you, Juwaisir. Those steps lead up to your terrace?'

Ibn Saud in the lead, all his men climbed the steep, narrow stair to the flat roof, a terrace edged by a waist-high crenelated wall. It was not pitch dark. Everyone lay flat for the fort was only three hundred feet away. Sentinels in the corner towers could, if observant, see movement below. Abdul Aziz raised himself slowly and studied the menacing bulk for a long moment: an infinity of brilliant points in a dark firmament outlining silent towers of jet bounding a black oblong. Nothing moved. 'They don't know we're here. Let's go!'

Cautiously, all straddled the low walls separating the terraces of the two houses. Ibn Saud and ibn Jiluwi descended silently into the darkness of the stair in the second house. A stifled scream and two unfortunates lay tied and gagged in their bed. Back on the roof, Abdul Aziz dispatched two of his eight men (sons of ibn Jiluwi) to summon those waiting at the enceinte of the town. 'When you come back with them, don't bunch up, and stay inside this place until I send for you,' he warned.

Then, much taller than his companions, he leapt high, grappled the bounding wall of the governor's terrace and pulled himself up and over it. Feet on shoulders, upstretched arms pulled, and in moments the six were beside him. With their daggers loosened, Abdul Aziz led them down into the menacing, stygian blackness of the upper floor.

'Make sure that the slaves don't make a row, men,' he whispered. Then to ibn Jiluwi, 'Light the candle. Let's see if Ajlan is here, or not.'

The two moved warily from room to room in the silent house, the taper in ibn Jiluwi's hand guttering as they peered into each. A brass bed in this one—only a shaikh could afford that! Abdul Aziz held his rifle ready to fire into one of two mounds under the quilts. Ibn Jiluwi lowered the candle and went to the head of the bed: the light showed the two heads to be women.

A high-pitched, sleepy voice, 'Who is it? Who is it?'

'Abdul Aziz ibn Abdur Rahman. Quiet woman! And you too!' he added as the other bundle stirred.

'Oh, it's you, Father of Turki. What do you want? You are in the harem.' The woman had known Ibn Saud as a child, and was not afraid. Honest women were never molested.

'No impudence! I want your husband, wicked woman who married a Shammari! Where is he?'

'I married only after you ignored me! He is in the fort with his men. When he comes back after morning prayer you had better be gone, if you value your life.'

'If you value yours, you and your friend will not raise your voices. Or do you prefer to be gagged?'

The two women were herded into a lower room where four terrified slaves huddled: three Somali men and a woman. All were again warned to silence.

'The others must be here by now. Have the slaves open a passage into the other house. It shouldn't take long to loosen these mud bricks. But keep an eye on them. No noise!' ordered Abdul Aziz. 'Have the cook make coffee and bring whatever there is to eat upstairs.'

The troop of twenty-three was soon reunited, the newcomers voicing satisfaction at the handiwork of the nine. The room behind the latticed alcove facing the fort was large and furnished comfortably with cushions and rugs. All lounged at ease as a trembling slave served coffee, dates, and unleavened bread, stumbling in the darkness, for a light in the room behind the grated opening would have been visible to anyone in the fort.

'Only two hours to sunrise,' ibn Jiluwi commented, 'we should get some rest.'

'Yes. We'll take care of Ajlan when he comes home. Find out which slave opens the door and select one of us of similar build to don her clothes so that Ajlan will suspect nothing when the door is opened,' Ibn Saud replied.

'Abdul Aziz lay back against the cushions behind him. 'Let's recite a few *surahs* [n. 7] together before we rest. Allah, look favorably on our affairs!'

The muezzin's predawn call brought all to their feet for sleep had been fitful at best. Two lines of men, Ibn Saud before them, began the morning prayer, *al fajar*. The murmur of the prescribed orisons accompanied the ritual of kneeling and prostration toward Mecca.

Waiting began. The pale salmon-orange of the pre-dawn gave way to the brassy brilliance of sunrise. A dark shadow of the fort wall leapt into existence, its edge ruler-straight on the tan, trodden earth in front of the governor's house. Ibn Saud and ibn Jiluwi peered anxiously through the lattice while sipping coffee. Bright lozenges of early morning sunlight marked their white robes as they knelt behind the screen. Four riflemen knelt behind them, ready to open fire when targets appeared.

Suddenly a loud grating groan broke the silence. The massive, iron-studded, wooden portal of the fort swung slowly inward. Ajlan ibn Mohammed ar Rashid and six of his retinue stood framed in the panel of light at the foot of the high wall. All bore arms, but carried them with the carelessness of the unsuspecting. This morning the amir had decided not to ride the mare held in check by a groom, for as the weighty gate shut behind him he sauntered into the open, sword at his side. Abdul Aziz saw his arrogant bearing, stiffened, sprang to his feet, threw off head rope and scarf, and muttered, 'I'll kill him.' He dashed down the stairs shouting, 'Let's go! Now! Come On!' threw open the door and raced toward the amir, bawling as a war cry, 'Akhu Nura [Nura's brother!] (She was his favorite sister [n. 8].) The others streamed after him, ibn Jiluwi at their head.

Ajlan, a stately figure in his padded winter cloak, blue trimmed in scarlet, was startled and for a moment only stared, then drew his sword and held it high while backing toward the fort. As Ibn Saud neared him he slashed down. The young warrior parried with his rifle. Ajlan, seeing his adversary a giant, began to turn away. Abdul Aziz fired hastily, and the amir, hit in the shoulder, dropped his blade and ran toward the great door. His guards had already retreated. One of them stooped to pass through the small wicket (n. 9) that had opened at the right end of the portal (Pl. III, fig. 9).

Ibn Jiluwi and the others in the forefront of the attackers engaged the retreating guards who battled courageously, sword against sword, but fell back continually toward the wicket. One of them fended off two assailants until he fell with a great gaping cut in the neck. Ibn Saud caught the fleeing amir from behind as he bent to pass through the wicket and wrestled him to the ground. Desperately, the fallen man lashed out with a kick that caught Ibn Saud in the groin, doubling him up in pain. Thus freed, Ajlan again ran to the wicket. As he bent low to go through it, ibn Jiluwi threw his spear with tremendous force, but missed. Its point struck the door just to the right of the opening. Aided by men inside, Ajlan struggled over the high sill, and was at last pulled into the courtyard. Ibn Jiluwi, drawn blade in hand, bent low and plunged through behind him, braving a possible sword stroke that would have cut off his head. Ibn Saud was behind him in a flash. The defenders fled, Ajlan lagging behind because of his wound. The two paladins rushed to unbar the great portal, pushed open at once by a swarm of shouting attackers brandishing swords.

All pursued the fugitives, most of whom sought refuge in the guard room not far from the gate. Ibn Jiluwi caught up with Ajlan and cut him down. Led by Abdul Aziz the others hunted out those who resisted, and took the surrender of the rest. Many asked for mercy in the time-honored way: dropping their weapons they put the thumbs of both hands between their teeth with fingers widely spread. All was over in less than an hour.

Ibn Saud, flushed with victory, took Ajlan's head to the battlements and threw it into the street, shouting, 'Who is on my side—Who? Your own amir is with you again!'

*Most writers who describe the taking of Riyadh say that the casualties inflicted on the defeated were heavy. They report that nearly half of the eighty defenders were killed or wounded;*

*the remainder jailed or pardoned.On the other hand a few minimize the number of casualties.
According to a 'reliable source', Ibn Saud lost two killed and four critically wounded—a fourth
of his force.*

# Early Battles (1902–1903)

News of the coup spread throughout Nejd in a flash. A number of shaikhs
came to Riyadh to pledge their support, their allegiance to the Saudi cause.
Shortly after the exploit Abdul Aziz commanded that the palace and its amenities
be refurbished. He then sent to Kuwait for his family, thus underscoring the
permanency of the change in régime both to the people of Riyadh and to the
nomads. Abdur Rahman arrived from Kuwait in May and in a public audience
gave Abdul Aziz the sword of ceremony inherited from *his* father, Faisal ibn Turki,
with its scabbard of enchased silver, its hilt of gold. Thus he ceded to his son the
title of amir, but Abdul Aziz insisted that his sire still be considered imam, the
religious head.

The defenses of Riyadh were put in order at once in preparation for an
attack by ibn Rashid, but that chief was occupied with revolt and pillage elsewhere and did not appear for ten months. Ibn Saud and his relatives used this
time for whirlwind visits to the tribes in the south that had never been subject to
Rashidi domination. They got pledges of support from the villagers of Hariq, the
Kharj area, and the Hauta and Aflaj districts, all south of Riyadh. The Murra tribe
promised to aid him, but the Ajman refused.

One day near the end of October, Saudi scouts reported ibn Rashid's army
approaching from the northwest. The defenses of Riyadh were by now in excellent condition. Abdul Aziz was sure that his father could hold the town, and went
back to the Hauta area, recruiting for his army. His brother Sa'ad *(Pl. XI, fig. 42)*
raised a force at Hariq.

Dilam: After further delay caused by sickness among his soldiery, ibn Rashid
moved on the town of Dilam, some sixty miles south of Riyadh, where a Saudi
force was already in place awaiting him. He arrived too late in the day to mount a
full-scale attack and encamped near the town. Ibn Saud arrived that night with
2,000 reinforcements for the garrison, but his numbers were still inferior to those
of ibn Rashid. In the morning the Shammari cavalry advanced with the usual display of caracolling horses and shouted challenges. Hidden among the palms and
behind walls, the defenders opened a withering fire, blunting the attack. In its
turn the Saudi cavalry charged, and fierce hand-to-hand combat between foot and
horse continued until sunset. Then Ibn Rashid broke off the fight and retreated to
the northeast. Three days later his force was at Hafar al Atj, ninety miles north of
Riyadh. Saudi horsemen had followed him but could not attack, for their rifles
were empty.

*Years later, Ibn Saud revealed that in the early morning fusillade his men had expended
nearly all of their ammunition. If ibn Rashid had not decided to quit the field, the outcome of
another day's fight would have been in doubt.*

Fig. 5. A wall of Riyadh in 1917

Fig. 6. The Mismak in 1918
(viewed from the roof of the Royal Palace)

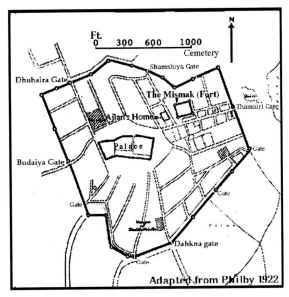

Fig. 7. Riyadh in 1917 (in black: wall and
buildings mentioned in the text)

Fig. 8. The Mismak Portal

Fig. 9. The Wicket
(Soldier points to ibn Jiluwi's embedded
spear point)

PLATE IV
Figs. 10-12

# THE WALLS OF HOFUF

Fig. 10. This Turkish stronghold in al Hasa was protected by thirty-foot walls...

Fig. 11. A deep, dry moat paralleled the walls...

Fig. 12. Officers in the Mosque of Ibrahim Pasha ... surrendered at noon
when threatened by the explosion of a mine placed under the domed edifice.

**Seesaw:** Ibn Rashid (Abdul Aziz ibn Mitab) had not been disheartened by the loss of a battle. Next time he would crush this upstart. In the meantime he continued his oppressions, ending up near the town of Kuwait. Mubarak alarmed, asked Ibn Saud for help. In February 1903 the new amir hastened to the aid of his mentor with a large force and together with Jabir, Mubarak's son, raided the Mutair, then allied with ibn Rashid.

The wily ibn Rashid who had planned this sequence of events sped to Riyadh hoping to take the defenders by surprise. In spite of his draconian precautions, Suhul *Bedu* (nomad, Bedouin) succeeded in eluding the net of his spies and warned the town about the fast-moving force. The town alerted, an attack on its walls would be too costly, so ibn Rashid, after a few minor skirmishes on 3–4 April, headed north never to see Riyadh again. En route, he constructed a new fort at Tharmida in Washm, and installed stronger garrisons in the towns of the Qasim.

# Strategic Gains (1903–1904)

In spite of this strengthening of ibn Rashid's defenses, shortly thereafter Nejdi forces invaded Washm. Because the people were exacerbated by the impositions of ibn Rashid the aggressors had little difficulty in occupying all the towns in Washm and the Qasim except Anaiza and its neighbor Buraida, the well-fortified capital of the Qasim region. Elsewhere, garrisons nominally allies of the Rashids fled or offered little resistance. Shagra, Tharmida, Thadiq, Ghat, Jalajil, and Raudhat as Sudair came under Saudi control.

*When the winter of 1903 came, the Saudi army, including the garrison of Riyadh that had followed on ibn Rashid's heels, had been well repaid with loot from the newly occupied towns. Ibn Saud now controlled not only the southern arid provinces but also much of the most fertile land in Arabia. When he returned to Riyadh a congress of the* Ulema *(religious authorities) and notables from all the towns and tribes declared him amir and imam of the Wahhabis.*

**Buraida Taken:** After the first rains of winter when good grazing was in prospect, Ibn Saud went again to the Qasim to take the two towns still under Rashidi control—Anaiza and Buraida—on the caravan route from Kuwait to the Hejaz. Early in March 1904, at Raudhat as Sirr, fifty miles west of Shagra, he defeated and killed the principal opponent barring his route to Anaiza. He arrived at that town by night, and at dawn on the 22nd sent to the assault a partisan contingent from Anaiza that had joined his forces, supported by ibn Jiluwi with a hundred men from Riyadh. The partisans and Nejdis routed ibn Rashid's followers. Before the town was taken, Ibn Saud with his mounted Bedu attacked a cavalry force in Wadi ar Rumah, dispersing it and taking all the enemy's stores.

With the stores were some of the grandsons of Saud the usurper, the *Araïf (n. 11)*. Had they been captives of ibn Rashid, or had they solicited his help to combat Ibn Saud? In any event they were welcomed by their cousin who took the charitable view. In a report to his friend, Shaikh Mubarak of Kuwait, he wrote: 'And we broke them and slaughtered of them three hundred and seventy men.

And God restored to us our kinsmen of the family of Saud who were prisoners in their hands.... And by Almighty God, but two Bedouin on our side were slain.'

Buraida was only fifteen miles north of Anaiza. Early in June while the watch was at evening prayer, partisans opened the gates. The garrison held out for ten weeks in the citadel waiting for succor. The Shammar force intended to relieve these beleaguered defenders was driven off in defeat. Its leader, a certain 'Ubaid ar Rashid, was captured. Ibn Saud killed him, literally carving him up as he stood, wielding his sword deftly to expose his captive's entrails. 'Ubaid had murdered the amir's uncle, Mohammed, sometime during the 1890s.

In only eighteen months Ibn Saud had retaken almost all of his family's former holdings except al Hasa and the Hejaz. Ibn Rashid held the western Qasim and was still a formidable opponent.

*After taking Buraida, Ibn Saud left long-time amirs in charge, the Al Muhanna family, who had headed the partisan attack as leaders of the local opposition to ibn Rashid. This choice of governors resulted later in a conspiracy to free the town from Saudi control. The complot involved both the Rashids and the Mutair as allies. Once this treachery saw the light, Ibn Saud entrusted the governance of his conquests only to relatives.*

**Bukairiya**: Ibn Rashid had not been able to stop this firebrand of an upstart. So, early in 1904 he appealed to the Turk, the *Wali* of the *Vilayet* of Baghdad, for help. The Ottomans sent him stores, weapons, and money with which he was able to raise contingents of the Harb and Hutaim along with his own tribesmen, the Shammar and townsmen from his capital, Haïl. And he was promised support by regulars of the Turkish army. In late May, six battalions of Turkish infantry, 2,400 men, with six field guns, set out from Samara to meet ibn Rashid in the Qasim. Before these troops arrived several inconclusive encounters between tribesmen of the contending forces occurred, first one and then the other holding the edge in the skirmishes. Although Ibn Saud had not yet fought Turkish regulars, their reputation was formidable. So when he learned that Turkish troops were in the field to aid ibn Rashid, he sent a message asking for his government's intervention to the recently appointed political resident for the Persian Gulf stationed in Bushire, Major Cox (A. IV).

*This was not the first message Ibn Saud sent to British agents in the Gulf. Shortly after his success in Riyadh in January 1902, he wrote the political resident announcing the coup. In 1903 he asked for a treaty like that made with the shaikh of Kuwait in 1898, and in that same year told the captain of the British gunboat* Sphinx *that during his visit to a Muscovite warship he had been offered rifles and money by a Russian official. In 1904 he reiterated his request for a treaty that would protect him from Turkish domination. It appears obvious that a prime factor in these attempts to win British support was his confidence in the inviolability of a commitment by Her Majesty's government, gained during his stay in Kuwait. He was disillusioned regarding this only in 1914 during the preludes to World War I.*

The commander of this Ottoman force, Colonel Hassan Shukri, warned Ibn Saud of the futility of resistance, and offered coöperation in return for submission. But the amir would not bow. He left Buraida's walls, sure to be breached by the enemy's cannon, and went to the sands and palm groves of Bukairiya, twenty miles west of Anaiza, where he could maneuver in the open.

# REGIONAL LOCATIONS

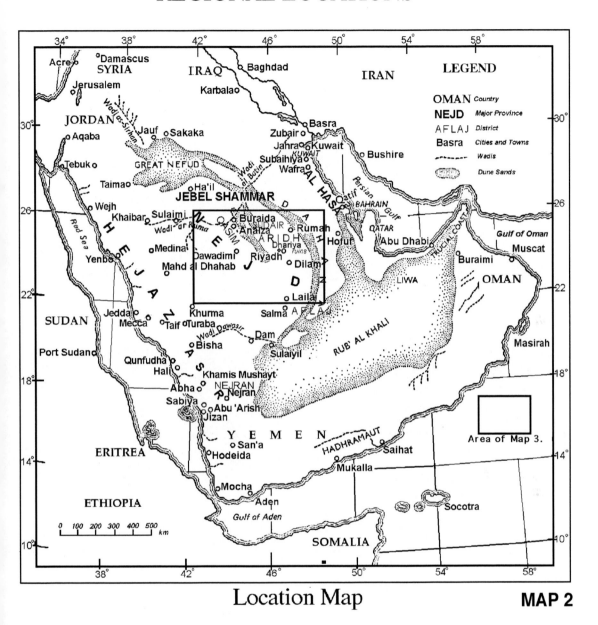

Location Map

**MAP 2**

Many of the localities mentioned in the text are shown on this map. It indicates the names but not the boundaries of the countries bordering Saudi Arabia, and gives the approximate location of the provinces and some of the districts recognized in the Kingdom of Saudi Arabia during Ibn Saud's reign. The placement of a number of the towns and villages in the peninsula is included. Map 1, an insert on the back cover, is somewhat more detailed in all respects. None of the maps herein provides topographic, hydrologic, or geologic data.

# CENTRAL NEJD
## Notable Events

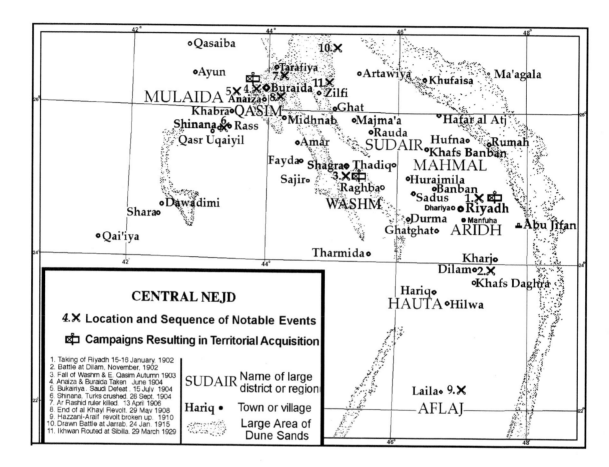

**CENTRAL NEJD**

**4.✗ Location and Sequence of Notable Events**

⛫ **Campaigns Resulting in Territorial Acquisition**

1. Taking of Riyadh 15-16 January, 1902
2. Battle at Dilam, November, 1902
3. Fall of Washm & E. Qasim Autumn 1903
4. Anaiza & Buraida Taken June 1904
5. Bukairiya . Saudi Defeat . 15 July 1904
6. Shinana. Turks crushed. 28 Sept. 1904
7. Ar Rashid ruler killed. 13 April 1906
8. End of al Khayl Revolt. 29 May 1908
9. Hazzani-Araif revolt broken up. 1910
10. Drawn Battle at Jarrab. 24 Jan. 1915
11. Ikhwan Routed at Sibilla. 29 March 1929

SUDAIR **Name of large district or region**

Hariq • **Town or village**

**Large Area of Dune Sands**

## MAP 3

Most of the towns and villages in central Nejd mentioned in the text, notes and addenda appear on this map, as well as the names of districts. It lists the location and sequence of events in central Nejd that marked important steps in the development of the Saudi seigneurie. Several of the events were crucial in the expansion of Ibn Saud's hegemony; others only removed obstacles to his upward progress. Map 1, an insert in the back cover, tallies these decisive events, along with those in other areas of the kingdom.

At dawn on 15 July the two forces met. Ibn Saud attacked, driving the enemy Bedu back again and again with townsmen from Nejd and his mounted nomads. But the Turkish infantry held its square firmly, and late in the morning the six guns of the artillery opened fire. Casualties mounted. The bark of the guns and the crack of exploding shrapnel daunted the attackers who retreated. A shell-burst near Ibn Saud wounded him—a splinter in the left hand, and, some say, a ball in the knee. He left the field to have his wounds bound, then returned to the action. His followers were in full flight.

He thought the day lost and with the main body of his troops fell back to Midhnab, fifty miles from the battlefield. Townsmen from the oases of the Qasim, although eager to be free of ibn Rashid's yoke, did not arrive in time to take part in the battle. When they at last reached the field the enemy was looting the abandoned Saudi camp. The townsmen attacked them. But with no effective leadership they too were forced to retire. Some 1,500 Ottomans are reported to have died in the actions of this day, including a dozen Turkish officers, along with 500 men from Haïl.

**Shinana:** A Saudi night assault forced a large body of Shammar besieging the town of Khabra to flee, leaving a good part of their stores behind. Ibn Rashid and his Turkish allies moved to a more defensible position near the walled town of ar Rass, thirty-five miles south-southwest of Anaiza. From that base they attacked the town, forcing Ibn Saud's brother, Mohammed to leave. Its people were then subjected to the usual program of harassment and looting. Ibn Saud used the time thus given him to attract reinforcements from the 'Ataiba and Mutair. With them, he advanced to confront the enemy. Under the broiling sun of August the tents of the two camps were within sight of each other near the village of Shinana twelve miles southwest of ar Rass. After a month of eventless confrontation cholera broke out in ibn Rashid's camp. The long wait became intolerable to nomads and many of ibn Rashid's Bedu decamped. Some of Ibn Saud's recruits too were on the verge of desertion. He suggested a suspension of hostilities to ibn Rashid who scornfully refused.

But it was ibn Rashid's Shammar who moved first, for after two months of confrontation forage for animals and brushwood for fires had been used up near the camp. The proximity of the enemy made distant excursions for these necessities perilous. His men begged ibn Rashid to pitch the tents elsewhere. So his army moved northwest followed by Ibn Saud. A portion of his forces under the command of his brother Mohammed occupied a small oasis and fortified grange, Qasr ibn 'Uqaiyil near Wadi ar Rumah.

On 27 September Ibn Rashid began the battle by opening fire on the grange. After less than a day's inconclusive fighting at this site where the Saudis had the upper hand, the Turks limbered their cannon and moved off to the north, protected by the Rashidi horse. That night, encamped in Wadi ar Rumah, ibn Rashid was persuaded that he should consider ending his campaign and under cover of darkness sent off camels laden with the season's loot toward Haïl. Ibn Saud's scouts detected the departure and a part of the Saudi cavalry and camelry followed the trains to capture the booty and to destroy its escort. The infantry stayed in contact with the main body of the enemy.

On 28 September 1904, in the broad bed of Wadi ar Rumah the Rashidi forces deployed between the low banks marking its course—the Turkish infantry and cannon in the center, flanked by Bedu. The combat was fierce and bloody. Ibn Saud's right flank wavered, so, with the best of his cavalry he charged the center. The Turkish square broke, and the rest of the Rashidi army fled. Five hundred and fifty Turks lay dead and their camp was overrun. The survivors could not live without food and water. For days those wandering in the desert could be killed for what they were carrying. But there was no organized pursuit of ibn Rashid and his Shammar, for the vast quantity of plunder, including a pay chest, six small-caliber rifled cannon, tents, foodstores, and weapons, glued the victors in place. Ibn Saud left Anaiza to return to Riyadh on 12 October.

Two Turkish fugitives who reached the Gulf told a British agent a story that may explain in part why poorly armed Bedu defeated six battalions of the much-feared Turkish army. Rumors in Constantinople were in agreement: Ibn Rashid himself had shot the Ottoman commander because he refused to spearhead an attack on Ibn Saud, and then had turned his nomads against the Turks in the full of the fight, killing a hundred and wounding ninety.

*In a society where loyalties are fickle and the overriding consideration is personal advantage such an action is not unwonted. Almost certainly relations between the Turks and the shaikhly Arabs had not improved on acquaintance.*


# Intermission


**Guile:** Less than a month after the victory Ibn Saud offered his submission to the sultan and begged his forgiveness in a series of obsequious and fawning letters signed by his father, Abdur Rahman. 'I am submissive to every desire and order of the Shadow of God.... I am the obedient servant of our lord the Great Caliph, God preserve his throne until the Day of Judgment.' He also wrote the governor of Basra, Fakri Pasha, to intercede for him with the Sublime Porte.

Why?

*He knew that Turkish power applied with its full might could end his plan to reëstablish the Saud hegemony. He would become a desert prince with a beggarly following, if he were not imprisoned or beheaded. Delaying a riposte could not worsen his position for, if rumors were true, uprising in Yemen and war in Tripolitania would force the Ottomans to send more troops to support their garrisons. Then operations against him might well be tempered by obligations elsewhere. But a better reason for his attempt at appeasement, and a more credible one, was the fear that a Turkish subsidy, which, according to some reports he received regularly, would be terminated.*

In February 1905, these placatory messages, together with Mubarak's efforts on behalf of the Sauds, and more important, the fate of their expeditionary force, caused the Turks to request that Abdur Rahman visit Zubair, a town in southwestern Mesopotamia, for negotiation of territorial boundaries. The Ottomans proposed to form a buffer state between ibn Rashid's holdings to the north and Ibn Saud's to the south. The buffer would be the Qasim district to be garrisoned by Turkish troops stationed in Buraida and Anaiza. The governors for the towns in the new state would be selected by the occupying force. The Turks proposed to recognize Abdur Rahman as master of southern Nejd and give him the title of *Qaimaqam* (district governor). (This is the smallest of the three Turkish administrative subdivisions then recognized: the two larger ones were called *Vilayet* and *Sanjak*, ruled respectively by a *Wali* and a *Mutaserrif.*) Apparently Ibn Saud agreed to carry out the duties of this official, but only as a means of removing this powerful enemy without resorting to the overt use of arms.

The Ottoman occupation troops, some 4,500 men (Goldberg says 7,000) again with six field guns, arrived in Buraida on 15 April to a scene of joyous welcome according to the report of the Turkish commander, the luckless Colonel Faizi Pasha. Ibn Saud ordered his Bedu to waylay their supply trains, a welcome source of plunder, and in June 1906, directed the shaikhs and tribes to stop communicating with Ottoman officials and to cease carrying mail and supplies to them. From Medina a relief force of 600 under Sami Pasha reached the Qasim in August 1906 with the mission of keeping lines of communication open. Ibn Saud, alarmed, once more asked Mubarak to try to get British support, again without success. He then negotiated with Sami. In October, Sami, owing to the miserable state of the troops, agreed to the face-saving device of allowing two dozen Turks to remain in Anaiza and Buraida, provided they did not interfere with the administration of the district. Two years later they were still there.

Before the arrival of the relief force, those left alive had been reduced to semi-starvation and were in rags. Many had deserted in order to escape constant harassment by the local population. The remainder of the army left in October-November 1906. According to Goldberg (*p. 75*), 1,200 troops with twelve guns set out for Medina on 3 November, and an equal number left for Basra six weeks later. He bases his statements on reports by Lorimer and messages to the Foreign Office. Other authors suggest an earlier departure and say that less than a thousand of the original 4,500 survived. There are two reports about the withdrawal. One says that the troops were escorted by Saudi forces to Medina in the Hejaz and to Basra; the other states that they straggled back alone to Baghdad and the Hejaz. In any event the Turks left central Arabia and never returned.

Even before the arrival of the contingent of Turks in the Qasim Ibn Saud withdrew his men, leaving the towns at the mercy of ibn Rashid who did not delay in resuming his overbearing despotic government and widespread pillage. Several of Ibn Saud's chroniclers find this withdrawal odd and offer several interpretations of his motives.

Their explanations for his departure seem unlikely. They are three: 1. The ruler of Nejd despaired of resolving the conflict between two factions of the Al Muhanna contending for power in the Qasim, and hoped that one or both of them would attack ibn Rashid. Without his support they would surely lose and then must ask for his help. 2. Ibn Saud had a call for assistance from the shaikh of Qatar whose brother, assisted by the Murra, was attempting to take authority. 3. He was short of money, so that the motive for his withdrawal was mainly lack of funds, and his journey to the littoral which caused anxiety to the British and their client states, was made in order to borrow from the coastal shaikhs (*n. 9*).

But there were other probably more compelling reasons for the departure from the Qasim in the early spring of 1905 and, in August, for the journey to the shores of the Persian Gulf. First, he had to demonstrate to the Turks the sincerity of his repentance and his desire to stay in their good graces. A withdrawal before their arrival showed his good will and his desire to comply with the new dispensation. Second, after three months of observation of the Turkish occupying forces he was sure that the Ottomans had no plans to encroach on his fief. He could make a journey without fear of invasion. Third, farther away from the Turks, his rôle in their discomfiture would be less suspect. Fourth, and the most speculative, nearly four years after his seizure of Riyadh and the recovery of some of his inheritance, it was time to reassert his primacy among the tribes of the littoral that were a part of his legacy. While at Qatar, he is quoted as having said, 'By God, I will explore the country belonging to my father and grandfather from Muscat to Ja'alan!' [province of southern Oman] But in this regard the protectorates of the Trucial Coast asked Britain to intervene, and Ibn Saud found it expedient to heed the warning given him. He did not invade Abu Dhabi or Oman.

He did convoke the shaikhs of the Murra, Bani Hajar, and Ajman of al Hasa, ordering them to cease intertribal warfare, and, more importantly, requiring them to acknowledge his authority. He also appointed three shaikhs to hear complaints, and gave them the right to confine transgressors pending his own decision as to punishment. The son of the shaikh of Qatar who had attempted to seize authority fled to Bahrain.

When the amir of Nejd returned to Riyadh he found letters from Mubarak urging action against ibn Rashid and a delegation from the Qasim asking for help. With Turkish forces present in force in Anaiza and Buraida, for a time he answered these appeals only by sending his brother Mohammed on raids into the region, but in the first days of 1906 he went north himself with Bedu and townsmen to carry out a joint campaign with a contingent from Buraida. Once arrived, he began to doubt the loyalty of their leader, Salih al Muhanna, and sent the men from Buraida home. Shortly thereafter he found proof of his suspicions in intercepted correspondence showing that the amir of Buraida was communicating with the Shammar leader, and that his friend Mubarak had been urging the Muhannas to become allies of the Rashids. It seems clear that the success of his protégé had roused jealousy or suspicion in Mubarak who still dreamed of being paramount in northern Arabia.

At Majma'a, 120 miles northwest of Riyadh, Ibn Saud got word that ibn Rashid was raiding in the eastern desert and set out to find him, although his own troops were fewer than the force ibn Rashid usually employed in his raids.

# Death of an Enemy (13 April 1906)

**The Hunt:** For three months Ibn Saud tried to close with the current head of the clan, Abdul Aziz ibn Mitab, who kept moving his camp to avoid confrontation. For the first time the renowned shaikh of the Mutair, Faisal ad Duwish, allied his tribe with the Sauds. But the Shammaris remained elusive. What finally happened is in dispute. The only points common to all the narratives of ibn Rashid's death are: the Saudi troops were on foot; the clash began before dawn; ibn Rashid was killed by bullets and the death took place in the early morning at a place known as Raudhat al Muhanna, probably about twenty miles east-northeast of Buraida, where there are a number of raudhat (depressions in which rain accumulates). The winter of 1905–1906 was particularly wet, so forage must have been abundant, a good reason for ibn Rashid to site his encampment there.

**The Kill:** Most accounts suggest that ibn Rashid's scouts were not alert and did not detect the proximity of the Saudi forces. One Arab tale, supposedly told by a participant, has ibn Rashid surprised by a night attack. His standard is captured without his knowledge. Running toward its Saudi bearer, he calls out to him, is identified and shot down, five wounds killing him instantly. Another, by Howarth, has him tracked to an encampment in a palm-grove, surprised by an attack before a stormy dawn, and shot as he shouts encouragement to his men. Philby (1930) has him riding to collect troops from outlying camps. Returning with reinforcements he mistakes a Saudi bivouac for his own and is brought down by rifle fire as he rallies his men. In that event surprise was involved only at the moment of entry into the bivouac. Rihani confirms Philby, saying that ibn Rashid rode into a Saudi outpost believing it one of his own, and was killed when recognized. Dickson and Rihani both state that the death was an accident. If so, the word 'accident' refers only to ibn Rashid's error, not to any desire of the Saudis to spare him.

Arab historians report that Ibn Saud's losses in this affair were thirty-five men killed, and that he carried the severed head to Buraida where it was thrown to the dogs.

# Consolidation (1906–1912)

**Cleanup:** Ibn Saud considered pressing northward to Haïl, to take advantage of the disarray caused by the death of an autocratic ruler, and the inevitable struggle for power among possible successors. But his men had been in the field for months, and needed a respite. Haïl was nearly four hundred miles by caravan trail from Riyadh, and the Al Muhanna, still powerful and liked in Buraida, were strongly opposed to Saudi hegemony in the Qasim. These malcontents were a danger to the stability of his government. It was time to quench hostility to his rule; to make himself paramount, and if possible, well liked. The first step was to eliminate the faction opposing him in the Qasim. Its head, Salih, although accepted by the Turks, was also popular with the Qasimis. In May 1906, less than a month after Abdul Aziz ibn Mitab's death, Salih and two brothers were seized and sent to prison in Riyadh. Eighteen months later they escaped, were recaptured, and two of the three were executed. They were among the last to be disposed of in this fashion. With one exception, condign punishment was henceforth to be forced residence, prison, or in many instances a reprieve.

For Ibn Saud now changed his policies with regard to opponents of his hegemony. The new procedures proved successful: by the end of 1912 he had eliminated opposition to the régime by the tribes of Nejd. But to achieve that end he had been involved in an almost continuous round of raids, battles, alliances, marriages of state, one incident of kidnap and ransom, and one multiple execution by decapitation. The endurance and pertinacity of the amir of Nejd were admirable, but the mercy shown recidivists was a carefully considered policy of conciliation which in essence was: Show the inevitability of retribution for wrong doing, but withhold punishment.

For his plan to succeed the possibility that malfeasance would be found out must become a certainty. But even well-merited punition was certain to arouse hatred and desire for vengeance among the Bedu tribes, in which every individual of each discrete sept considered himself bound by ties of blood. Consequently, Ibn Saud pursued and captured all malefactors, but almost always withheld a severe penalty, provided that the offender promised to behave. Even backsliders were spared. The result was a host of grateful but chastened supporters. Only once did he allow multiple executions, a salutary lesson for potential protesters against his régime.

Some of the more striking events of the years 1906–1912 are:

**Revolt:** On 29 December 1906, the new head of the Rashid clan, Mitab ibn Abdul Aziz, was murdered after only eight months in power. Ibn Saud then attempted to take Haïl, but failed, and the Mutair chief, Faisal ad Duwish, recently an ally, joined the Shammar forces. In May 1907, an uprising began in the Qasim involving ad Duwish and a Muhanna, Abd al Khayl, governor of Buraida. At the head of a sizable army Ibn Saud forced an entry into Buraida and cowed this disloyal governor who had been negotiating secretly with the Rashids for independence from the Saudi hegemony. A large contingent of Shammari came down from Haïl to help the Muhanna faction. Ibn Saud first attacked ad Duwish at Majma'a and crushed his Mutair nomads. Their chief surrendered, was pardoned, and again took the field to support his new allies. In the battle that followed Ibn Saud worsted the Mutair once more.

On 22 September, shortly after the second defeat of ad Duwish, and at the same site, At Truffiyah, the Rashidi army attacked, was beaten, and fled to Buraida. From there the current leader of the ar Rashid, Sultan ibn Hamud, retreated to Haïl where, in 1908, he too was murdered, and was replaced by Saud ibn Hamud.

Left with only one opponent Ibn Saud returned to Buraida where he was again refused admittance. On 29 May 1908, secret negotiations opened one of the gates at the time of evening prayer. The governor sheltered in the fort for a day, surrendered, and was allowed to leave with his family to exile in Iraq. Ahmed ibn Mohammed as Sudairi, Ibn Saud's relative by marriage, was named governor in his stead.

**Insurrection:** After their return to the Saudi fold in 1904–1906, the *Araïf* (n. 11), nine grandsons of Saud ibn Faisal the usurper had been installed in Riyadh with their families. (Three married two of Ibn Saud's sisters.) For years they had claimed the right to govern based on the fact that their fathers were senior to

Abdur Rahman, and therefore that they outranked their cousin, Ibn Saud. But they had been denied posts of authority, and were in fact only guests of their kinsman.

Early in March 1910 Ibn Saud visited Shaikh Mubarak and was photographed for the first time by the new representative of the British government, Captain Shakespear (Pl. XI). Less than three months later in the latter part of May 1910, Ibn Saud left Riyadh leading a force to the aid of his old friend, but in a battle at Hadiya on 16 June, the Kuwait–Nejd contingent was routed by the Muntafiq, a powerful tribe of southern Iraq, at that time allied with the Rashids. Taking advantage of Ibn Saud's absence, the *Araïf* left Riyadh for al Hasa, and joined the Ajman. They planned to set up a government to rival or to replace that of Ibn Saud. Early in 1911, leading their Ajman allies, they skirmished near Anaiza with Ibn Saud's tribal supporters. Outmatched in numbers the rebels went to Kharj in southern Nejd to gain support. Failing to win converts there, they went farther south to Hariq.

There they met kindred spirits. In 1905–1907 internecine executions among the Hazzani family of southern Nejd had forced Ibn Saud's intervention and a demand that the dispute be settled according to Koranic law. The offenders refused, were besieged, captured, and imprisoned for two years in Riyadh. Freed, they were still rebellious and ripe for further action against authority. The two rebel groups joined forces and began to mobilize their resources in men and arms.

**Ransom:** Ibn Saud became aware of this alliance immediately, and sent his brother Sa'ad to recruit men for his army among the 'Ataiba of western Nejd. Husain ibn Ali, then only two years in office as sharif (n. 13) of Mecca, used this crisis to invade Nejd, an enforcement of his demand that Ibn Saud pay a yearly sum for his tenure of the Qasim, and perhaps also to support the activities of the insurgents. Husain (A. V) captured Sa'ad at Qai'iya and held him for ransom. In the autumn, Ibn Saud wrote to Mubarak, telling him that the sharif demanded as the ransom for freeing Sa'ad a yearly rental of six thousand Maria Theresa dollars (£600?, see n. 25) for the Qasim, and Saudi acknowledgment of Ottoman sovereignty. Ibn Saud agreed to both conditions, made costly presents to the sharif, recovered Sa'ad and immediately reneged on his engagement. The negotiations had taken several weeks.

**Punishment:** Nevertheless, the rebels were still not prepared for action when Ibn Saud with twelve hundred men reached Hariq. He chased them by way of Hauta to the town of Laila, where the Saudi governor had already captured one of the chief conspirators, Saud ibn Abdullah. Most of the rest of the Araïf fled to Mecca, one or more went west to al Hasa where they found support, and one to Oman. The Hazzani who had backed Saud ibn Abdullah were rounded up, and with Ibn Saud present in Laila, eighteen were beheaded. Saud ibn Abdullah was spared, and Saud ibn Abdul Aziz, presumably the head of the complot for he was later dubbed Saud 'al Kabir,' (literally, the Big One, the Great) must have escaped to the Hejaz (n. 11).

After this 1910 debacle, both Abdullah and al Kabir became Ibn Saud's fervent and reliable supporters. Before the insurrection al Kabir had married the amir's sister, Nura. As al Kabir's mother was Ajman, Ibn Saud may have proposed the union to court the support of this powerful but unruly tribe. The aborted attempt of 1910–1911 was not the last incitement to sedition by the Araïf. In al Hasa they kept the Ajman aroused and in revolt until late in 1916 when the remaining insurgents fled to Kuwait, defeated after three years of bitter conflict. This ended the agitation by the few cousins still unreconciled to Ibn Saud's supremacy.

## Plan for Power (1912)

**The Foe**: In 1912 Ibn Saud was still confronted by enemies. To the north the Rashids and their Shammar; to the east the Turks and the Ajman, and to the west the sharif of Mecca who had already invaded his territory and even now sheltered relatives opposed to his rule. Although he had succeeded in overcoming, deterring, or winning over his Nejdi foes, the defects of his army had never been more apparent. Villagers and townsmen who had won his victories and could be counted on to defend themselves as he enlarged his hegemony could not be asked to leave their fields and shops for long periods without serious harm to the economy.

The Bedu, although fully mobile, were untrustworthy for the most part, prone to leave the field of battle with their spoils and to scatter to the *dirah* of the tribes. They fought for gain at the least possible risk to life. His great-great-grandfather had armies that conquered all before them and at the beginning of the nineteenth century brought the As Saud to a pinnacle of power. Their impulsion: religious fervor directed to the spread of the tenets of reform—Wahhabism. Townsmen still professed its dogma and the *Ulema* were strict proctors of its precepts in Riyadh. Ibn Saud's ties through marriage with the descendants of Abdul Wahhab, known as 'As Shaikh,' ensured him the full support of the clergy.

**The Weapon**: But at best nomads paid only lip service to the true faith. Ibn Saud could send out *Mutawwa'in* (deacons) to the tribes to preach the word, but that alone would not make nomads immediately available, and did nothing to curb their fickleness in the field. The answer was clear. Newly roused zealots for the faith must be gathered in communities where many could be called up by a single appeal for their services. Their fervor would be kept ardent by a preacher living with them, preferably an ascetic impassioned in belief. And life in community would lead to a sense of unity of purpose, a brotherhood of the elect. Provided with tools and seed, the converts would become farmers, at least nominally self-sufficient.

## The Ikhwan (1912–1930)

**Taxis**: The first of the communities came into being in 1912 at the wells of Artawiya, 150 miles north of Riyadh in the *dirah* of the Mutair tribe. The Mutair peopled it, led by their great shaikh, ad Duwish. Ibn Saud provided the agricultural equipment for what was planned as a farming settlement, and arranged a subsidy for the villagers. Shortly thereafter a second community was founded at Ghatghat, a few miles southwest of Riyadh. This was in the *dirah* of the 'Ataiba led by their paramount shaikh, Sultan ibn Bijad ibn Humaid.

Spurred by Ibn Saud's preachers the Bedu flocked to become a part of the newly redeemed who would not only propagate the faith but also be rewarded by spoils from the ungodly. In fifteen years nearly 200 of these *Hujar (n. 12)* had been founded, adult males making up a fighting force of at least 150,000, perhaps more. Only a small part of this total was on active service at any one time. The occupants of the *Hujar* called themselves *Ikhwan* (the Brethren), for they had quit nomadic life to live in sanctified fellowship. Their badge of brotherhood was an open-topped turban of white cotton, which was wrapped around the head cloth. It replaced the otherwise ubiquitous black woolen rope with its dangling cords, the *agal*, a putative camel hobble.

The sense of superiority, of being closer to the revealed truth and to the way of life prescribed by the Prophet so influenced the conduct of the new 'Elect' that they became a scourge to those not of their order. As arbiters of dress and conduct they punished violators of their code by beatings or worse. Silk clothing was forbidden, as well as smoking, gambling, fortune-telling, and adornment of any kind. Robes must not touch the ground and facial hair must not be over-luxuriant. The more bigoted refused to reply to greetings from the non-elect, and averted their faces if addressed. Refusal to accept Ikhwanian standards of piety or conduct was on occasion punished by death, and it is reported that even those lacking knowledge of pertinent *surahs* of the Koran met the same fate.

Ibn Jiluwi, amir of al Hasa, had warned Ibn Saud against his sponsorship of the new force, and in his province he punished excesses of bigotry severely. Elsewhere in the Saudi ambit little was done to curb such immoderation, although in Riyadh Ibn Saud himself restrained the inordinate pretensions of some of the *Ulema*, and in 1919 forbade forcible proselytization.

**Potency**: Whatever its defects, the *Ikhwan* was an army unequaled in mobility and fanatical courage, requiring little or no logistical support. Led by the amirs of their *Hujar*, some of them paramount shaikhs, they fought with complete disregard of danger, even courting death on the battlefield, for the fallen were assured of a place in Paradise. The great green banner of the faith led the formal attacks of the *Ikhwan*. Inscribed in white, 'La illah il Ullah'—No god but God— it streamed in the wind of the advancing camel-mounted legion, flanked by cavalry on the blooded mares of the desert. The riders were followed by a horde of running footmen, shouting war cries, 'The winds of Paradise are blowing, where are ye who seek it?' The *Ikhwan* neither sought quarter nor gave it. In the early days some of these warriors were armed only with clubs, spears or swords. Later, all carried rifles and were girded with a bandolier closed by a dagger at the waist. At prayer time the rifles were laid down in long straight lines, butt to muzzle, as the imam led the kneeling figures in their prostrations toward Mecca. All plunder taken was delivered to a representative of Ibn Saud for distribution. Four-fifths were returned to the soldiers, and one-fifth was allotted the state. As the *Ikhwan* wore no jewelry the state profited, although animals and agricultural products were welcome in the *Hujar*.

After 1914 the *Ikhwan* participated in many of the campaigns of the Saudi forces, and by 1918 was the backbone of the armies. Its warriors sometimes spared neither women nor children, in direct contravention of the long-honored code of Bedu warfare, and as a consequence their reputation as bloodthirsty killers spread terror. Contrary to Bedu custom, animals were killed when they could not be driven off by the raiders. Yet their punishment after the rebellion of 1929–30 left much resentment over the manner in which infidel forces (British airmen) had been used to help quell the revolt.

# Al Hasa Recovered (1913)

**Overture:** By the end of 1912, through battle and diplomacy Ibn Saud had insured his hegemony over all of Nejd. However, his position with respect to the Ottoman government was equivocal. Although certainly anti-Turkish, he had no objection to a pledge of allegiance to the Sublime Porte when it seemed expedient.

In March 1911, Ibn Saud had his first long talk with Captain Shakespear *(A. VI)*, the new political agent in Kuwait *(Pl. VI, fig. 18)*. He explained to the Englishman that he wanted the Turks driven out of al Hasa for it had been a part of his ancestors' domain. Furthermore, Turkish control over the littoral of the Gulf made it difficult for him to control the tribes between Nejd and the coast. If the British would protect him from invasion by sea after he had driven the Turks out, he would be pleased to receive a British political agent. The Ottomans were now in difficulty in the Balkans and North Africa and the moment was opportune. Shakespear transmitted the proposal to London, but explained to the amir that the government was in no position to aid him. The official posture remained that Turkey was the sovereign power in Arabia. Ibn Saud must be given no encouragement. Shakespear was severely reprimanded by Whitehall for his contacts with the amir. Nevertheless, during a trip into northern Nejd he conferred with Ibn Saud for four days at Khafs, only a month before the amir's attack on the Ottoman power that had held al Hasa since 1871.

**Performance:** On the night of 4 May 1913, Ibn Saud and 800 picked men, mainly townsmen, approached Hofuf. This Turkish stronghold in al Hasa was protected by thirty-foot walls of sun-dried brick and sandstone in good repair *(Pl. IV)*. Great palm groves offered concealment to the attackers, but the walls overlooked a cleared flat several hundred yards wide. A deep, dry moat paralleled the walls and three outlying forts protected the approaches. The five gates were barred and guarded, and the walls were studded with watch towers. But there were no towers on the north wall. Somewhere along its 2,000-foot length it would be scaled, although the citadel, called the *Kut,* and two of its barbicans formed the middle of the rampart. After midnight the scaling party crept from concealment loaded down with rope and the trunks of tall palms. Young men trained from childhood to pick dates accompanied the stalwarts carrying these boles. The advance was cautious, for any loud sound would alert the garrison. Silently, they laid trunks across the dry moat and set others upright against the wall. Then, in a trice, young bare-footed climbers were on the battlements. They paid out the cord wrapped around their waists, and hand over hand were soon pulling up the heavy rope ladders attached to the dangled ends of the cords. In moments, twenty cutthroats armed with daggers had reached the street behind the wall and were away to open the south gate where the main body awaited entry. Some reports suggest that an active fifth column participated in opening the gates, headed by the Al Gosaibis, leading merchants and Ibn Saud's agents in Bahrain.

The slap of bare feet, several half-stifled groans, and the now unguarded south portal swung open to allow ingress to a horde of armed attackers who then attacked the military barracks and the *Kut*. Shots rang out as the sleeping garrison awoke to its danger and fired both rifle and cannon. But the assailants were merciless. The surviving defenders huddled in the citadel, for the populace, ired by Turkish misrule and exactions, had aided the attackers in dispatching their oppressors. Officers who had taken shelter in the mosque of Ibrahim Pasha (*Pl. IV*) where they continued to resist, surrendered at noon when threatened by the explosion of a mine under the domed edifice. When terms for evacuation had been negotiated the whole of the Turkish force, 1200 men, was escorted to the port of Oqair, some seventy miles east, where it embarked for Bahrain.

Ibn Saud moved north and occupied the ports of Dammam, Jubail, and Qatif, where a ninety-man garrison sailed to Bahrain before his arrival. The Turks made two efforts to return: one at Qatif, the other at Oqair, but both failed. So, in a matter of weeks Ibn Saud recovered a province held by the Turks for 42 years. Nevertheless, he complained to Cox about British acceptance of the Turk's use of Bahrain as a staging area for invasion, although he did not mention that the Ottoman troops attacking Qatif had been transported from Basra to Bahrain in a British steamship.

In an attempt to avoid retaliation he sent several messages to the Turks expressing his subservience and loyalty, at the same time pointing out that he had only retaken what was his family's. He feared greatly a Turkish riposte from the sea, manifest in his repeated efforts, vain for over a decade, to obtain British protection, although briefly the official position of Whitehall favored intervention on his behalf. So, on 29 May 1914, Ibn Saud signed the treaty forwarded to him in Riyadh by his agent in Basra. The wali of Basra had signed it on the 15th (*n. 30*).

**Turkish Treaty:** The terms of the treaty guaranteed him lifetime recognition of his status as Wali of Nejd, the services of a military officer as joint commander of the forces, and troops at their joint discretion to be stationed in the ports; the government would supervise customs, taxes, etc. Surplus funds from these sources would be sent to the Porte, but arms and ammunition would be provided free. A postal service would be established and Ibn Saud would have direct communication with the Ministry of the Interior. He was prohibited from conducting foreign affairs, negotiating treaties or granting concessions. If war or insurrection came he was to provide troops to combat the common enemy. He was spared any effort to comply with the provisions of the treaty by the declaration of war between the Turkish government and Great Britain on 5 November 1914. When a copy of the treaty was found in Basra in 1916, Cox wrote on the flyleaf, 'This is the treaty which Ibn Saud was obliged in self-defense to make when we left him to his own devices in the early part of 1914.' *(See n. 30 for a discussion of the authenticity of the document.)*

# World War (1914–1918)

According to one author, before war was declared Ibn Saud had envisioned a plan to take Basra provided that Britain gave him a free hand. Shakespear told him that the government would never allow it. In any event, with the onset of hostilities Ibn Saud received a letter from the acting political resident (Knox) assuring him that for his aid he would be granted everything he had ever requested. Basra was seized by troops from India before he could assemble a force, but he said in his reply to the letter that he would further the common interests of the friends of the 'Illustrious Government.'

**The Sharif**: Meanwhile, Ibn Saud's enemy, the sharif of Mecca, Husain ibn Ali, an aged descendant of the Prophet's daughter and son-in-law, made a proposal through his son Abdullah to Lord Kitchener in Cairo: given aid to effect Arab unity he would lead a revolt. He was known to the several groups of Arabs in the Middle East that were planning an uprising to gain freedom from the Turks. His sons were in contact with these insurgents, and as sharif he had much prestige and influence among them. Husain controlled many thousands of tribesmen who, provided with modern weapons, could combat the Ottoman garrisons on the Red Sea coast, and perhaps drive them from the Hejaz. When the Allied Gallipoli campaign of 1915–1916 failed, an Arab uprising became imperative for many of the Turkish soldiers fighting for the Dreibund were Arabs and their defection would weaken the enemy. This fact, as well as the worsening military situation in Mesopotamia late in 1915 led in February 1916, to the establishment of the Arab Bureau (Allied Intelligence in Cairo) headed by D. G. Hogarth. This new entity promised Husain lavish supplies of military equipment and a subsidy in gold reported to be as much as £200,000 a month in return for his heading a revolt. The high commissioner of Egypt, Lord Kitchener, who had begun secret discussions with Husain, was drowned when his ship was torpedoed on the North Sea. His replacement was Sir Henry McMahon.

Perhaps even more tempting to the ambitious sharif than the Arab Bureau's offer was Sir Henry's pledge (in the third of four secret communications) to support Husain's designs for the independence of the Arab peoples. England would aid to establish Arab autonomy in those Turkish provinces in Asia where Britain could act without detriment both to French interests and to those of some indigenous governments that would be supported and maintained. Small states and shaikhdoms already protected by treaty with Great Britain were excluded. Husain took it that his plans to head an Arab confederation would be backed by the Allies. Not long afterward he assumed the title, 'King of the Arab Lands.'

The revolt began on 5 June 1916. After a good start during which Husain's forces freed Mecca, the advance lagged. T. E. Lawrence was sent to spur progress, with the well-publicized results which Glubb (1959) characterized as, 'a valuable contribution to victory.' The story is told by Lawrence in his magnificent epic. Baker (1979) gives a more prosaic but valuable summary that focuses on Husain's aspirations, his plaints, and his disillusion.

On his side of the peninsula Ibn Saud had gone into action against his great enemy, the Ar Rashid, over a year before the revolt in the Hejaz began. But he did not choose to aid the British in their battle to drive the Turk from Mesopotamia. Several authors state categorically that he did nothing to aid the Allied war effort. That is demonstrably false, although after the Ajman revolt ended he could have helped more than he chose to, and it is probable that he furnished supplies and transport animals to the Turks during the first two years of the war.

**Shakespear:** Early in February 1914, Shakespear, then a vigorous 35, began an adventurous trip across Arabia as the first step of his return to London for long leave. Ibn Saud had invited him to Riyadh, and his eager requests for consent to visit the Saudi capital were supported by Sir Percy Cox. The Secretary of State, Lord Crewe, at last granted him permission for the journey, for once contravening Whitehall policy with regard to Turkish sensibilities about British contacts with Ibn Saud. Shakespear arrived in Riyadh on 9 March and left three days later heading north. On 17 May he arrived at Kontilla at the Egyptian frontier of Sinai, thus ending one of the longest camel rides across Arabia ever made by a foreigner, 1810 miles. He reached London late in the spring, reported on his trip and reiterated his plea for recognition of Ibn Saud's worth. When war was declared in August, he went to Aldershot where he began to train recruits while hoping for transfer to France. The Foreign Office found him there, and in short order he was on his way back to Arabia.

On 31 December 1914, he reached Ibn Saud's war encampment in the desert not far north of the recently established *Hijra* of Artawiya. Shakespear, now resident representative of Britain to the Saudi court, bore proposals from Whitehall concerning the ways in which the amir of Nejd could aid the war effort in return for arms and money. But Ibn Saud was more concerned over the promises of the letter sent him at the outbreak of the war. Were its provisions valid only for the duration of hostilities, or would they continue indefinitely? Would he be required to accept other conditions to insure that they would continue in force?

Shakespear inferred from these questions that Ibn Saud wanted a signed treaty before breaking the neutrality which he had maintained with great difficulty because of Turkish pressures to join with them. Together, the friends prepared the draft of such a treaty, setting out Ibn Saud's desires and the conditions he was prepared to accept. Shakespear forwarded the draft to Cox early in January. But he was destined never to see it in effect.

**Jarrab:** On 31 December when Shakespear met the amir in the desert north of Zilfi the latter had been in the field for several weeks preparing for combat with the Ar Rashid. Ibn Saud's army of about six thousand included 1,500 Nejdi townsmen and over 4,000 Bedu of the 'Ataiba, Suhul, and Harb, as well as a mounted contingent of Ajman. Some *Ikhwan* from Artawiya were present. Ibn Saud twice urged his English friend to return to Kuwait. Shakespear refused. As an ardent photographer he wanted pictures of a battle in the desert between Arabs, a spectacle no Westerner had ever seen. So, when Ibn Saud moved his camp the captain accompanied him, as usual in the uniform of the 17th Bengal Lancers. Although most foreigners adopted Arab garb, both comfortable and inconspicuous, Shakespear had worn khaki on all of his desert journeys.

At dawn on 24 January 1915, the Shammar and Nejdi forces, nearly equal in strength, met in battle near a village called Jarrab, well to the north of the town of Zilfi. The Saudis deployed their infantry along the north bank of Wadi ar Rumah between two bodies of mounted men. The Shammar army advanced along the broad floor of the wadi from the southwest, and the men of Nejd charged into their flank. Sabers flashed and clashed; men bent low over camel or mare fired blindly into the clouds of dust veiling the battlefield. At the wadi's edge the Saudi infantry poured lead into the struggling mass. Behind them on a hillock of sand, a lone field piece fired into the Shammari forces not yet engaged. Clad in khaki, and with pistol as sidearm, Captain Shakespear stood nearby, snapping the shutter of his bulky camera to record the action. He put it down and raised his binoculars.

'Up fifty, Husain!'

The Ajman cavalry and camel corps broke suddenly from their positions on the left flank of the Saudi line and rode off southward in the direction of the Shammari camp, then completely undefended. The Shammari mounted reserve on which the cannon had been firing charged into the gap and began to roll up the Saudi infantry which retreated in wild disorder. The gunner removed and buried the breechblock of his light cannon, and urged his companion to flee with him. 'Take off your topee and come with me,' he urged. Instead, the officer drew his revolver and fired it at the advancing horde. Shot in the leg he continued firing. Then as the Shammari camelry came close, he was hit in the arm. He fell as a bullet found his head. The greed of the Ajman had lost both the day and a friend for Ibn Saud. The enemy was in no better plight. Both sides would require time to recover, but Ibn Saud was given little respite:

Hearing that Ibn Saud was mobilizing for a confrontation with ibn Rashid (then Saud ibn Abdul Aziz ar Rashid), Sharif Husain sent his son Abdullah into Nejd at the head of a Bedu force. To the British in Cairo Husain explained the invasion as a support for Ibn Saud. The Hejazis stopped at Shara, southwest of Anaiza, some 170 miles from the battle, and went no farther. Although Ibn Saud counted the battle at Jarrab a defeat and many Bedu abandoned him, the sharif's army returned at once to the Hejaz, its true purpose unknown and unrevealed.

The abandonment of the fight at Jarrab by the Ajman camelry that caused the rout of the Saudi infantry was followed by an even more baneful defection by the tribe. It cost Ibn Saud a brother even dearer to him than Shakespear.

**Ajman Revolt:** The freeing of al Hasa in 1913 and the installation of Abdullah ibn Jiluwi (he of the Riyadh exploit) as its amir had not been welcomed by the *Shia* community along the coast (*n. 13*). Ibn Jiluwi was known and feared because of his rigorous enforcement of *Shari'a* law. But he was instructed by Riyadh to leave the

Shiites free to practice their heresy in private. More trouble arose when ibn Jiluwi began to collect taxes on agricultural products and cattle. Egged on by two of the still uncowed Araïf the Ajman revolted and were joined by the Murra. Ibn Jiluwi, outmatched, sent to Riyadh for help.

In August 1915, Ibn Saud seconded by his brother Sa'ad headed for Hofuf leading a scratch force of 300 townsmen and 900 Bani Hajir whose *dirah* was in southern al Hasa. Sixty miles northwest of Hofuf at Jebel Kinzan he intercepted the Ajman dissidents and began to discuss their grievances. His brother, anxious for revenge, suggested that the situation was favorable for an ambush. Ibn Saud agreed, probably with reluctance, and in the ensuing early morning fire-fight Sa'ad was shot dead. A bullet deflected by a cartridge pouch bruised Ibn Saud. In all, 300 men were killed in this failed ambuscade.

The rebels outnumbered Ibn Saud's and ibn Jiluwi's combined forces, and in October the two were behind the walls of Hofuf waiting for help. Mohammed, Ibn Saud's brother, headed the relieving force from Riyadh, and two letters to Kuwait brought to al Hasa Mubarak's son Salim leading many Kuwaiti tribesmen. With these reinforcements Ibn Saud began a series of raids and attacks on the rebels. On one dawn raid, he is said to have been wounded high on the thigh. His men thought the wound even more serious and to reassure them he requested that a marriage be arranged. He consummated it on the spot, and thus calmed their fears. This feat at once became part of the Ibn Saud legend. The razzias and skirmishes continued with a ruthlessness rare in desert combat and culminated in a confrontation in central al Hasa at Ridha where the insurgent Ajman and the scheming Araïf suffered a major defeat. A few days later Ibn Saud had an important rendezvous with Sir Percy Cox.

**British Treaty:** Before the battle of Jarrab Shakespear sent to Cox the draft of the treaty that he and Ibn Saud had prepared. Cox emended it and sent it on. Vetted by the India Office and Whitehall, it was returned to Ibn Saud who suggested other changes. Before the end of August the text had been agreed upon by both parties. Ibn Saud, occupied in putting down the rebellion, arranged a late December meeting with Sir Percy. They met on Tarut Island near Qatif on the 24th, and the treaty was signed 26 December 1915.

It gave Ibn Saud the protection of Great Britain that he had been after for twelve years. He was recognized as the ruler of Nejd and al Hasa and as chieftain of the tribes therein. He could name his successor. In return he promised to refrain from entering into treaties with other nations, from giving up territory, or from granting concessions to any foreign power. He would keep roads to the Holy Places open, and would not interfere in nor attack the territories under British protection along the Persian gulf. The treaty was ratified by the viceroy of India 18 July 1916.

In October 1915 by letter, Cox had promised Ibn Saud three hundred captured Mausers (he had asked for 3,000) and ten thousand rupees, but the guns were not delivered until the spring of 1916. In June 1916, he was given a thousand more guns, two hundred thousand rounds of ammunition for them, and a loan of £20,000.

**Ajman Defeat**: In addition to their support of the Araïf the Ajman had refused to accept Saudi control of their affairs including a demand that they stop imposing a transit tax on caravans crossing their territory en route to Nejd. Just before his December meeting with Sir Percy, Ibn Saud, leading the combined forces from Kuwait, Riyadh and al Hasa, decisively defeated the Ajman in the aforementioned battle at Ridha. Then Salim and his Kuwaitis went back to Hofuf. There he and Ibn Saud's half brother Mohammed quarreled. It must have been a bitter and long-lasting dispute, for deeply offended, Salim took his contingent home. At the same time he offered the defeated Ajman shelter in Kuwait which in an 1899 treaty the British had promised to protect from any aggressor. It was the beginning of a long enmity.

In spite of a crushing defeat, the Ajman had not given up. Ibn Saud, with his usual persistence and aided by the guns and cash provided by the British, continued the fight until September 1916, when the last Ajman force crossed into Kuwait. Methods of warfare on both sides had lost the chivalrous aspects of previous conflicts. Women killed the wounded, and wells were fouled.

**Imperial Durbar**: Sir Percy had been vindicated in his long campaign to make the British government recognize Ibn Saud's importance, for, after subduing inter-tribal bickering on his return to Riyadh in September, the amir of Nejd controlled unchallenged the whole of Nejd and al Hasa. But he feared that British support for Husain would end in subordinating him to his hated rival. On 11 November 1916 Sir Percy met Ibn Saud at Oqair to calm his fears. The amir expressed a wish to meet Jabir, Mubarak's elder son, now shaikh of Kuwait.

Nine days later on 20 November an Imperial Durbar (here a formal British military reception in the style of Indian rajahs) was held in Kuwait. It is probable that Cox had already planned this conclave of shaikhs, for wartime difficulties in communication made it unlikely that such a gathering could have assembled with only a week's notice.

Other reasons for a Durbar existed aside from a demonstration of Britain's power and an expression of its deep appreciation for Arab support: Whitehall had already suggested that better use could be made of the new Nejdi ally, and a meeting of leaders would make possible coördination of the activities of all the Arab tribes under the control of the India Office and would serve to improve the strained relations between them and the sharif of Mecca. The Durbar was attended by Ibn Saud, Shaikh Jabir of Kuwait, (his father, Mubarak, had died in October 1915) Shaikh Khaaz'al of Muhammera, then a Persian district, and other important shaikhs from al Hasa and southern Iraq. Ibn Saud was dubbed Knight Commander of the Most Eminent Order of the Indian Empire.

At the conclusion of the ceremonies he made a speech, certainly tongue-in-cheek, for it followed by less than a month Husain's announcement that he was now, 'King of the Arab Lands.' Nevertheless, in accordance with Sir Percy's urgent recommendations for harmony, he condemned the Turks, praised the British, and urged all to coöperate with Sharif Husain in forwarding the Arab cause of liberty from the Turkish yoke. But more important, Ibn Saud was given a monthly subsidy of £5,000, three thousand rifles, a sword of honor and four machine guns. (The machine guns ended up in Hofuf and were never used because the gunners forgot how to operate them.) In return, Ibn Saud promised to keep a force of four thousand men in the field to checkmate the Rashids and to help prevent supplies from Kuwait reaching the Turks to whom he had covertly sold camels during the two previous years.

After the Durbar Ibn Saud was taken to Basra where he saw a display of British arms, an airplane in flight, and an x-ray of his hand. He rode on a train and in an automobile. On the ship to Basra he was present at a Sunday service led by a vice admiral. The reverence paid Isa, a Jewish prophet of the 'Time of Ignorance,' was remarkable, and confirmed his views that although they were infidels, the British were pious believers in God.

**Riyadh Mission**: Throughout the winter of 1916–17 and for months thereafter Ibn Saud kept in the field the four thousand men that he had committed to at the Durbar. Considerable difficulty arose in maintaining the blockade of goods to the Turks. Merchants in Kuwait and in the Qasim conspired to run it, probably aided by the new shaikh of Kuwait, Salim. Salim was dour and against all change, including acceptance of Ikhwanian Puritanism. His sponsorship of the Ajman was contrary to the commitment entered into by his brother Jabir who had died early in 1917, only eighteen months after assuming his father's duties.

In September 1917, a caravan of three thousand camels from the Qasim reached Kuwait under a pass signed by Turki ibn Abdul Aziz then in charge of the blockade under his father's orders. The caravan was loaded and returned to the Qasim with the sanction of Salim although he had been ordered by telegraph to detain it. This deliberate flouting of a British command resulted in a naval blockade of Kuwait.

After the Durbar both the India Office and Whitehall considered that the £5,000 monthly subsidy to Ibn Saud should yield more substantial help to the war effort. The failure of the blockade of supplies to Ottoman forces in Syria lent substance to their plaint. Perhaps Cox and others had learned that Ibn Saud himself had conspired to supply the Turks besieged in Medina. So, on 30 November 1917, a British military mission arrived in Riyadh, headed, after a dispute, by H. St. J. B. Philby *(A. VII)* who was to remain with Ibn Saud for thirty-five years after the war. Philby's mission had three objectives: 1. Improve relations between Ibn Saud and Sharif Husain. 2. Determine Ibn Saud's requirements for taking the field against the Rashids. 3. Improve relations between Kuwait and Nejd. They had deteriorated after Salim had given asylum to Ajman who in 1917 had twice raided Nejd and then fled back to Kuwait. Kuwaiti grievances included the fact that Ibn Saud had taxed the Awazim, nominally subjects of Kuwait.

Husain refused to allow Ronald Storrs, who was to represent Cairo in the mission, to go from Jedda to Riyadh because he could not assure his safety in Nejd. On his side, Ibn Saud vetoed sending the mission on from Riyadh to Jedda. But in the Saudi capital some progress was made. Colonel Cunliffe-Owen, accompanying Philby as military adviser, sat in on the discussions of the armament necessary for a successful campaign against the Rashids. The requirements were determined as: £50,000 per month for an estimated six months; four field or siege guns and crews; ten thousand rifles, and ammunition for them. Ibn Saud would provide fifteen thousand men. Philby submitted this agenda to higher authority thus fulfilling one of the objectives of the mission.

But another objective—that of improving relations between the Hejaz and Nejd—aborted completely. Instead animosity worsened. Philby increased the tension between the two chiefs by making an uneventful journey, not authorized by Husain, from Riyadh to Taïf, thus refuting Husain's contention that insecurity in Nejd made Storrs' trip unwise.

Consequently there was no improvement in the relations between the rulers and Philby was in Husain's bad books for a time. Matters were not improved by Philby's arguments with the sharif, so vehement that he was barred from Hogarth's meetings with the self-styled 'King'. Philby was forced to return to the Gulf by sea via Cairo and Bombay for Husain refused authorization for an overland journey. He found Ibn Saud in the desert at Shaib Shauki only on 11 April 1918. He had been instructed to tell the amir that the assault on the Rashids had been canceled. Cairo feared that he would use the new arms given him to attack Husain, and British successes in the Middle East made an encounter with ibn Rashid needless.

**Failure at Haïl**: In an attempt to salvage something from the cancellation, and perhaps also to help Ibn Saud divert the *Ikhwan* from their ever-increasing insistence on retaliation for the sharif of Mecca's attacks on the faithful at Khurma, Philby, flouting Cairo's orders, promised Ibn Saud £20,000 if he would mount an attack on Haïl. Ibn Saud agreed to do so, but only after the *Hajj*.

In August 1918 preparations for the foray began. Philby was not allowed to stay with the army after it passed Buraida on its way north. *Was the ban only because the amir feared the loss of another British officer?*

The columns met with relatively slight resistance in their advance and collected loot in quantity, mainly camels and sheep. The garrison at Haïl was strong and determined, the walls high. After several half-hearted attacks the Saudi army, now predominantly *Ikhwan*, returned to Riyadh in December. The war had been over for some time—the armistice with Turkey was signed 30 October—but British support for Husain was still official policy and Ibn Saud berated Philby for its continuance. The expedition had occupied large numbers of the *Ikhwan*, and temporarily distracted them from their insistence on a riposte to Husain's attacks on Khurma. This was taken officially as justification for Philby's decision to turn over the £20,000 in gold to Ibn Saud in return for undertaking the offensive. Perhaps in a covert attempt to lessen Ibn Saud's bitterness at the paucity of British support for his régime, but officially as thanks for his help during the war, the Saudi amir was invited to visit London shortly after Husain had launched his first failed attempt to take Khurma. He sent his 14-year-old son, Faisal (*A. VII*).

# Sanguinary Disputes (1918–1920)

**Khurma–Turaba:** The inhabitants of Khurma, a town on the main caravan route from Nejd to the Hejaz, were converted to Wahhabism during the eighteenth century dispersion of this dogma from Dhariya. Their descendants, some four thousand souls, readily accepted the puritanical austerity of the *Ikhwan*. The amir of Khurma, Khalid ibn Luwai, was nominally under the hegemony of Husain ibn Ali, sharif of Mecca and ruler of the Hejaz. Early in 1917 Khalid was jailed after having been humiliated publicly by a blow across the face from Abdullah, the sharif's son. Ibn Luwai had refused Husain's order to remove the town's *qadi* (judge) who advocated that the people transfer their allegiance from Husain to Ibn Saud. In November 1917, ibn Luwai announced his independence from the Hejaz, presumably after consulting the Nejdi prince.

In May 1918, Husain sent a force of eight hundred Bedu under orders to seize the judge. These nomads were later reinforced by eighty-two soldiers of the army, two old guns, and two machine guns. On 1 June this joint contingent led by a sharif, Hamza, lost fourteen men and all of its guns in an unsuccessful attack on Khurma. The Bedu of this force then disbanded. In July, Husain sent another force of eight hundred armed with four field guns and six machine guns to occupy Khurma. A part of this array under Amir Shakir of the 'Ataiba was driven off with heavy losses.

The British counseled Husain against further attacks, and at the same time warned Ibn Saud not to invade the Hejaz. Ibn Saud wrote the British representative in Jedda that he would accept arbitration to determine who would have jurisdiction over Khurma, but he wanted the British to guarantee that its inhabitants would be safe from molestation by Husain.

In August, Shakir clashed with the *Ikhwan* at Ain Hannu, sixteen miles east of Khurma. He was again defeated, and a part of his 'Ataiba defected to the Saudi forces. On 16 September ibn Luwai attacked a similar detachment, and in October another push by Husain's 'Ataiba was repulsed. Ibn Saud promised the British not to intervene personally, but would not agree to continue curbing reprisals against Husain by the inhabitants of Nejd.

Turkey surrendered to the Entente on 30 October 1918 in a ceremony on board H.M.S. *Agamemnon* off the town of Mudros on Lemnos Island in the Aegean Sea, but the Ottoman commander in Medina, the obsessed Fakhri Pasha, held out for two more months, until 1 January 1919. Until Medina fell, all the attacks on Khurma had been made by poorly-armed Bedu aided by a few soldiers with modern weapons. The reason: half of the sharifian army was besieging Medina, the other half was heading toward Damascus with Faisal (Husain's third son) or Lawrence.

Husain was determined to keep Khurma and to topple the Nejdi barbarian. In May 1919, Abdullah, with an army of five thousand well-armed regulars equipped with ten field guns and twenty machine guns, advanced from Taïf toward Khurma. He was joined by many Bedu hoping to share in the spoils. On 20 May an attack on the invading force by 4,000 *Ikhwan* failed. On the 21st Abdullah advanced to seize Turaba, a town sixty miles east of Taïf and forty miles from Khurma. He established a camp and boasted that he would move on east-ward to al Hasa after having taken Khurma. He ordered all the tribes and villages to send him representatives within six days or suffer the consequences.

For months the *Ikhwan* had become increasingly insistent that action be taken to stop harassment of true believers by the heretics of Sharif Husain, only to be held back by Ibn Saud. Now unleashed, the initial setback did not deter them. Ibn Saud himself took the field with an army of twelve thousand, but he and his army were far from the decisive battle that took place during the night of 25–26 May.

From the *Hijra* of Ghatghat near Riyadh eleven hundred camel-mounted *Ikhwan* rode in seven days the three hundred miles to Khurma where they joined townsmen under Amir Khalid ibn Luwai. Commanded by the devout *Ikhwan* leader Sultan ibn Bijad ibn Humaid of Ghatghat, the combined forces attacked Abdullah's army after midnight and destroyed it. Many victims awoke only as their throats were slit. Witnesses of the slaughter say that blood formed pools in the sand. Nearly all of Abdullah's army were killed. Only 150 Hejazis, mainly officers in undress, escaped to Mecca with Abdullah to report the massacre to his father, old Husain.

Ibn Saud restrained the victors at Turaba from invading the Hejaz, for the British had warned him that if his men did so he would lose his subsidy and the protection of the treaty of 1915. He could afford to wait. British motivation to protect his enemy would soon be gone now that the war had ended. But he did not foresee the extent to which wartime acquiescence to Husain's pretensions to leadership of all the Arabs would become government policy in support of Hashemite suzerainty.

**Kuwait:** Jabir ibn Mubarak had ruled only eighteen months after his father's death in 1915 when he too died early in February 1917. His brother Salim, who then became amir, was different in many respects from his cosmopolitan and easygoing sibling. He was a stern Moslem, supporter of an austere sect inimical to the Wahhabi dogma (*n. 4*), and very obstinate. Before his accession he had spent his life in the desert and refused to accept modern inventions. Salim's sudden departure from al Hasa after the battle of Ridha in November 1915 had already estranged Ibn Saud and his protection of raiding Ajman tribesmen in Kuwait antagonized the Nejdi ruler even further against Salim, already in his bad books.

The sea blockade of Kuwait that began in February 1918 lasted until 10 August 1920. It played havoc with the economy of the town by stopping imports, for transshipment of these goods by camel train to the interior was a major source of revenue. Salim blamed the blockade on Ibn Saud's reports to the British about Kuwaiti merchants having run guns and supplies to the Turks in Syria, although he himself had Turkish sympathies and may well have been involved in the traffic. So when a question of territorial limits arose in 1919, the two amirs were already on bad terms.

According to the text of the treaty entered into between Ibn Saud and the British government on 26 December 1915 on Tarut Island, the frontier between Kuwait and Saudi territories remained undefined. But the Anglo–Ottoman Convention of 1913 gave Kuwait indirect control over and the right to levy taxes on tribes in a large area 130 to 160 miles south and west of Kuwait town. (Gold-berg [p. 90] says that the Convention was signed 29 July 1913 after three years of negotiation; but because of the war the paragraphs concerning al Hasa and Kuwait were never ratified.)

To forestall territorial claims by Ibn Saud, Shaikh Salim proposed to construct a fort on the coast at Dohat Balbul 100 miles south of Kuwait (see Map 1). In February Ibn Saud countered by sending Mutair tribesmen to seize the wells at Qariya'Ilya. Their leader began to build a *hijra* there, and Salim riposted by sending a large force to Hamdh, fifteen miles east of Qariya'Ilya, in an attempt to overawe the Badawi. This force was attacked by *Ikhwan* under Faisal ad Duwish and routed with great loss, its leaders narrowly escaping capture. On its return to Kuwait, Salim, in fear of further attacks, ordered that the town be walled. In two months a twenty-five-foot mud-brick rampart four miles in length enclosed the town. It was constructed in panic haste by all the able-bodied—men, women, and children.

Salim asked for British help in negotiations with Ibn Saud, and was told that he had not been a party to the Anglo–Ottoman Convention, but was protected in any event by Clause VI of the 1915 treaty. (This treaty specified that Ibn Saud would not interfere in British-protected territories—Kuwait, Bahrain, Trucial Coast states.) Late in August, under British pressure both parties agreed to arbitration of the dispute, but Faisal ad Duwish attacked before negotiation could begin.

On 9 September a large force of *Ikhwan* reached Subaihiya, less than fifteen miles south of Kuwait town. The new walls were manned at once, but no assault came. However, on the morning of 10 September, another troop of *Ikhwan* attacked the village of Jahra twenty miles west of the town.

The *Ikhwan* began their attack at six o'clock, and by nine had cleared the village. The surviving defenders, some six hundred, took refuge in the Qasr al Ahmar, the Red Fort, a square building with walls fifteen feet high where negoti-ations for their surrender continued throughout the day.

That night the *Ikhwan* made three determined assaults on the fort. All were repulsed. In the morning over eight hundred dead lay around its walls, and an equal or greater number of wounded returned to Subaihiya, five hundred dying on the way. Kuwaiti losses were some two hundred. On 18 October a Saudi dele-gation visited Kuwait, demanding that the population embrace Ikhwanian reforms. Shaikh Salim received it only on the 24th.

The British government now intervened, threatening reprisals if the town were attacked. Major More, the political agent, delivered the warning in person to the delegation, and a copy was dropped on the *Ikhwan* encampment from an airplane. On the 26th the *Ikhwan* army withdrew. British warships in Kuwait bay, and the presence of R.A.F. aircraft probably had a part in the decision to leave.

The discord between Ibn Saud and Salim ended abruptly with Salim's death on 27 February 1921 at Jahra where he had been ill only four days. Ibn Saud said at once that there was no longer any quarrel to settle, and no need of a boundary between his territory and Kuwait's.

Clearly, ad Duwish's raids, ostensibly to force proselytization, were in fact punitive. It is known that they had been ordered by Ibn Saud. That the feud was a clash of personalities is proven by Ibn Saud's declaration of friendship to Kuwait after Salim's death. Although many anecdotes relate Ibn Saud's sudden anger, quickly over, the Kuwait affair shows him capable of enduring hatred.

# Expansion (1921–1923)

Asir: Early in the seventeenth century much of Asir, a mountainous area south of the Hejaz with a narrow coastal plain, the Tihama, was invaded by the Turks. Their rule was tenuous and disputed by the people, who after adopting Wahhabism, came under the influence of a holy man, Ahmed ibn Idris, a devout Sufi from Morocco. He became revered as a saint. After he died in 1837 pilgrims flocked to his tomb and shortly thereafter the Idrisi, headed by Ahmed's son and later his grandson established a small theocratic state. With Italian help, in 1909 they revolted against the Turks. The struggle continued intermittently throughout the next decade. As a consequence, at the end of the Great War Asir was declared independent by the victorious allies who were concerned that the holder of the Farasan Islands be friendly because of the strategic importance of the archipelago in controlling maritime traffic. During the war, British troops occupied Hodeida and the islands against a possible Turkish invasion. Sharif Husain, who before the revolt had fought at the side of the Turks in Asir, at war's end disputed Idrisi hegemony himself and was allowed to hold the port of Qunfudah in spite of Idrisi claims to the region.

According to an Arab source, Hassan al Aidh, the amir of Abha, the largest town in the mountains, allied himself with Sharif Husain and attempted to subjugate the tribes and villagers who again professed Wahhabism. Delegations appealed to Ibn Saud for aid. He warned al Aidh to respect religious liberties, and received a threat in reply. In 1921 he sent 3,000 *Ikhwan* to Asir under the command of one of his cousins, Abdul Aziz ibn Musa'ad al Jiluwi, who had been one of the nine paladins of Riyadh. The oppressor was taken to Riyadh where he remained in prison for more than a year before returning to Abha. A Saudi-appointed amir replaced him but the Idrisi were allowed to hold the coastal plain and the port of Hodeida. In July 1922, Faisal, Ibn Saud's second surviving son, led 6,000 men to Asir to punish the recalcitrant al Aidh who had revolted against Saudi hegemony and with the aid of Sharif Husain had taken Abha again. Faisal easily defeated both Aidh's and Husain's contingents, and in May of the following year returned with his prisoner to Riyadh, where he was welcomed by his father (*n. 14.*)

While Ibn Saud was tightening his hold on the mountains still contested for by sharifian forces from the Hejaz, the Idrisi chieftain died. His two sons fought over the succession. One, Ali, aided by the Imam Yahiya of Yemen, took power. His uncle, Husain, deposed him in 1924. The Imam Yahiya seized the opportunity offered by the discord to occupy Hodaida and Jizan, the Idrisi capital on the coastal plain. The Idrisi ruler, fearing that the imam would take all of his holdings asked for Saudi aid. It was granted (Treaty of Mecca, 21 October 1926), but on the condition that the Idrisi possessions would be annexed to the Saudi domain upon his death. In 1934, after a Saudi clash with the Imam Yahiya of Yemen, the province was incorporated into Saudi Arabia.

**Haïl Taken:** In 1919 the Shammar were no longer supported by Turkey and it was easier for Ibn Saud's missionaries to penetrate the large tract north of Buraida occupied by nomad supporters of the Rashids. Among these nomads their prose-lytizing met with some success, but the townsmen of Haïl, although troubled by the murder of successive rulers, accepted with little demur the changes in régime caused by the several seizures of power by competing branches of the Rashids.

Early in 1920, the last of the assassinations connected with the struggle for power resulted in a thirteen-year-old becoming the amir of the Shammar, with his uncle as regent. Ibn Saud took the opportunity offered by this change in régime to conclude an agreement between himself and the new rulers of Haïl. Its terms allowed the amirate to remain independent in internal affairs, but ultimate control of the state was henceforth in Saudi hands. This arrangement was soon abrogated by another takeover.

In 1914, the Ruwala chieftain Nuri as Sha'lan, most of whose *dirah* was in Syria, had occupied the villages of Jauf and Sakaka at the northern limit of Shammar influence in Nejd. As the sudden deaths of successive Rashidi amirs continued, Nuri's son easily enlarged the sway of this powerful tribe. To combat this menace, the guardians of the new child amir named as leader of the Shammari army a brother of the latest assassin. In 1920, he, Mohammed ibn Talal, regained control of these northern towns held throughout the war years by the Ruwala and then returned to Haïl and took over the amirate, the deposed ruler, Abdullah ibn Mitab, age 13, fleeing 17 July 1921 to the Saudi camp where he was well received.

Ibn Talal was arrogant but a good warrior. In the spring of 1921 forces probing his dispositions were under young Faisal, and in the summer Ibn Saud's brother, Mohammed, led a second contingent into the arena. The Mutair shaikh, Faisal ad Duwish, then joined the heir to the throne, Saud, in a combined offen-sive. All three were put in difficulty by determined opposition and broke off the ineffectual campaign when the young Abdullah came to them. Alone, ad Duwish renewed the attack, and after a long chase trapped ibn Talal at the village of Juhamiya, north of Haïl. The Mutair leader then demanded that the Shammar accept Wahhabi doctrine. Summoned to witness the proposed conversion, the Ar Rashid attacked the Mutair in a pitched battle and won. Ibn Saud learned of the setback and ordered ad Duwish to await his arrival.

Late in April 1921 Ibn Saud was informed of the outcome of the Cairo conference where Churchill had chosen the best of the sharif's four sons, Faisal ibn Husain, as candidate for king of Iraq (nine months after his expulsion from Syria by the French in July 1920), and his brother Abdullah as amir of the new state of Trans-Jordan (later renamed Transjordan). The southern boundaries of both states were as yet undefined.

He could wait no longer to secure his northern frontier. After observing Ramadan in Buraida, on 4 September he arrived with a large force of Mutair, 'Ataiba and Qahtan at a town east of Haïl where ibn Talal's army was concen-trated. Aided by the troops under his sons and brother, mainly *Ikhwan*, in successive attacks he drove ibn Talal and many of his army westward to seek shelter behind the walls of his capital, while other forces of the Shammar yielded. The usurper then offered to surrender provided that he remain amir of Haïl. Ibn Saud refused the proposal, and the town was put under siege by the whole of the Saudi army nominally headed by Saud ibn Abdul Aziz, the heir-apparent.

The Turkish guns captured in 1904 were brought up but not used. After more than two months of assaults costly in the lives of fanatical warriors, entry into the town was reportedly achieved through secret negotiation with partisans in Haïl opposed to the usurpers, the as Sabhan family. According to this version of events a gate opened at night. Two thousand men entered and occupied the walls and the streets of the town on 4 September 1921. Abdul Aziz ibn Musa'ad al Jiluwi, fresh from his victory in Asir, was named governor.

Another explanation of the capitulation has it that Ibn Saud threatened bombardment if within three days the town did not surrender. The townspeople and refugees who had sought shelter within the walls were short of food after two months of investment, but the gates were opened only after assurances that the *Ikhwan* would be prevented from looting and mayhem. Ibn Talal held out for a month in the fort, but, after a pledge of personal immunity, surrendered on 4 November and joined his relatives in Riyadh where, after two years in jail, he was held in residence until his death.

**Move North**: In 1922 the *Ikhwan*, accompanied by Saudi missionaries, rode to Jauf and Sakaka, three hundred miles north of Haïl at the limit of Shammari influence. Nuri as Sha'lan, the paramount shaikh of the Ruwala, had taken these border towns twice: first during the Great War and again late in 1920 during the final difficulties concerning the succession at Haïl. Ibn Talal, who had just recovered them, was then fully occupied in defending his capital against Ibn Saud. With the aid of a faction in Sakaka favorable to the Saudi cause the *Ikhwan* occupied the two towns with ease, the son of Sha'lan having little stomach to battle the redoubtable soldiers of Allah. (According to Musil, *Ikhwan* tenets flourished at Jauf as early as 1914.)

Ibn Saud's warriors did not stop at Jauf but continued north into Wadi Sirhan, the only feasible route for caravans from Arabia to the riches of the Levant. They occupied strong points and did not stop until they had reached the frontier of Syria, now in the hands of the French in accordance with the provisions of the Sykes–Picot Treaty. *(n. 15)*.

The Ruwala, whose *dirah* extended from central Syria south into the area of Jauf and Sakaka, accepted Saudi overlordship in Arabia. The Shammar Bedu of the region were given the choice of accepting Saudi rule or of moving to Iraq. Faisal, the king of that new country, made no attempt to prevent the many emigrants of the tribe into his domain from raiding into Nejd, a policy that caused many deaths on both sides.

# Boundary Problems (1922–1924)

Ibn Saud was perturbed by these Shammari raids which were immediately countered by Mutair incursions into Iraq. In March 1922, one of these forays two thousand strong, led by ad Duwish, was turned back by a contingent of Iraqi desert police.

**Muhammera Treaty:** In order to stop such confrontations, Sir Percy Cox, then high commissioner of Iraq, proposed a conference. It met late in April 1922, and a draft treaty was signed on 5 May at Muhammera by representatives of King Faisal and Ibn Saud. The treaty provided for the punishment of raiding tribes and the safety of pilgrim routes. It suggested that the frontier between Iraq and Nejd should be drawn according to tribal *dirah*. But before becoming effective the covenant had to be ratified by Sir Percy and by Ibn Saud who had been named sultan by the *Ulema* and notables in May 1921, reportedly at his own request.

The sultan rejected the treaty on the grounds that the territory and tribes formerly ibn Rashid's were now his by right of conquest. In particular, the treaty specified that the Dhafir and Amarat tribes were based in Iraq. According to the sultan they spent most of the year in Nejd. Probably this specification had been accepted by the Saudi delegates only because they had been instructed to accept under protest clauses proposed by the British, but to refuse those offered by the Iraqis.

Sir Percy was determined that bounds between Iraq and Kuwait, Iraq and Nejd, and Kuwait and al Hasa must be established, in other words that the provisions of the rejected Muhammera document should be revised and made acceptable to Ibn Saud. The matter became urgent for in July the *Ikhwan* occupied Jauf, and to the south and west, took Taima, along with Khaibar in the northern Hejaz.

In the scorching heat of August fifteen hundred Mutair from Shagra crossed a thousand miles of desert to a village, Umm al Ahmad, only a few miles from Amman the capital of the new state of Trans-Jordan. There they slaughtered all the inhabitants and killed most of their animals. The warriors of the aroused Bani Sakhr pursued the intruders who abandoned their booty as they fled south. The R.A.F. helped, using the improvised armored cars on Rolls-Royce chassis used during the war and the fragile, two-seater wooden biplanes (De Haviland 9A's) of the period armed only with machine guns. They hunted down the hapless warriors of God. Only a few escaped slaughter. Armstrong says that the eight survivors were punished by Ibn Saud. According to Besson (*p. 151*) they got only three months in prison and a lecture, but what a lecture! Rihani quotes a part of it: 'Do not forget that there is not one among you whose father or brother or cousin we have not slain. Aye, by God! It was by the sword that we conquered you, and that same sword is still above your heads. Beware, O *Ikhwan!* Encroach not on the rights of others.'

In September Cox sent Colonel Dickson to Bahrain to establish contact with the sultan in order to set an early date for a conference. Reluctantly Ibn Saud agreed to attend. In November, a few days before the conference was scheduled to begin Rihani arrived at Oqair and met Ibn Saud in the desert between Oqair and

Hofuf. The sultan told his Lebanese–American guest that his main purpose in meeting Sir Percy was to stop the noxious propaganda against him circulated by Husain and his sons. When he learned that representatives of Iraq and Kuwait were to be present he feared bad faith, but could not avoid the conference that was to convene on 21 November. It began four days late because Cox and the representatives of Iraq and Kuwait had been delayed en route.

**The Oqair Protocols:** *(A. IX)* Ibn Saud, sultan for just eighteen months, and envoys from the newly hatched kingdom of Iraq wrangled for five days over the bounds between their dominions. Sir Percy lost patience. He told both sides that at that rate nothing would be settled in a year. In a private meeting he told the sultan that he, Cox, would decide the type and position of the frontier. Ibn Saud accepted this dictum, perhaps because of his respect for Sir Percy, to him the epitome of British fairness. The high commissioner penciled red lines on a map, representing bounds recognized to this day. (Recently contested by Sadam Husain.) In order to render lip service to Ibn Saud's contentions concerning the importance of tribal *dirah*, a rhomboidal 'Neutral Zone' was drawn on the boundary between Iraq and Nejd, and another, a broad arc, on the new frontier between Kuwait and al Hasa. *(See Map 1.)* The demarcation between Iraq and Nejd gave Iraq a large tract claimed by Nejd, but as compensation Ibn Saud was ceded most of the territory considered Kuwaiti in the Anglo–Ottoman treaty of 1913, unratified because of the war. In addition, Cox promised Ibn Saud that he would be assigned the villages and salt mines of Qariyat al Milh in Wadi Sirhan when the southern border of Transjordan had been fixed by treaty. Thus the principal loser in this high-handed procedure was Kuwait, the smallest and weakest of the three states. Although under British protection since 1899, this shaikhdom was reduced to one-fifth of its former area of jurisdiction with a concomitant loss of both the support of and the taxes from two tribes of al Hasa.

The two protocols were signed 2 December 1922. That of Iraq-Nejd permitted the free movement of nomadic tribes across the frontier and the free use of wells near the frontier. Article 3, written to satisfy Ibn Saud's contention that difficulties would arise from a fixed boundary, prohibited construction of forts and concentrations of troops in the border area. This article was to become one of the pretexts for armed rebellion against him.

At the time, Cox's drawing the limits of states on a map did nothing to stop incessant raiding from both sides of the new boundary between Iraq and Nejd. The British government wanted to put an end to this scourge and at the same time to address two other matters: one, to end wartime subsidies in the Middle East, and the other, to establish and safeguard the frontiers of Transjordan.

**Kuwait Conference:** To reach these objectives, on 17 December 1923, after months of delay, a conference convened in Kuwait. Representatives of all the parties concerned: Iraq, Transjordan, Kuwait, the Hejaz, and Nejd were present, but Husain refused to send his son Ali or even the young Zaid as a delegate, and for a time held back his representatives because ad Duwish had raided in his kingdom to within eighty miles of Medina. The agenda was largely that of the rejected Treaty of Muhammera. But an important addition was negotiation to counter the menace posed by the *Ikhwan's* recent occupation of Wadi Sirhan and the area to the east up to the Syrian border. In June the *Ikhwan* had occupied the fort at Qaf near the northern end of Wadi Sirhan. They were driven out with some difficulty by Abdullah ibn Husain's Transjordanian forces spurred on by the British. The presence of the Saudis in that place menaced the keystone of Whitehall's postwar policy in the Levant: a contiguous chain of client states from the Red Sea to Persia. The route of a proposed railroad from the Mediterranean to the Persian Gulf would pass near Jauf, already in Saudi hands.

The chairman was Colonel S. G. Knox, senior political officer, Iraq. He announced the termination of subsidies to become effective 31 March 1924. That decision removed the strongest of Britain's means of exerting pressure on the negotiators. Nevertheless, after long debate almost all the provisions of the Muhammera draft were accepted, although Ibn Saud's demands for the return to his lands of groups of Shammar and other tribes that had fled to Iraq were ignored. Britain's hopes for resolution of the problems caused by the *Ikhwan* occupation of Wadi Sirhan were not realized because the conference ended before the matter was broached officially. Two events caused its demise before any agreements were initialed:

One was a raid into southern Iraq by a lieutenant of Faisal ad Duwish. *(See Map 4 in n. 20)* On 20 March some two hundred and seventy men, women and children of a defenseless shepherd tribe were killed and their animals taken. The raiders escaped without harassment by Iraqi forces. After this debacle the Iraqi delegation did not return to the conference.

The other was the assumption by Sharif Husain on 5 March 1924, of the title of Caliph of Islam, the spiritual head of all Moslems, Successor of the Prophet. Just two days before his proclamation, the new government of Turkey headed by Kemal Atatürk had announced the abolition of the Caliphate after four hundred years of Ottoman claims to the leadership of Islam.

Although two of the sons of Husain ibn Ali—the king of Iraq and the amir of Transjordan—aroused some support for this arrogation, other Islamic countries had been antagonized by Husain's overweening pretensions to leadership of an Arab confederation. British officials had given lip service to this megalomaniac to ensure his coöperation during the war, but offered no support for his claims thereafter. His eccentricities, together with the extortionate treatment of pilgrims and his lack of concern for their health and welfare had become notorious.

Colonel Knox reported to Whitehall the lack of progress in reaching final agreement, and after the two events mentioned, despaired of reconciling the disparate views thus occasioned. He was also ill with dysentery and on the verge of retirement. His illness had already been the cause of a long recess in January. On 11 April the conference ended with no positive results. The matters comprising the agenda of the conference were not to be addressed again by the British government until late in 1925 when Ibn Saud was engaged in the conquest of the Hejaz.

# Conquest of the Hejaz (1924–1925)

**Motives**: Ibn Saud's upbringing as a follower of the strict tenets of the Wahhabi creed and his own profound faith in its verity made the whole way of life in the cities of the Hejaz anathema. The tombs of the 'saints,' and all the sinfulness of a religion debased by idolatry and schism must be rooted out and the true faith installed in the Holy Places. The heretic who in his pride and greed had oppressed and robbed the pilgrims and had tolerated, even approved, of these evils must be removed. In spite of repeated provocation (*n. 16*), Ibn Saud had been restrained in his activities against Sharif Husain by the fear that the British subsidy of £5,000 a month would be withdrawn. At the time of the Khurma–Turaba incidents he had been threatened with its loss. It seems clear that the menace of its forfeiture together with that of annulment of the Treaty of 1915 (which promised him protection from foreign adversaries) was in 1919 so weighty that he leashed the *Ikhwan* and accepted a three-year truce with the sharif of Mecca.

Now, in March 1924, the subsidy had been withdrawn and the final six-month allotment had been paid in advance. Sir Percy Cox, his friend, had left his post as high commissioner of Iraq, and Ibn Saud's request that he be allowed a permanent representative in London had been denied. The new political agents in the Gulf region were less considerate than before. Perhaps in itself this new freedom from restraint might not have precipitated action, but he was now sure that the British government no longer supported the king of the Hejaz with the earnestness of the war years. The subsidy to Husain, like his own, had ended. (In fact, Whitehall had decided not to interfere in a war of religion, but he was not aware of this.) These considerations were as nothing against the sacrilegious actions of the sharif. How dare he call himself Caliph, the Commander of the Faithful? It was the ultimate blasphemy! A doddering but dangerous old fool, he and his seed must be extirpated.

Ibn Saud's approach to the invasion of the Hejaz was systematic and well-planned. The campaign would begin only after all pilgrims had left the Holy Land. He must justify his course of action not only to his people but also to all believers. The *Ikhwan* needed no explanations. They were ready for battle and booty.

**Notice to Islam:** Called by Abdur Rahman, a great assembly of the four estates met in Riyadh on 5 June 1924. Ibn Saud attended but left the conduct of the meeting to his father. The first item on the agenda was a justification for invasion. Ibn Bijad, paramount shaikh of the 'Ataiba and leader of the attack at Turaba on Abdullah, spoke at length. He listed the grave faults of Husain ibn Ali and his administration, ending his condemnation with a peroration on the shame and impiety of unilateral assumption of the Caliphate by a heretic. He demanded that Ibn Saud lead them to Mecca for the pilgrimage, a rite which had been denied Nejdis for the third year in succession. The *Ulema* agreed that this was a valid ground for war. Ibn Saud replied that an armed march into the Holy Places would be a great sacrilege unless all Islam agreed that it was necessary, for 'the Holy Cities were a common possession of all Muslims.' A notice over the signature of Faisal, his second living son, was sent to all Islam asking their assent to a Saudi takeover in the name of all. The nature of the future government would be decided on by a congress in Mecca.

Many recipients of the notice feared butchery of fellow believers by the ferocious *Ikhwan*, and some knew of the desecration that had occurred during the Wahhabi occupation of Mecca in 1803. Only a reformist group in India replied affirmatively, and its answer arrived well after the war had begun. Their delegation arrived in Jedda 24 December 1924, and left 6 February after unsuccessful attempts at mediation between Ali and Ibn Saud.

**Attack**: In August, another raid into Transjordan by a large body of the *Ikhwan* met the same fate as the one in 1922. The population of the village of Qastal near Ziza was butchered like that of Umm al Ahmad two years before. Armored cars and airplanes killed a great number of the assassins. Bertram Thomas, later the first non-Arab to cross the Rub' al Khali, described this ghazzu in a letter to a friend (*n. 17*). He had been on leave in India from his duties in Transjordan when it took place. Because of the great size of the force and the date of the invasion, (less than a month before the massacre in Taïf) it is possible, even probable, that it was the first strike of the coming war.

In Riyadh, Ibn Saud planned his offensive. (According to Philby, his apologist, the invasion was but a series of probing attacks, the encounter at Taïf due only to chance.) Late in August three columns of *Ikhwan* began to march: one toward Mecca, one to the northern Hejaz, and one toward Iraq.

**Taïf Massacre**: On 1 September the southern column, some three thousand strong under Sultan ibn Bijad and Khalid ibn Luwai, approached the outskirts of Taïf. Its advance guard assaulted Klak, an outpost fort. The defenders were captured or fled to the barracks of the central garrison, commanded by the sharif's oldest son, Ali. The other Hejazi outposts did not wait to be attacked. During the afternoon of the third the entire garrison, accompanied by a number of townspeople, left Taïf in the direction of Mecca. Those remaining in Taïf sought to forestall an assault by arranging a cease-fire with ibn Luwai's fanatical townsmen from Khurma, for the main body of *Ikhwan* from Ghatghat were still at some distance.

On the afternoon of the fourth, in accordance with the terms of the cease-fire, the north gate of the town was opened. The *Ikhwan* entered. Suddenly the compact group scattered, daggers were drawn and slaughter began. Why, has never been discovered. Was some tenet of the *Ikhwan* code breached or did an impulse to punish the apostates become general? More probably the lure of loot was paramount. One report has it that a police post not aware of the cease-fire began a fusillade. The carnage went on through the night. Bodies were buried in the rubble of pillaged shops and homes or hurled into wells. Torture yielded hidden treasure. The *Ulema*, pursued into their sanctuaries, were murdered in the mosque of ibn Abbas among the tombs of saints, silent testimonials of their heresy. At least four hundred men and boys had died when at noon of the next day ibn Bijad put a stop to the killing and succored the survivors, mainly women and children.

Still in Riyadh, Ibn Saud is said to have wept when he heard of the events at Taïf. Immediately he sent messages to his two field commanders by racing camel forbidding further murder and looting on pain of execution. In the vicinity of the Holy City fighting must not occur. But the sultan did not go immediately to the Hejaz.

Terrified refugees fled Taïf, and were soon sowing panic in Mecca and Jedda. Ali and the Taïf garrison strengthened by reinforcements from Mecca took up a position at the village of Hadda between Taïf and Mecca where in contrast to their previous pusillanimity they put up a stiff defense. Probably Ali feared his father as much as the *Ikhwan*. The defenders, overwhelmed, retreated to Mecca on 26 September. Ali went on to Jedda but the indomitable old man remained in the Holy City where he was plagued by telephone and telegraph demands from Jedda notables that he abdicate in favor of his son. These demands were particularly galling to him because of Ali's ignominious abandonment of Taïf.

Husain asserted that he would never give up. In his usual egocentric and irascible way he attempted to arrange a defense. In vain, for only his police remained loyal and many of the population had gone to Jedda and beyond: to Port Sudan, opposite Jedda on the Sudan coast, or to Egypt or India.

**Abdication**: In Jedda, Ali began to organize resistance. On 3 October over a hundred notables of Jedda, headed by Abdullah Alireza, a rich merchant and governor of the town, asked Ali to beg his father to abdicate. They hoped that Ibn Saud would then consider a cessation of hostilities. On the same day at nine o'clock in the evening the king of the Hejaz signed his abdication. Ali was named 'Constitutional Sovereign of the Hejaz.' He was short and slim, described by Hogarth as a 'very conscientious, careful, pleasant gentleman without force of character....' On 6 October, in hopes of an armistice or better, Ali asked the terms that Ibn Saud would accept to end the war. He was told that there weren't any. A few days later the sultan made his position clear: the war would stop only when Husain and his sons had left the Hejaz.

Husain took his time to quit Mecca for he was engaged in collecting his goods and treasure. He arrived in Jedda 9 October 1924 in a five-car* entourage, his own Mercedes crammed with his household and £800,000 in gold sovereigns sealed in kerosene cans, profits from the pilgimages and what he had skimmed off British subsidies during the war. On 16 October he left on his ramshackle yacht for Aqaba, the town at the head of the gulf of the same name, and the northernmost port in his relinquished kingdom.

With the approval of the Foreign Office the newly created amir of Transjordan, Abdullah, had annexed Aqaba to serve as the port for his new domain. His brother Ali, still under siege in Jedda, could do nothing to stop him, even if he would. On 16 June 1925 the exiled Husain was winkled out of Aqaba and taken to Cyprus by the British because Ibn Saud threatened to occupy the town if the ex-king remained there.

Husain, who thought he had been promised leadership of all the Arabs in return for his revolt against the Turks in 1916–1918, finished his days in Cyprus in house arrest. Baker (1979) says that after having a stroke he was allowed to go to Abdullah in Amman for the last few months of life.

---

\* Some say only four motor cars were in the Hejaz in 1924.

Although his conduct as king had been reprehensible, he was at the last considered as having been misled by promises, and a figure worthy of respect for his indomitable stance in the face of misfortune and what came to be considered his honorable refusal to yield to British pressure regarding Palestine. Many authors enlarge on mistakes in British policy regarding Husain, and carelessness in the tenor of the undertakings made him.

**Mecca Occupied:** The *Ikhwan* did not approach Mecca until more than five weeks after the fall of Taïf. Ali's stand at Hadda had delayed them about three weeks. Overawing the local tribes did not require much time. Perhaps part of the army had been engaged in taking loot to Nejd, but almost certainly it had been ordered not to enter the Holy City. There, many residents had left for fear of the *Ikhwan*. Local Bedu began to steal from deserted shops and homes. Ibn Bijad learned of this pillage, and may have acted on his own initiative.

In any event, at dawn on 16 October four soldiers of the *Ikhwan* clad only in the two white seamless cloths of the pilgrim, the *Ihram*, entered the silent and shuttered city. Shouting, they proclaimed that no one need fear for his person or property; the sacred precincts were now under the protection of ibn Bijad. The following morning two thousand of the *Ikhwan*, all clad as pilgrims but bearing arms, marched silently into the hush of deserted streets and bated breath. They occupied the strong points, looted the sharif's palace and other public buildings, destroyed some of the domed tombs and images of people, broke some hubble-bubble pipes, but no one was molested. Even the *Ikhwan* feared ignominious death from the thin curved blade of the Somali executioner if they disobeyed the sultan's edicts.

**October Message:** Ibn Saud remained in Riyadh for two weeks after the occupation of Mecca. To calm the fears of Islam, he sent another message worldwide: As soon as his assumption of power in the Hejaz was assured, all were invited to a conference in Mecca to determine the form of government acceptable to the majority of his coreligionists. He left Riyadh on 12 November and after a slow, triumphant progress arrived at Mecca on 3 December 1924. His tents were set up in the hills behind the city.

On the fifth, clad as a pilgrim, he entered through the Gate of Peace, repeated the prescribed phrases several times, 'Labbaik! Allahuma! Labbaik!' (Here am I at thy service, O God, at thy service), visited the Great Mosque, kissed the Black Stone (*n. 31*) in the wall of the Ka'aba and walked around that stone cube seven times performing the rites of the Lesser Pilgrimage, the *'Umra*. Meticulous in religious matters, he was also considerate in mundane affairs. Knowing how difficult it would be for the people of Mecca to be ruled by the rude Bedu of his army, he established a consultative body of local residents, the *Majlis as Shura*, which advised him about local administrative problems on which he himself made the decisions.

**Wahhabi Rigor:** But despite Ibn Saud's concern, the Meccans were for several years not spared the rigors of Wahhabi intolerance. Untutored Bedu from the desert served as proctors of the 'Committee for the Encouragement of Virtue and the Suppression of Vice.' They roamed the street armed with stout staves. When the call to prayer sounded they beat on the closed doors and shutters of the shops shouting, 'As-salat! As-salat!' (To prayer! To prayer!) Laggards were helped on their way. Sometimes the names of the faithful were recorded as they left the mosque. Five times a day life was interrupted by attendance at a ceremony soon changed from a rite of faith to an obligatory, supervised exercise. Whoever intentionally neglected his prayers was subject to imprisonment for up to ten days and a stiff fine. Wine drinkers were punished according to the judgment of a *Shari'a* court.

Koranic punishments were introduced: beating with a cane or palm frond for drunkenness, amputation of a hand or foot for theft, stoning for adultery, hanging or decapitation for murder. After a time the Nejdis were sent back to their villages or *Hujar*. Their functions taken over by Hejazis, in general less zealous guardians of morals. Penalties were exacted in the public square, most often after the noon prayer on Friday. Foreigners were seldom accused of wrong-doing and pilgrims were pardoned minor derelictions.

**Siege of Medina**: While this régime was being installed in Mecca and later in Jedda, the *Ikhwan* were engaged in imposing order on rebellious tribes: a section of the Harb, and the Billi of northern Hejaz. The supporters of King Ali in Medina and Yenbo, its port, were besieged by a large force of *Ikhwan* under Faisal ad Duwish who had been ordered not to make an all-out assault. Saudi artillery reportedly damaged the dome of the mosque that sheltered the tomb of the Prophet. Ibn Saud was informed that the garrison feared to surrender because of the ferocity of the blockaders. In the end, he had food smuggled to them by sea, while awaiting his son Faisal with a large fresh force from Nejd. One contingent of the newcomers was commanded by Mohammed, his third surviving son. It replaced the *Ikhwan*. The Medinans opened their gates on 5 December. Yenbo yielded on the 15th.

**Siege of Jedda**: Ali assembled a motley force including many destitute West African pilgrims, three hundred 'volunteers' from Transjordan, Syrian, Egyptian, and Russian soldiers of fortune, and a Turkish general, Tahsin Pasha al Kakir, a Syrian who had seen long service in the Turkish army. In addition to a variety of rifles, armament included three 'armored' cars, cannon of several calibers, machine guns, and three obsolete aircraft. Their White Russian pilots were very close to parodies. One landed at Taïf and was killed at once. Their greatest exploit was dropping a bomb on Mecca the day that Ibn Saud entered the city. It destroyed a house where on occasion Ibn Saud had stayed. All of this preparation for battle, the trenches, barbed wire, machine gun posts, served for nothing. The Saudi attack began on 3 January 1925, with desultory cannon fire that ceased at the beginning of Ramadan, never to be resumed.

Nevertheless, the blockade was tight. In the moist heat of summer food ran short, and fresh water supplied by a coal-fired steam desalinator became precious as the supply of fuel shrank. The population, swollen by refugees, began to starve and disease became widespread. Hundreds died. Ali was strongly supported by the merchants of Jedda who did not see commerce flourishing under the Wahhabis. They envisioned the Hejaz as independent, after having forced Ibn Saud to withdraw. A dissident group headed by Qasim Zaimal, nephew of the governor of Jedda, attempted to negotiate an armistice. He was caught and sentenced to death. The sentence was not carried out.

The Turkish general repeatedly promised victory, even after one of the 'armored cars' (a truck covered with thin sheet-iron plates), sortied, and was at once immobilized by hordes of *Ikhwan*. The recoil of cannon installed on the roofs of tall houses for counter-battery fire caused the buildings to collapse. As at Medina, Ibn Saud did not order a determined attack. He wanted no repetition of Taïf. Too, a few diplomats and Amin Rihani who had visited him in Riyadh were in the town. Conditions in Jedda continued to worsen. The prime minister and foreign minister of the constitutional democratic government went to Egypt to 'secure assistance,' and the élite of the unpaid soldiers mutinied. After Medina surrendered, Ali, aided by Jordan, the British consul, made arrangements to go to his brother Faisal, king of Iraq since 1921. On 20 December he left Jedda on the British sloop, H.M.S. *Cornflower*.

**Victory:** On 17 December a party of notables, mostly merchants, visited Ibn Saud's headquarters at Raghama, a farm seven miles from the city. Agreement was reached on a number of conditions which demonstrated once more Ibn Saud's magnaminity and generosity: amnesty for all supporters of the previous government of the Hejaz; fares and pocket money for the return of foreign soldiers; all civil servants of the former government to retain their posts; the property held by the Hashemites before the accession of Sharif Husain to be kept by that family. On 23 December, accompanied by Jordan, the notables arranged a reception for the sultan just outside the walls of the town at which he reinstated the merchant-prince governor, Abdullah Alireza, in his position as *Qaimaqam*. Ibn Saud entered the city that night or the next day and on 25 December announced that the war was over.

**King of the Hejaz:** The restraint of the conqueror's demands on the captured cities, the evidences of a functioning home rule (the *Majlis as Shura*) in Mecca, and the establishment of adequate security there impressed the notables of Jedda most favorably. Too, his well-judged arrangements for the reception of pilgrims at three fishing ports while Mecca was still besieged had impressed the few Moslem palmers brave enough to enter a war zone, and had shown the beleaguered merchants that Ibn Saud was not a godless tyrant. But being incorporated into a sultanate and governed from afar by a ruler whose reputation internationally was that of a savage would be bad for business. The *Majlis* of Mecca and the *Ulema* of Riyadh and the Hejaz were consulted by these businessmen. The consensus—a new ruler for the Hejaz must be chosen at once.

Only one choice was possible. In order to prepare Islam for this step, on 7 January 1926 Ibn Saud issued a statement in which he voiced his regret for the apparent indifference of Moslems to his several requests for consultation about the governance of the Holy Places so that the choice was now up to the people of the Hejaz. The next day, 8 January, after the noon prayers in the Great Mosque of Mecca, a venerable imam made a short statement announcing the name of the new king of the Hejaz. Cannon boomed a salute; people crowded to offer their allegiance. Ibn Saud must have been satisfied. He had at last reassembled his ancestors' domain.

# Stabilization (1925–1927)

Ibn Saud was to spend two years in the Hejaz without returning to Riyadh. But even before the war had ended the British, seeing the inevitable outcome, thought it desirable to tie up a loose end that might have endangered their post-war plan for a chain of client states to serve as a barrier to further expansion by the new strong man and as a secure route for overland communication and trade between the Mediterranean and Baghdad.

**Hadda–Bahra Agreements:** On 10 October 1925 Sir Gilbert Clayton with his aide George Antonius met Ibn Saud and two of his advisers, Hafiz Wahba and Yusuf Yassin, at a camp near Bahra, a then-abandoned village halfway between Jedda and Mecca where Ali had held off the *Ikhwan* after the Taïf massacre. The siege of Jedda was still in progress, but luxurious tents were comfortably furnished and the best cook in Jedda saw to sustenance. Twenty sessions ended on 2 November with two protocols, one for Iraq, the other for Transjordan. The Hadda treaty concerned mainly the delineation of a boundary between Nejd and Transjordan. Sir Gilbert had been instructed to make every effort to have Saudi forces withdraw from Wadi Sirhan, the main artery of trade between Nejd and the Levant, but was successful only in retaining a corridor north of it as Transjordanian territory. The two aides to the sultan were extremely difficult and obstructive negotiators. Nevertheless, the treaty was satisfactory to England for if the *Ikhwan* had remained at the Syrian frontier Transjordan and Iraq could not have been contiguous.

At the conference Ibn Saud again protested the seizure of Ma'an and Aqaba by Abdullah, now amir of Transjordan, but was persuaded not to attack Aqaba after Sharif Husain was deported to Cyprus in July. With the war still in progress he would not press his right to the two towns, although British support for Abdullah's claim was clearly specious, both towns having been taxed by the sharif. He did get two prizes. One was the villages and salt mines of Qariyat al Milh promised him by Sir Percy Cox at the Oqair meeting of 1922. The other was the fortifications at Qaf that guarded the north end of Wadi Sirhan. Thus he retained control of the only feasible route of access to the Levant, although at the same time accepting a boundary between the Hejaz and most of Transjordan. The dispute over the location of the remainder of the boundary and the Saudi claim to Aqaba was not settled until August 1965.

The treaty of Bahra concerned the regulation of tribal movements across the Nejdi–Iraqi border and the establishment of a tribunal to inquire into claims by one tribe against another for recompense of loss due to raids. It proved unworkable.

**Praxis of Peace:** While the sieges of Medina and Mecca were still in progress, other Saudi troops were engaged in establishing order among the tribes of the Hejaz that, in a search for valuables, had been prone to harass and even to kill pilgrims. To impress upon his new nomad subjects the necessity for stopping such molestation, Ibn Saud ordered that one erring band that had robbed a caravan and murdered some of its people be made an example. The group of more than two hundred men, women, and children was tracked, surrounded and annihilated.

He explained to a foreign diplomat the reasoning behind this massacre:

> You, like all the others from the West, think of us as wild, rough fanatics, backward and narrow-minded people.... We have often acted severely, even mercilessly, and with Allah's help we have beaten a wicked enemy. This country shall now at last have security, peace, and order and will know justice.... Bedouin have to be treated in a very hard way for only then do they learn their lesson and, Insh'Allah, once they have learned it they will never forget it. We teach them the hard way, not to be cruel, but out of mercy. And once we have punished them we shall not in the mercy of Allah have to do it again as long as we live.... We can often make justice effective in the remoteness of our deserts only by the reports spread of the justice we dealt out to the dogs of the Hejaz, those robbers of the Bani Malik of whom we killed several hundreds. Far away in the deserts this news will be applauded because it will mean that caravans can at last travel in peace and security where till now they were kept away by fear.... You punish year in year out and yet it does not seem to be effective. I punish in such a way that it does not have to be repeated. We know the Bedu and we know how he has to be ruled *(van der Meulen, pp. 99–100)*.

Law-abiding chiefs were given instruction in the administration of justice so that the army would not be called on too often. Each tribal shaikh and amir was ordered to report to Ibn Saud all crimes committed in his *dirah* or community and the punishment he meted out for each offense. All those responsible for judging criminals were ordered to take note of the activities of their peers, and to report any neglect in reporting a crime or its punishment. Negligence by either party would be penalized.

In the Hejaz more and more leniency was accorded small violators of the Wahhabi code of conduct, but in a few years crimes involving theft were almost nil throughout the kingdom and the king's subjects could journey freely without fear of molestation. Pilgrims were received and passed through quarantine with only a moderate and fixed demand for tax and much less bilking by those licensed as guides. The lives of *Hajjis* arriving overland were no longer in danger from marauding bands.

**Islamic Congress**: Even before the fall of Jedda a delegation from India had reached the Holy Land to discuss the form of government to be set up in the Hejaz. After Ibn Saud declared himself king with the approval of at least some of the population, the delegation envisioned that he would take charge of foreign policy, defense and finance, whereas internal administration would be run by some kind of international body in which all the Islamic states would be represented.

The congress met in Mecca after the *Hajj* of 1926. The seventy delegates represented all of Islam except Transjordan, Iraq, and the *Shia* community of Persia. Ibn Saud prevented any discussion of the form of government in the Hejaz, including the legitimacy of his assumption of the throne. His opening speech listed the topics permitted for debate: the participants were invited to investigate every avenue that could lead to improvement in the religious and moral climate of the Holy Land. They went home with nothing accomplished because of their inability to agree on a common policy, a discordance of views symptomatic of the disunity within Islam. Thereafter, according to most sources Ibn Saud refused to take part in any pan-Islamic or even pan-Arab movement. Nevertheless, in a 1935 interview with Landau *(1938, p. 88)* he is quoted as having said, 'Pan-Arabism is a necessity.... Each Arab state within that federation will preserve its own ruler and its individual forms of government and administration.' Saudi Arabia and Egypt were founding members of the League of Arab States formed in March, 1945. The League is till functioning.

**Treaty of Jedda:** In the autumn of 1926 Ibn Saud left the Hejaz, but returned in 1927 to meet Sir Gilbert Clayton. The British government had at last recognized that the treaty signed in 1915 at Qatif guaranteeing protection to the Saudi state had lost its significance, for it no longer expressed the true relationships between the United Kingdom and the man who held sway over a domain extending from the Red Sea to the Persian Gulf. On 20 May Sir Gilbert, trusted by Ibn Saud after the bargaining at Bahra, negotiated a treaty that was ratified by Britain some months later. Valid for seven years, the treaty recognized the complete independence of the Saudi state and formally accepted the frontiers lately established through protocol and negotiation. However, the inclusion of Aqaba and Ma'an in Transjordan was not accepted by the Saudis. The treaty was renewed in 1936 and 1943.

This formal recognition of Ibn Saud's status by Great Britain was followed by that of France, Holland, and the Soviet Union. A little later Belgium, Turkey, and Switzerland also established formal diplomatic ties. But his right to rule was soon to be challenged in his own country. The good feeling engendered at the January conference in Riyadh was soon dissipated by the king's renewed insistence that all raiding must cease. In the early summer of 1927 Ibn Saud continued discussions in Jedda with Sir Gilbert. They reached agreement that the king would respect the frontiers of Iraq and Transjordan as established, and that infringements of any kind by any state or individual would be the subject of peaceful negotiation.

# Ikhwan Unrest

**Genesis:** The forces of the *Ikhwan* had been sent back to Nejd within a year after they had taken and pacified the Hejaz. One Arab source relates that while the siege of Jedda was still in progress ibn Bijad and ad Duwish came to Ibn Saud's camp at Raghama with the proposal that in return for their services one should be made governor of Mecca and the other of Medina.

Whether or not this imprudence occurred, the *Ikhwan's* task in the Hejaz was ended, and its continued presence was an embarrassment *(n. 18)*. Its ouster was much resented by both the leaders and the rank and file. They had been prevented from looting the richest of prizes and they had not been compensated satisfactorily for their restraint. In their eyes Ibn Saud had neglected them, preferring his new subjects whom he had shamefully allowed to slight their religious duties. He had parleyed with the Nasrani and had not destroyed those inventions of the devil, the motor car and telephone.

In the autumn of 1926 Ibn Saud returned to Riyadh by car for the first time, although camels were not banished from his train for another nine years. He had stayed almost two years in the Hejaz fully occupied in arranging facilities for receiving pilgrims and in setting up a reliable civil administration. He was aware of and concerned over the increasing unrest of the *Ikhwan* and of their murderous raids into Iraq despite his ban on such forays.

Dhaidan al Hithlain, paramount shaikh of the Ajman, joined Faisal ad Duwish and Sultan ibn Bijad ibn Humaid of the 'Ataiba, two leaders of the *Ikhwan*, to form a triumvirate. They vowed mutual support in the event of punitive measures by Ibn Saud, and together would push for freedom of action. Late in 1926 they held a conclave in Artawiya during which they catalogued their grievances. Of the three, ibn Bijad was said to be motivated only by religious considerations; the two others were judged to be opportunists. The putative leader was Faisal ad Duwish, who since the surrender of Haïl in 1921 had been a loyal lieutenant of the ruler. Ibn Bijad had routed Ali at Khurma in 1919 and sometimes acted independently, as he had when he occupied Mecca.

**1927 Conference:** The situation became so tense that Abdur Rahman convoked some three thousand of the *Ikhwan* and notables to Riyadh so that their grievances could be aired and their validity judged by the *Ulema*. Of the *Ikhwan* leaders only ibn Bijad was absent. The conference discussed and condemned such disparate particulars as the king's acceptance of Satanic innovations like the telephone and motor car; his consent to Faisal's visits to godless England in 1919 and 1926 and Heir-Apparent Saud's tour in Egypt; his failure to have coerced the *Shias* of al Hasa into accepting Wahhabism; and his laxity in allowing the tribes of Iraq to graze their herds in Nejd.

These accusations occupied the congress for a long time after its first meeting on 29 January. The king was eloquent in defending his actions. The real cause of the *Ikhwan's* unrest was that Ibn Saud no longer sanctioned them to spread God's word; in other words to loot at will. They wanted *jihad*, a holy war, against Iraq and Syria. After long consultation, the *Ulema* decided that only the king had the right to declare *jihad*. But the sting of this judgment was deadened for the moment by the ample funds and lavish gifts bestowed on the conferees by the king from his gleanings in the Hejaz. As a result, all applauded the decision of Ibn Saud, who, supported by the *Ulema*, had on 19 January added the title, 'King of Nejd and its Dependencies' to that of 'King of the Hejaz.' Philby says it was done only to make him equal in rank to King Faisal of Iraq.

The good feeling engendered at the January conference in Riyadh was soon dissipated by the king's renewed insistence that all raiding must cease. In the early summer of 1927 Ibn Saud continued discussions in Jedda with Sir Gilbert. They reached agreement that the king would respect the frontiers of Iraq and Transjordan as established, and that infringements of any kind by any state or individual would be the subject of peaceful negotiation.

**Busaiya Incident**: This arrangement worked fairly well for several months although with fugitives, refugees, occasional raiders, and smugglers, incidents at the frontiers were common. It was terminated abruptly during the night of 5 November, 1927. The Iraqi government, counseled by British advisers (although Captain John Bagot Glubb dissented), had ordered the construction of a police post in southwestern Iraq at a site known as Busaiya. Work to construct buildings there had begun in September. Ibn Saud protested their presence as a violation of Article 3 of the Oqair protocol that prohibited the construction of forts near the frontier. He was compelled to act, for if he has not done so he would have lost control of his tribesmen. Perhaps he admired their exploits against an old enemy, although as king he could not condone them. The tribesmen argued that construction of the forts was the beginning of a plan to restrict their movements and to hinder the raids necessary to their way of life. Ibn Saud must have known that the post was fifty-five miles from the border, although his Bedu could not read a map and would have rejected any concept that limited their freedom of movement.

On that November night, some forty Mutair commanded by a lieutenant of Faisal ad Duwish attacked the post, still under construction, and killed all but one of the twenty occupants of whom only six were policemen. The British government at once informed Ibn Saud that compensation must be given for the killed and wounded, and assurance provided that adequate measures had been taken to prevent more raids.

On 8 December, Ibn Saud warned the high commissioner of Iraq in a telegram sent to the political agent in Kuwait that a party of *Ikhwan* was marching northward in defiance of his orders. The next day R.A.F. airplanes spotted two groups of raiders, together nearly a thousand, and attacked. The raiders had plundered both shepherds and Bedu. On the 22nd, ad Duwish himself struck at shepherds in the western corner of the Iraq Neutral Zone, amassing booty, mainly sheep.

On 19 February, two parties of raiders were strafed and dispersed, but one airplane was shot down and the pilot and his gunner killed. On the 20th and 21st a large camp of white tents was bombed with unsatisfactory results.

# Rebellion

Early in March ibn Bijad set out from Ghatghat asking for others to join him, but at the king's command Khalid ibn Luwai persuaded him to return to his *hijra* at Ghatghat although he left his war standard in the field. On 24 March he was again on the march and again was induced to hold his hand until the king had talked to him.

**Peace Efforts**: To this end Ibn Saud left Riyadh on 10 April. On the 14th he arrived at Buraida. Ibn Bijad and ad Duwish were encamped twenty-five miles to the north. Ibn Saud asked them to come to Buraida but they refused, suggesting a venue in the open desert. The possibility of an armed clash between the redoubtable force led by his best captains and his own small escort was all too likely. So the king of the Hejaz and Nejd and its Dependencies spurned the flung gauntlet, but go-betweens arranged that the *Ikhwan* leaders would cease raiding until Ibn Saud had conferred with Sir Gilbert Clayton.

On 7 May Ibn Saud reached Jedda and talked with Sir Gilbert from the 9th to the 20th. He reiterated his stand that the police posts were in contravention of Article 3 of the treaty and pointed out that the attacks by the R.A.F. on tribes in Nejd territory violated the provisions of the Oqair protocol. Furthermore the troop he had sent to punish the raiders had been bombed. He demanded that the posts at Busaiya, Salman, and elsewhere be demolished. Sir Gilbert could not agree, but transmitted the demand to the government of Iraq.

From 2 to 9 August the talks were renewed. Ibn Saud repeated his demand that the posts be destroyed. He explained that his tribes and townspeople had been told the provisions of Article 3. If they were to find that the treaty he had signed was worthless and he did not then break with the British (which he would never do, he said) he would lose prestige and all his influence over the *Ikhwan*.

**1928 Conference**: This failure to reach an understanding made imminent a general uprising led by the *Ikhwan*. To forestall an insurrection Ibn Saud returned to Riyadh from Jedda on 8 September and sent messengers to all the tribes and dignitaries of Nejd convoking a conference of notables. For several weeks the delegates streamed into town. Although the meeting was delayed in hopes of their attendance, the three chief malcontents did not appear. Many of their followers did come, each small group led by its amir. They were the élite of the desert fighting men, proud, arrogant, and determinedly independent. The other delegates were governors of towns and provinces, heads of tribes, and men prominent in business or trade.

So it was that some eight thousand men (Besson says 13,000), representing the four estates of Nejd—the townsmen, the *Ikhwan*, the Bedu and the *Ulema*—met in Riyadh on 5 November. Their number made it necessary for the meeting to be held in the courtyard of the palace. The *Ulema* sat on the king's right, the amirs of the towns and provinces on his left. Seated in the middle of the enclosure the tribal chiefs or their representatives faced this assembly. At the outset Ibn Saud made a speech castigating the rebels of the *Ikhwan* for their acts of violence, violations of the frontier, and wanton attacks on the caravans and property of other tribes. The accused in the audience replied that they were only fulfilling their religious obligations by attacking those who strayed from the true faith.

They were ready to fight against the king's enemies and would ostracize those of their brethren who disobeyed his commands. But the injunctions of the Koran should be observed by all with the utmost strictness and without exception. (A stricture on the king himself who had allowed the *Shias* of al Hasa to perform in private the rites of their sect.)

The monarch replied that the conference had been called to discuss the causes of discontent among the *Ikhwan*, and to let the *Ulema* rule on the validity of their accusations. Although the leaders of dissent were not present, those of the *hujar* who did attend made three demands: The supplemental tax levied in excess of the usual *zakat* must be removed; all infidel inventions, motor cars, wireless, radio, telephone, etc. must be destroyed; the frontier posts of Busaiya and Salman must be demolished.

At that point the king delivered a long diatribe. In the entire kingdom there was not a single province, town or parcel of land that he had not won with his sword on the field of battle. He said in effect, 'I do not wish to govern a people who do not want me. Choose any member of my family to rule you,' pointing dramatically toward his assembled relatives, 'and I will bow the knee to him with you.' He would avoid the sin of arrogance in prolonging his stay in power and would be happy in retirement. It was a shrewd ploy. No one else in his family commanded the respect, the admiration of all.

Stunned by this pronouncement the assembly was silent for a long moment, then broke into roars of dissent. Ibn Saud, taking advantage of the confusion, asked each member of the *Ulema* if, in his opinion, the king was good or bad, and whether or not his rule should continue. Of course all replied favorably to both questions. Each individual of the other two factions, the amirs of the towns and the tribal chiefs, was questioned in the same way and gave the same answer. 'That being so,' the king said, 'I ask a new oath of allegiance to me.'

Then the plaints of the *Ikhwan* dissenters were discussed and adjudicated. Ibn Saud agreed to remove the supplementary tax. To the second demand he answered that he was ready to destroy all infidel inventions in his possession if the *Ikhwan* would at the same time destroy all of their arms and ammunition which were the invention of and had been made by infidels. The *Ulema* decided that all of these contrivances could be used lawfully for there was no Koranic prohibition on their use. The third demand was a stumbling block. The best that Ibn Saud could do was to obtain a commitment that no raiding would take place for two months while he attempted to have the forts demolished through negotiation. He knew that he would not succeed, but he had sounded the loyalty of the delegates and found many among the townsmen who, although approving most of the exploits of the *Ikhwan*, swore allegiance to him and would fight, even against the redoubtable soldiers of God. All went home with lavish gifts of swords, incense, money, food, and some were given jewelry for their wives.

**Raids Renewed:** In December 1928, at Jumaima near the Iraq frontier a detachment of ibn Bijad's 'Ataiba raiders pillaged a caravan and killed a number of the men from Buraida that were escorting it to Damascus. This attack on home-folk caused many former supporters of the *Ikhwan* to become skeptical of the validity of the religious motivation of the attackers and aroused resentment against them.

In February 1929, raids by small parties of *Ikhwan* resumed in Kuwait and southern Iraq. Ibn Saud ordered all the towns of al Hasa and northeastern Nejd to be provisioned and fortified against siege. Late in April and early in March larger bodies of raiders operating from Nejd and from Iraq took booty from both nomads and shepherd tribes. The increasing tempo of raids and the murder of an American missionary raised grave anxiety both in potential targets of the attacks and in official circles in London. There, it was assumed that the king of Nejd could no longer control his army.

**Battle of Sibila**: To calm these fears and to restore order, Ibn Saud decided that he must act. In mid-March 1929, with an army of loyal followers, its contingents headed by his brother and his sons, he moved to the Qasim and encamped at Zilfi. Only after dislodging a troop of 'Ataiba was he able to water his beasts. The next morning ad Duwish's son Azaiyiz and another young Mutair arrived with a message: 'As representatives of our tribes (Mutair, Ajman and 'Ataiba) we ask pardon. We wish to settle our differences peacefully, without war.' The young men offered to pay for the camels taken during the December raid on the caravan.

Ibn Saud replied that a court would decide, implying that the *Ikhwan* leaders would be tried for their misdeeds. To confirm his position on this matter, he sent letters to the shaikhs of the tribes involved in the killings, asking them again to accept trial for their crimes in a *Shari'a* court.

After a delay, a reply came, presumably dictated by ad Duwish. 'If you want a trial, have it at our camp. Bring your own judge' (an outstanding member of the *Ulema* named al Ungari). Ibn Saud's counselors deemed this offer a ploy to entrap the king and refused it. In the other camp ibn Bijad differed with ad Duwish. He refused a trial on the grounds that a religious court whose members were dependents of Ibn Saud would not give a fair judgment.

The king's army then moved to a plateau above the Tuwaiq escarpment tilled for wheat. (Sibila=stalk of wheat.) Neither party trusted the other, but after several exchanges of proposals, it was agreed that that one of the *Ikhwan* chiefs would come to Ibn Saud's camp to parley, his safety guaranteed. The following day ad Duwish arrived, weaponless, with an armed bodyguard of eight horsemen. As in a cinematic depiction of a meeting of hostile Dons of the Mafia, these guards lifted simultaneously all four of the entry flaps of the tent chosen for the parley. Inside, the king was seated, alone. He gave ad Duwish the usual pledge of security, 'You are under my protection,' and the two embraced.

Together in solitary conference during that day and the next, interrupted only for food and prayer, the two debated their differences. On the second evening Ibn Saud tried once again to persuade ad Duwish to agree to a trial. He replied. 'I will speak with ibn Bijad and tomorrow we may return. If we do not come, our absence will mean war.'

After a night of uncertainty, the king made a last effort to avoid combat by sending an emissary to the opposing camp asking for an answer. Not receiving one, he ordered the army to advance. It was the dawn of 29 March 1929. The throng of Nejdi infantry marched forward guarded on the right flank by the camelry of the 'Ataiba and a section of the Mutair and on the left by hosts of 'Anaiza, Hutaim, Harb, and Shammar. The brightly colored war banners lent an air of pageantry to the advancing array.

A messenger from the enemy rode into the path of the great force, asking for the king. Finding him, he said, 'Imam, we ask you to spare our people. Whatever compensation you want for our misdeeds we will pay, be it camels or whatever else you ask—just spare the lives of our people.' Ibn Saud replied, 'It is not only a question of camels. You have killed men and your chiefs must answer to the *Shari'a* and abide by its decision.' Then the king's emissary returned to report that he had been fired at and could not deliver his message.

Ibn Saud dismounted from his beautifully caparisoned war horse, and, honoring tradition, stooped to the sand at his feet and threw it in the direction of the enemy. 'Trust in God and prepare to fight,' he said. As the advance continued, both sides began a heavy fire. According to Almana the *Ikhwan* were behind a breastwork of stones on the uphill bank of a large wadi. The king's outposts, in position throughout the night on its lower side, began to withdraw. The *Ikhwan* could see their movement and thought they were retreating because of the fusil-lade. In small groups rebels quit the sheltering wall and ran toward the retiring pickets. A dozen machine gunners that had been ordered to await such an ideal target opened fire on the *Ikhwan* and mowed them down. The infantry ran forward and the cavalry on the right flank charged and caught many of the fleeing foe. Some escaped because Ibn Saud called off the pursuit of a beaten enemy. The battle of Sibila was over in half an hour. Ibn Hithlain, the Ajman leader, was not involved. He was away to the east guarding the flank of his allies from an attack by ibn Jiluwi's son leading a band of Awasim from al Hasa.

The account of the battle in Glubb (1960) differs greatly from Almana's. The preliminaries are similar, with the addition of a proposal by ibn Bijad to assassinate Ibn Saud in a night attack led by Azaiyiz. In this version the main action of the conflict is a clash of infantry: The townsmen of Nejd, burning to avenge their comrades slaughtered by ibn Bijad at Jumaima, run to assault the fanatical *Ikhwan* from Ghatghat and Artawiya. Two of their attacks are repulsed, but after the second the men of ibn Bijad are ready to retreat, and are put to flight by a cavalry attack from the rear led by shaikhs of the 'Ataiba and Mutair opposed to the *Ikhwan* movement.

All accounts agree that ad Duwish was wounded by a ball piercing his paunch. He had lost much blood and appeared to be dying. His men carried him to Artawiya in seven hours. Other requests for mercy having failed, his wives went to Ibn Saud and asked that their lord be allowed to die in peace. The king refused, but later, when he went to Artawiya and saw his old captain on a stretcher, granted him a full pardon. Perhaps this was a ploy to trap ibn Bijad who had escaped in a fighting retreat of great skill. Shortly thereafter this 'Ataiba chief surrendered and was imprisoned in Riyadh. Ibn Saud's son Abdullah razed ibn Bijad's *hijra* at Ghatghat.

**Resurgence**: After the loss of the battle at which he had not even been an onlooker, Dhaidan ibn Hithlain and his Ajman returned to al Hasa where he was treacherously murdered by ibn Jiluwi's son (*n. 19*). Soon thereafter the Ajman again raised the standard of revolt. The whole of northern Nejd and al Hasa from Jebel Shammar to the Persian Gulf was in tumult. Most threatening was the rising of sections of the 'Ataiba whose *dirah* lay between Riyadh and Mecca. Faisal ad Duwish having recovered in secret from his wound joined the Ajman on 19 June with a hundred thousand camels and five thousand men representing Mutair, Ajman, and ibn Bijad's section of the 'Ataiba.

In Mecca, Ibn Saud formed a motorcade and headed for Shagra through terrain controlled by the 'Ataiba who confronted him at Duwadimi. In a moving speech he persuaded their leaders to remain uncommitted. From Shagra he moved north to the Qasim and in the end assembled a force of eight thousand men, mainly villagers and townsmen, but including many Bedu. Each tribal chief joining the army got six gold pounds, each of his men, three.

The British now coöperated with him, reporting by wireless the movement of the rebels as observed in air reconnaissance and by loyal tribes of Iraq and Kuwait. Colonel Dickson, the political agent in Kuwait, warned the shaikh, Ahmed ibn Jabir as Sabah (he had succeeded Salim on 29 March 1921), not to allow the rebels to enter his territory.

In June, through an emissary, ad Duwish tempted Shaikh Ahmed to join him with the prospect of recovering both the territory taken from him in 1922 by the Oqair Protocols and control of the two tribes lost to him. Dickson, recently appointed political agent in Kuwait, lauded him for rebuffing this prospect, and he was later made a Knight Commander of the Most Excellent Order of the Indian Empire (K.C.I.E.).

In July, Ajman rebels were at the Abu Jifan wells and had cut the Riyadh-Hofuf road. From a base soundly located strategically, Faisal ad Duwish made a number of raids. One killed a small troop of Suhul tribesmen escorted by Saudi soldiers. As a result, Ibn Saud's advance party at Hafar al Atj returned to Riyadh. On 10 August the *Ikhwan* severely handled a Nejdi detachment at 'Nta in central al Hasa, and on the 15th destroyed fourteen trucks of the baggage train of Amir Saud, the king's eldest living son.

The rebels were successful everywhere during August, but ad Duwish lost a son (*n. 20*). Ibn Saud stayed on the defensive, his plan being to hold only the towns until the coming of cool weather. As a result, more and more Bedu joined the insurgents. On 22 August, Faisal ad Duwish moved to Hafar al Batin where his force was joined by a section of the Mutair of at least a thousand men.

**Counterattack**: In September, Ibn Saud began his offensive. In the east, the Awazim supported by men from the towns of al Hasa were ordered to move north and drive the rebels to the Kuwait border. In Nejd, using both diplomacy and force, the monarch stopped the defection of more of the 'Ataiba. The British government gave him reports concerning movements of the insurgents obtained by air reconnaissance.

The Awazim ordered to the offensive were defeated on 5 October at Inqair in central al Hasa where the tribe lost two hundred and fifty dead and many camels. But Ibn Saud continued his campaign. Moving part of his forces by car and truck, he at last defeated in battle a large body of Mutair and Ajman led by ad Duwish. The rebels then retreated northward toward Kuwait from Wafra in the Neutral Zone where the conflict had been waged.

Ad Duwish was deeply affected by the death of his son, but continued to hope for victory. If he could leave his women and looted camels in safety, greater mobility might allow a return to Nejd. A victory there, if sufficiently memorable, would gain him more allies, or at the least reasonable terms of surrender.

So he asked Dickson to get answers to three questions. Two of them concerned the protection of his womenfolk and his captured camels. They were addressed both to the British airmen guarding the borders of Kuwait and Iraq and to the shaikh of Kuwait: Would they take responsibility for the safety of his women and of his loot? Both replies were vague and indecisive negatives. So ad Duwish was denied both the greater mobility which would have been his without women and children and the significant increase in manpower resulting from an influx of herdsmen and guards freed from their tasks. The third question asked if he, ad Duwish, would be held responsible by the British if a Saudi airplane with an English crew were shot down. It was answered by an emphatic affirmative. The collapse of the rebellion began then.

Ad Duwish made no more attacks, and advised all who could to leave him and make peace with the king. On 10 November, the rebel forces, shrinking daily through desertion, moved to a site some seventy miles from the Kuwait border. On 28 December they were attacked by the shaikh commanding the left wing of the Saudi army, although negotiations for peace had already begun. Taken by surprise, the rebels nevertheless drove off the aggressors with relatively small loss.

Ibn Saud's army occupied a broad arc south of the rebels; to the west a separate Saudi force was captained by ibn Musa'ad, amir of Haïl; to the north, on the Iraq–Kuwait frontier, Royal Air Force ground troops with armored cars were stationed to prevent incursion into the two states. On 31 December, a large body of Mutair attempted to escape to the south past Ibn Saud's right flank. All were killed by troops under the command of sons Mohammed and Khalid. Early in January, another group of Mutair tried to turn his left flank and were intercepted by a car-transported force commanded by Ibn Saud himself. All males were killed. Then the main body of the rebels moved northeast toward the Jahra oasis, twenty miles west of Kuwait town, where they were met by an armored column of the R.A.F. and herded into the oasis where airplanes of Squadron 84 held them under threat of bombing.

**Surrender**: On 9 January, Dickson persuaded the leader of the Ajman, Naif al Hithlain, to surrender to a force of armored cars of the R.A.F., and on 10 January ad Duwish gave himself up, leaving his immediate family in Dickson's care. Along with another Mutair shaikh, the two were flown to Basra and sent to a Royal Indian Marine transport, the *Patrick Stewart*, lying in the Shatt al Arab. Later they were transferred to the sloop H.M.S. *Lupin*, anchored in the Bay of Kuwait. There, they awaited the end of negotiations to insure that their lives would not be forfeit. On the twelfth Ibn Saud asked for their extradition. A mission to Ibn Saud on the twentieth headed by the then political resident in the Persian Gulf, Sir Hugh Biscoe, was successful in getting the king's promise that their punishment would not be capital, and on 28 January the three *Ikhwan* leaders were flown from Kuwait to Ibn Saud's camp at Khabari Wadha where an elaborate ceremony of surrender was held, attended by a deputation of British officials including Col. Dickson. The many thousands of surviving tribesmen were handed over to the Saudi army on 4 February 1930. Ibn Saud promised to temper his punishment of the rebels with mercy.

The leaders of the rebellion were confined in Riyadh. Faisal ad Duwish died there on 3 October 1931, apparently from an embolism in an artery of the throat. The others remained in prison in the capital until 1934. An attempt to escape led to their transfer to the old Turkish dungeon in Hofuf. Nothing more is known about them.

The last threat to Ibn Saud's hegemony had been overcome. Militant *Ikhwan* would never again dispute his rule. In two years only a few diehards still wore the white turban. Nevertheless, some of the *Hujar* continued to thrive. But for many of his subjects Ibn Saud was no longer 'imam,' but was stigmatized as 'Al Wahhabi' for they felt that he had treated the *Ikhwan* harshly and were resentful of his having called on the infidel British to aid him. Some of the *Ikhwan* were convinced that he had used their zeal cynically *(n. 21)*.

**Rifada Rout:** In 1932, ibn Rifada leading six thousand men of the Billi tribe of the northern Hejaz attempted a revolt. It was quickly put down by armored vehicles and cavalry units of an army of ten thousand called up by radio to assemble at Taïf and then sent to Dabha. The malcontents, who had been egged on by Amir Abdullah of Transjordan, lost three hundred and fifty killed, including ibn Rifada and two of his sons. But criticism of Ibn Saud was muted because his authority was absolute and he was supported by townsmen, tribes, and a religious hierarchy loyal to him. After 1932 none of his own subjects seriously contested the king's power, although during the *Hajj* of 1934 three Zaidi (Shiite sect) Yemeni soldiers tried to stab him as he was making a ritual circumambulation of the Ka'aba. They were shot dead by guards as the Amir Saud shielded his father from the daggers, taking deep wounds in his left shoulder.

This attempt to kill the king came after a war, the last that Ibn Saud's army carried to a successful conclusion. In 1931 the heretical ruler of a neighboring country, the Imam Yahiya of Yemen challenged his authority by attempting to annex a small peripheral element of Saudi territory. The imam's version of the Moslem faith included intercession with the Almighty by saintly persons, himself among them as God's representative on earth. As such, he was anathema to the Wahhabis.

# Yemen War (1931–1934)

**Origin:** Even before Asir was declared independent at the end of the war in 1918, a dispute began between the Idrisi and the Imam Yahiya over the boundary between Asir and the Yemen. It continued until 1923 when the relatively weak Idrisi family, rulers of coastal Asir, gave up their autonomy and the whole state became a Saudi protectorate. In 1934 after the death of the last amir, Asir was annexed by Saudi Arabia.

Although not a part of Asir, a fertile oasis, the Nejran, lies in the interior near the Yemen–Asir boundary. The area had been the haven of the sharifs of Abu Arish, nominally subject to Yemen, for much of the nineteenth century. It was not of great interest to Ibn Saud who was content to leave it as a semi-independent buffer between him and the imam. But during the winter of 1931–32 a Yemeni force occupied Nejran and harassed the inhabitants who then sought aid from the king.

In the spring of 1932, Khalid ibn Luwai, amir of Khurma, was sent to the scene and with considerable difficulty ousted the intruders. Other Yemeni aggressors in the mountains and on the coastal flatlands of southern Asir held their ground and ibn Luwai was killed. Ibn Saud then accompanied some of his own men part of the way to Abha, and ibn Musa'ad led a contingent of Bedu from Haïl. A 1933 meeting between Yemeni and Saudi envoys at Sana'a, the Yemeni capital, did not bring a settlement and tempers flared.

**Invasion:** On 5 April 1934, Ibn Saud sent two armies into Yemen, one under his son Faisal along the coastal plain, the other under Faisal's older brother Saud, the heir-apparent, inland toward Sana'a. The unfamiliar mountains with precipitous slopes and passes defended by tribesmen at home in the area were too much for the desert warriors of Nejd of whom only a fraction were *Ikhwan*, no longer so brave now that they were fighting for territory and not the faith. Along the coast, Faisal made much better progress. After an initial hold-up at what is now the northern boundary of Yemen at Maidi, resistance was slight and in three weeks Faisal had taken Hodaida, the major seaport. The Imam Yahiya was thoroughly cowed, sending the message, 'Enough! Enough! Enough!' to Ibn Saud.

**Treaty of Taïf:** British, Italian and French warships arrived before Hodaida at the moment of its capture. Ibn Saud, perhaps fearful of international repercussions, ordered a halt. A truce was declared, and a conference began at Taïf watched by a commission of conciliation, whose members came from Syria and Egypt. After some delay and a threat to resume hostilities caused by the reluctance of Imam Yahiya to sign the treaty (dated 13 May but signed only on the 21st), Saudi troops left the Yemen. The imam was given back nearly half of the territory that had fallen into Saudi hands including part of the coastal strip that Yemeni forces had occupied before war began. The Saudis kept the port of Jizan and the Nejran oasis. An indemnity, said to be £100,000 in gold, was paid over to Ibn Saud in compensation for his mobilization, and a boundary commission made up of representatives from neutral Moslem states met in 1935. Border markers were installed before the end of 1936 and they have been respected ever since, in spite of later turmoil in Yemen.

This brief passage of arms was the last time Ibn Saud's army was employed to acquire territory, although a small contingent was used once in an attempt to claim sovereignty over a large tract in the hinterland of the Trucial Coast and in the interior of Oman held during the heyday of the eighteenth century Saud family hegemony (*n. 23*). The authority of the state was never questioned or challenged until Saud ibn Adul Aziz mismanaged the throne some years after his accession. Aided by the army as well as police, governors and amirs settle disputes arising from inter-tribal raids and squabbles. Problems arising from disagreement between labor and management were for a long time dealt with harshly, for the state employed many workers, although for the most part through foreign contractors.

# GROWTH OF THE SAUDI DOMAIN
## 1902-1934

PLATE V
Fig. 13

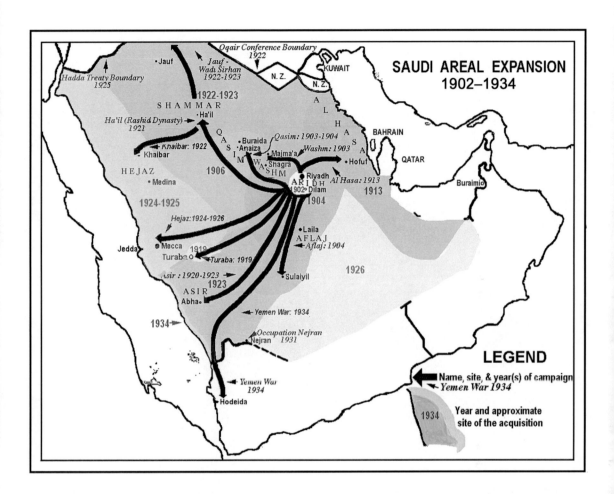

This figure shows the dates of acquisition and approximate limits of the territories that Ibn Saud added to his domain during three decades of struggle to restore and hold his patrimony. The dates in red are the years in which these areas were acquired. The black sinuous arrows show only the directions of the military or punitive thrusts associated with territorial acquisitions, not their actual route.

# Summary

The preceding pages recount how in the years 1902–1934 the kingdom was created and united by force of arms and astute maneuvering. Enemies foreign and domestic were defeated in war and battle. Two decades of tight-rope diplomacy that involved temporizing with the Ottoman overlord and professing trust in Britain ended in removal of the Turkish yoke of subservience, a very welcome subsidy, and a guarantee of imperial protection. After World War I, when the British founded the two Hashemite states—Iraq and Transjordan—along his northern frontier, Ibn Saud threw off the ties of gratitude and custom that had for so long bound him to alliance with Britain. The conquest of the Hejaz made him independent and earned him the recognition of the Great Powers. But his creation, and principal weapon, the *Ikhwan*, proved to be a two-edged sword. After he sheathed it his autonomy was strengthened by two events. One was the discovery of oil in his kingdom which led to a supply of funds from an American oil company; the other was the Second World War which gave him both money and know-how.

As the indigenous crude oil stocks of the United States were drawn down by wartime activities, the necessity for other sources of supply became obvious. Consequently, when the enormous size of Saudi oil reserves became apparent, the government of the United States made every effort to win the approval of the régime by supporting it both financially and with arms and technical assistance. The preponderance of American resources over those of Great Britain was another factor in the loss by that longtime ally of the Sauds of its privileged position as the most valued counselor of the monarch.

Despite the aid and counsel offered by both of these benefactors Saudi Arabia remains completely independent, basically a family autocracy. During Ibn Saud's lifetime it was truly governed by one all-powerful ruler. After 1932 his authority was never in question. Although raiding ceased and theft was almost inexistent, the monarchy functioned poorly in protecting the rights of the individual and in providing for his welfare and progress. It was plagued by graft, bribery, and corruption and was always in debt, yet it never faltered, probably because the king was not aware of or refused to acknowledge the existence of major failings. Only shortly before his death did he attempt to broaden the bases of power and decision-making.

*Part II of this document, 'The Saudi State,' looks at the structure and mechanisms of the higher echelons of government in the first half of the twentieth century, the vicissitudes of the exchequer, and developments in foreign policy. Most higher officials were members of the Saud family or related to the monarch by marriage. The exchequer remained in a precarious state throughout the half-century. His advisory council was made up almost entirely of foreigners, but all policy decisions, foreign and domestic, were Ibn Saud's alone. He brooked no independent implementations of judgments or decisions. The examination of government begins with a brief review of the discovery and early development of its resources of oil, without which it could not have continued to exist in the form described here.*

# Part II:

# The Saudi State

# THE SAUDI STATE

## Creation

**Name Changes:** The Saudi state was reborn 16 January 1902 when Abdul Aziz standing on the town wall of Riyadh said, 'Your own amir is with you again.' Its growth in area and power are marked by the changes in Ibn Saud's appellations. On 8 January 1926, Ibn Saud, already recognized for more than five years by his followers as 'Sultan of Nejd,' added the title, 'King of the Hejaz.' On 17 January 1927 he assumed the appellation, 'King of Nejd and its Dependencies.' On 27 September 1932 he united the two into one: 'Kingdom of Saudi Arabia.' Early versions of the country's dark green flag with its declaration in white script: 'There is no god but God; Mohammed is the Prophet of God,' are ornamented by crossed swords under a palm tree, but now only a sword underlies the text. The flag represents a country of some 865,000 square miles; larger than all of western Europe. For the most part it is desert, but the largest single producer of crude oil in the world has maintained its identity until now as a sovereign state ruled by the Saud family. But the kingdom would surely not have survived intact with the same system of government if crude oil in vast quantities had not been found within its limits.

**Oil?:** Most accounts of the acquisition of rights to explore for oil in Arabia take the view that Ibn Saud did not think that oil existed in his realm. Three facts militate against that view: 1. In 1920 Ibn Saud commissioned a European to be his commercial representative in London. One of his duties may have been to facilitate inquiries about concession rights, but in any case the agent (Dr. Mann) would not have accompanied a potential concessionaire to Arabia without Ibn Saud's consent. 2. At the Oqair conference of 1922 an Arab adviser to the then sultan of Nejd said to Sir Percy Cox that one of the reasons for decrying a 'Neutral Zone' to be shared by two states was the belief that the area might be petroliferous. 3. Dickson, a British political agent, knew of a secret Turkish report of oil seeps near Qatif and, presumably with Ibn Saud's permission, had made several trips to the area in an attempt to find them. In any case if *he* knew of them, so did Ibn Saud.

The negotiations to acquire a concession to explore for and to develop the petroleum resources of Arabia began late in 1922.

# The Concession Story

1922–1930: At the Oqair conference *(A. IX)* when Sir Percy Cox drew the lines on a map fixing the limits between the new kingdom of Iraq, the shaikhdom of Kuwait and the domain of the sultan of Nejd, another and much less prestigious person was at the camp. That individual and his mission have been described by Rihani and by Dickson. Both were present, Rihani as a guest of the sultan, Dickson as aide to Sir Percy Cox, then high commissioner of Iraq.

He was Major Frank Holmes, a short and corpulent New Zealander, an ex-Royal Marine, whose receding hairline was hidden under a white sun-helmet like those then issued French troops in North Africa. In a photograph taken during the meeting he stands, dressed in a suit and stiff-collared shirt, just to the rear of a seated Ibn Saud, monumental, and the slight, trim Sir Percy in a trilby and bow tie, hands clasped, sitting bolt upright *(Pl. XII, fig. 48)*.

Major Holmes was accompanied by his interpreter, Dr. Alex Mann, a physician who had been on Sir Percy's staff and was now Ibn Saud's commercial representative in London. Ibn Saud had appointed him to that post in 1920, with British government (*i.e.* Sir Percy's) approval. Major Holmes reached Oqair from Bahrain on November 17, four days before the date set for the opening of the conference. Accompanied by Dr. Mann he set off at once on a Rosinante to consult Ibn Saud who was in Hofuf. But it was surely not Holmes' first visit to the Arabian mainland.

From the timing of events at Bahrain before the conference and a report by Dickson that Holmes had hired dhows, it is more than likely that before the negotiator's arrival at Oqair he had visited an oasis six miles north of the town of Qatif. There, a copious artesian source forms a small lake. Dickson *(1956)* could not find the seep of crude oil reported in a secret Turkish document to be near the lake. Holmes was not more fortunate. If a seep existed, its dark stain had been buried under drifting sand.

Nevertheless, after the protocols had been signed Major Holmes was eager to present his offer. Ibn Saud heard him out, and not only because he had brought many expensive gifts. With Sir Percy and Dickson present, the Major indicated the area he wanted. It was roughly rectangular, bounded to the south by a line extending sixty miles inland from the base of the Qatar peninsula, and to the west by a line parallel to the shore running north nearly two hundred miles to a point some twenty-five miles southwest of the just-drawn Kuwait–al Hasa Neutral Zone. It included nine of the giant fields found and developed two to three decades later. *(See Map 9 on Pl. XII.)*

Sir Percy preferred that a British peroleum company negotiate through him for a concession in Arabia. If Holmes' company, Eastern and General, acquired a large tract, then an oil company could obtain rights to it only through this middle man that would profit from selling the rights to its holdings. So he tried to persuade Ibn Saud not to make a deal with Holmes. He was successful only for the duration of the conference. Three months later, Ibn Saud, perhaps counseled by Rihani, accepted Holmes' offer. In July 1923, the concession agreement was approved and signed in Jedda. For the sum of £2,000 a year the Eastern and General Syndicate had a concession valid for seventy years permitting explo-ration for and extraction of minerals in an area of about twelve thousand square miles.

Philby (1964) says that the syndicate hired a Swiss geologist who worked in al Hasa for two years during the cool season, but in 1926 the annual rental was not paid, so his report must have been negative. Ibn Saud canceled the concession in 1928.

The lapse made Holmes' subsequent bids for rights in Arabia nugatory. He was more fortunate in Bahrain where the concession he had acquired for Eastern and General was sold at a profit to Gulf Oil of Mexico in December 1927. The Red Line Agreement (n. 22) forced Gulf to sell its rights to Standard Oil of California the following year.

As mentioned above, a number of writers suggest that Ibn Saud did not believe that oil or any other exploitable mineral would be found in al Hasa. But the protest by Abdul Latif Pasha al Mandil* against Sir Percy's delineation of a Kuwait–al Hasa Neutral Zone shows that at least one of Ibn Saud's party thought otherwise, and most probably had freely expressed his opinion. In reply to Sir Percy's asking the reason for his objection, Abdul Latif replied, 'Quite candidly, because we think oil exists there.'

**1930–1933:** Whatever Ibn Saud's opinion of oil prospects, no other efforts were made by anyone to obtain a concession in al Hasa until 1930 when Major Holmes, now under the aegis of the Standard Oil Company of California, approached the royal court in Jedda. He was rebuffed. All remembered the abandonment of the concession that he had taken in 1923 and for which Suleiman (A. X), the minister of finance, had obtained only £4,000 in rental.

Whether or not Abdullah Philby (he had become a Moslem in August, 1930) played an important part in the negotiations that led to the acquisition of a concession by Standard of California is moot. Several British authors make little of it, but Yerkin (1991) gives him a leading rôle, and Philby himself (1964) with minute details about negotiations suggests that he was indispensable. In any event, impetus to an evaluation of the mineral wealth of the kingdom came from Mr. Charles R. Crane, son of the founder of the Crane Bathroom Equipment Company of Chicago and a millionaire Arabophile. Member of a commission appointed by President Wilson to investigate the matter, he had recommended against Jewish colonization in Palestine. In this King–Crane report (see Howard 1963) he also advocated that the French not be granted preferential status in Syria or Lebanon, recommending instead that Arabs govern these countries. So he was welcome in Arabia.

Crane had attempted to see Ibn Saud many times. Early in 1929 he narrowly escaped death in Kuwait when his car was shot at by Ajman raiders under Dhaidan al Hithlain. On 25 February 1931, he at last met the king and was given a royal welcome in Jedda. Before his departure he is said to have made two gifts to his host. One was a magnificent rose-pink bathtub that ended on the roof of the king's quarters in Jedda because water could not be spared to fill it in a

---

\*    A Nejdi merchant and banker stationed in Basra as Ibn Saud's representative.

town where almost all fresh water came from a decrepit steam desalinator. The other, better documented and far more practical, was his offer to send a qualified engineer to survey the mineral prospects of the country, a Mr. Karl S. Twitchell, who had worked for Crane in Yemen.

Twitchell arrived in Jedda in April. He studied the water resources and gold mines of the Hejaz for several months. In December, at the king's request (another indication that Ibn Saud hoped for oil) he crossed the country to al Hasa. In nearby Bahrain island an exploratory test well was about to start drilling, so when he met the king in Hofuf on 12 January 1932, Twitchell recommended that negotiation await the results of this test. If it was successful, then prospects for oil in eastern Arabia would be greatly enhanced, for the two areas, only twenty-six miles apart, must be very similar geologically. Both Bahrain island and a hill near the coast in Arabia, Jebel Dhahran, probably had the same origin—upward movement of salt.

Almana says that a copy of the report on oil prospects that Twitchell prepared in Jedda for the minister of finance was sent to London with Faisal on his fruitless trip to raise money. He must have been instructed to offer a concession to the British government, for shortly thereafter the legation in Jedda informed the Saudi Court that Whitehall was grateful for the offer but was not interested.

On 1 June 1932, oil in modest quantities was discovered by BAPCO (Bahrain Petroleum Company) a Canadian subsidiary of Standard. The company had been set up to conform to the provisions of the nineteenth century treaty with the local shaikh declaring Bahrain a British protectorate. The treaty prohibited the shaikh from granting rights to a company not based in a member state of the British Commonwealth.

Twitchell returned to the United States in July 1932, making known his knowledge of mining prospects, and, as instructed by the king, offering a concession in Saudi Arabia. Several mining companies along with the petroleum-producing Texas Company declined to enter into negotiations for rights in such a completely unknown area. But after acquiring a concession in Bahrain island Standard of California's geologists had been urging the company to go after rights in Arabia and welcomed Twitchell who had actually been in al Hasa.

On 11 July, Philby, then in London, had been approached by a former under-secretary of state, Francis B. Loomis, now a Standard executive, to discuss under what terms Ibn Saud would grant a concession in eastern Arabia. As a member of the king's inner circle, Philby was fully aware of the financial crisis in Arabia and told Mr. Loomis that the king needed much gold, now. Negotiation for rights could be undertaken at once.

Keeping the promise he had made before his departure from Arabia, Twitchell reported to Ibn Saud Standard's interest in a concession. Philby's interview with the Standard executive confirmed the validity of that interest which was reaffirmed in subsequent meetings, cables, and correspondence. Standard of California was invited to send to Jedda persons empowered to negotiate. Philby knew of the invitation (he says he sent it) and informed friends in the British petroleum industry about it.

On 15 February 1933, Twitchell arrived in Jedda with Mr. Lloyd Hamilton, head landman for Standard. Their wives accompanied them. Negotiations dragged on. After a time Philby was employed by the Americans as interpreter and go-between. The representative of Iraq Petroleum, Stephen H. Longrigg, was out of the running from the start because his instructions limited his offer to payments in rupees, and were restricted to a down payment of £10,000.

The Americans were not aware of the limitations imposed on Longrigg, but Philby knew of them, for he met with the British negotiators as an official of the Saudi government. At the same time he accepted a retainer of £1,000 a month from Hamilton. But his loyalty to Ibn Saud cannot be faulted, for he supported Suleiman in his insistence that the king would agree to a concession only if a large loan was included as the down payment. With the menace of a higher bid by the British ever-present, the Americans finally dropped their objections to a very large down payment and agreed to an interest-free loan of £35,000 in gold payable on the granting of a concession.

The concession agreement was presented to the king's council for approval on 9 May 1933. Ibn Saud, who had dozed through the reading of the terms of the contract, awoke when the droning voice ceased. Asked his opinion he said, 'Put your trust in God and sign.' Abdullah Suleiman did so. He had been advised by Sir Andrew Ryan, the first British minister to Saudi Arabia, to accept the American offer because it was most unlikely that there was oil there anyway. *(See A. VII for another version of Sir Andrew's thinking.)*

The terms of the agreement were stiff, but the area opened to exploration and development was large. The concession covered all of eastern Arabia as far west as the Dahana sands, and included preferential rights on other areas to the west and north including the Saudi half-share of the Kuwait Neutral Zone. The boundaries were not precisely defined in the initial grant, and were subject to negotiation later. A second concession agreement was signed in 1939, increasing the area of the concession westward to the 'outcrops of basement.'*

In addition to the £35,000 down, another £20,000 loan was due in eighteen months, along with a yearly rental of £5,000. If oil in commercial quantities was found, two more loans of £50,000 would be payable at yearly intervals. All loans would be recovered from royalty on production of four shillings gold a long ton. There would be no taxation and no customs duties.

**1933–1953:** In 1949, Saudi Arabia claimed a large area in the Rub' al Khali as far east as the Buraimi oasis *(n. 23)*, including four-fifths of the shaikhdom of Abu Dhabi. *(See Map 7 in n. 23.)* The oil company, then known as ARAMCO (Arabian American Oil Company), aided the Saudis by transporting officials and soldiers to Buraimi, and at the bargaining table by providing documents supporting the Saudi assertions. The dispute was not settled until 1974. Most of the contested area near the coast is now in the hands of the United Arab Amirates. In support of

---

*    Rocks on the surface whose potential for generating or storing petroleum has been destroyed by heat or great pressure. Usually both are involved in the destruction of these capacities.

his claim Ibn Saud cited the Wahhabi conquest of Oman in 1797 and his ancestors' taxation of the villages and tribes of the Buraimi area until 1857.

Oil in commercial quantities was discovered on Dammam Dome, the
geological term for Jebel Dhahran, on 4 March 1938, by well No. 7, a 'Deep Test.'
Wells 1 through 6 had penetrated only to the levels productive in Bahrain and had
yielded small quantities of oil and gas or were dry. Well No. 7 was drilled deeper.
Below a thick stratum of white, impervious rock called 'anhydrite' ($CaSO_4$) it
encountered four levels of partly biogenic limestone, porous enough to hold oil
and gas. The lowest of these levels is known as the 'D' member of the Arab Zone
and has proved to be the most widely distributed and most productive of the four
(*n. 24*). Exploitation of the fields was slowed by the war. Production rose to 5.1
million barrels in 1940, dropped slightly during the remaining war years but
climbed to nearly 60 million barrels in 1946. In 1953, the year of Ibn Saud's death,
production was 308 million barrels and revenue to the state was $110 million,
although only two of the five fields already discovered were in full production.

Much of this revenue went to satisfy the wants of the king, mainly for
construction of palaces and the importation of western goods—arms, motor vehicles, and communications equipment. Of what was left, some built roads and
some repaid debt and the interest on it. Little was spent on providing an infrastructure for the development of the economy or for the welfare of the people. As
might be expected under this régime, the lower echelons of government and its
administration were often impoverished, but functioned reasonably well because
the higher posts were filled by the king's sons or relatives and nepotism was the
rule.

Foreigners were employed in government only in the king's entourage
and in the Hejaz where they dealt with the complexities of overseeing pilgrims,
traders, and diplomats. For many years Ibn Saud ruled as a complete autocrat,
making all decisions. He did solicit the views of a group of advisers, all but one
Arab, almost all of them foreigners, and permitted the establishment of several
ministries. In the last year of his life when he felt that he was no longer able to
direct and transact all the essential business of the monarchy the king ordered the
installation of a Council of Ministers to be organized by the crown prince, Saud
ibn Abdul Aziz.

Books by Almana, Wahba, and Philby are the source for most of the
following—an overview of the mechanism of government.

# The Saud Autocracy

'We raise them not above us, nor do we place ourselves above them. We
give them what we can; we satisfy them with an excuse when we cannot. And
when they go beyond their bounds we make them taste of the sweetness of our
discipline.' This statement of policy reflects Ibn Saud's concept of good government. His word was law. If his people obeyed they were rewarded; if not, they
were punished. That they should have a voice in choosing their destiny was alien
to his thought.

**Personnel**: Governance of all major towns and provinces was, after unfortunate experiences with entrenched families, entrusted only to relatives of the king. In the early days, Abdullah ibn Jiluwi and Abdul Aziz ibn Musa'ad, Ibn Saud's cousins and participants in the coup in Riyadh, were named amirs of Hofuf and Haïl. In 1950 the ibn Jiluwis were still governors of al Hasa and the Sudairis (close relatives: offspring of Ibn Saud's mother and two uncles) were heads of thirteen provinces and towns including outposts like Sakaka, Tebuk, and Abha (mountain town in Asir), as well as a holy city, Medina.

With the taking of the Hejaz Ibn Saud had seen, however reluctantly, that it brought problems that his two previous conquests, al Hasa and Jebel Shammar, had not presented. Both of those provinces could be administered by men of his own stamp, all linked by consanguinity, and all convinced of the rightness of feudality. But the government of the Hejaz, long controlled by the Turks, was more complex socially and more rewarding financially, but less amenable to Wahhabi precepts.

As early as 1917 he had as his principal adviser Dr. Abdullah Said Damluji, later given the title of foreign secretary. It was he who signed the Oqair protocols in 1922. A native of Mosul in Iraq, he had a degree in medicine (Constantinople) and was fluent in French and Turkish. He had come to Arabia at the outbreak of war with Turkey in 1914 and in 1926 was in Jedda as provisional minister of foreign affairs.

In 1927 when the Treaty of Jedda was signed, Damluji was aided by Fuad Hamza, who replaced him at the end of the decade. Fuad Hamza was a Palestinian, a Druse shaikh, who had been a journalist and then a schoolmaster under the British mandate. He spoke English fluently. With them during the negotiations were two more of the king's advisers, Yusuf Yassin, a Syrian from Latakia, also formerly a teacher in the Palestine mandate, and Hafiz Wahba, an Egyptian lawyer and journalist, later ambassador to London.

Almana says that Yassin was a thorn in the side of the British, for he was outspoken, and made no attempt to be courteous and restrained. He was made minister of state, the head of the foreign section of the Court, in effect the foreign minister. Glubb describes Yassin as a curious mixture of journalist and Wahhabi fanatic, who used threats in ordinary discussions. Clayton who dealt with them during the negotiations for the Hadha-Bahra treaties described Hamza and Yassin as, 'the familiar type of "pinch-beck" politician employing a certain amount of low cunning and resorting at all times to a policy of consistent obstruction.'

Other foreign advisers were: Rushdi Mulhas, Ibn Saud's political secretary, a Palestinian strongly opposed to the British mandate; Shaikh Khalid al Hakim, a Syrian; and Shaikh Khalid Bey al Ghargani, a Libyan from Tripoli particularly interested in mining and petroleum prospects. All of them were members of a committee dealing with foreign affairs. Philby was a member too, but attended only at his discretion.

Faisal was named viceroy of the Hejaz in 1926 and minister of foreign affairs in 1930. Saud was appointed viceroy of Nejd in 1930, and in 1932 was named crown prince. His selection as heir to the throne had to be accepted by the tribes and notables of the kingdom as well as by the Saud family. Other blood relatives became advisers of the Court or ministers of state. A Ministry of Defense and Aviation was established in 1944 under Mansour (*Pl. IX, fig. 34*), the king's twelfth son, and in 1951 Ministries of the Interior, Agriculture, Communications, and National Economy were set up, the first three under sons of the king, the last controlled by the Ministry of Finance where Abdullah Suleiman had been appointed minister in 1932. Ibn Saud's brother Abdullah, twenty-five years younger, was, at twenty-five, one of his chief counselors, replacing in his affections the lost first-born, Turki.

In addition to a discrete foreign ministry, a 'foreign court' came into existence, in fact a translating and news-gathering bureau. In Ibn Saud's time it was small: a chief, two or three typists, translators (from 1926 until 1935 Almana was one), and a secretary-scribe. The 'court of internal affairs' or 'domestic court' included a hall for the king's *majlis* and seating for petitioners. The small staff dealt with the townspeople and Bedu visitors. An official received petitions and prepared them for submittal to the king. Both of these departments were in Riyadh. The clerical system in the Hejaz was patterned on that of Ottoman times, and initially employed the same people.

**Court Routine:** When the king traveled his 'court,' some thirty functionaries, went with him. The 'foreign' and 'domestic' courts totaled eighteen–twelve clerks and their six servants. The Chamberlain's section sent three receptionists with their three servants. The king had three personal servants and three cooks, along with soldiers to assist them.

The retinue included fifty or sixty of the ruler's personal guards who were relatives or long-time friends. Armed Negro slaves, nearly all of them Somalis in brilliantly colored robes, numbered at least thirty. Other soldiers brought the total of armed men in the caravan to more than two hundred. By 1937, two hundred and fifty cars and trucks were used to transport men and impedimenta. Camels had been retired.

On visits to the Hejaz the monarch took with him a wife or two, their youngest children and their servants, together about twenty-five. A doctor and his assistants had their own transport. In pre-highway days ten or fifteen Indian and Indonesian driver-mechanics attended to breakdowns.

When radios improved, a portable transmitter and receiver, operators, and supporting staff accompanied the caravan. News reports were received and translated routinely both in the field and in the larger towns where an official was instructed to pass on at once any happening of importance.

In Riyadh or in the cities of the Hejaz Ibn Saud followed an almost invariable daily schedule. He rose at 4:30 A.M., before the pre-dawn prayer, and after these devotions slept for another hour. The entire day was molded about the five periods of worship. At about eight, the Chief Chamberlain would give him the names of people with matters of importance to discuss. They were received in the order of their consequence. When the more eminent had been dealt with he began work on the day's correspondence. Almana describes the king's Napoleonic ability to dictate two letters at once and to carry on a conversation at the same time.

Anyone could attend the general *majlis* held in a large hall later in the morning. The attendance was seldom less than eighty and often rose to one hundred and fifty. The sovereign opened the sitting with a verse from the Koran which he subjected to exegesis. He then chose a subject of importance and expounded on it for some time, making a methodical disquisition with heads and subheads. An open forum followed in which he answered questions on any subject, even rendering judgments on disputed issues. However, the sessions lasted less than an hour.

All who attended the *majlis* received a present. Their names were listed and presented to *As Shiyukh* who noted what gift each should get. For a Bedu the usual was three gold pounds, a robe and a cloak. In addition, he got sacks of rice, dates, and small packets of coffee, tea and sugar. These donations insured the loyalty of the tribesmen for they constituted a large part of his annual income. However, the people of Riyadh seldom came to these daily meetings, and townsmen and villagers living elsewhere rarely visited the capital.

A modest lunch (the king was never greedy for food because he suffered from digestive upsets) was sometimes followed by a visit to the harem, but often by a short nap. Later in the afternoon he usually held a meeting with his consultative council on foreign affairs, always bringing up a subject for their consideration and advice. The council had no executive authority. Most of the time it had but eight members.

Nearly every day at the conclusion of this meeting the king motored out of the town. Sometimes he remained abroad so long that he said the evening prayer in the open. After supper and another prayer, he convened the evening *majlis*, which was more relaxed and less formal than that of the forenoon. The participants were dignitaries and high officials of the town and distinguished visitors. After a half-hour of instruction by the head of the *Ulema* concerning the life of the Prophet or religious history, the king allowed discussion on any topic of interest, including on occasion the charms of a favorite concubine or slave-girl.

When the guests had departed the ruler made a tour of the offices of his court where matters that had come up during the day were brought to his attention. No one else was permitted to make a decision, even on a matter of small importance, a fact that to some degree slowed the routine of government, and made his staff wary of exerting authority or making independent judgments.

The king usually went to his quarters after nine in the evening, but slept little before midnight. The routine of his daily life was unchanging except for the month of Ramadan and the occasional hunting trip or picnic. As he aged, his staff made every effort to spare him tiring encounters and needless effort. But in the year of his death, learning of unanswered petitions, he issued a warning to his representatives that all appeals addressed to him must be brought to his attention.

Ibn Saud's government functioned, but it was hampered by a virtually permanent shortage of funds due to his munificence versus his meager income. The treasury was more often than not insolvent. Only in the last years of his reign was income even remotely linked to expenditure, and the exchequer was always in arrears because of the extravagance of the monarch and his family. The story of his rise from rags to riches is more interesting than that of a Horatio Alger hero.

# The Saudi Exchequer

**Early Days:** Abdur Rahman and his family in exile in Kuwait lived on the meager allowance of the Turkish authorities (60 Turkish pounds a month) granted them as insurance against the improbable chance that they would eventually regain the ancestral holdings. When Abdul Aziz took Riyadh he gathered loot in the form of arms and cattle, an unknown quantity of specie, and probably more of both as contributions, voluntary or not, from his lieges. In addition to their services he collected *zakat*, here a tax, on crops, the production of cereals (wheat, rice, and millet), fruit (mainly dates, but including apricots and figs), and on cattle (camels, horses, sheep, and goats). In April 1918, when Philby was returning to Riyadh with Ibn Saud, the amir was much concerned over the paucity of his revenues, and discussed them with his guest at length. On sheep and camels *zakat* was levied at the rate of one sheep or five Maria Theresa dollars *(n. 25)* for every forty sheep, and one goat or five dollars for every five camels. This yielded some $MT20,000 annually.

On crops irrigated by surface waters the tax was twenty per cent of production, and on harvests watered by wells ten per cent. The revenue from this source was a little more than $MT200,000.

Customs duties levied at one-eighth *ad valorem* on imports through al Hasa supplied only 460,000 rupees annually during the war years. In sum, at the rates of exchange then current his income from taxes was about £100,000 a year. Hence the importance of the subsidy of £60,000 paid him by Britain.

Until 1917 he had additional revenue from the capture of livestock and other booty, taken from recalcitrant tribes who opposed his rule. Because of the prospect of peace and his success in subduing his opponents this income practically ceased thereafter.

Ibn Saud insured the loyalty of his subjects and demonstrated his preëminence by largesse. In the early days this was for the most part food, meals supplied daily to hundreds of followers in Riyadh, but it included clothing, camels, money; and more rarely to visitors of high rank a watch, a jeweled dagger, a horse, a woman. Any Bedu who came to visit him with news or to show his loyalty was rewarded.

**The Hejaz and After:** With the conquest of the Hejaz completed late in 1925, from 1927 to 1930 duty and tax on trade and the pilgrim traffic increased his revenue to over £5,000,000 annually. But in 1931 the worldwide slump reduced his income from all sources to less than £2,000,000, while his expenditures for gifts and construction which had risen in proportion to receipts could not in his view be decreased in the same proportion.

As revenue increased he floated a currency, the riyal, which lost some of its value as the depression continued, so that merchants began to buy gold and export it to their banks abroad. The debts of the two kingdoms climbed to more than £300,000, much of it owed for imports of arms, radio equipment, cars and trucks, even aircraft. A part was due Indian contractors for the construction of roads and palaces. Interest on loans from the Indian government and sums advanced by the great merchants, the Al Gosaibis and the Ali Rezas, were not inconsiderable.

Building projects for himself, family, and friends proliferated. On excursions, he threw coins from the sedan by handfuls. As long as money was available the king would spend it or give it away, believing that discontent and dishonor must surely follow if he did not maintain a princely standing.

After 1930, employees of the government were paid only after long delay. As a result, they went on short rations or used their post to demand bribes. The drought in revenue continued throughout the decade.

In 1932 the situation had become so critical that the Amir Faisal, the second surviving son, and Fuad Hamza, an adviser to the court, were sent to Europe to raise money. The Bank of England and private investors in London were not interested, but the Russians rolled out the red carpet. On 29 May the would-be borrowers arrived in Moscow and thereafter were feted by commissars from Leningrad to the Caucasus.

Molotov offered to overlook a debt of £30,000 incurred by Suleiman's seizure of a shipload of gasoline and kerosene for the use of the Court, and to make a loan of £1,000,000 in return for removal of the trade embargo (placed on Russian goods at the request of Jedda merchants after the arrival of a Soviet cargo ship) and the signing of treaties regulating commerce and friendship. The loan was not made for the treaties were never signed. Ibn Saud presumably retained some regard for the British and feared the unknown and untested.

Concession Income: An imbalance between receipts and expenditures lessened temporarily in 1933 when the California Arabian Standard Oil Company (CASOC) obtained its concession. The down payment of £35,000 in gold sovereigns was placed in Suleiman's unpracticed hands and in 1934 another £20,000 in gold reached the Saudi coffers.

In 1938 CASOC paid the first royalties, about $340,000, on production of oil, and, as had been promised in the event of a commercial discovery, loaned the Saudi exchequer £50,000 against future royalties. Another loan for the same amount was made in 1939. But when the Second World War began in August 1939, the kingdom's recurrent financial crises had not ended. In 1940 the British government began granting subsidies that rose to more than a million pounds a year. Advance payments against royalty on oil topped $10 million a year, although production then was limited to some 30,000 barrels a day. Finally, on 18 February 1943, Lend-Lease funds from the United States were released to Saudi Arabia and in the two following years over $33 million in cash and goods poured into the country in addition to more advances against royalty.

But after the war, in March 1946, when the minister of finance, Abdullah Suleiman, tried to draw up a budget based on 1945 royalty income he found that expenditures would be £17.5 million but income only £13.2 million. The exchequer was again chronically short of cash in spite of ever-increasing revenue from production of oil, and after 1950 from a half-share in the profits of the oil company. No matter what the amount, much of it passed into the king's hands every year to be disbursed at his pleasure to himself, to his male progeny, and to his entourage. Very little went for public works. Corruption and mismanagement made merchants and entrepreneurs rich, but the richest was Suleiman. Undoubtedly the king learned of Suleiman's improbity, but knew his loyalty to the régime, and thought his laying up of a fortune a matter of no moment. Nevertheless, in 1944 he threw out one of Suleiman's aides who had a reputation for venality.

By the summer of 1950 the pay of the army and police was four months in arrears, and the value of the currency was wavering, but in that year Suleiman decreed a tax on income. The royal family and the *Ulema* were exempted.

In 1951 Saudi revenue from oil was $110 million (for the first time it was half of Aramco's net profit, not just royalty) but the budget set spending at $125 million, of which two-thirds was allotted 'State Palaces, Princes and Royal Establishments.' In 1952 the expenditure on Palaces, etc., was reduced to one-fourth of a budget of just over $150 million. Defense was next in line. Repayment of debt was set at $26 million. A new item was $8 million for the Department of Health. That same year taxes on pilgrims equivalent to $55 a head were eliminated, an annual loss of $6 million to the exchequer. In 1953, the outstanding debt was somewhere between $150 and $200 million.

In 1952 Saudi gold coins minted by the Bank of France arrived in Jedda and were used at the same time that the price of silver bullion rose. Millions of silver riyals were smuggled out of the country every month and sold by weight. Under the Point Four aid agreement of 1951, American advisers set up the Saudi Arabian Monetary Agency in May 1952. (It still existed in 1975.) In less than a year SAMA had stabilized the value of the riyal by depreciating silver against the dollar, but none of this remedial work lessened the extravagant expenditures of the royal family. Suleiman squeezed the oil company using every possible means. The king, now old and crotchety, supported him. But a year after the monarch died his successor, Saud ibn Abdul Aziz forced Suleiman to retire. Ironically, he had tried to curb Saud's expenditures, even more prodigal than those of his father.

The meager income that plagued Ibn Saud in the first three decades of his rule clearly played no small part in his continued acceptance of British tutelage and protection during that time. Not only were loans and arms provided (never enough!) but also guidance for his relations with other states. His restraint during the Khurma–Turaba incidents in 1918–19, the Oqair protocols, the Hadha–Bahra agreements, even his warnings to British client states during the *Ikhwan* rebellion and his reconciliation with Faisal of Iraq in 1930—all showed his continued respect for the former ally, in post-war years beset by its own difficulties.

Yet already in 1922 he told Rihani of his resentment of British high-handedness. 'See what they have done to me, Ibn Saoud their friend and ally. They spin and spin—spin nets for me. They have surrounded me with enemies—set up states that they are supporting against me' *(Rihani 1928)*. The seizure of Aqaba by British troops in 1925 and its inclusion in Transjordan certainly increased his ire, for the town had been taxed by Husain as part of the Hejaz, now his by right of conquest. The British mandate of Palestine was worrisome because of Jewish immigration, and by 1937 when Dickson visited Ibn Saud, was a major concern to the king, then 60. All of these incidents certainly lessened his confidence in the integrity of his old ally. To Rihani he had said, 'and we will keep faith with them, even through loss and injury, so long as they keep faith with us.'

# Saudi Foreign Policy (1902-1953)

The eighteenth century leaders of the Wahhabis recognized no limits to the spread of their faith, a basic requirement of their dogma. The concomitant rapid territorial expansion accompanied by brutal rapine ended in the destruction of the first Wahhabi régime in 1811–1818 and its suppression in 1838–1840. The military campaigns that accomplished this were ordered by the Sublime Porte, for centuries the ruler of an Ottoman Empire. Perforce, the Porte found Wahhabism a threat to its hegemony and acted to abolish it *(A. II)*.

**The First Thirty Years**: Ibn Saud, the leader of the Wahhabis after 1902, differed from his ancestors in one basic respect. He understood that pragmatic considerations set a limit to the propagation of the faith. And he was intelligent enough to recognize that in spite of the prescriptions of dogma, compromise would be necessary to insure that his realm survive. He had some conception of the strength of both the European powers and the Ottoman Empire and had seen an example of how their rivalries could be used to advantage by a weaker adversary. This he had learned at the *majlis* of his mentor, Mubarak as Sabah, who, in the late nineteenth century had received German, Russian, and French emissaries, in addition to threats and menaces from the Turks, and finally in 1899, had obtained a treaty of protection from the British.

The treaty worked—the Turks no longer harassed Mubarak, although he was let down by the Anglo–Ottoman treaty of 1913 (signed but never ratified). In consequence, from the beginning of the struggle to regain his patrimony Ibn Saud never ceased his efforts to obtain protection from the English comparable to that given Kuwait. His attempts began in 1902, only four months after he had taken Riyadh. He sent a letter to the British political resident (C. A. Kemball) in which he wrote, 'I request of your benevolent government to consider me as one of their protégés.' This letter showed that his political acumen was already well-developed, for in it he mentions that he had ignored a Russian offer of aid in his stand against the Rashids because, 'I have no wish to look to anyone but yourself because of the favors and protection you extend to all those who place themselves under your eyes.'

This maneuver was repeated in 1903 when he visited Kuwait and again reported to Kemball that he had had another offer of money and arms from the Russians. Early in 1904 he had news that the Turks were sending a force to aid ibn Rashid. By messages sent through the political agent in Bahrain he suggested to Cox, the new political resident in Bushire, that he would drive the Turks from al Hasa if the British would protect him from attack by sea.

But after the battle of Shinana (28 September 1904) Ibn Saud, perhaps despairing of British aid, used his father's name to write the *Wali* of Basra, Fakhri Pasha, protesting his loyalty and explaining that only *his* orders to the populace had stopped the people of the Qasim from a massacre of the surviving Turkish troops. The news that the Turks were sending a second expeditionary force caused him on 16 November (again under his father's name) to send a telegram to the sultan requesting him to reconsider because the Arabs of Nejd would not tolerate such support for ibn Rashid. He also asserted his hereditary ownership of the Qasim and his right to leadership of its people.

Half of the 4,500 (–7,000?) man expeditionary force started from Medina and the other half from Samara in southwestern Mesopotamia. Having had news of its size, in December Ibn Saud wrote the sultan: 'I have no idea of revolting against the Ottoman government. As I am the lawful ruler of Nejd and have defeated the usurper Ibn Rashid, I am willing to accept any reasonable terms you impose on me. I am sorry to have fought the Ottoman troops in Nejd, but as they were helping my antagonist Ibn Rashid, I was obliged to do so in self-defense.'

He sent more placatory correspondence in the same vein while Mubarak attempted to persuade Knox, the political agent in Kuwait, that he should obtain British aid for Ibn Saud. If his efforts failed, Mubarak was instructed to arrange a meeting between the Saudis and the Turks. This he did. On 8 February 1905, Abdur Rahman arrived at Safwan, near Zubair. In two meetings with Mukhlis, *Wali* of Basra, it was arranged that Abdur Rahman would become *Qaimaqam* of southern Nejd, to include the districts of Washm and Sudair with Riyadh as his capital. The Qasim, however, would be administered and garrisoned by the Turks, with governors for Buraida and Anaiza appointed from the local population. This relinquishment of jurisdiction over territory taken only recently from the enemy aroused protest among the *Ulema*, but Ibn Saud had a plan to recover it without battling superior force.

In August, secure in the knowledge that the presence of Turkish troops prevented the Rashids from retaking the Qasim, although their harassment of its people continued, Ibn Saud went to al Hasa. There, he reasserted his authority over the three major tribes of the region, in the process restricting Turkish jurisdiction to the areas guarded by troops. When he returned to Riyadh, he again undertook action in the field against the Rashids through campaigns directed by his sons. At the same time he protested his devotion and allegiance to the Turks in letters which always included denigration of his Shammar enemy, as molesters of Qasimis through, 'acts of tyranny, bloodshed and robbery.'

In April 1906 the death of his major opponent, the Rashidi amir, Abdul Aziz ibn Mitab, brought a pause in the campaigns against Haïl. The withdrawal of the Turks from the Qasim in November marked the beginning of a six-year period during which Ibn Saud was able to mend his fences at home, climaxed in 1910 with the quelling of the major effort of the Araïf to establish a new régime, and in 1912 with the establishment of the first *hijra*. Until 1907 he kept up a flow of correspondence with the British designed to obtain help. One such letter received by Prideaux, political agent in Bahrain in November 1906, indicated that Ibn Saud had become aware of Britain's desire to maintain friendly relations with the Ottomans. He proposed to obtain from the Turks the governorship of al Hasa, after which he would declare himself independent at an opportune moment. Or else he could drive the Turks out, provided that Britain would guard him against a counterattack from the sea. He proposed that his attack to remove the Turks be made only four or five years hence and that he would appeal overtly for British protection only after the seizure of al Hasa had been completed. That was the last of Ibn Saud's calls for protection by Great Britain until 1911 when he sent to Cox in Bushire an emissary who was turned away for lack of credentials.

But on 7 March 1911 Shakespear met him in the desert near Thaj and sent his proposal on to Cox, accompanying it with a note to the effect that a Saudi presence in al Hasa would be advantageous to Britain. As political agent in Kuwait, he warned the amir that the policies of his government required that Turkey be recognized as the dominant power in the Middle East. Britain was concerned only with those states that fronted the Persian Gulf where it intended to remain the supreme authority and guardian of its protectorates, but it had no interest in the interior.

Ibn Saud was forced to the conclusion that he would have to take al Hasa without a promise of British protection. But his reasoning had told him that once he held a portion of the coast, the British would be forced to reconsider their position. His talks with Leachman in December 1912 at Riyadh had given him news of the grave difficulties of the Ottoman Empire, then fighting wars in both Tripolitania and the Balkans. Even if these actions ended, the Turks would find it difficult on short notice to mount a large force for action in the Persian Gulf. His conversations with Shakespear at Khafs on 30 March–2 April 1913 *(A. VI)* confirmed that Britain would not consider his move into al Hasa a hostile act. These two desiderata and the reports of his agents in Hofuf concerning Turkish unpreparedness made it clear that the time was ripe for action.

Once he had secured al Hasa, Ibn Saud lost no time in attempting again to establish relations with Great Britain and to mollify the Turks. During June and July his efforts to effect a change in the British position were unsuccessful, as shown by Cox's letter to him of 9 July 1913, which reaffirmed a policy of non-interference in Turkish–Saudi relations. After the Anglo–Ottoman Convention was signed on 29 July, Foreign Secretary Edward Grey changed his hitherto adamant opposition to contacts with Ibn Saud. Cox wrote the amir on 11 September. His letter stated that if the Saudis undertook to respect the integrity of the Gulf shaikhdoms, British representatives were ready to meet him in order to determine how the friendly regard of the government could be demonstrated.

The meeting took place on 15–16 December in Oqair. The British were represented by Major Trevor, the political agent in Bahrain, and by Captain Shakespear, the agent in Kuwait. Ibn Saud wanted their assurance that the British would block any Turkish effort to invade al Hasa by sea. He did not get it. But in a reversal of its long-standing policy of non-intervention in central Arabian affairs, on 9 March 1914 Whitehall discussed with the Sublime Porte Ibn Saud's relations with Turkey. It protested the provisions of an agreement that Turkey offered Ibn Saud in return for recognizing his *de facto* seizure of al Hasa. Two of the six points of the agreement required that foreign merchants be excluded from al Hasa and that the Porte would determine and carry out foreign policy there. Britain would accept neither.

The two political agents persuaded Ibn Saud to delay his reply to the Turkish proposal for three months while London was consulted. But with war in the offing, and with Turkey officially neutral, the Foreign Office reverted to its previous stand. The Ottomans increased their pressure on Ibn Saud. Arms were sent to ibn Rashid, and troops arrived by sea and landed at Basra. To counter these moves Ibn Saud began to assemble an army. When Shakespear arrived in Riyadh on 9 March 1914 on his way to Egypt overland he found mobilization under way. The Saudis might have to repel an attack by ibn Rashid or a Turkish invasion in al Hasa. And the attacks might be simultaneous.

The India Office interpreted the *démarche* of 9 March by the Foreign Office as an intervention on Ibn Saud's behalf. It informed the amir that the British government was trying to arrange the matter of his status with the Porte, and that, 'He should not take any independent action in the matter.' This was good news. Britain was on his side. But the Turks put on more pressure with three letters, one of which informed him that the sultan was resolved, 'to guard zealously what was left to Islam.' Other letters followed. Ibn Saud could delay no longer.

On 16 April he left Qatif for Kuwait and arrived at Malah ten miles south of the town on the 26th. Lt. Col. William Grey, then political agent, informed him that Whitehall had decided not to intercede because the Turks had declined an offer of mediation. He was on his own for the moment, but would again attempt to induce British intervention. The conference began at Subaihiya on 2 May. The Turks insisted that al Hasa return to the *status quo ante*, except that under Ottoman suzerainty Ibn Saud would head the local government. However, they demanded that Turks man all forts. Ibn Saud protested, but was told that if he did not accept the garrisons he would be compelled to do so. Thereupon he rose, half-unsheathed his sword, and ordered the speaker to leave. Negotiations ended abruptly with both sides returning to their bases.

With a German–Ottoman alliance a real possibility, the Foreign Office reverted to its non-intervention policy and left Ibn Saud unsupported. He was forced to bargain with the Turks through his agent in Basra. The result was the Turkish Treaty, signed in Basra 15 May 1914 by Suleiman Shafik ibn Ali Khamali, Wali of Basra. The terms of the treaty are mentioned briefly above (*pp. 29–30*). Ibn Saud signed it 29 May in Riyadh. The main point of contention, the size of the Turkish garrisons in al Hasa, was resolved to Ibn Saud's satisfaction, for he was to decide on their strength in consulation with the Turkish officer detached to Hofuf. The outbreak of war negated any necessity to comply with the provisions of the treaty which later was declared by Saudi negotiators never to have existed (*n. 30*).

In July 1914, three months before war was declared between Britain and the Ottomans, the Turks instructed Ibn Saud that in the event of hostilities he would stop fighting ibn Rashid and move north to protect Basra against a British advance. He would be given arms and money. He immediately told the British of this order. On 3 November Knox, then acting political resident, promised him protection from an Ottoman attack from the sea, and recognition of his independence in Nejd and al Hasa, with a treaty to guarantee it, if he would: 1. Coöperate with Shaikh Mubarak and the shaikh of Muhammera in liberating Basra, or 2. Act to prevent Turkish reinforcements from reaching Basra. He did neither, but did not comply with the Turkish order. His excuse: he must remain in Nejd to protect his domain. Presumably caution was the reason for his hesitancy to aid either contestant. He did not know which would win.

The Turks continued to press for his help, and sent four envoys to Nejd, along with four *Ulema* to preach *jihad* against the infidels. Ibn Saud promptly confined the mullahs and ordered read publicly in one of his *majlis* the British proclamation guaranteeing that the Holy Places would not be attacked. But until he had the protection of a British treaty he had to keep the Turkish envoys guessing. In December 1915 he told Keyes, political officer in Bahrain, that he concluded a treaty with the Turks after he had lost faith in British promises, but that he meant never to honor it.

Through Knox in Bushire, Ibn Saud learned that Shakespear, carrying an official proposal from the government, was on the way to him. In correspondence with Knox prior to Shakespear's arrival at Khufaisa on 31 December, and in discussions with his English friend afterward, Ibn Saud remained cautious and non-committal regarding aid to the British. Their promises to date had been informal and he had no assurance that pledges made now would be honored after the war. He wanted a treaty, but did not want to commit himself to a military rôle. So he pointed out to Shakespear what might happen if he were forced to carry out his commitment to Turkey as specified in the treaty of 15 May. Shakespear recognized the implied threat. He prepared the draft of a treaty in accordance with Ibn Saud's desires and forwarded it to Cox. Cox added five amendments and sent the draft on to India. Nowhere in the draft was any reference to the active military assistance specified in Knox's proposals of 3 November.

The Turks supported ibn Rashid with arms and money. After the battle of Jarrab, which was not the victory he had envisioned, Ibn Saud's negotiations for a treaty with Britain continued. Cox's draft reached him in mid-May, forwarded to him in Riyadh by his agent in Basra, Abdul Latif Mandil. His counterdraft reached Cox on 24 June, and was sent by sea to India and then to London. Cox, then chief political officer of the British Expeditionary Force, was not free to meet the amir until early December, and until his victory at Ridha early in December Ibn Saud himself was occupied in quelling the Ajman revolt.

The signing of the treaty on 26 December 1915 ended Ibn Saud's quest for protection against the Turks that he had sought since 1902. He obtained it only because Britain had accepted his benevolent neutrality in lieu of active support. This was truly a triumph of negotiation on his part.

His skill in diplomacy was tested again. Britain wanted him to coöperate with Sharif Husain who had been his enemy since 1910. He feared that in their desire to keep the sharif's forces active the British would bow to Husain's pretension of being 'King of the Arab Countries' and would force him, who had fought for independence, into vassalage. After much preliminary correspondence Cox assured Ibn Saud in a letter dated 18 October 1916 that no understandings with Husain would alter Britain's observance of the terms of the Qatif treaty. Saudi aid to the revolt in Hejaz, perhaps by attacking ibn Rashid, would be appreciated, but the sharif would be constrained to recognize the total and complete independence of Nejd. The reassuring effect of this missive was negated by Husain's reply to Ibn Saud's request for guarantees of his autonomy: 'Only a man bereft of his reason or of an absent mind' could have written such a letter which was returned so that, 'you may reflect on what you wrote to us.' Ibn Saud was convinced that such a reply could be written only if Husain had an understanding with the British regarding his eventual kingship. He asked to meet Cox.

The meeting was held in Oqair on 11 November 1916. Ibn Saud reported growing opposition in Nejd to his pro-British policy, in part because the blockade on trade with Syria that he was enforcing greatly reduced the income of many of his subjects, and in part because his people were distrustful of alliance with a power that supported their enemy, the sharif. He showed the letter from the sharif to Cox who agreed that it was 'extremely discourteous and arrogant.' Nevertheless, as a gesture of alliance, but only at Husain's request, Ibn Saud stood ready to send fifty men under one of his sons to the Hejaz 'as a token of identification with the Sharif's cause.' He could begin operations against ibn Rashid if Britain would assist him with money and arms.

At the Durbar the tension of Ibn Saud's ongoing feud with Shaikh Salim of Kuwait (because of Kuwait's harboring dissident Ajman) may have been eased, for the amir met Mubarak's successor, his son Jabir, the then current head of the family, and found that young but urbane ruler congenial. Unfortunately, Jabir died only a year later, and Salim replaced him.

Early in 1917 the Turks sent to Riyadh a deputation from Medina, still under siege by Husain, to protest Ibn Saud's seizure of seven hundred camels destined for Syria. It also asked for supplies and more camels. Because the deputation was accorded audience, it may be that the seizure had taken place only as a show of compliance with British desires. Although Saudi records are not available, it appears that as early as 1915 Ibn Saud was clandestinely providing camels and supplies to Turkish forces in the interior. If so, Turki's pass for the enemy caravan to Kuwait may not have been just an error by an inexperienced commander. Such actions would have been compatible with Ibn Saud's caution— to straddle the fence until the outcome was certain—and with his shrewdness— to realize that a quick victory by sharifian forces at Medina would increase the prestige of Husain to the detriment of his own.

The causes of Ibn Saud's distrust and hatred of the Hashemite Husain are listed in Note 16. In a letter to Husain dated 13 August 1916 the Nejdi reveals his abiding mistrust: 'If you are desirous of our services and coöperation, then we desire you to give us a promise so that our mind may be at rest regarding your attitude especially regarding the question of interference with our tribes and subjects.' During the war, the Saudi amir kept his army of zealots from the Hejaz because he would not fight one enemy while another (the Rashids) could attack his rear. More important, he wanted the protection of the British as well as their subsidy which they threatened to stop if he made aggressive moves against their well-paid ally. Of interest are British attempts to stop Husain from using British gold to suborn Saudi tribes, attempts that occasionally were successful. In 1918 and thereafter they tried to prevent an overt clash of arms by reining in the sharif's invective against the Sauds and by ignoring his pretensions to leadership of all Arabs. They refused to recognize Husain's use of the title, 'King of the Arab Lands,' and as early as the winter of 1916 sent him letters of reprimand for insulting Ibn Saud and the shaikhs of Kuwait and Muhammera.

Ibn Saud's statecraft during the war years is shown by three skillful ploys: 1. He avoided a campaign against the Ottomans in Iraq that both the British and Husain would have approved, but would have required his leaving Nejd. 2. He sidestepped coöperation with the sharif that would have involved fighting the

Turks, would have left Riyadh open to attack and would have suggested that he was subservient to Husain. 3. He managed to achieve these negative victories without alienating the British who had urged that he do one or the other. Their agents found him friendly and trustworthy—a masterful performance. In fact, the 1919 invitation for him to visit England was an expression of gratitude for his help in the war.

In 1921, the establishment under British auspices of the Hashemite states of Iraq and Transjordan heightened Ibn Saud's disillusion with British friendship and guidance in foreign relations. He was not unaware of the postwar economic and political problems of the nation that for seventy years had kept the peace in the Persian Gulf, and this knowledge probably influenced his decision to begin the conquest of the Hejaz.

Both before the beginning of hostilities and after Mecca was occupied he showed great concern to calm the apprehension of Islam as to his intentions regarding the Holy Land and its future administration. In June and October 1924 he issued statements that were sent to all the Moslem nations and enclaves of the world. The first asked for the consent of Islam to his taking power in the Hejaz in the name of all, and promised that the nature of the future government there would be decided by a congress in the Hejaz itself. The second message was an invitation to the conference. Neither elicited much response, except that a delegation from India arrived even before the war ended. The congress took place after the *Hajj* of 1926 with seventy delegates in attendance. Ibn Saud allowed no discussion of the legitimacy of his takeover or of the form the government would take. It was a skillful use of dictatorial power to avoid endless controversy and criticism concerning the legality of his takeover, but it also showed a regard for world opinion that his ancestors had ignored.

In spite of his disenchantment with their policies, Ibn Saud's continued respect for and coöperation with the British is evinced by the series of discussions with Sir Gilbert Clayton beginning with the Hadda–Bahra agreements of 1925, followed by the Treaty of Jedda in 1927, and ending with the 1928 arguments regarding the 'forts' in Iraq. He was obliged to maintain his uncompromising posture concerning the destruction of the forts because of the intransigence of the *Ikhwan* and the loss of credibility and stature that would have ensued from any change in position. The *Ikhwan* revolt might have succeeded in overturning his government had he accepted a settlement that did not include removal of the police posts.

Ibn Saud could not have been comfortable during his meeting with King Faisal of Iraq on H.M.S. *Lupin*, 20 February 1930 *(Pl. VII, fig. 22)*. The encounter had been arranged by the British immediately after the *Ikhwan* revolt was crushed in an attempt to mollify the bitterness between the two monarchs after a decade of cross-border raids ending in the Busaiya massacre. Faisal could not forget that both his father and his brother had lost a kingdom to the aging giant who sat next to him. Ibn Saud remembered the long series of insults and worse that this man's father had inflicted on him.

For his part, Ibn Saud never overcame his hatred of the Hashemites. It colored his foreign policy throughout his lifetime. Nevertheless, on this occasion he signed two treaties with Iraq, one of 'Friendship', the other of 'Good Neighbor-liness'. Obviously, Faisal's British advisers had proposed this gesture.

Although he resented British king-making, Ibn Saud may have preferred that British interests take the concession in al Hasa, for otherwise his son would not have been given a copy of Twitchell's 1932 report to take to Whitehall. Old ties were difficult to break. Proof: at British behest his prohibition in 1936 of the importation of slaves.

Official America was slow to recognize the importance of Ibn Saud. The first U.S. minister to Saudi Arabia, Bert Fish, was named in 1931. He resided in Cairo, where he was also minister. He first visited Arabia in February, 1940. Long before, Russia and Britain had promoted their consulates in Jedda to legations, but the Russian representative left in May 1938 and disappeared in the Stalinist purges.

**Second World War:** As he had in 1914–1918, during the Second World War Ibn Saud, ever the prudent ruler, hedged his commitment to the Allied cause. In January 1939, he opened diplomatic relations with Germany, and in February sent a messenger to Hitler with a personal letter saying that he wished to see friendly and intimate relations with the German Reich developed to the greatest extent possible. In that same period the king received Dr. Fritz Grobba, the German minister in Baghdad, for long discussions. In July 1939, he committed himself to buy 4,000 German rifles and to have an arms factory constructed near Riyadh.

During this period he continued to protest his friendship for Great Britain and throughout the war years the British and Americans had no inkling of his contacts with the Axis. That some of his advisers, including Yusuf Yassin and one of his doctors, Midhat Shaikh al Ardh, ardently favored the Axis was well known, however. They cheered early German victories and Philby predicted the collapse of British efforts because of the success of submarine warfare.

But Ibn Saud did not assist the Axis cause at any time, at first because he feared the activities of Italy in Eritrea. In 1934 he blocked Mussolini's efforts to get a foothold in Yemen. During the Second World War he made no attempt to arouse enmity to the Allies among the Arabs of the Levant and the Moslems of northern and western India, whose rising in a *jihad* could have severely hampered British war efforts. During the crisis in Egypt caused by Rommel's advance he sent his son to talk to the Indian troops.

As Allied campaigns began to succeed, Ibn Saud no longer straddled the fence. He did not pay for the German arms, and declined to allow Japan to obtain rights to his oil in spite of a treaty of friendship. On 1 March 1945 he declared war on the Axis and sent delegates to the inaugural meeting of the United Nations in April. But he refused a British request to repatriate Rashid Ali al Gailani, the leader of the April 1941 'Golden Square' revolt in Iraq (assistance provided by Germany and Vichy France), although he had aided neither that astute politician nor the four generals who arranged the uprising. The revolt forced the pro-western prince regent, Abdul Illah, to flee and caused many deaths among British troops.

The exigencies of war changed the pattern of international relationships. In 1944 the British government saw its position as principal counsel to Ibn Saud threatened by American investment and government subsidy. At the same time awakening Arab nationalism in the Middle East revealed the strong dislike of the Raj after a century of colonialism. As a result Whitehall fostered a seven-member Arab League (Saudi Arabia, Egypt, Iraq, Jordan, Lebanon, Syria, Yemen) to promote political and economic coöperation among the Moslem states, and incidentally to dim Arab recollections of British imperialism.

The League held its first meeting 22 March 1945 and is still in existence. But Britain lost its bid to regain prestige in the Middle East. The members of the League had only two aims in common: to reduce British rule and influence and to intervene in the conflict between Arab and Jew in Palestine. Since Britain supported Jewish aspirations, the League at once became an ideal means of coördinating anti-British activity in states otherwise widely divergent in form of government and policy. But direct action by Saudi Arabia was limited in scope, whereas Egypt and Jordan eventually went to war with Israel.

In spite of Saudi Arabia's membership in the League, most writers say that Ibn Saud was opposed to the establishment of any pan-Islamic or pan-Arab political formation, and refused to support any plan that aimed to group the newly independent Arab states in a larger supranational entity. The propaganda of the Muslim Brothers in Egypt and the Arab nationalists in Syria did not interest him. On the contrary he insisted that the separate and discrete existence of each Arab state be maintained. His opposition to any kind of union was based on the realization that for Saudi Arabia such a union would certainly challenge his family's dynasty as a system of government, and would eventually destroy Saudi independence. In his time the shortage of manpower and resources along with the military weakness of a country without heavy industries would have worked against a position of leadership in any such combine.

**Palestine Problem:** In November 1917 Arthur Balfour, British foreign secretary, declared that the government favored the foundation of a Jewish homeland in Palestine. The declaration was intended as a ploy to spur Jewish help, mainly financial, in the prosecution of the war. It included the phrase 'nothing shall be done which may prejudice the civil and religious rights of existing non-Jewish communities in Palestine.' Two years later Balfour had changed his position radically: 'In Palestine, we do not propose even to go through the form of consulting the wishes of the present inhabitants of the country.... Zionism ... is of far profounder import.'

Jewish immigration into Palestine began during the First World War and continued thereafter as refugees from central Europe entered the country, sometimes illegally. The British were given a mandate over Palestine at an April 1920 conference in San Remo sponsored by the League of Nations. Before the mandate took effect Ronald Storrs had been military governor. On 30 June he handed over direction of the protectorate to the new administrator, Sir Herbert Samuel.

Although pro-Zionist, Sir Herbert followed the official policy and opposed the clandestine entry of Jewish refugees to the territory. He was charged with establishing a Jewish national home; at the same time he was responsible for respecting the rights of all the inhabitants of Palestine. Riots and attacks by

Arabs protesting the influx of settlers occurred sporadically throughout the decade, as high commissioner replaced high commissioner. By 1936 an augmented force of British troops (well over 25,000) in the mandate was being systematically attacked by Arab guerrillas, some of whom were armed secretly by Ibn Saud. Publicly, Ibn Saud issued a statement jointly with the rulers of Iraq, Transjordan and Yemen asking for moderation in the conduct of the rebellion. In 1937 the Peel Commission was set up to heal the breach. It recommended the establishment of discrete Arab and Jewish states. Because immigration was still strictly controlled, Jews began to harass the British in a series of murderous clashes. Counter-measures caused more bloodshed.

A conference in London called to settle the dispute among the three parties ended in deadlock on 17 March 1939. The Amir Faisal attended this fiasco where Arab and Jew refused to sit at the same table. In 1940 refugees from central Europe were turned away forcibly in order to maintain the numerical balance between disparate populations. In consequence, Jewish attacks on British troops grew in number and severity. The problem was then referred to the United Nations. After much debate, on 29 November 1947 that body declared in favor of partition, thus increasing the furor of the Arabs. On 15 May 1948 the British mandate expired. The Arab League declared it would exterminate the Jews.

Undeclared war began on 16 May, although Arab forces had begun to occupy objectives months before. Arabs from five countries faced sixty thousand trained and desperate soldiers of the *Haganah* determined to protect their land and families to the last. They repulsed their Arab antagonists on several fronts but were forced to withdraw elsewhere. The war, punctuated by three unsuccessful cease-fires and the deaths of two mediating diplomats, ended definitively 7 January 1949. The Arabs demanded *de facto* international recognition of their annexation of much of the territory they had seized.

Egypt and Transjordan had provided most of the Arab troops. Egypt took the Gaza Strip, Transjordan two thousand square miles on the west bank of the Jordan River and half of Jerusalem. Saudi Arabia sent a brigade and took nothing. In 1950, Abdullah of Transjordan asked for recognition of his territorial *fait accompli* in the name: Hashemite Kingdom of Jordan. Saudi Arabia did not support him, for the king's resentment of the existence of both Hashemite states still lingered.

**America's Posture:** During World War II the Department of State belatedly recognized the importance of Arabian oil to the West and urged friendly relations with the Moslem states of the Middle East, but in the autumn of 1945, soon after he had taken office, President Truman put the United States on the side of Zionism. The Chiefs of Mission from Arabia and other countries involved in the Palestine problem reported the anger in Arab countries because of his support of Jewish aspirations. He replied. 'I'm sorry, gentlemen, but I have to answer to hundreds of thousands who are anxious for the success of Zionism. I do not have hundreds of thousands of Arabs among my constituents.'

Subsequent American policy was dichotomous, but the administration, dependent on votes, supported the UN proposal to divide the country into separate Jewish and Arab states. In November 1947 Faisal headed a delegation to plead the Arab cause before the General Assembly in New York. His arguments found favor only with a minority and he himself was vilified and spat upon by Jewish demonstrators. The United Nations voted the State of Israel into existence on 14 May 1948. Possibly the balloting was influenced by behind-the-scenes lobbying by U.S. delegates. The United States was the first nation to recognize the new state, thirty minutes after it was born. President Truman had overruled his pro-Arab Department of State which had assured Faisal of U.S. support for his position. The prince never forgot the betrayal of his cause by self-styled friends.

This support of Jewish aspirations was in direct contradiction of promises made Ibn Saud at the end of the war: On 12 February 1945, the king and an entourage of forty-eight, among them his younger brother Abdullah, two of his sons and five advisers, boarded the destroyer U.S.S. *Murphy* at Jedda along with only seven of a flock of ninety-three sheep and a few sacks of rice and vegetables taken from several dhows fully loaded with the king's bounty. His tent and throne were set up on the foredeck, the admiral's cabin spurned. His followers bunked down in every possible clear space. As the ship moved rapidly up the Red Sea the king was notified of the bearing to Mecca for each of his five daily prayers.

The president met the king on the Great Bitter Lake of the Suez Canal on 14 February *(Pl. VII)*. The monarch was piped on board the cruiser U.S.S. *Quincy* after two nights and a day on the *Murphy*. Through Colonel William Eddy the two leaders, one arthritic and walking with a cane, the other within two months of his death, discussed for five hours the problem of the Jews in Palestine and the need for Allied bases in Arabia. Roosevelt stressed the suffering of the Jews under Hitler, the mass exterminations. Did His Majesty have any suggestions as to how they should be compensated? Ibn Saud replied, 'Give them and their descendants the choicest lands and homes of the Germans who oppressed them.' The president tried another tack. The survivors did not want to stay in Germany where they had suffered so greatly, and feared more reprisals. Traditional Arab hospitality could help solve the problem of Zionism. The king said that he could see no reason to fear a thoroughly defeated enemy and no reason why the Arabs of Palestine should welcome the Jews. Arabs had not massacred Jews. 'Make the enemy and the oppressor pay, that is how we wage war.' The survivors of the holocaust should be distributed among the fifty victorious nations in proportion to their resources. Palestine was small and poor and had already taken its share of immigrants.

In his desire to be gracious, Roosevelt promised the king that 'he would do nothing to assist the Jews against the Arabs and would make no move hostile to the Arab people before consultation with them.' Ibn Saud took this as a promise by a head of state, his peer, and not by an individual. This view was confirmed by a letter from Roosevelt dated 5 April in which he made it clear that his undertakings were made, 'in my capacity as Chief of the Executive Branch of this Government.' A week later he died.

At the end of the interview Ibn Saud consented to the lease of a site for an air base near Dammam, the lease to run until 1950. In exchange, there would be no military occupation of his country, and America would support any move on his part to aid Arab peoples under foreign rule. No moves in this direction ensued, but immigration into Palestine would raise the problem of Jewish dominance there, and Roosevelt's promise would not be honored.

**Ibn Saud's Stand:** Many years before the State of Israel was recognized by the Great Powers, Ibn Saud proclaimed his opposition to a Jewish presence in the Middle East. As a child he had read in the Koran the echoes of the Prophet Mohammed's struggle with the Jews of Medina nearly 1,400 years before. God's Holy Word as revealed by his Prophet must be heeded by a king whose every action was in obedience to the Word, but, as Philby and van der Meulen both realized, only as he interpreted that Word. His interpretation was colored by the necessities of the moment, although perhaps he did not see his problems in that light.

He used every vehicle possible to make his views on Jews and their colonization of Palestine known to the British government. On 23 October 1937 the king talked for ninety minutes to Dickson, whom he had invited to Riyadh. At that time the political agent had retired from government service, but promised to transmit to the proper authority the sovereign's remarks. A few sentences of the very earnest, low-voiced diatribe give its tenor:

> Our hatred of the Jews dates from God's condemnation of them for their persecution and rejection of 'Isa and their subsequent rejection of His chosen Prophet. It is beyond our understanding how your government ... can wish to assist and reward these very same Jews who maltreated your 'Isa.... It were far, far preferable from every point of view, that Great Britain make Palestine a British possession and rule it for the next hundred years, rather than to partition it in the way they propose.... Your government must at once further restrict the immigration of Jews into Palestine ... allowing no more to come in.... We are being placed in the most difficult and most invidious of all positions by the British Government, our friends.... Your government should remember that I am the Arabs' religious leader and thus the interpreter of the scriptures. God's word to them cannot be got round.

In March 1943 he invited representatives of *Life* magazine to visit Riyadh, and considering his hatred of the Zionists, issued a relatively measured statement of his views on the immigration of Jews to Palestine. He reviewed history and concluded that they did not have a valid claim to a homeland there, and that pursuance of their attempts to colonize it were against the interests of the Allies as well as of the Arabs.

He was more vehement in 1945 when van der Meulen encountered him unexpectedly in the desert. The king was en route from Riyadh to his secret conferences with Roosevelt and Churchill. That night the monarch addressed a crowd of *Ulema* and notables and shaikhs from the Marrat area, giving them a précis of the progress of the war and the place in the world for Arabs when it ended. He then enlarged on the dangers to Arab progress from the *Yahud*—the Jews. He reviewed their history, full of rebellion against Allah, and the disaster of their presence to nearly every nation in which they had lived. The Zionists in Palestine dared to drive out a small and weak Arab nation from a land that they claimed as the land of *their* fathers, curse them! Listen to Allah's word as it is given in the Holy Book. Then followed the bitterness of the *surahs* in which Mohammed recites his quarrel with the Jews. The passion of a born orator convinced of the righteousness of his cause swayed the crowd, which was ready for blood.

A few days later, after a two-day voyage on an American warship he repeated the same arguments to Roosevelt, albeit in a less sanguinary vein. He then went on to Cairo where he met Churchill at a rather *louche* resort hotel *(Pl. VII)*. The prime minister told the king that he should be grateful for twenty years of subsidies and should assist Britain in the problem of Palestine where a strong Arab leader could restrain fanatical Arab elements, insist on moderation in Arab councils, and effect a reasonable compromise with Zionists. Perhaps confusing régimes he said later, 'You'd think they'd be grateful, after all we did for Faisal and Abdullah.'

**The Last Act:** During his sunset years, Ibn Saud, although still in autocratic command of his country was less sure in his conduct of foreign affairs because of the rise of nationalist sentiments and the consequent changes in government in neighboring countries. He refused to be drawn into commitments requiring joint action with other states, including the activities of other members of the Arab League, but accepted those actions when they did not involve his country. However, happenings abroad that affected Saudi Arabia became too numerous to be handled adroitly by an aging king, or by his partisan ministers.

In Arabia, Ambassador Childs found universal resentment of America's support of Zionism, and had difficulty in renewing the lease of the airbase at Dhahran. The airbase had been constructed in 1945 when a five-year lease had been signed. Using his personal relationship with the king, Childs succeeded in renewing the lease for five years from 1951 in return for a commitment to supply arms, to train the army, and to equip and train a small navy and air force. Did the king harbor a plan to chasten his long-time Hashemite enemies? Probably not, for by that time he was losing interest in affairs of state, and according to a U.S. medical mission in April 1950 he was: 'considerably aged and enfeebled ... increasingly senile.'

Because the construction of the Trans-Arabia pipeline (Tapline) began late in 1947 it was imperative that transit rights be obtained across Syria. Transit dues had to be negotiated and general agreement reached on the flow of oil to the port of Sidon in Lebanon, the Mediterranean terminus of the line. Yusuf Yassin now had plenty of money to interfere in the politics of his native land, Syria, and did so much to his satisfaction. Probably he had something to do with the frequent changes of régime there. More openly, Saudi Arabia offered to lend Syria $6 million and with some delay paid it, even after a change of dictators.

Abdullah ibn Husain of Jordan *(Pl. VII, fig. 24)* was murdered in 1951. Perhaps as a gesture of reconciliation his son Talal was invited to Saudi Arabia and made much of with visits to Jedda and Mecca and many gifts. However, this young man was an Anglophobe. Declared mentally ill, in August 1952 he was replaced by *his* son Husain, then aged sixteen, and a wise and respected monarch until his death on 7 February 1999.

Ibn Saud visited Egypt in January 1946. Later, he counseled King Farouk to reach a settlement of the dispute over the British occupation of the Suez Canal Zone. When in October 1951 the Egyptian foreign minister abrogated the Anglo–Egyptian Treaty, Saudi Arabia cheered. Ibn Saud probably had little or nothing to do with the matter, for he was already in decline. The revolution, already brewing, that would exile King Farouk and bring a military junta to power occurred after he was gone.

In his last two years the king began to relinquish the reins of power, but too late to give the crown prince experience in government. Only in 1953 did Prince Saud go to the Hejaz, a province nominally under Faisal, to reorganize the administration. That same year he was given the responsibility of setting up a Council of Ministers. Nevertheless, Ibn Saud remained head of the government until his death, and required obedience from all up to his last illness.

This account of Ibn Saud's saga of battles and his handling of foreign and domestic concerns (Sir Percy Cox said that he always made the right decision in foreign affairs) brings to the fore only some aspects of this gifted and multifaceted man. His sophistication in matters of human relations is shown by his ability to impress the highly educated, like the Dutch consul in Jedda, with his grasp of world affairs, and his ability to seize the essentials of a situation at once. Yet his upbringing had focused on the Wahhabi view which was concerned primarily with man's relation to God. He did not know that the world was round.

The final section is an attempt to depict the man, not only his appearance, but his character and demeanor, his foibles and his strengths. Several who have written about him never saw him. Of those who did, only Philby who lived in his shadow for twenty-five years paints his actions in a consistently favorable light, although questioning his professedly religious motives for establishing the Ikhwan. Gertrude Bell (*n. 26*), besides an unsurpassed description of his person at forty, foresaw his ultimate eminence in the Middle East. Rihani gives an account of him and his court in 1923 before the conquest of the Hejaz and the ubiquity of the automobile and telephone: a man kind enough to visit him every day to see to his comfort while he was ill with malaria.

Armstrong portrays a warrior, lithe and dangerous. Howarth limns an embattled statesman, and Goldberg too sees a cautious and astute master of diplomacy, striving for personal autonomy. Glubb describes a benevolent patriarch who nevertheless used massacre to gain his ends. Lacey employs anecdote to support his portrait of an earthy, uxorious, plainspoken but eloquent and forceful ruler whose manipulation of the polity was ably supported by the clergy. McLaughlin reveals his complex and contradictory personality and its effects on his ascent to power. Van der Meulen shows sympathy for a man who at the last outlived his time. Although some question his motives, all insist on the sincerity of his religious convictions.

These accounts and others listed in the bibliography, together with the glimpses given by the memoirs of envoys to his court and the biased narrations of Wahba and Almana, both on his staff for years, together provided me with a comprehension, certainly imperfect, of the man as he may have been. All inferences and interpretations are colored by the prejudices of the individual, but mine are perhaps less affected by circumstance or partiality than some of the others.

# FRIENDS AND ENEMY

PLATE VI
Figs. 14-20

Fig. 14. Husain ibn Ali, Sharif

Fig. 15. Mubarak as Sabah

Fig. 17. Ibn Saud in 1935

Fig. 16. H. St. J. B. Philby

Fig. 18. Captain Shakespear

Fig. 19. Yusuf Yassin

Fig. 20. Abdullah ibn Jiluwi

# THE KING'S PEERS

PLATE VII
Figs. 21-24

Ibn Saud and Churchill at the Auberge Hotel near Cairo, February 1945

Ibn Saud and Faisal aboard H.M.S.
*Lupin*, February 1930

Ibn Saud and Roosevelt on U.S.S.
*Quincy*, 14 February 1945

Ibn Saud with Abdullah ibn Husain, King of Jordan, 29 June 1948

# IBN SAUD

PLATE VIII
Figs. 25-29

Fig. 25. Oqair, 1922

Fig. 26.
Official photo, 1922

Fig. 27. Kuwait, 1910. First photo

Fig. 28. Riyadh, 1925

Fig. 29. Circa 1950

Saud (2)

Faisal (4)

Mohammed (6)

(4) = Order of birth

Khalid (7)

Mansour (12)

Mishaal (18)

Fig. 36. With four young sons in Taïf, 1934

# THE KINGS OF SAUDI ARABIA

PLATE X
Figs. 37-41

Fig. 37. Saud (1953-1964)

Fig. 38. Faisal (1964-1975)

Fig. 39. Abdul Aziz (1902-1953)

Fig. 40. Khalid (1975-1982)

Fig. 41. Fahd (1982- )

Fig. 42. Younger brother Sa'ad

Fig. 43. Elder half-brother Mohammed

| Brother ? | | Sa'ad | | Brother ? | |
| Ibn Saud | Turki | | Mubarak | Abdullah | Mohammed |

Fig. 44. Abdul Aziz never traveled without his binoculars and used them often.
This photo was taken by Shakespear in March 1910 in Kuwait town where Ibn
Saud was visiting his old friend Mubarak as Sabah.

Fig. 45. Turki ibn Abdul Aziz

Fig. 46. Binocular case

# Part III:

# The Man

# (1876–1953)

# THE MAN

## Aspect

**Attaints of Time:** I met the king when he was sixty-two. He had been named king of Saudi Arabia only seven years before but had ruled in Nejd since 1902, in al Hasa since 1913, and in the Hejaz since 1926. The habit of command had long since been his and was visible in his regal bearing. His face showed the ravages of the long years spent in establishing and maintaining his dominion, for forehead and cheeks were lined deeply and the dark and piercing right eye was ringed by crepy skin. I assumed that the black patch over the left one hid an orb lost in battle. Only while preparing this screed did I learn that the loss of sight had been caused by a disease that attacked him, probably in May or June of 1923 (*n. 27*).

Even before this illness Ibn Saud's vision required help, for in 1922 at Oqair he wore glasses occasionally. Later, his sight must have dimmed more, for he required guidance even in mounting the steps of his residence in Jedda. Glubb in Jedda with Sir Gilbert Clayton in 1928 mentions that the king wore spectacles at all times during their talks (*1960, p. 210*). Sir George Rendel who saw him in 1937 mentions that, 'he ... was already becoming very short-sighted.' Before being photographed he sometimes removed his glasses, for in many snaps he has none. To supplement my impression of his appearance when he was long past his prime, herewith my observations concerning a few of the hundreds of his published photographs.

**Photo Pastiche:** The first known photograph of the amir of Nejd was taken in Kuwait by his new acquaintance Shakespear in March, 1910 (*see frontispiece, Pl. VIII, fig. 27 and Pl. XI*). He was thirty-three years old. Flanked by his family and notables he sits, impassive, or perhaps slightly bored, looking directly at the camera. His head is covered by a red- and white-patterned cotton cloth, the *ghotra*, which covers his ears and hangs to his chest, framing a long, narrow visage. Faint lines mark his forehead, which is half-covered by the *ghotra*. Arched narrow eyebrows swoop to the root of a broad, fleshy nose separating rather small, heavy-lidded eyes. A black, drooping but clipped mustache covers almost all of his upper lip, and joins a well-trimmed arc of beard that leaves a semi-circle of tan flesh in which a small imperial is visible below a prominent lower lip. He is not wearing spectacles.

The sleeves of his *thobe* (the long white gown) under the *bisht* (the brown camel-hair cloak edged in gold) seem too long, for the cuffs are folded back leaving little more than the knuckles and long fingers of his hands exposed. He holds a string of amber prayer beads and on the little finger of his right hand is a ring of shiny metal. A similar ring on the same finger can be seen on all of the photographs in which his right hand is visible: at the Durbar of 1916, with his family in Riyadh in 1918, at Oqair in 1922, with King Faisal of Iraq in 1930, with his grandchildren in 1935, with General Spears in 1940, with Roosevelt in 1945, and in the several poses taken at the palace in Riyadh in the 1950s. Was this band, seen in some photos to be ornamented with a flat stone *(Pl. VIII, fig. 28)*, both a signet and a symbol of power? Probably, for Faisal removed a ring from his dead father's finger and handed it to the heir-apparent, Saud, presumably as a sign of fealty.

Other evidence supports the conjecture that the ring was a signet, an intaglio seal, a token of authority and validity: Rihani's description of a gesture of the king is one: "'I will put my seal'—he punched the palm of his left hand with the knuckles of his right,—"if Great Britain says You must. But I will strike when I can'" *(p. 68)*. Another is Clayton's statement that the sultan put his seal on the Hadda-Bahra agreements, and a third is De Gaury's *(1946, p. 64)* mention of the king's signet, '... silver and cornelian (*red chalcedony*). His name, without a crest or emblem, was alone engraved on the seal.' Khatib *(Vol. 2, p. 5)* confirms de Gaury.

At the 1916 Durbar in Kuwait, wearing the ribbon and insignia of a Knight Commander of the Indian Empire, Ibn Saud faces Colonel Cox, trim in uniform, topee, and sword together with Miss Bell in an ornate, broad-brimmed hat. Abdul Aziz holds binoculars in the right hand, a camel stick in the left, and his unprotected eyes squint against the sun.

In a photograph taken by Major Dickson at the Oqair conference of 1922–23 he is mounted, with reins of heavy rope in his left hand and a long, thin camel stick in his right. He smiles down at the camera and the light is such that the fleshy cheeks stand out, along with the prominent nose. He has no glasses, *(Pl. VIII, fig. 25)* but in another photo taken there in company with Sir Percy Cox and Major Holmes he is wearing a pair *(Pl. XII, fig. 43)*. His aspect changes greatly from one photo to another. In some he seems a refined aesthete, in others a coarse brute.

In many of the pictures published after 1922 he wears spectacles. In 1930, aged 53, on H.M.S. *Lupin* during the meeting of conciliation with King Faisal of Iraq he has metal-rimmed eyeglasses *(Pl. VII, fig. 22)*. They appear in a photo with Amin Rihani in the early 1930s, in one with American military envoys in 1943 and another with Roosevelt in 1945 *(Pl. VII)*. Signs of aging other than spectacles appear in his photographs only late in life, for his figure is hidden under voluminous robes. When I met him in 1939 he wore no glasses, probably because he had covered his blind eye with a patch for protection against the dust of the trip. He still moved freely, although his face was lined and his body was clearly somewhat heavier than it had been in youth. Photographs of his face made during his 1946 visit to King Farouk in Egypt reveal fatigue. From then on he declined rapidly. Arthritis in his knees became so painful that he stopped walking with a cane and took to a wheel-chair, like but larger than the one given him by Roosevelt. He wore slippers and woolen stockings to keep warm and to aid circulation in his legs. His chroniclers report the changes in his person:

Philby wrote, 'the fire had gone out of him.' When van der Meulen saw him in 1952 his beard and hair had been dyed black. His hands had become stiff and their skin wrinkled. The once mobile face was set and expressionless, the once brilliant eye weak and lusterless. The voice so musical and full of conviction had become a hoarse croak of mumbled words. The keen intellect must have waned, although still with periods of the old lucidity. An aura of command remained, but on occasion he dozed in the course of an interview.

How great the change from the feral giant who led his men at the seizure of Riyadh and threw his foe's head from the battlements; the man who charged the Turkish square and carved up 'Ubaid in 1904; in 1913 regained al Hasa in a daring night assault; in 1924 directed the conquest of the Hejaz; in 1929 had taken the field again to lead his army in the battle of Sibila and in 1930 to complete the defeat of the *Ikhwan!*

*Senescence did not change the essential qualities of the man, displayed best during the years when he was fighting to establish his kingdom, but he became a Lion in Winter, for when Asad saw him in 1951 'his face was ... bitter and withdrawn.' Philby says he was disappointed in the outcome of his life-long efforts, for his last words to his old friend from England were, 'A man's possessions and his children are his enemies.'*

*Age impaired his body and darkened his spirit, but what were the qualities, the* salient traits *of mind and character, that gained him his kingdom? Many can be deduced from his conduct in a variety of trying circumstances. A few have been offered tentatively by acute observers, and others can be inferred by induction from the whole corpus of his acts.*

## Salient Traits

Bodily strength and endurance were required for most of his early exploits, and other qualities required from the outset—courage and tenacity—became even more necessary as his hegemony grew. He possessed them in full measure as shown by the saga of exploits recounted in Part I. But strength and courage alone would not have won him a lasting kingdom. He had not only to defeat his enemies, but also to insure the support of the clergy, and insofar as possible to earn the loyalty of his subjects and their consent to his founding a dynasty.

**True Belief:** None of those who have written about Ibn Saud question the sincerity of his belief—a profound faith in God and his Oneness and Omnipotence as set forth in Wahhabi dogma and in the Koran. But he upheld the authority of all of the *Ulema*, although privately condemning the sanctimony of some, and it has been mooted that he used faith cynically. Philby is not sure that he founded the *Ikhwan* without taking into consideration the value of religious fanaticism as a source of valor. In his book, *The Heart of Arabia (p. 298)* he says, '... his tendency to allow his interpretation of doubtful points of principle or practice to be influenced by political motives led me often to wonder whether his domestic policy was dictated less by his religious convictions than by political ambition and the desire to weld the centrifugal human forces of Arabia into a mighty empire for himself and his descendants.'

Van der Meulen is more charitable. The astute and widely traveled Dutch Counsel in Jedda who spent many hours with Ibn Saud, said in his 1957 book, *The Wells of Ibn Saud (p. 60)*: 'Was he a Wahhabi merely because he had proved faith to be the only way to weld into a durable fighting force undisciplined beduin, whom normally only quick success kept united? Was he, in short, a Wahhabi by materialist calculation rather than by religious conviction? I did not believe it. Yet I believe both factors were there and both were strong.... His strong convictions as a believer impressed me more than his qualifications as a worldly ruler, as a man who loved power.'

Whether or not Ibn Saud used religious fervor cynically, his founding of the *Hujar* gave him a striking force of unparalleled mobility and bravery. The fact that before the walls of Haïl he threatened to punish a man who questioned why the higher clergy did not do themselves what they urged on others—to court death in battle to gain the immediate rewards of Paradise—suggests that Philby's questioning of his motives may have been valid *(n. 21)*.

Ibn Saud is quoted by Landau *(pp. 86–87)* as saying that politics must be based on religion. If not, 'they are not good; political conduct cannot be separated from ethical conduct.' To de Gaury he was more specific: 'In all things, surely it is known to you, I am reasonable: in all things will decide on the merits of a case, save only when my religion is touched. By God—I have it here close to my heart—without it I die—none shall take it from me. By God above I swear it!'

**Tolerance:** Whatever his motives for founding the *Ikhwan* may have been, he was tolerant of beliefs other than his own, with the exception of a hatred of Jews, intensified when Palestine was opened to their settlement. He worked closely with the *Ulema* (his ecclesiastical council and arbiter of both religious and temporal matters), some of whom were descendants (known as *As Shaikh*) of Abdul Wahhab and related by marriage to the As Saud. He supported unfailingly its rulings and its position as guide and judge in matters theological and mundane. In return, its exegeses of the *surahs* and interpretations of *Shari'a* law were sometimes slanted in favor of the king's stand. His acceptance of the tenets of Wahhabism never wavered, but his intelligence kept him from the bigotry shown by some of the *Ulema*.

In 1911 Shakespear wrote to Cox, 'He and his brothers did not show a trace of the fanatical spirit which might have been expected from the ruling Wahhabi family.... I feel convinced of the correctness of this impression for I frequently discussed matters of doctrine, customs, and religion which are held to be anathema by the Wahhabi sect and I was always answered with calm and intelligent reasoning.' Nevertheless, Ibn Saud was zealous in maintaining the religious structure he inherited and in increasing its authority, although he did not persecute the *Shias* of al Hasa and forbade ibn Jiluwi to do so.

But his subjects' execration of unbelievers led Ibn Saud to deny other faiths entry into his domain. Although after the discovery of oil many Christians were granted ingress, they were prohibited from overtly practicing religious rites or building places of worship. In Dhahran, the tiny, white-garbed 'angels' shivering in the cold to proclaim 'tidings of great joy' from the roof of the recreation hall on Christmas Eve were, theoretically at least, subject to immediate expulsion. Missionaries based in Kuwait and Bahrain were allowed into the country for limited periods only as doctors to treat the Royal Family. However great his personal sufferance of foreigners and their infringement of Wahhabi strictures on drinking and smoking, in public he himself conformed to the standards of conduct of the most conservative of the *Ulema*. When away from the dour divines of Riyadh he welcomed a song, but did not condone musical instruments, except drums. He romped with his sons in the *Ardh* sword dance, but disapproved of Lucille Ball's being shown in the cinema on the U.S.S. *Quincy*, although he himself had watched only a patriotic film.

In spite of his unfavorable opinion of a female movie star because her antics on the screen had distracted his men, including two of his sons, Ibn Saud did not tolerate sanctimonious abuses of piety. When such excesses were brought to his attention he did not hesitate to bring the offender to heel, although even he did not dare challenge openly the rigid interpretation of Wahhabi tenets that kept Riyadh a cheerless town. Too, as the imam of the *Ikhwan* he could not overtly condemn the extremism of their venial pride in being the elect of God, or in the graver fault of indiscriminate slaughter and rapine, for all was in the name of a righteous crusade which he himself had initiated. Only when his authority was seriously challenged did he crush the triumvirate heading the revolt and send their followers home. But he had ways to propagate the faith other than the *Ikhwan's* redoutable force:

Nominally, the religious jurisdiction of the country was independent of his control. It was a recognized state hierarchy with its headquarters in Riyadh. In the early days, six of its members were at Riyadh, three in the Qasim and in al Hasa, and one each in the other districts and provinces of Nejd, over twenty in all, together comprising the *Ulema*. Ibn Saud laid before the *Ulema* all questions of law and those disputes involving the legality or validity of his own actions, for in Arabia civil as well as ecclesiastical matters are judged by *Shari'a*, religious law, which in the usual course of events is administered by a judge, the *qadhi*. Lower in the hierarchy are *Mutawwa'in* (deacons) in Ibn Saud's day entrusted with the religious instruction of the Bedu, one for each fifty men.

To aid these deacons, sometime missionaries to the unenlightened, Ibn Saud directed the preparation, publication and distribution of religious tracts based on the writings of eminent theologians, including those of the founder, Mohammed Abdul Wahhab. The original treatises of these divines were printed too, but in limited numbers. It is questionable that printed exhortations helped to effect the conversion of unlettered Bedu, but their chiefs and some villagers could read, and a mention that the *Ikhwan* were coming was probably a convincing argument for the immediate adoption of a new creed, particularly among those with no strong convictions.

That the king did not rely exclusively on the persuasions of his warriors to spread the gospel shows that his own upbringing had made him aware of the power of the printed word. By the standards of the time and place he himself was well educated. It seems strange to us that when his position was secure he did not establish more schools. Possibly he would have found them a danger to his autocracy. Yet most of his advisory council was made up of foreigners, all of whom had a formal education. Two of this select group who wrote about their service with him express their admiration of his superior intellect, as do many of the westerners who had dealings with him. Of all Ibn Saud's qualities, his outstanding intelligence and quick comprehension aided him most. They were the *sine qua non* of his success.

**Intelligence:** Judging from the published comments concerning Ibn Saud's mind it must have been phenomenally acute. That it enabled him to be a shrewd judge of human nature is less obvious, and a thirst for information is mentioned even more rarely, although his awareness of the latest happenings outside Arabia astounded seasoned British observers. The most fulsome, even rhapsodic evocation of Ibn Saud's mental capacities is by Almana *(1980, p. 249)*: 'His Majesty was gifted with powers of memory, perception, observation and wit which were utterly out of the ordinary.... His Majesty's memory was more impressive than that of any man I have known. He ... had a talent for instant recall which would put a computer to shame.' Granted that this was written by a fellow Arab proud of his association with a great man, some credence must be given his effusion.

Other observers too report extraordinary qualities of intellect. Philby *(The Heart of Arabia, p. 327)* describes an ability Ibn Saud shared with Napoleon Bonaparte: 'I received a summons to the presence and, entering the royal pavilion, found Ibn Sa'ud seated by the old camel saddle with a secretary on either side of him, dictating letters on different subjects simultaneously to both with a rapidity and precision that astonished me.' *Interrupted by a Bedu petitioning for redress:* 'with scarcely a check either in his conversation with me or in the composition of the letters in hand, he elicited its salient facts from the plaintiff.'

Cheesman, an ornithologist, was impressed by his knowledge of the native and migratory birds of al Hasa, as well as by his curiosity concerning the capabilities of several motor vehicles he had ordered. To the Englishman, Ibn Saud's questions concerning the General Election in England and the course of the reparations talks between France and Germany demonstrated an amazing familiarity with foreign affairs, better than his own. At that time *(1924)* Ibn Saud received the Damascus newspapers by courier and undoubtedly had access to others. This interest in world affairs had begun during his childhood in Kuwait. It resulted eventually in the establishment of the news service (the 'foreign court') of which Almana was a member.

Reader Bullard, British minister to Saudi Arabia in the late 1930s wrote, 'Ibn Saud's most remarkable quality was his political wisdom. It had grown with the extension of his responsibilities until it was equal to any situation.... He managed to be better informed on international affairs than many educated Europeans.' Roosevelt said that he learned more in five minutes from Ibn Saud about the Jewish problem in Palestine than from all of his advisers in days.

The American diplomat, J. Rives Childs, was in Arabia from 1946–1950 as minister and ambassador. In his book, *Foreign Service Farewell* he says, 'His natural endowment of exceptional astuteness and judgment of men, along with an indomitable will, had enabled him to weld the warring tribe into the kingdom which bore his name.'

Sir Percy Cox who met Ibn Saud often in his position as political resident for the Persian Gulf and later as high commissioner in Iraq writes in his foreword to Cheesman's book: 'The intercourse of fifteen eventful years has left in me feelings of strong personal affection for the man and the friend, and profound admiration for the great qualities of self-reliant courage and statesmanship which have contributed so much to the shaping of his destiny.'

That courage, together with a superb physique, started Ibn Saud on the upward road, but he would never have reached his destination without a comparable superiority of mind. In Part I his exploits are recounted serially; his courage in performing them can only be inferred. But courage must be in any list of the traits responsible for his success.

**Courage:** The many scars of battle on his limbs and body (43, Benoist Méchin says) attested Ibn Saud's disregard for danger. According to Almana he was able to ignore pain: his doctor, Rashad Pharaon, about to inject anesthetic before removing two spent bullets from the then sultan's lower abdomen was told that it was unnecessary. As proof, Ibn Saud himself removed the mangled flesh of the wounds with a knife. If the legend of consummating a marriage while wounded in the upper thigh is true, it confirms that he did have the faculty of bearing pain. But this shows courage only in the limited sense of refusal to allow the suffering of the body to daunt the will.

The courage required to face adversity or sorrow is a different and perhaps more admirable category, true gallantry. Ibn Saud had that courage, as well as the more common bravery that accepts the possibility of death in battle. Perhaps he was less comfortable under the threat of assassination that must certainly have existed while the Araïf were contesting his right to lead them. Dickson mentions rumors of attempts at poisoning by members of the family, and a knife or a bullet was a real possibility, given their all too common use at Haïl. When traveling, his meals were prepared by his own cooks, and when dining in public at home he chose his generally frugal repasts from the common dishes. No certainty exists that these practices were precautionary, and the same may be said for the maintenance of a large bodyguard, which served mainly as a retinue consistent with the dignity of a monarch. Yet the guard provided sentries at tentrances and in the halls of the palaces and was at hand when the king gave audience. Its size, several hundred, made the approach of an unknown to the king's person impossible. But every member of the family had access to him and rumors of plots against his life had wide circulation, perhaps with reason. Ibn Saud himself said to Rihani, 'I have to be aware of my own people—the nearest to me. Treachery we have discovered among the closest of our allies.' One of his black slave guards told Rihani that the amir gave his full trust only to them.

That his pattern of life guarded him against assassination may never have occurred to Ibn Saud. But Glubb noted with professional approval that when he visited a place other than his own locales, armed slaves investigated the site thoroughly before he entered, even asking where he was to sit. His guards remained standing and alert while he prayed, as I saw during his visit to Dhahran in 1939.

The protection thus afforded him was in keeping with his well-documented foresight and caution, both of which were aspects of his superior intelligence.

**Prudence and Caution:** In all of his attempts to free himself from Turkish domination and to regain his patrimony, Ibn Saud exercised restraint to a remarkable degree. In spite of his impatience to retake al Hasa he waited more than ten years from his initial success at Riyadh before acting. He had to be sure that the British would not object to his hegemony on the shore of the Persian Gulf, and he struck only when the Turks, occupied with war in the Balkans and in Tripolitania, had reduced the size and quality of their garrison in Hofuf.

When the British withdrew their brief and tentative support of his position with respect to the Turks just before the outbreak of the hostilities of 1914–1918, he did not scruple to sign with the hereditary enemy a treaty that pledged his aid to them in the event of war. Yet in the negotiations before his acceptance of the treaty, his true attitude surfaced. When threatened with coercion if he did not accept Turk-manned garrisons in al Hasa he half-drew his sword and broke off the conference. This was a break in his long-held subservient posture toward the Ottomans which after each of his transgressions against their rule caused him to write fawning and servile letters professing submission and obedience. It paid off in that the final treaty specifies that recognized as *Qaimaqam*, Ibn Saud would specify the number of Ottoman soldiers to be stationed in al Hasa. In pursuance of this policy of caution he may have aided the Turks covertly during the early years of the war *(Musil, p. 288)*. It is recorded that he sent a mission to the Turks in Damascus at the end of September 1916, just two months before the Durbar in Kuwait. Only after he had a promise of protection and a subsidy from the British did he undertake to interdict Turkish supply routes, and even then continued to provision Medina with food in order to discredit his enemy Husain, whose forces were then besieging the town.

All of this double-dealing, including his transactions with the Axis during World War II, was merely a manifestation of his caution—his intention to safeguard his dominion against any eventuality, even remote. He showed prudence in many other respects. Even his nepotism may have had at its roots a fear of treachery. His policy of withholding punishment for sedition was probably not based entirely on respect for family, but included recognition of the peril posed by the traditional revenge for blood. But his caution was not for his person but for his realm, as his scars of battle demonstrate.

*These attributes—firm belief in the omnipotence of God and the justice of his cause, strength and endurance, pertinacity, high intelligence, courage, prudence, and well-judged tolerance—were essential to regaining his patrimony. But other less lofty traits of character are apparent in his conduct—his demeanor. Some helped him in his quest.*

# Demeanor

**Attitude:** Cited by many are his generosity, perhaps calculated; his simplicity, perhaps cultivated; and his charm, perhaps deliberate. The qualifiers imply cynicism, a trait which is not consonant with the widely-held view that Ibn Saud's belief in the omnipotence of God was complete and sincere. The innuendo proposed may be completely invalid and cannot in any case detract from the greatness of his achievements. He himself said that he gave to the Bedu in times of plenty so that they would give him their all in time of need. And it is true that his generosity often exceeded any reasonable degree of necessity, although he himself set the scale governing the value of presents to be made his guests based on their rank and importance and his sense of what his position demanded in this regard. Almana reports that one of his wives requested a palace for herself. It was constructed, but it was not to her taste, so it was torn down immediately and another built. This when money from production of oil was in short supply.

Many have remarked on the magnetic and engaging nature of Ibn Saud's smile. In repose his face was stern and rather sullen (Clayton says, 'in repose rather sad, even at times slightly sulky'), but changed to an attractive, even captivating expression when he so wished. Van der Meulen confirms this, 'His smile made his face radiate kindness.... In repose his features were grim and forbidding, but when he smiled it was completely transformed and he became extraordinarily attractive.' Some observers doubted the sincerity of the emotion thus expressed. One of them was Sir Andrew Ryan, first British minister to Saudi Arabia in the 1930s, who suggested that the famous magnetic smile was switched on and off a little too readily. But Ryan had been requested to quit the court. On the other hand, Childs says that when greeting a favored person, 'his face was suffused with a graciousness almost tender in its nature,' and Asad reports that 'a gentle smile ... gives an almost spiritual quality to the beauty of his face.'

**Ferocity:** Displays of ferocity and what we would call callousness were not rare. An example: Ibn Saud described to Rihani how he killed 'Ubaid ar Rashid at Buraida: 'I struck him first on the leg and disabled him; quickly after that I struck at the neck; the head fell to one side—the blood spurted up like a fountain; the third blow at the heart—I saw the heart which was cut in two, palpitate like that (*a gesture*). It was a joyous moment—I kissed the sword.' *Homo homini aut deus aut lupus.*

**Rage:** Another unpleasant trait was his anger which was sudden, violent, and often excessive with respect to the cause. Several chroniclers report incidences of it. Rihani (*p. 52*) is perhaps the most graphic. 'His mouth becomes like iron, the lips shrunk and taut, white and trembling.... All the charm of his features gives way to a mordant, savage expression.' Philby was astounded when he saw Ibn Saud beat Fahd ibn Jiluwi, son of the governor of al Hasa, for having struck one of his own guards. He mentions one of his encounters with the monarch's 'ungovernable rage—an inevitable weakness of despots, however benevolent—and he was certainly one of them ...' (*1948, pp. 287–288*).

Both his sons and his advisers quailed before his volatile wrath and the flow of his superlative invective. 'O swollen whore.... You are nothing but a strayed beetle!' Any penance prescribed was carried out at once, but often a penalty was later indemnified by a present, for the anger quick to rise was equally prompt to subside. Even when adult his sons were not spared beating and vituperation, even confinement. But long-lasting true anger and hate were reserved for the enemies who menaced his hegemony or flouted Wahhabi precepts. The arch-villain was the sharif of Mecca. Another was a shaikh of Kuwait, Salim ibn Mubarak as Sabah, who was not only contemptuous of Wahhabi dogma but also had sheltered his enemies and accused him of connivance with the Turks.

His anger was well-controlled when circumstances arose requiring decisions that involved a course of action, particularly those vital to his future. Several writers describe how patiently he awaited the moment when all was favorable, how he weighed all the factors that might affect the outcome of a bold action. Such caution was almost always rewarded by success.

**Sensuality:** Another trait was a life-long preoccupation with sexual pleasure and satisfaction amounting to concupiscence, and a well-documented propensity to ribald jokes and what we would consider salacious discussions of sexual enjoyment with other men of his class. The customs of the time and place saw these as normal, and they were not proscribed in the Koran. That *al Malik* kept four girl slaves for his pleasure was reasonable. They were chattels owned at his discretion, and could be given in friendship or as a choice present. As the king aged, they became progressively younger. His adviser Yusuf Yassin helped to find them, youth being thought to be a powerful stimulant to flagging potency. Yet Ibn Saud was no libertine, but a good father who loved his children, and several of his twenty-two recognized wives.

He was no insensitive brute, but a lover of the beauty of poetry and the chanting of *surahs* from the Koran by five blind reciters stationed in the dark corridors of his palace. He himself confessed to having written verses, often at moments of grave decision, to his most beloved wife, Jauhara bint Musa'ad al Jiluwi, his cousin, who died during the epidemic of influenza in 1918–1919. Although this side of Ibn Saud's life was closed to others, it is reported that his relations with the wives established in Riyadh were always proper, if not always intimate. The time he spent with women, often his relatives, during short periods in the afternoon and evening, is said to have been the most carefree of his hours, a time of relaxation before prayer.

For many years those hours were few. Ibn Saud managed all the affairs of his demesne and all decisions were his. None of his aides was permitted to exercise independent judgment even on matters of little importance. As a consequence, the routine of administration was delayed until he authorized a course of action. This was not a great constraint on good order, for Ibn Saud worked very long hours and slept little during the years his hegemony was increasing. After the Hejaz was added to his dominions he realized the necessity of ceding some degree of discretion to others, but with few exceptions chose only his sons or close relatives to exercise it.

**Eloquence:** Ibn Saud possessed great powers of persuasion. He used them to attain preëminence and to keep it. Persuasive oratory stood him in good stead on many occasions. It helped him in 1918 when he turned the *Ikhwan* toward Haïl and away from Khurma and the Hejaz. In 1927 it helped him to gain time at the conference in Riyadh where he was accused by the *Ikhwan* of consorting with infidels, encouraging the use of devices made by them, and laxity in spreading the faith. In 1928 a second convocation, summoned to forestall a general revolt, was won over by a speech reminding his audience that he alone had united them. This, and his offer of abdication, rallied everyone to his person.

In 1929 when many of the *Ikhwan* were in full revolt, oratory may have saved his régime. Before his army was fully mobilized, while he was en route from Mecca to a confrontation with his dissident chiefs in the Qasim, he was blocked by sections of the 'Ataiba at Duwadimi. In a long, moving speech he convinced them neither to delay nor to oppose him. The fanaticism he fanned and the loyalty he inspired or bought gained him his kingdom, but to keep it required full use of every weapon in his arsenal of strategy and stratagems. Sexual prowess served to strengthen alliances and to engender his successors; eloquence, charm, and a dash of ruthlessness along with condign punishment helped him to keep his subjects in hand. In addition, he had *Hadh* (luck). In his own belief this was not good fortune, but rather a blessing from and a protection by the Almighty. Instances of his ever-repeated good luck were recounted in innumerable tales passed from mouth to mouth—clearly a gift of Allah and a requisite for a leader of Bedu.

*This attempt to scrutinize a man dead nearly fifty years and to present a reasonably coherent synthesis of his character and its effects on the governance of his country now turns to what has been said about his interests, his prejudices, his predilections, his taste and his foibles. All are considered valid bases for inferences regarding his stature as a man, but all must be judged in the light of his background, upbringing, and ever-changing circumstances.*

## Analects of a Man's Life

*We start with what are often considered trivia. They offer insights of interest into commonly neglected aspects of a psyche.*

**Quirks and Foibles**: In day-to-day relations Ibn Saud was utterly unassuming in speech and unpretentious in demeanor. He despised snobbery and was completely democratic in his dealings with the ragged and dirty nomads who attended the *majlis* of *as Shiyukh*, Abdul Aziz. His manner was simple and direct. He spoke freely about himself and his experiences, concealing, perhaps without hypocrisy, his insights into the minds and motives of others and the complexity of his own multi-faceted personality. Unlike many of his contemporaries he was unconditionally loyal to his friends and supporters and more often than not generous in his treatment of a vanquished enemy.

Ibn Saud spoke a correct Arabic replete with old proverbs and quotations from the Koran. When he wished to affect the candor of the Bedu his vocabulary was laced with words and expressions used by the Murra with whom he had spent two years of his boyhood. Foreign names he found awkward were deliberately mispronounced, and later in life his rapid enunciation was sometimes imperfect. Sir Gilbert Clayton remarked in his diary, 'he speaks fast and rather clips his words.' When King Farouk of Egypt visited him in the spring of 1945, Ibn Saud, realizing that his guest did not understand him, asked one of the Egyptian monarch's aides to translate. Foreigners noted his harshly accented Nejdi pronunciation so different from the speech of Egypt and Palestine. In gatherings, his formal and even ordinary conversation was like a lecture with heads and subheads. When marking a point in one of these discourses, the long staff in his right hand struck the ground forcefully, and his questioning 'Na'am?' (Yes, do you agree?) would interrupt the flow of words. This staff was plain and unpainted. In addition to its use for punctuation and emphasis, it served as a prop when he told the story of one of his exploits: a support for his head to underscore weariness, across his knee to underline a pause, held aloft to emphasize an attack. But when he was angry it was a club or stick to punish the object of his wrath. A cane replaced it in later years when arthritis crippled his knees.

Ibn Saud believed that dreams had a real significance, and insisted that his always came true. Hafiz Wahba relates that his employer once dreamt that Sharif Husain rose from his chair and offered it to him who later became king of the Hejaz. Dickson tells of another: On a night before the battle of Jarrab the amir dreamed that he was pulling a leather bucket (*dallu*) brimful of water from a well, bringing it up hand over hand. When only a span from the top, the cord broke and the bucket fell back into the well. As interpreted by one of the *Ulema*, the dream meant that he would suffer a great setback, but would persevere in building his kingdom. After the battle half of the tribes deserted him, but he continued to rule and to enlarge his hegemony.

Mohammed Asad reports one more. While still a young man in Kuwait, Ibn Saud dreamt he was riding alone in the desert and saw Abdul Aziz ibn Mitab[*] coming toward him on horseback. Asad reports the king's words: 'We were both unarmed but Ibn Rasheed held aloft in his hand a great shining lantern. When he saw me approach, he recognized the enemy in me and turned and spurred his horse to flight; but I raced after him, got hold of a corner of his cloak, and then of his arm, and then of the lantern—and blew out the lantern. When I awoke, I knew....' This was the man killed in 1906 at Raudhat al Muhanna by Bedu followers of the amir of Nejd. For several months they had been led by Ibn Saud himself in search of the leader of the Shammar.

Ibn Saud was fond of perfume and used it liberally. At the conclusion of a meal he sometimes drew a phial from his robe and as a mark of favor drew the long, thin applicator over the back of a guest's hand. Although all his scents were heavy and strong, mostly essential oils, he did not use them to hide odor. Even in the early days his private quarters included a bathroom, at that time provided with a movable metal tub and a wood-fired water heater filled from goat-skin bags. The visit to his choice for the night was regularly preceded by a bath and a change of robes. In any event custom required that the body be washed completely after intercourse. At that same period his legal wives were each housed in discrete, well-furnished apartments in the palace. Later, when affluence came, several favorites had palaces of their own.

Rihani says that Dr. Mann's medicines were neglected in a storeroom of the palace, but Ibn Saud used the services of physicians regularly. He allowed missionary doctors in Kuwait and Bahrain to visit Riyadh, but only to treat his own family. Prohibited from proselytizing, the missionaries attempted to undo

---

[*]  He who became amir of the Shammar and ruler of Riyadh in 1897 when Mohammed the Great died.

the ravages of barbarous and harmful treatment, and the damage caused by resort to the cautery to drive out the devils of illness. He later employed his own physicians, most of them from the Middle East. They came only after the Hejaz was added to his domain. Two of them, Drs. Pharaon and Khashoggi stayed with him for many years. Dr. Pharaon remained a trusted friend of the family even after Ibn Saud's death.

Dr. Dame of the mission of the Dutch Reformed Church in Bahrain treated him for the severe case of erysipelas he suffered after Rihani's departure in February 1923. Philby reports that specialists from Egypt were summoned to treat the infected eye. At other times Dr. Mylrea of the American mission in Kuwait visited him. When his potency flagged at age sixty a whole battery of aphrodisiacs and vitamins were prescribed by his staff physicians and taken copiously. Nevertheless, the characterization of hypochondriac suggested by some authors seems overblown.

Ibn Saud sometimes indulged in heavy-handed practical jokes, among them a loudly-voiced order for the arrest of a newly-arrived guest, who was almost at once reassured after being subject to an initial shock. Diversion in the stiflingly restrictive religious rectitude of Riyadh was mainly escape from the presence of the dour divines who peopled the streets and had access to all public gatherings, including those in the palace. In addition to the almost daily custom of evening prayer outside Riyadh, most often at a limestone prominence, Abu Makhrouq, picnics were a favorite device for quitting the oppressive atmosphere of the town and the king often found an occasion to propose one. Games, races, and other impromptu amusements supplemented the al fresco meal, often taken in the shade of the king's own gardens. Sometimes the penalty for the loss of a wager was an arduous or demeaning task, almost invariably remitted before its completion, but prizes in specie were a common reward for the winners.

The young children and their slave companions, children of about the same age chosen to grow up with them, accompanied the indulgent father on his picnics. At the age of seven the sons were assigned a teacher from the ranks of the learned, usually one of the *Ulema*. But even then they were allowed to visit their father and to demand his attention while he was busy.

According to Philby, Ibn Saud's deference to his father included avoidance of being in a room above his head. Van der Meulen saw Abdur Rahman use his son's back as a dismounting block while in Jedda and several authors remark on Ibn Saud's habitual effacement when his father was in the same room. This was a part of his pride, his regard for the family, which extended even to those of the Araïf who attempted to take power, for not one of them perished at his hand although all were held under ward. That other relatives were placed in positions of authority may have been due mainly to considerations of security, but nepotism was also a factor.

In the first known photograph of Ibn Saud binocular field glasses are at hand (*Pl. XI*), as they are in a snap taken at the Durbar of 1916. Until he aged they were always within reach and often used. Rihani mentions his scanning the waters of the bay of Selwa with them while awaiting Cox, and again reports their use in following the progress of an impromptu horse race in Riyadh. Field glasses must have served him often in the battles and skirmishes of the early years of his rise to power, and were even more necessary because his sight required assistance early in life.

The king was passionately fond of hunting in several forms. He had a mews with dozens of hawks, mainly varieties of Sakers that came young and untrained to Riyadh from southern Iraq and Persia. The falconers of the king lived with the birds, training them to fly from the arm and to remain with the kill until they were recovered. In 1923 when Rihani was at Riyadh with him Ibn Saud already had a motor, an open touring car, which he used not only for long excursions in the desert, but also for the hunt. Earlier on, it had been a blooded mare that carried the king as his falconer removed the hood and jesses from favorite birds and launched them from the wrist in search of a bustard or in pursuit of a herd of gazelle. Later it was from the seat of his car that the sultan followed the chase, undoubtedly eyeing the soaring falcon through his binoculars until it stooped to strike its prey. But his interest in birds was not limited to those of the chase, raptor or prey, for when Cheesman, the ornithologist, talked to him in Hofuf, he was impressed by the breadth of the sultan's familiarity with other birds, native and migratory.

As he aged, the king chased and shot gazelle from his car. At thirty-five miles an hour the open sedan pursued the frantic, leaping herd, white scuts flashing as they bounded into the air. As game began to be depleted by this exercise, the chase went farther and farther afield for the king was followed by all the hunters of his court. On my way back to Dhahran I helped one of the princes with my spare jerrycan of gasoline when he was stranded eighty miles from Riyadh.

One of Ibn Saud's passions, rather more than a foible, was to have a railroad. Was it because he rode one in Egypt in 1946 during his visit to King Farouk, or did he remember the narrow-gauge relic he had ridden in Basra when at the Durbar of 1916? In any event the then incongruous sight of two huge yellow Diesel locomotives head to head on a single track greeted us in Dhahran in 1949 as Bechtel began the construction of a line from a seven-mile, deep-water pier at Dammam port to a terminus at Riyadh. At a cost of $50 million the 370-mile line was completed in October 1951 and the king helped his son Saud to drive the golden spike. With the increasing industrialization of Saudi Arabia the line may by now have become profitable.

Swords were used in close combat long after every warrior in Ibn Saud's army had a rifle. The king had a collection of them. Perhaps the most prestigious was the sword of honor that Abdur Rahman gave him in 1902: *Rahaiyan*. With a pearl-encrusted hilt of massive gold this heirloom dates from the time of Abdul Wahab himself. De Gaury cites their names: '*Rahaiyan*,' the grinder; '*Al Ajrab*,' the rusty from blood; '*Al Khafiq*,' the cleaver; '*Khataf*,' the snatcher; '*Raqban*,' the severer of necks. It was *Al Khafiq* that he used to carve up 'Ubaid at Buraida in 1904. In 1945 his guards still carried swords. Others existed in his collection, probably all named. Was one of them the sword given his grandfather Faisal by Pelly in March 1865, 'a Wilkinson sword made to please the Arab taste'?

The king was a creature of habit. Besides the unvarying daily routine of the court described above, he enjoyed and ate most often only a few dishes: for breakfast—bread, honey and *leben* (curdled milk); for lunch and dinner—preparations of lamb and chicken along with rice and the vegetables and fruits grown at the state farm at Kharj which was supervised by an American. After dinner or a rare late supper he had a desert. The favorite beverages: freshly drawn camel's milk served in a perennial, chipped blue-enamel mug, and water brought him from a well in Mecca. He was a connoisseur of coffee and dates of which some varieties grew in his own groves.

The gift offered honored guests and friends was sometimes a blooded mare. Philby was given one which won races in Europe. The one presented to Sir Gilbert Clayton never reached England. The king had a breeding stable at Yamama, near Kharj, whose products were in later years used mainly in races ridden by his sons, although some may have been sold abroad.

The lavish gifts the king gave and those he received were judged by his own sense of values. In 1945 when leaving the destroyer U.S.S. *Murphy* to board the cruiser *Quincy* on the Great Bitter Lake of the Suez Canal he gave every crewman $40, and gold daggers and swords to the senior officers. In return he got a pair of binoculars and two submachine guns. Roosevelt gave him a wheelchair. When Churchill belatedly sent a right-hand drive Rolls to make up for the totally inadequate selection of perfumes presented as a gift during their interview in Cairo he spurned it. Honor would not allow him to sit to the left of the chauffeur. On the other hand, the DC-3 complete with crew lent him for a year by the United States was used enthusiastically.

His gifts to both statesmen were collections of jewels, daggers and swords along with the costly clothing worn by Arab princes. But although more valuable than the gifts offered less eminent persons, they were of the same kind. Perhaps he could not conceive any other way of expressing appreciation.

*This narrowness of vision did not extend to other fields. He had a penchant, or rather desire or craving to be well-informed, to be abreast of all happenings at home or abroad that might affect him or his régime. This bent led him to establish a system of information gathering that became more efficient as means of communication improved.*

**Newshound:** As soon as he had reached a position of authority as amir of Nejd, Ibn Saud began to glean information from all sources open to him. In the early days and even later the Bedu who came to Riyadh to get what was in fact an annual or semi-annual stipend were welcomed and questioned. In the Bedu encampments and in the towns and villages his custom was to hold audiences to which all were invited. His encouragement and advice were interspersed with questions. Rumors and opinions were sifted and compared. In the end he had a coherent view of the degree of loyalty of each of the tribes and its subdivisions, where they were encamped, the health and state of mind of the chiefs, the condition of the herds, their pasture, who had and who had not paid *zakat* (tax). The quantity and location of rain were important. Drought was a recurrent menace that could change the plans for a campaign and signal the start of a revolt.

During the decades when communication was by camel-mounted messenger, placing his relatives in positions of authority in towns and provinces was more than a wise precaution. Along with insuring unswerving loyalty to his régime, their use permitted a frank and usually unbiased evaluation of the local polity, the state of the economy and all other matters of concern to government, including subversion and espionage. Ibn Saud himself uncovered more than one spy in Riyadh and meted out punishment, on occasion a beheading. Undoubtedly he set up an intelligence service active both at home and abroad. In a conversation with Philby he said, 'I have long been undermining the House of Rashid by "*siyasa*,"' which may mean spying and subversion as well as the more usual translation, 'politics'.

His long relationship with the British political resident for the Persian Gulf and his agents began in 1902. The number of messages back and forth and the relative rapidity of interchanges shows the existence of an efficient dispatch service. The establishment of a corps of couriers mounted on fast camels must have been a priority for the newly proclaimed amir of Nejd. Dickson (*1949 p. 510*) says Ibn Saud told him that in 1915 when the British troops won the battle of Shuaiba in Iraq his picked messenger brought the news from Zubair to Riyadh, 530 miles, in five and a half days. The *dhalul* died on arrival. Ibn Saud's express riders between Oqair and Hofuf, 60 miles, covered the distance regularly in five hours. Messengers between Kuwait and Riyadh, just under 500 miles, took ten days for the journey. (*Cf. Lawrence, p. 338*: miles in a day's journey—easy stage, 50; good, 80; emergency, 110.) Normal progress for a camel is four miles an hour at a walk; six, walking and trotting; eight at a trot, and thirteen miles an hour going all out for a short distance. Messages from Ibn Saud to the British political resident were delivered by hand to his agents in Kuwait or Bahrain and sent on by cable and telegraph (*n. 28*).

On Philby's advice, early in 1929 a contract was let with the Marconi company for wireless telegraphy. A net of stations eventually covered the whole country. It proved useful, not only for normal communication, but also to call up forces for duty and to speed help in case of catastrophe. Later, portable transmitters and receivers accompanied the monarch on his travels and a news digest was prepared for him daily.

A concomitant of information on events is intelligence about individuals and their doings. In addition to his own inquiries among the tribes and the reports of the Bedu coming to Riyadh for their stipend, Ibn Saud presumably had agents among them, perhaps the deacons preaching the faith, whose reports served him well when dissidence came to the fore in 1910–16 and again in 1928–30. He maintained contact with other rulers—the imam of Yemen and the Idrisi, the king of Egypt, even the sultan of Turkey (before his overthrow in 1923) and with Moslem communities throughout the world. Like those of other nations his official establishments overseas had intelligence services, avowed and clandestine. They provided dossiers on heads of state and leaders of factions.

*Ibn Saud's efforts to get timely reports of significant happenings throughout the world were only a part of his vigilance over the security of his realm. In an attempt to insure that his line would remain in uncontested power after his demise he required both Bedu and townsmen to accede to the nomination of his eldest surviving son as heir to the throne, an event rare in Arabia where contests over succession were the rule. Perhaps he envisioned all of his sons in positions of authority, for he sired them in numbers unequaled except in legend.*

**Paterfamilias:** The number of legitimate sons that Ibn Saud fathered has been quoted variously between forty-three and forty-five but the number of his daughters has never been revealed and perhaps never counted. Legitimate wives totaled at least twenty-two with some probably uncounted because of very prompt divorce. His last living son, Hamud, was born in 1947, after a spate of births in 1941–43. Long before this last arrival the king had begun to seek help to maintain his vigor, and it is known that his doctors prescribed many aphrodisiacs and tonics kept in a chest that accompanied him everywhere.

But in the years of exile in Kuwait no such remedies were necessary. His first wife, bint al Fikri, died in 1896, six months after the marriage. His second wife, Wadhba bint Hazzam, gave Ibn Saud his first son, Turki, born in 1900, and another, Saud, in 1902. In the interim he had taken a third wife, Tarfa bint Abdullah, who bore Faisal in 1904. By 1910 he had wedded at least seven. One of them was Jauhara bint Musa'ad al Jiluwi, already mentioned. Another was Hassa bint Ahmad ibn Mohammed as Sudairi (daughter of an uncle on his mother's side) whom he divorced and five years later remarried, saying that he could not forget her. She gave him eight sons and five daughters. In 1917 he took to wife his brother Sa'ad's widow, Jauhara bint Sa'ad as Sudairi, whose children he brought up as his own. She died giving birth to the third child sired by him. He then married her sister Haiya to bring up the brood. She gave him  three more sons. For other motives he married Shahida, a Syrian from Latakia, mother of Mansour, at first a concubine in his harem.* For reasons of state he wed Fahada the widow of the tenth amir of Haïl and most certainly she was not the only one of her kind.

In accordance with the Koran's teaching *(Surah IV, verse 3)*: *Marry women of your choice, two or three or four, but if ye fear that ye will not be able to deal justly with them then only one*, he had only four wives at any one time. In the years when he was establishing his domain Ibn Saud usually had three wives in Riyadh, letting the fourth position open to be filled by any girl to whom he might take a fancy during his absences from the capital. Such a procedure also permitted a quick marriage for reasons of state. In 1918 he told Philby, 'Wallah! In my lifetime I have married five and seventy wives and insh'Allah, I have not done with wiving yet.' By 1930 the total had risen to 135 virgins and about a hundred others. In the early days at least, many of these brief marriages were made to cement the allegiance of the tribes in his realm.

He asked Philby, 'Why is it that you English allow divorce to be so difficult? Among us when a wife no longer pleases, we get rid of her by thrice repeating a simple word: *Talliq, talliq, talliq!*' He once told Shaikh Ahmed ibn Jabir as Sabah (ruler of Kuwait after 1921) that there was no pleasure on earth comparable 'to put his lips on the woman's lips, his body on her body and his feet on her feet.' With his friends he told bawdy jokes and discussed the merits of his concubines. But in the privacy of the harem he was very different if the few scraps of indirect information can be trusted.

In accordance with his almost invariable routine he left his friends at nine in the evening for his quarters. But there was no headlong rush to the companion chosen for that night. Instead he bathed and dressed afresh, telling a grandson who saw him that as his wife was preparing herself to receive him, so he readied himself to go to her. The favorite of his old age Umm Talal, was once asked by a

---

\* McLoughlin (p. 144) says that he did not marry her.

son how she fared with her husband given his volatile temper, replied, 'You do not know your own father. He is a different man with us than the one you see.'

On one occasion he told Philby: 'I love my family very much indeed, but I don't always let them know it! But what do you folks know about love after all, who take one wife and then sleep on different beds? Why I—well the longest winter night is all too short for me! Even when I settle down to rest, I wake from time to time to embrace my companion, and sometimes I do it in my sleep!' (*Arabian Jubilee, p. 139*).

He loved his children. When they were small he allowed them to be with him on every occasion possible, and took them with him on outings with friends and guests. In 1922 he told Rihani: 'I train my children to walk barefoot, to rise two hours before dawn, to eat but little, to ride horses bareback—sometimes we have but a moment to saddle a horse, leap on his back and go.' When adolescent, the boys were sent to an informal school under the eyes of a venerable member of the *Ulema* to learn the Koran by heart, and to acquire respect for their elders. Ibn Saud himself had memorized many of the chapters, the *surahs*, of the Koran, as well as the *Ahadith*— collections of the acts and sayings of the Prophet and his companions.

His children were considered adult at sixteen or seventeen. Turki, born in 1900, was in 1917 in charge of a large force responsible for preventing smuggling into the Qasim from Kuwait. Faisal, born in 1904, saw his first son in 1921. In spite of their early assumption of responsibility, Ibn Saud demanded the same filial respect from his sons as he had shown all his life to his father, Abdur Rahman. At the daily *majlis* the sons sat lower than their father and paid close attention to his words, never interrupting. But their submission to his authority, although real and based on fear as well as respect, did not prevent delinquency when away from his eye. The king could not have been aware of all the peccadilloes and worse of many of his offspring. He did not foresee the effects of almost unlimited funds, and of contacts, even infrequent, with the fleshpots of the West.

In 1947 when Prince Nasir, born in 1920, held a drinking party following which seven of his guests died of wood alcohol poisoning, he was flung into jail and later caned by his irate sire in front of his princely peers.

In November 1951, Prince Mishairi, then nineteen, killed Cyril Ousman, a British citizen employed in Jedda since 1929 by the Saudi government and the British consulate. This minor official and his wife were acquainted with several of the princes. Mishairi, refused a drink and a favor, brooded for four days, returned to the consulate and shot Cyril as he jumped from a window after the prince had blasted the door with a shotgun.

Ousman's wife was asked to choose between the death penalty and blood money. Her friends persuaded her to accept the money (£70,000). Mishairi hid in Faisal's residence for two weeks waiting for the king's wrath to cool. Ibn Saud is reported to have said, 'Where is Mishairi's head?' This form of capital punishment was not inflicted on the erring prince but he was sentenced to life imprisonment. He was released only when amnesty was granted many prisoners after Ibn Saud's death.

The incident resulted in a fiat forbidding the importation of alcohol into Saudi Arabia, and a boom in the construction of stills by foreigners in al Hasa where the processes causing the fermentation of fruits and grain became a major interest.

Ibn Saud based his rule on the threat of swift, sure punishment for any misdeed. Although for a time high-ranking rebels against his authority were granted clemency, common criminals were never spared. Even today, although many foreigners live in Saudi Arabia, violent crime is still less common than in most western countries.

**Justice:** From the early days of his rule Ibn Saud had been reluctant to punish blood kin, no matter what their misdeeds. Even Saud ibn Abdullah captured in Sulaiyl in 1910 and guilty of treason was spared the decapitation meted out the Hazzanis. Perhaps because the fall of the house of Rashid was due in large part to repeated assassinations of close relatives he shrank from such measures. Too, the catastrophic results of the long rivalry between two of his uncles may have moved him to avoid bloodshed within the family because of the certainty of attempted revenge. Even so, he was the target of at least two plots by members of his family to murder him, one of them by poison. Nothing and nobody stopped him from punishing other miscreants, although during the decade that he was establishing his primacy over Nejd his forbearance was exceptional. He himself told Philby, 'I have made it my aim to be patient with all men. Be patient with God and be patient with the stiff-necked; for these will either repent and be cured or come out in their true colors openly, when they can be struck down once and for all' (*Arabian Jubilee*, p. 106).

His method of reaching this end demanded strength and endurance. In the ten years after the capture of Riyadh when not campaigning against his enemies he was almost always on the move: to cement an alliance, often by marriage; to settle a dispute between tribes; to collect taxes; to retrieve animals stolen in a raid; to capture a thief or murderer; to arrest a rebellious shaikh or governor. Once in hand, any high-ranking miscreant, even a hardened recidivist rebel against his government, was almost always pardoned and returned to his *dirah* or post. The amir's message: You cannot escape me. If I choose to be merciful, be grateful! It was an effective course. By 1912 the tribes of Nejd were his, although revolt still simmered among the Ajman and Murra of al Hasa.

He was peculiarly sensitive to disrespect to himself, to his family, and to his guests. When Sir Gilbert Clayton was at Hadda in 1925 he and his secretary took an evening walk near an *Ikhwan* camp, and were cursed as 'Dogs of Christians.' They attempted to apologize to Ibn Saud for trespass. The king summoned the two culprits, cursed them, and ordered a flogging. Spread-eagled face down, they were given thirty thwacks with palm staves wielded by brawny Negro slaves, then imprisoned.

Crimes involving murder, adultery, incest, and sexual aberration were usually punished by death in one of the several forms prescribed by Koranic law. When these crimes were brought to his attention the king was always in favor of strict application of the statutes. On the other hand, in spite of his deep religious feeling, he frowned on the bigotry of zealots, and in particular on the witch hunt for and severe punishment of minor offenses against Wahhabi tenets—smoking, dressy apparel, singing, even minor delinquencies in attendance at prayer.

However, he had no qualms about the removal of a hand or foot for theft. Beatings severe enough to cause death were not infrequent in his capital, and even more common in al Hasa where ibn Jiluwi was his lieutenant.

In addition to death inflicted as a penalty or as a result of excessive punishment, it was an ever-present threat from disease, accident, famine, and war. Perhaps one of the causes of the seeming disregard of death was its frequency at all ages (*n. 10*).

**Death:** Other sources of an apparent indifference to maiming and death among the Arabs of the desert were harsh living conditions and the Wahhabi faith, a creed in which the dead are not to be mourned, and their resting places are unmarked. Perhaps Ibn Saud's seeming unconcern over the death of his soldiers stemmed from these verities. Philby implies and Dickson suggests that his willingness to send them into battle when the odds were against their survival demonstrates that he used their religious zeal cynically. During the siege of Haïl in 1921 he apparently felt no compunction about ordering charge after charge of his men against walls when the chances of success were minimal. Neither ibn Bijad nor ad Duwish, his principal lieutenants, were more solicitous. Yet family and tribal ties were of great importance to all of shaikhly extraction. Ibn Saud was no exception, as can be seen in his sparing the lives of cousins and uncles who had repeatedly conspired against his hegemony. And his reactions to death in his immediate family ranged from sorrow to agonized bereavement.

The worldwide epidemic of influenza of 1918–1919 killed indiscriminately in Riyadh. Among the victims was Ibn Saud's first-born, Turki, just nineteen and already well known as a warrior. According to Philby he was 'a particularly pleasing and gallant lad' (*n. 29*). He had sired a son and three daughters.

Two other sons of Ibn Saud died then. One was Fahad, about fourteen, and the other a five-year old, Sa'ad. The British government sent a note of condolence to which he replied, 'you have participated with me in my sorrow ... the loss of my son in the glory of his youth.'

Too, he lost the greatest love of his life, Jauhara bint Musa'ad al Jiluwi who had given him Mohammed and Khalid. (Both achieved fame, Mohammed for his part in the surrender of Medina, and Khalid as king in 1975.) It is said that even many years later the mention of her name brought tears to his eyes. Four other sons died in infancy during Ibn Saud's lifetime. One adult still in his twenties, Mansour, was minister of defense until his death in 1951.

The king's mother, Sara as Sudairi died in 1910. She came from a prominent family living north of Riyadh that through marriage became uncles and cousins of the Sauds. All were tall and raw-boned. It is clear that Ibn Saud owed his stature and heavy frame to her, for Abdur Rahman was small and slight. The Sudairi family was entrusted with many important posts including the governorship of cities and towns.

In June 1928 Abdur Rahman died in Riyadh while his son was in Mecca. Abdul Aziz held his father in great respect always, and showed his filial devotion at every opportunity, ceding when possible the place of honor to him, and sharing some of the burden of government with him. An eyewitness, Mohammed Asad, describes the strong emotions aroused in the monarch when informed of the death: 'the uncomprehending stare with which he looked at the messenger for several seconds and the despair which slowly and visibly engulfed the features normally so serene and composed.' He sprang up, crying, 'My father is dead!' and ran from the room, his *bisht* trailing behind as he leapt up the steps repeating, 'My father is dead! My father is dead!' He was now both amir and imam. For two days he refused to eat or drink or to see anyone, spending both night and day in prayer.

In the summer of 1950 his older sister, Nura, passed on. She may have shared a camel with him in 1891 in the flight from Riyadh and her name was on his lips in January 1902, when he attacked Ajlan. She ruled the distaff side of his family and was a critic and adviser of value. When the telephone was installed in Riyadh she was the first to be connected with her brother.

None of the defunct mentioned here is in a marked grave. Neither is the king himself. He died in Taïf on the night of 9 November 1953, in the arms of Faisal, who, when Saud, the heir-apparent, arrived from Jedda, took a ring from the dead man's finger and gave it to his brother as a sign of fealty. Saud reciprocated by naming Faisal crown prince and heir-apparent. Only Mohammed, the third eldest of Ibn Saud's living sons refused to swear allegiance, but later relinquished his claim to the succession.

# Envoi

*Ibn Saud—King by Conquest* was begun as a distraction from the pain of a great loss. It has ended with an enhanced appreciation of this man's outstanding abilities and a better understanding of his character. Viewed in the perspective of lasting worldwide significance his accomplishments are important only in that they let the vast resources of energy in the kingdom he created be discovered and developed. In a narrower sense he founded a Middle Eastern kingdom that stands with the West against totalitarian government, although now it is in effect a benevolent dynastic oligarchy which has been both a bulwark for and a burden to the West.

As a man Ibn Saud stood above most of his compeers both in physical endowment and in mental capacity. He used both to the full in restoring his patrimony. At the same time he established a central, unifying government that in his day included almost none of the essentials of the infrastructure of a modern state. Nevertheless, that government has endured a century in spite of insurrection and grave unrest, a feat never before achieved in inner Arabia. Given his upbringing and the mores of the time and place his conduct is understandable, although not all of his actions are laudable when judged by the criteria of the western world today. In our ethical code he was licentious and brutal. Licentious, because in fleshly relations he exceeded the norms of his own milieu. Brutal, in the sense that he countenanced or ordered the death of many men, and once, as a salutary lesson intended to strike fear into all, of an entire sept including women and children.

It cannot be gainsaid that he used his warriors for purposes other than to propagate his creed. Often his army protected or enlarged his domain or chastised his enemies. Glubb says, 'Ibn Saud, an entirely benign patriarch, breathing benev-olence and the service of God, employed massacre to rise to power' (*1959, p. 221*). That he did so consciously, as a policy, is debatable (*but see p. 53*). In the lines following those quoted, Glubb suggests that he did not. Van der Meulen, although hesitant, concurs.

As a statesman Ibn Saud won the admiration of most Europeans who came into his venue. After the fact almost all recognized the wisdom and foresight needed to make the series of tactical decisions that would achieve his strategic objectives—the recovery of his heritage and the establishment of a lasting govern-ment headed by his progeny. Article I of the 1915 treaty recognizes these aims: 'The British Government do acknowledge and admit that Najd, El Hassa, Qatif and Jubail, and their dependencies and territories ... and their ports on the shores of the Persian Gulf are the countries of Bin Saud and of his fathers before him, and do hereby recognise said Bin Saud as the independent Ruler thereof and absolute chief of their tribes, and after him his sons and descendants by inheritance....' The Treaty of Jedda of 1927 is at once more concise and more liberal: 'His Britannic majesty recognises the complete and absolute independence of His Majesty the King of the Hejaz and of Nejd and its Dependencies.'

From 1902 to 1915 he walked a tightrope between repeated refusals of his requests for British protection and professed obeisance to Turkish power. For a short period late in 1913 and early in 1914 a change in Whitehall's protocol of refusal to consider his proposals seemed imminent, but as war neared British policy conciliatory to the Sublime Porte denied him the protection against the Turks that he sought. This led to his signing a treaty, negated by the hostilities, accepting Ottoman supervision of his rule in al Hasa. Thereafter, British subsidy and arms helped him maintain his ascendancy while he avoided acceptance of tasks that would have taken him out of Nejd or made him appear subservient to Husain. Political agents calmed his fears that British support for his enemy Husain would end in forced subordination to him, but did not temper his indig-nation at the vast difference in their subsidies.

Turkish aid to the Rashid dynasty ended with the armistice, but some British officials favorable to Husain advocated that the Shammar chieftains be provided with arms and a subsidy to restore their hegemony and thus to reëstab-lish a balance of power among the three centers of strength in central Arabia. Ibn Saud was aware of this proposal and of Husain's efforts to create a coalition against him, but he had used his subsidy to good advantage by creating more *Hujar* and by providing all warriors with arms. The weapon he thus forged served him well in engagements at Khurma and Turaba, Haïl, the Asir and Kuwait, while he awaited the waning of British support for Husain.

To forestall criticism he made his conquest of the Hejaz in the name of all Moslems, promising a say in government there to other nations and communities of believers—an unfulfilled pledge. But he maintained ties with Britain in spite of the installation of Hashemite régimes on his northern frontier, an example of the prudence that governed all his important decisions.

Perspicacious as none of his ancestors had been, Ibn Saud saw the Hejaz as the last addition to his kingdom. Perhaps, as Besson suggests, he planned to use the *Ikhwan* to harass the two Hashemite states on his northern border, always keeping its transgressions within the bounds delimited by the strength of British reaction. But he had not foreseen the greed of its leaders who in the guise of religious ardor repeatedly attacked tribes in the new states. The two great assemblies of 1927 and 1928 in Riyadh, called ostensibly only to judge the validity of criticisms of his government, gave Ibn Saud a measure of the temper of his new adversaries, but even so, the rapid growth of the revolt found him unprepared.

A successful conclusion to this imbroglio left Ibn Saud undisputed master of his kingdom, but still a prey to the financial problems that had plagued him from the outset. At first, the paucity of revenue from taxes and imports kept him poor, but after the Hejaz was acquired, his own lavish lifestyle and his 'l'État c'est moi' system of government kept him in debt. Only in the two years before his death did he attempt to broaden the bases of decision-making although his older sons were given posts of authority in the early thirties.

The Second World War, like the first, found him assuring the future of his kingdom by maintaining good relations with both sides. Throughout the war years he managed, as in 1914–1918, to avoid active military participation, and only when Allied victory seemed certain did he accept loans from Britain and the United States. Thereafter that nation replaced Britain as his principal adviser in financial matters and also played a minor rôle in his decisions on foreign policy. The Arab League was formed in the last year of the war, but because of established policy and his increasing debility, Ibn Saud had little interest in its doings. When Arab nationalists began to effect changes in the governments of several states in the Middle East he did not assist them, although more than one revolt was against his old enemy, the Hashemites.

Even against the Jews in Palestine his efforts were not in keeping with his sentiments. The contests in the Levant resulting from the acceptance by Europe and the United States of a Jewish homeland induced him to send a brigade of his troops abroad for a short time, and for a longer period to provision in arms Arab guerillas and irregulars in Palestine.

Any discussion of Ibn Saud the man must stress the strength of his religious convictions, and their effects on his policies. That he nurtured the faith of his followers and then used their fervor to foster his end is undeniable, but that he did so consciously, as a planned policy, is debatable. He himself wrote:

اللهم ان كان في هذا الملك خير لي وللمسلمين ، فابقه لي ولأولادي .
وان كان فيه شر لي وللمسلمين ، فانزعه مني ومن أولادي !

عبد العزيز آل سعود (١)

Freely translated: Allah, if this power has some good in it for me and all Moslems, may I and my children keep it. If, on the contrary it bodes some evil for me and all Moslems, take it from me and my children!

Abdul Aziz Al Saud

This prayer expresses one of Ibn Saud's most cherished beliefs: All that he had done was by Allah's will, by His grace. It also reflects his concern about the dynasty he had restored and includes one of the themes repeated frequently in his discourses—the responsibility of a ruler toward his subjects, a topic on which he quoted the Prophet: 'Every man is a shepherd entrusted with responsibility for his flock.' Yet his modest efforts to improve the general welfare with doctors and hospitals were completely inadequate. He had a lively sense of the value of medical care and measures to safeguard public health as shown by the steps he took to prevent epidemics among the pilgrims when the Hejaz fell to him, and his life-long concern for adequate advice and therapeutic treatment for himself and his family. But at the time of his death hospitals were in operation only in Riyadh, Mecca, Jedda, and Taïf. In al Hasa the oil companies provided for their employees and families medical facilities not found elsewhere in the kingdom. It was only in 1952 that the budget of the ministry responsible for public health was increased from $2 to $15 million.

Education for all never became a matter of policy during Ibn Saud's lifetime. Like most of his generation he regarded learning unnecessary for women. He believed it permissible for them to listen to the Koran and other scriptural literature, but reading and writing were unsuitable accomplishments, although not forbidden. For men, his opinions were less uncompromising. Although as early as 1927 a kind of religious college was set up in the Hejaz, the authority of the *Ulema*, which even Ibn Saud had to respect, insisted that all education must be based on the sacred texts. Consequently, primary education lagged in Arabia. In 1950 fewer than 20,000 boys were in public schools. However, he belatedly installed facilities in Riyadh for the education of young princes. Before his death in 1953 hundreds of Saudis, some on stipends from the king himself, had been sent to study in Egypt, Lebanon and Syria; a lesser number to England and the United States. The oil companies set up training schools for their employees and fostered contracting services run by nationals. But this initiative was not followed elsewhere in the kingdom where foreign contractors were used almost exclusively.

As a result, during Ibn Saud's lifetime almost nothing was done by the government toward establishing an economic infrastructure that would better the standard of living of the people. Ibn Saud had only contempt for the benefits of 'modernization' other than those that concerned him directly—the latest in armament, electric light, radio, telephone, motor cars; paved highways and new buildings. In 1937, when fretting under the economic hardships of the depression the young people of the Hejaz were demanding more freedom, an article purporting to reflect his thought appeared in the Mecca newspaper. It condemned as a temptation of the devil the attitude of those youths who wanted, 'modernization, progress, civilization, liberty and whatnot.' He censured especially those women who attempted to associate with men, citing 'progress' but neglecting their duties as mothers and wives. A 'welfare state' was unthinkable to a Nejdi prince who would certainly have condemned the idea had he been capable of conceiving it. His largesse in the early days was not for the commonweal but a means of showing his ascendancy and seigniory, as well as a way of insuring loyalty to his person.

His outlook on the duties of government, unchanging throughout his life-time, was, as mentioned elsewhere, a reflection of his certainty concerning his right to rule. The consummate autocrat speaks: 'We raise them not above us, nor do we place ourselves above them. We give them what we can; we satisfy them with an excuse when we cannot. And when they go beyond their bounds we make them taste of the sweetness of our discipline.' But it would be unjust to judge this man's social conscience by the standards of a twentieth century industrialized democracy.

He was reared in a society in its essentials unchanged since the time of Abraham—a society in which many were unlettered and engaged in nomadic or pastoral pursuits under a patriarchal dispensation, and governed by an elite chosen by birth or by elimination of rivals. Yet some writers condemn his failure to better the lot of these nomads and their farmer relatives.

When asked why he did not try to organize his state on a less personal basis, so that his sons could inherit a structured government, he said, 'I have conquered my kingdom by my sword and by own efforts; let my sons make their own efforts after me.' In defense of his ignorance of other forms of administration, consider this fact: until well after World War I all of the 'independent' states bordering his realm were either kingdoms or shaikhdoms.

This brief recapitulation of Ibn Saud's career and rationale for his failing to found a modern state ends with the thought that in spite of the overwhelming weight of a tremendous accumulation of wealth and the pressures of a burgeoning society his sons still observe the principles that guided their father. The legends based on his deeds inspire his grandsons with pride in their heritage and convinces many Saudis of the family's right to rule in spite of derelictions by individuals. Yet at the end was he himself uncertain of the future course of the dynasty that he had labored unceasingly to restore? Was the disillusion and sadness that marked his last year a judgment that he found his life's work wanting? His last words are reported to have been: 'There is no power and no strength save in God.'

# Notes

# NOTES

1.   Only custom dictates the writing of Abdul Aziz as two words, for Abdullah is nearly always written as one. Both mean the slave or servant of God. In the name Abdulaziz, God is designated by one of His reputed ninety-nine names: *The slave of the Beloved (One)*. The apostrophe sometimes used in the family name (Sa'ud) indicates a separation into two syllables in pronunciation and the presence of the Arab glottal stop, *Ain*. The 's' is a sibilant, as in the word sod; the 'a' is like that in father; the 'ud' is clearly separate and is pronounced like the 'ud' in rude or the 'ood' in the word snood. Ibn Saud objected to its use in reference to himself, for in Moslem countries the family cognomen is not commonly used in naming an individual. He is *Ali*, the son of *Yusuf*, in turn the son of *Turki*. The confusion that often arises is overcome in some cases by a nickname. Before the death of his first-born son many referred to Abdul Aziz ibn Abdur Rahman as 'Abu Turki' (the father of Turki). Later he was often called 'As Shiyukh' (the plural of shaikh.) After his father Abdur Rahman, *the Slave of the Compassionate (One)*, relinquished the dignity, he was in fact the 'imam' (religious leader), and was always called so by the *Ikhwan*. 'Al' means 'of the house of,' or 'of the family of,' 'ibn' (pronounced *bin*) 'the son of.' The inversion of letters is a widely accepted convention.

     In this work the names of individuals are spelled in English as they are spoken, although written Arabic does not indicate the sounds produced in the linkage between spoken words: the 'sun-moon' relationship. For example: the 'l' in 'ul' before the consonant 'r' changes in sound to 'r' in Abdur Rahman, for example, and to 'd' in ad Duwish, but remains 'l' before the 'a' vowel sound in Abdul Aziz. In other words, in speech the 'l' is elided before certain consonants.

2.   Many publications give 1880 as the year of birth of Abdul Aziz ibn Abdur Rahman. Lacey *(1981)* presents arguments for 1876, and McLaughlin, *(1993)* concurs, quoting Zirikli *(1970)* who says that Ibn Saud's brother, Abdullah, confirmed that 1876 was the true date. The authors of the several books that indicate 1880 seem to have been misled by the Arab historians Mutluq and ibn Nasr. Winder *(1966, p. 266)* remarks that 'the date [1880] is almost certainly only traditional.' Two writers who had access to Ibn Saud himself state clearly that he was born in 1876: Rihani, who visited Riyadh in 1922–23, wrote this *(1928, pp. 86–87)*: 'Ten years later (1318 A.H.—1900 A.D.) his *(Abdur Rahman's)* son Abdul Aziz, then twenty-four years of age, joined the forces.' Gertrude Bell *(n. 26)*, in her widely quoted description of Ibn Saud at the Durbar of November 1916, wrote: 'Ibn Saud is now barely forty, although he looks some years older.'

With Lacey's findings as confirmation, 1876 seems to be established as the true year of his birth, and the date of birth was probably in November, if Miss Bell's comment is apt. (Khatib says September.) Van der Meulen is more precise as to the day, stating: 'The exact date of his birth is not known as his mother could not read or write but it must have been about the 20th of Dhul Hija 1297 A.H. corresponding to the 26th of November 1880 A.D.' *(1957, p. 37).*

3.    The most readily available reference to the history of the Saud family is probably Philby *(1955)*. McLoughlin *(1993)* presents a detailed study focused on Ibn Saud with new data from late research. Lacey's 1981 work is more easily digested than most. Other studies are G. Rentz's thesis *(unpublished, University of California, 1947)* and the outstandingly researched book by R. Bayly Winder *(1965)*. The sources for these works are documents in Arabic by Uthman ibn Abdullah ibn Bishr, Ibrahim ibn Salih ibn Isa, Abdur Rahman ibn Nasr (period 1885–1936), Saud ibn Hidhlul al Thunaian As Saud (period 1885–1940), and Mutluq ibn Salih and his son Ali Ahmed (period 1880–1940). Several writings in English and French by 19th century contemporaries add valuable information. Among them are Doughty, Palgrave, Pelly, Huber, and the reports of the British political agents in the Persian Gulf region, including Lorimer. For a bibliography more complete than that herein see Besson, Lacey, Winder, Alangari, and the 1988 bibliography *Saudi Arabia* by Frank A. Clements, in which the titles are more eclectic.

Summaries of the family history are given in Holden and Johns, Troeller, and more fully in Glubb *(1959)*. Addendum II is yet another summary of the history of the Sauds. A reasonably complete, uncritical but compact review of Ibn Saud's rise to power is given in Collin's introduction to Clayton's diary *(1969)*.

4.    *Wahhabi.* The name used by non-Moslems for the followers of the tenets of Mohammed Abdul Wahhab (1703–1787). His puritanical reforms found favor with the Sauds, the ruling family in Nejd (central Arabia), who used the religious fervor of adherents to increase the size of their hegemony *(A. II)*. They were not only secular leaders, but also the head, *imam*, of the religious polity. As Wahhabi dogma permits the use of force against *mushrikun* (polytheists), Moslem or non-Moslem, and against sinners, these crusaders of the eighteenth century, as well as their twentieth-century descendants, the *Ikhwan*, found justification for rapine and killing even among other followers of Islam.

The Wahhabi creed is based primarily on the Koran, but recognizes six collections of *Ahadith* (Traditions) and two books of *Tafsir* (Interpretations). These, together with extracts from the writings of Mohammed Abdul Wahhab, are the sources from which the dogma was derived. It condemns the veneration that the other branches of the *Sunni* pay the memory of the Prophet Mohammed, his relatives, and other religious leaders and mystics, for the concept of saints and prophets as mediators between God and man is rank heresy to the Wahhabi. Nevertheless, the descendants of Abdul Wahhab are still known as 'As Shaikh' in Riyadh where they have a privileged status.

5.    The number of participants in a battle is invariably exaggerated in the accounts of Arab historians.

6.  Almana pp. 274–275 (*Appendix 5*). Some doubt exists concerning the authenticity of some of the names, for one of the band mentioned by Dickson may not appear in Almana's list.

7.  *Surah:* One chapter of the 124 that constitute the Koran. Poetic imagery is common in many, and most have a descriptive name. The work is in part a guide to conduct.

8.  Often the name of a sister was used as a battle cry by noble families. Nura was held in high esteem by Ibn Saud throughout his life. She was one of sixteen sisters, but the only one older than he.

9.  Photographs of the wicket can be found in Dickson (*1949*) and Lacey (*1981*). Herein, see Plate III, 'Sites of 1902 Saga.' Photo taken from de Gaury (*1946*). The British had long considered control of the Persian Gulf vital to the safeguard of their position in India and to that end made Oman and Bahrain protected client states. (*See Kelly 1968.*) Ibn Saud's journey to the coast aroused fears that he planned to add Oman to other ancestral holdings recently regained. In 1903 the visit of the ships of foreign flags (Russia and France) to the Gulf had caused a sharp reaction by Whitehall, including a visit to Oman, Bahrain, and Kuwait by the viceroy of India, the imperious Lord Curzon, who stated to an Arab audience, 'The peace of these waters must still be maintained, your independence will continue to be upheld; and the British government must remain supreme.'

10. Thesiger (*1959, pp. 152–153*) who traveled with the nomads of Oman, and twice traversed the Rub' al Khali, wrote:

    > It is characteristic of Bedu to do things by extremes, to be either wildly generous or unbelievably mean, very patient or almost hysterically excitable, to be incredibly brave or to panic for no apparent reason. Ascetic by nature, they derive satisfaction from the bare simplicity of their lives and scorn the amenities which others would judge essential. Although on the rare occasions that offer they eat enormously. I have never met a Bedu who was greedy. Continent for months on end, not one of them, even the most austere, would regard celibacy as a virtue. They want sons, and consider that women are provided by God for the satisfaction of men. Deliberately to refrain from using them would be not only unnatural but also ridiculous, and Bedu are very susceptible to ridicule. Yet an Arab will use his sister's name as his battlecry, and Glubb has suggested that the medieval conception of chivalry came to Europe from the Arabs at the time of the Crusades.
    >
    > Bedu set great store by human dignity, and most of them would prefer to watch a man die rather than see him humiliated. Always reserved in front of strangers and accustomed on formal occasions to sit for hours motionless and in silence, they are a garrulous, light-hearted race. But, at the instigation of religious zealots, they can become uncompromisingly puritanical, quick to frown on all amusement, regarding song and music as a sin and laughter as unseemly. Probably no other people, either as a race or as individuals, combine so many conflicting qualities in such an extreme degree.

*(pp. 209–210)* As I listened I thought once again how precarious was the existence of the Bedu. Their way of life naturally made them fatalists; so much was beyond their control. It was impossible for them to provide for a morrow when everything depended on a chance fall of rain or when raiders, sickness, or any one of a hundred chance happenings might at any time leave them destitute or end their lives.

11.   *Araïf* (The Recognized). Term for camels stolen in one raid and recovered in another. Used by Ibn Saud to designate the sons of the male children of Saud ibn Faisal, brother of Abdur Rahman. Saud had five known sons: Abdur Rahman (killed, 1883); Mohammed, Sa'ad, Abdullah (all three killed, 1888); and Abdul Aziz (imprisoned in Haïl, 1888). Among them they had nine male children: By Abdul Aziz, four—*Turki, Faisal, Mohammed, Saud;* by Abdullah, two—*Turki and Saud;* by Sa'ad, two—*Fahad, Faisal;* by Mohammed one—*Salman. (See genealogical chart).* The two Sauds have been confused in at least one publication. Three, perhaps more, of the *Araïf,* either detained by or allied with ibn Rashid, were recovered by Ibn Saud in 1904 and others came from Haïl in 1906.

Because their fathers were older than Abdur Rahman the *Araïf* claimed precedence, and hence that they should govern. Their ties with the 'Ajman were strong, so that tribe backed their plots for seizing power. Three of the *Araïf* married two of Ibn Saud's sisters.

12.   *Hujar:* The singular of this plural word is *Hijrah (Hegira).* This name is given the move of the Prophet Mohammed from Mecca to Medina—from the home of the unbelievers to the site of the rise of Islam. The Muslim calendar begins with this move (A.D. 622). To the *Ikhwan, Hijrah* meant a move from nomadic life to fixed abodes (*Hujar*) where the true religion would be strictly practiced.

13.   *Shia.* The word *Shia* means proponent of or partisan of. In accordance with an express instruction by the Prophet himself the Shiites accept the prophet Mohammed's son-in-law, Ali, as his legitimate successor, and one of his sons, Husain, as a beheaded martyr. Those who claim descent from Husain can use the title *Sayid (Seyyid),* while those claiming descent from his brother Hassan are *Sharif.*

The *Shias* have faith in the efficacy of prayer to saints, a belief unacceptable to Wahhabis and other conservatives. Once a year they perform public penance by several methods of mortification, including flagellation with chains and chest-beating, in commemoration of the martyrdom of the Prophet's grandson, Husain. When possible the Shias visit the Shia mosque and Ali's tomb at Karbala in Iraq. The Shiites do not acknowledge the validity of *Sunna,* Mohammed's exhortations codified into law by the first three caliphs of Islam. The *Sunni* (the Path [*of Mohammed*]), those who do accept this law, are the largest sect of the Moslem faith.

14.   Some references say that Faisal led the expedition to Asir in 1921. The leader of that expedition was Abdul Aziz ibn Musa'ad al Jiluwi, Ibn Saud's cousin and one of the eight paladins at Riyadh in 1902. Rihani *(pp. 178–180)* describes Ibn Saud's actions when his victorious son returned to Riyadh from Asir in May of 1923, having led a successful second expedition that left the capital in July 1922. The sultan confided to his guest that he had to participate in a cavalry charge behind his son, for as an observer he would have shed tears of pride.

15.   Sykes–Picot Agreement. On 9 May 1916, Sir Mark Sykes for England and Georges Picot for France signed a document assigning spheres of influence in former Turkish territory when victory was won. As shown on Map 5 (a reduction of the original inserted in the Sykes–Picot protocol) a French zone extended from the Mediterranean coast of Syria inland to the upper reaches of the Tigris, and a British zone included all of lower Mesopotamia. Between the two, an independent Arab state or states would be created, albeit subject to European guidance as indicated on the map. Two rich areas where independence might be viable would thus be under European tutelage, making a mockery of Husain's British-nurtured aspirations for Arab unity and the support of the Raj for his leadership. The mandates granted in 1920 at San Remo are outlined on Map 5A.

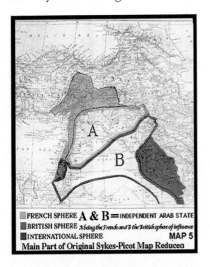

FRENCH SPHERE **A & B** = INDEPENDENT ARAB STATE
BRITISH SPHERE *A being the French and B the British sphere of influence*
INTERNATIONAL SPHERE                                      **MAP 5**
**Main Part of Original Sykes-Picot Map Reduced**

Middle East Mandates  1920   MAP 5A

Many an apologia has been presented in defense of Britain's fostering of Husain's illusions, but a written secret commitment to Husain signed by MacMahon, British high commissioner for Egypt *(See Antonius 1938 and Glubb 1959)* promised support for his leadership and agreed to recognize the Nationalists' aspirations for independence in specific areas.

Although aware of the Sykes–Picot agreement, Lawrence refrained from making it known to Husain, whose claims to leadership of an Arab confederation persisted, even after Russia's revolutionary government published the document. Perhaps in part as an expiation for his silence, Lawrence backed Husain's son Faisal, his own companion-in-arms, in his bid to become king of Syria. The French threw Faisal out five months after he was elected king of Syria in March 1920. A year later Lawrence persuaded him to accept the British offer to be king of Iraq. At a conference in Cairo in March 1921, Churchill with Lawrence at his side, approved the nomination, along with the sop of Transjordan for his brother Abdullah. Sir Percy Cox engineered Faisal's acceptance as king by the people of Iraq *(A. IV)*.

The area around Mosul and the upper Tigris, which had been in the French sphere of influence, 'A' of the 1916 protocol, became a part of Iraq mainly because British troops occupied the region before French forces could reach it. The mandates given France and Great Britain at San Remo in 1920 recognized the *fait accompli.*

16.  Confrontations between Husain ibn Ali, sharif of Mecca, and Ibn Saud:

> 1910. Sharif invades Nejd and kidnaps Sa'ad, Ibn Saud's brother. For his ransom, the sharif demands payment of a yearly rental for the Qasim and Washm.
>
> 1911. Husain protests Ibn Saud's taxation of the 'Ataiba. Threatens to loot caravans coming to the Hejaz from Nejd.
>
> 1915. Abdullah, Husain's son, invades western Nejd at the moment that Ibn Saud takes the field against ibn Rashid. Ibn Saud's riposte: If the British do not restrain Husain, we will.
>
> 1916. The sharif asks Ibn Saud to become an ally to help him fight the Turks. Ibn Saud demands a guarantee that his sovereignty will not be threatened. Husain calls him 'Bereft of reason.' On 5 November Husain proclaims himself 'King of the Arab Lands.'
>
> 1917. Husain charges that Ibn Saud aids the Turks because caravans are reaching the garrison in Medina while the amir is being paid to blockade their route.
>
> 1918. Husain attempts to retake Khurma: At least four major attacks fail. The Ikhwan are outraged.
>
> 1919. Abdullah marches on Khurma and is wiped out at Turaba after threatening to go on to the Gulf. Nejdi pilgrimage is canceled.
>
> 1920. Three-year armistice between Husain and Ibn Saud signed at British behest, but pilgrimage is again canceled.
>
> 1922. Husain publishes libelous comment on Ibn Saud, at the same time sending him letters professing friendship.

In 1918 Husain offered an alliance to the Rashids that would have involved a joint strike against Nejd. After the war Husain used some of his British subsidy and a part of the arms provided him to support a groupment of tribes in the north including the Harb, Hutaim, Shammar, Dhafir, the shaikhs of Muhammera and Zubair, Seyyid Talib of Basra and Salim of Kuwait, all united in their opposition to the *Ikhwan* and Ibn Saud. Through intercepted correspondence Ibn Saud became aware of these moves against him.

17.  Bertram Thomas, then assistant British representative in Transjordan under Philby, wrote in a letter to a friend, dated 25 September, 1924 (*first appearance in print*):

> T. J. has been in the limelight rather a lot lately. In my absence in India which incidentally coincided with the Amirs (*sic*) absence in Mecca on the Pilgrimage, much water chiefly seething and some of it muddy passed under the bridge. There was an invasion by the Wahhabis some 5000 of them—fanatical Arabs you know from central Arabia. They came along on camels with rifles and spears and swords (only 300 of them were mounted on horses) and emblasoned on their green war banners was their slogan لااله الا الله pronounced Lá illáh il Ulláh, meaning, 'There is no God but God.' And with this pious sentiment on their lips, they were athirst for loot and rapine. Our aeroplanes and armoured cars had a half hour's running fight with them, the contest was of course an unequal one, and the desert was strewn with 500 Baduin corpses for our Transjordan vultures and jackals and hyaena to batten on. The remains of their stricken army hared off into the desert from whence they came, but fearful of pursuit they avoided the usual route via known

wells, and taking pot luck along untried roads, many of them perished miserably with their camels from thirst.

18. During the *Hajj* of 1926 the Egyptian contingent escorted the *Mahmal*, an ancient litter holding the great black covering for the Kaaba, the *Kiswa*. This traditional offering, replaced annually, was guarded by armed Egyptian soldiers with a bugler and, some say, a military band. The bugle call to make camp sounded. The *Ikhwan*, already irked by the *Mahmal*, threw rocks at the soldiers who fired into the crowd of attackers killing some of them and a number of inoffensive pilgrims. Faisal, Ibn Saud's son, heard the shots, raced to the scene and stopped the clash during which 23 Egyptians died. Thereafter, the *Kiswa* was made locally. In 1936, the new king of Egypt, Farouk, restored diplomatic relations with the Sauds. They had ceased for a decade.

19. Death of Dhaidan: Late in April 1929 the paramount shaikh of the Ajman, Dhaidan ibn Khalid al Hithlain, was camped at Sarrar in central al Hasa seventeen miles from Awaina where Fahd ibn Jiluwi (son of the amir) was stationed. Fahd wrote Dhaidan, asking him to visit and offering a written safe conduct. Dhaidan, one of the three *Ikhwan* leaders who had protested Ibn Saud's strictures on raiding, had similar assurances of safety from Fahd's father and from Ibn Saud, because he had not participated in the battle at Sibila. Nevertheless the counselors among his two thousand followers advised him not to accept the invitation, because four years previously Fahd had treacherously captured and sent to Riyadh a shaikh wanted by the sultan.

Dhaidan showed the three letters of safe conduct to his men, and explained that it would shame him if he doubted the word of the king and his viceroy. So he rode the seventeen miles to Awaina on his mare, escorted by twelve of his followers, one a body slave. The party was well received with the usual coffee and ended with the customary scenting with the smoke of burning sandalwood.

As he rose to take his leave, Dhaidan was seized and manacled, along with eleven of his escort. One managed to escape, and galloped back to warn the camp at Sarrar. He arrived at sunset on his exhausted horse. After much discussion a midnight attack was chosen as the plan most likely to succeed. At night weapons must be only daggers and swords, for rifle fire in the dark could kill friend as well as foe.

The fifteen hundred of the rescue force met a patrol of Fahd's horsemen and all but annihilated it. A lone survivor alerted Fahd who rode out with two hundred to force a way through the attackers. He was driven back to his camp and killed by a young man who seized the reins of his horse, then shot him in the head and heart. Fahd had ordered a Negro slave, ibn Mansour, to kill the captives if the 'Ajman attacked, and, as the rescuers approached, did so by cutting the throats of the bound and helpless men. For this feat he was named ibn Jiluwi's chief executioner. That night, four hundred and fifty of Fahd's men were slain.

20. On 15 August 1929, Faisal ad Duwish sent his son Abdul Aziz ibn Faisal, called 'Aza-iyiz' on a raid into the southern 'Anaiza and Shammar country to show that the *Ikhwan* truly were a menace to Ibn Saud. The young man, about twenty-five, was accompanied by a group of experienced senior advisers and a picked force of six hundred and fifty camel-mounted warriors of the Mutair and 'Ajman. On a long

march that ended far to the north of Haïl (*see Map 4*) the raiders captured many hundreds of Amarat and Shammar camels and a Saudi convoy with ten thousand riyals of *zakat*. In the summer heat the captured camels began to drop from exhaustion as the party hastened homeward and their own *dhulul* had not drunk for four days. They learned that Ibn Saud's governor of Haïl, ibn Musa'ad, was trying to intercept them and had begun to guard the wells along their projected line of march. The elders in the party recommended an immediate change in direction but Azaiyiz refused to change his plan to water at the Umm er Radhuma wells, although his scouts told him that they had now been occupied by a force fully three times larger than his.

The old men counseled strongly against any attempt to water at Umm er Radhuma against such opposition. In the face of Azaiyiz's determination they left the party, taking a hundred and fifty men with them. Azaiyiz continued on for, he said, God was on the side of the *Ikhwan*. The force, now only five hundred strong, reached the vicinity of the wells at noon, and found them defended by fifteen hundred Shammar, Harb and Hathar Bedu. At this point none of the raiders had drunk for eight hours and the camels were faltering.

Azaiyiz ordered the noon call to prayer and rallied his force, saying, 'Are we not of the Brethren, and the elect of God?' A half-hour later the attack against entrenched defenders began. The repeated saber-wielding charges of the *Ikhwan* were aided by the mirage which made the aim of the holders of the well uncertain.

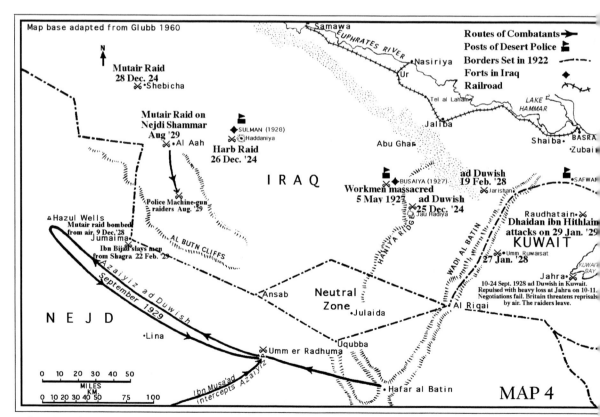

**Locations of some of the raids by the Ikhwan in the period 1924-1929. Azaiyiz's route and point of interception by Musa'ad shown.**

In spite of the desperate need of the assailants, the defenders' numbers prevailed as fresh reserves were fed into the fray. At sundown Azaiyiz had lost three-quarters of his men. Seeing the day lost he left the field escorted by five faithful servants. Their desiccated bodies and those of their camels were found two months later. Thirty-eight survivors of the attacking force eventually reached safety. After being disarmed they had been permitted to drink. Six Shammaris sent to execute them were killed by one Mutair who had managed to secrete his weapon.

21. Shaikh Mutluq of the Mutair had been Faisal ad Duwish's right-hand man for years. In 1921 during the two-month siege preceding the capture of Haïl, he participated in several attacks against the walls where many men were thrown off the scaling ladders or shot. The *Ikhwan* disregarded danger, for the dead in holy war were assured of immediate entry into Paradise, with its doe-eyed eternal virgins and flowing streams. Mutluq began to doubt the assurances of the head of the *Ulema* that this was the sure reward of valor, and challenged him, the *Alim*, to lead an assault. If he were so sure that delectable *houri* is awaited the fallen, he should be eager to do so. Mutluq was called before Ibn Saud and told to cease spreading despondency among the troops or face punishment. At that moment his eyes were opened to the uses of religion for political advantage.

22. The Red Line Agreement was a pact effective 1 July 1928 among the major international oil companies including Royal Dutch Shell, Anglo–Iranian, the Compagnie Française des Petroles and and an American consortium headed by Standard Oil of New Jersey. The pact required equal and joint participation by each company or group in exploration for and exploitation of oil discovered within the territory demarcated by a Red Line drawn around all of the pre-World War I holdings of the Turkish Empire in the Middle East, excluding Kuwait, but including the Sinai peninsula and Cyprus. Calouste Gulbenkian relinquished his 15 per cent of the 'Turkish Petroleum Company,' a consortium that he had formed in 1914 (Anglo–Persian, German and Turkish [British controlled] banks, and Royal Dutch Shell), and in return was awarded five per cent of all the oil produced, for which CFP would pay him the market price.

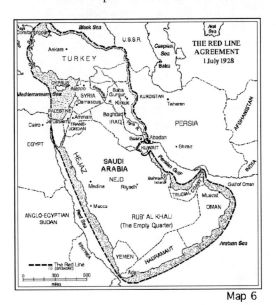

Map 6

Consequently, when in 1925 Major Holmes obtained a concession for Eastern and General in Bahrain, and tried to interest Anglo–Persian and Standard of Jersey in acquiring it, both refused. Gulf, with foreign oil only in Mexico took his offering in 1927. But in 1928 Gulf became part of the American consortium participating in the Red Line Agreement. As two of the members of the agreement had refused Holmes' offer, and any operation required unanimous consent, Gulf looked for a buyer of its Bahrain holdings. Standard of California, like Gulf on the lookout for foreign ventures, bought the concession, for it was not a party to the Red Line agreement. However, a clause in the British protocol with Bahrain and the other amirates under their protection required that development of oil resources be entrusted only to firms based in the Commonwealth. To satisfy this requirement Standard of California set up a Canadian subsidiary to operate the venture with the odd result that longshoremen from Liverpool and roustabouts from Texas found each other's speech a foreign language.

23.    The Saudi claim to the Buraimi oasis was based on these grounds: In 1797 at the beginning of the rapid expansion of the Saudi empire, Oman was temporarily occupied by the Wahhabis and in 1801 a Saudi leader took Buraimi and coöperated with the tribes of the Pirate Coast in seizing vessels, even British ships. Intermittently until 1859 the inhabitants of Buraimi paid tribute to the Saudi amirs, who struggled to obtain a hold on the coastal towns. Desert tribes, the Bani Yas and Awamir, acknowledged fealty and paid taxes, but when the As Saud lost their domain as a result of strife between brothers, the tribes and villagers stopped their contributions. In 1865, the year of Faisal's demise, Pelly demanded compensation from Riyadh for the death of a British subject in Sur, thus acknowledging Saudi sovereignty over Oman, but in 1869 the Saudis were expelled from the nine villages of Buraimi. In the 1920s Saudi tax collectors visited the Buraimi region, but were unable to get the villagers to pay *zakat*, although they extracted some tribute from the Bedu of the area.

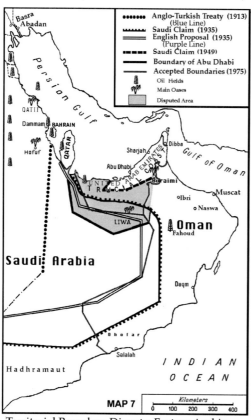

**MAP 7**

Territorial Boundary Dispute: Eastern Arabia
(Oman, Abu Dhabi, Saudi Arabia) including Buraimi Oasis

Data from Benoist-Mechin (1960) and Kelly, J.B. (1964) supplemented and
revised with information from the Oil and Gas Journal and Farsi Map Service, Jedda

The accompanying map *(Map 7)* shows the boundaries proposed by the interested parties. In gray, the area first claimed by the shaikh of Abu Dhabi. If Saudi Arabia's demand of 1949 had been accepted, the area north of the heavy dashed line is all that would have remained to Abu Dhabi and the other amirates of the Trucial Coast. Four-fifths of Abu Dhabi would have gone, including Buraimi and the Liwa oasis, the ancestral home of the shaikh of Abu Dhabi. The thin red line indicates the boundaries accepted under duress by the shaikh of Abu Dhabi in 1974, and also shows a provisional frontier between Saudi Arabia and Oman.

ARAMCO began sending its parties into the area south of Qatar in 1948–49, and planned exploration in the eastern Rub' al Khali, claiming Saudi jurisdiction over a large tract in the south and east. In 1951 Ibn Saud continued to press for his rights at the same time professing his respect for the British who were still a military and naval power in the Persian Gulf. In February 1952 a conference at Dammam on the Saudi claim ended in discord and was adjourned. Late in 1952 the British presence on land was given teeth by the creation of the 'Trucial Oman levies.'

This military unit was formed to counter Saudi plans for territorial aggrandizement and to end the trade in slaves to Riyadh from Oman. On 20 September 1952 a Saudi force of forty entered Hamasa, a village in the Buraimi area claimed then as now by the sultan of Oman. It was transported in ARAMCO vehicles and remained until 13 August 1954 when it was removed. Police detachments from both sides then established themselves in the area, awaiting the outcome of a tribunal to decide the issue of jurisdiction.

Ibn Saud, old and crotchety, said that he would see the force dead rather than withdraw it, but in April 1953, the year of his death, he agreed to arbitration. It was not until July 1954 that Saudi Arabia and Britain agreed to the form of arbitration, and it was only on 11 September 1955 that the tribunal met in Geneva. It was made up of representatives of four neutral nations. For the presentation of evidence Oman and Abu Dhabi were represented by Sir Reader Bullard, as Britain had nineteenth century treaties guaranteeing the integrity of both Oman and the Trucial Amirates. Yusuf Yassin represented Saudi Arabia. Yusuf was caught in attempted bribery of the tribunal and Sir Reader resigned. Shortly thereafter the conference disbanded. In October the British published evidence of large scale bribery of the desert tribes. That same month the Saudi police contingent in Buraimi was evicted by the Trucial Oman levies. Yassin lost face at the Saudi court, but Saud, king after his father's death in 1953, decided to do what he could to annoy the British. He broke off diplomatic relations and provided funds and arms to rebels in Oman. But he was eager to end the stalemate. The outbreak of civil war in the Yemen halted negotiations for a time. Faisal took power in 1958, but waited until 1964 to raise the question again. He rejected the British proposals. In Abu Dhabi leadership changed by force of arms. Faisal approached the new amir with a somewhat reduced demand and was rebuffed. But shortly thereafter Britain announced its plans to withdraw from the Gulf, before its departure setting up the United Arab Amirates, of which Abu Dhabi was the largest in area and resources.

After the British left, a revolutionary group centered in Aden threatened the territory of the sultan of Oman fronting the Arabian Sea. The shaikh of Abu Dhabi, fearful for his own territory, went to Faisal in May 1970 asking for aid. It was given only on condition that he accept the map prepared by Faisal's cohorts showing Saudi territorial demands. The amir kept the Liwa and Buraimi oases, but lost a small oil field in a corridor extending south from the Qatar peninsula. Finally, on 29 July 1974 the map was initialed by both parties.

24. On 8 July 1939 I was working in a small, makeshift laboratory peering into a binocular microscope at chips of rock taken in June 1938 from Well No. 7 when it had attained a depth of nearly a mile below the surface. This 'wildcat' (exploratory well) was the first to penetrate the main 'Arab D' reservoir of the Dammam structure, expressed in the topography as a hill known as Jebel Dhahran. As part of my indoc-

trination into the geology of Arabia I was looking at the sponge-like limestone in which oil had been stored for many tens of millions of years. The summer sun was hot on the corrugated iron roof of the wooden shack. I was about to remove my shirt when a high voice piped, 'Shoof, Sahib, Shoof!' And a small tan-faced boy in a dirty white nightgown pulled at my arm, urging me to come out.

Down the hill a half-mile away the tall metal derrick of Well No. 12 was collapsing into an inferno of orange flame above which rose a column of black smoke, spreading into a great billowing cloud. Under the weight of overlying rock, the gas in the reservoir had been compressed long ago into a volume many times smaller than that which it would occupy at the surface. That day, a part of the mile-long column of heavy mud that held the oil and gas in check had been removed in preparation for perforating the casing opposite the productive zone. Some of the gas escaped and by accident was ignited. Then, before the great valves that closed the well-head could be activated, the crew had been forced to run for their lives. Some were lost.

25.  Maria Theresa dollar. A large silver coin of Austria–Hungary, minted long after the dissolution of the empire destroyed by World War I. Although it bears the profile of a bosomy Maria Theresa, it has been widely used in the Middle East, for its content of silver does not vary.

Although all of these coins are dated 1788, the dollar was minted well into the twentieth century and used for trade in the Levant and North Africa. According to some reports its value was five or six to the English pound, but Lorimer, writing before 1908, says that in al Hasa its value was one shilling 10 1/4 pence. In Asir in 1922 Rihani found it to be worth fifty American cents. Cheesman in Hofuf in 1924 determined its value to be two shillings fourpence. Thomas in southern Oman in 1930–31 indicates that it was equal to one shilling fourpence there.... There and at that time it was the only negotiable currency among the tribes.

26.  Gertrude Bell was a rich Yorkshireman's daughter. Flouting Victorian convention, she traveled extensively in the Middle East, learning Persian in addition to the European languages commonly acquired by women of her class and intelligence. She became a well-known mountain climber, translated Persian poetry, and while traveling in the Levant and northern Arabia learned Arabic. She aided archeologists in uncovering traces of Sumerian and other ancient civilizations.

As the First World War began she was chosen to work in the Arab Bureau (British Intelligence in Cairo) but en route was drafted to Iraq where she was put on the staff of Sir Percy Cox, then chief civilian administrator with the British army. She wrote reports concerning Arab tribes and their posture in relation to the British army and the civil administration of Mesopotamia. In carrying out this work she met tribal leaders and compiled voluminous dossiers on their genealogy and the tracts they claimed as their *dirah*. Her critique of the war-time relations between army and civil authorities reached high levels at Whitehall and caused changes in the chain of command. After the war when the British government decided to install Faisal as king

she continued her work, judging the reaction of the population to the several procla-
mations regarding self-determination by the League of Nations and by the British. In
1926 she died in Baghdad, while working as curator of an archeological museum.
She was, perhaps, the first European woman that Ibn Saud met. After his return to
Riyadh from the Durbar she was a favorite in his repertoire of imitations. Her shrill,
'Ya, Abdul Aziz,' and her attempts to question him, and, perhaps, to instruct him
were a subject for jest in the court.

27. After Rihani left him in the spring, Ibn Saud remained in Riyadh for many months,
but on 15 January 1924 arrived in Hofuf on a visit to his cousin Abdullah ibn Jiluwi,
amir of Hasa. There Cheesman saw him. Although he does not mention a disfigure-
ment, the dedicated ornithologist reports that he discussed the illness with the
sultan, who described it as 'a fever of the eyes and face.' The ruler made light of the
malady, saying that Dr. Dame, fortunately in Riyadh at the time, had cured him. This
may have been only bravado for other writers say that all the left side of the face was
affected and that incompetent treatment failed to halt the very painful ravages of the
disease. When infection invaded the eye a specialist was called in from Egypt, but
came too late to save its sight. In 1925 at Bahra Sir Gilbert Clayton saw that the eye
still required treatment. The lid had drooped and the skin around it had puckered,
destroying the symmetry of the features.

In 1947 Dr. E. A. White of the American legation examined the king and reported
that 'the eyes reveal blindness of the left eye due to corneal scarring....' The doctor
assumed the injury to be the result of trachoma because of the prevalence of that disease in the Middle East.

Van der Meulen says that for months on end the monarch was unable to do his usual
amount of work and Philby mentions that his absences gave rise to rumors that he
had died, in turn provoking a rash of scurrilous obituaries in the Hejazi press.

28. The cables linking the Persian Gulf with India had been laid in 1864 from Gwadur, a
port in eastern Baluchistan owned by the sultan of Oman, to Malcolm's Inlet on the
eastern side of the Musandam peninsula where it joined a land link across the
mountainous spine of the peninsula to Elphinstone's Inlet on the western side. From
there a cable was laid to Persia. It reached Bushire in March 1864. Officially, direct
communication between India, Bushire, and London began only 27 January 1865
because, although the cable from Bushire to Fao had been tested in April 1964, the
overland telegraph of the Turkish government from Fao to Basra was not completed
until January of the next year after acrimonious dispute with the British concerning
the routing of the Baghdad–Basra line.

This circuitous route by sea and land was necessary to insure uninterrupted communication because the Persian government could not control the coastal tribes of
Baluchistan who would have destroyed an overland system repeatedly, or demanded
impossibly high bribes for allowing it to operate. Farther north, a land line from
Khanaquin to Bushire completed late in 1864 gave an alternate route for communicating with Europe. A cable laid down in 1860 from Egypt through the Red and
Arabian Seas to Karachi failed soon after its installation.

29. Turki ibn Abdul Aziz was the first of Ibn Saud's children. In *The Heart of Arabia (pp. 316–17)*, Philby describes him briefly as he was in 1918:

> Women had not the same attraction for him as for his father, and he told me that it was only for war and the chase he had any real passion. He had struck me ... as being exceedingly delicate ... and he was certainly exceedingly handsome. Shorter by a good deal than his father, but with several years of growth before him, he was of lighter build, and his thin pale face and dark eyes, set in a framework of plaited locks drooping on either shoulder from beneath his silk headkerchief, betokened a physique little suited to the rough environment in which he had been born and bred.

30. The Buraimi dispute (the topic of n. 23 concerning the limits of Saudi jurisdiction in the eastern Rub' al Khali, the Trucial Coast and western Oman), had curious repercussions during its adjudication, to the point of raising a question as to whether or not Ibn Saud had in fact signed the Saudi–Ottoman treaty dated 4 Rajab 1332. (15 May 1914, according to the United Kingdom *Memorial* of 1955. Rentz says that the Arabic date is actually some two weeks later.) If Ibn Saud signed the document on 29 May as Goldberg postulates, then the Saudis were legally bound by the treaties between the Ottoman government and Great Britain because they were then Turkish subjects.

If so, Ibn Saud had no claim to the Buraimi oasis for the Ottoman–British Convention regarding Turkish juridiction in eastern Arabia had been signed 9 March 1913. On the map accompanying it a 'Blue Line' running south on 20° E. longitude from near Oqair (*see Map 7, n. 23*) left a vast area to the east free of Turkish jurisdiction. This would explain the change in Philby's stance regarding the treaty. In his 1930 book, *Arabia*, he admits the existence of a signed Saudi–Ottoman treaty. The Buraimi dispute had not yet erupted. But in his 1952 volume, *Arabian Jubilee*, he states that negotiations, 'resulted only in a verbal understanding that Ibn Saud should formally recognise Ottoman suzerainty.' In *Saudi Arabia (1955)*, he backs off even farther: There was no agreement but 'a tentative understanding was reached, in which Ibn Saud gave a verbal understanding to recognise the Sultan's suzerainty.'

This same tactic was followed by the authors of the Saudi Arabia *Memorial* who stated: 'The Saudi archives have failed to yield any text of a perfected Saudi–Turkish Agreement' and supplemented that argument by saying, 'If it existed it was certainly not entered into good faith by Turkey.' G. Rentz *(1977)* argued that since no treaty was signed at Subaihiya, Ibn Saud could not have agreed to one. Goldberg (*Article, 1984*) shows that Ibn Saud's agent carried the treaty to Riyadh for his signature, and that Ibn Saud himself informed British political agents that he had signed a treaty and outlined to them its terms and their possible consequences in relation to his future dealings with England.

The British position in 1955 at the Hague Court of Justice was: A treaty between Ibn Saud and the Turks had been made and signed. It was valid because in the 1914 Convention which was ratified (the 1913 Convention was not) the 'Blue Line' is mentioned, and is shown on the map accompanying this Convention at 20° E. longitude where the 'Purple Line' running at 45° northeast from Aden joins it. Like the

'Blue Line' the 'Purple Line' marked a proposed eastern limit of Turkish influence. (*See Map 7, n. 23.*)

31. Black Stone. Probably a meteorite broken up on entry into the atmosphere. It consists of three large pieces and some fragments of nearly black stone, held in a ring of lighter stone banded in silver. The rite of kissing and touching it was incorporated into the ritual of the Pilgrimage by Mohammed the Prophet (Mohammed ibn Abdullah ibn Abd al Muttalib). It is embedded in the east wall of the Ka'aba, a large cube of gray stone and marble in the courtyard of the Great Mosque of Mecca. The Ka'aba was already an object of reverence and pilgrimage in pre-Islamic days, presumably because it held the Black Stone.

# Addenda

# I. The Tribes of Arabia

In the time of Ibn Saud the Arab of the desert thought himself the élite of the race. Some claimed descent from Ishmael, son of Abraham and Hagar, others from an even older patriarch named Qahtan. His townsman brother found the nomad overproud of his lineage, and both fickle and untrustworthy. But the teachings of Mohammed Abdul Wahhab (1703–1787) gave to both a religious dogma that united them in one purpose—to propagate Moslem Unitarianism. In furthering the dissemination of their beliefs they also shared the dangers of the battlefield, although far apart in the rhythms of everyday living. The Bedu looked down upon the *hadhari*, a man who lived a soft life in a fixed abode and had access to the fleshpots of the town; the villager thought his nomadic cousin, a *Badawi* (Bedu), a slothful, untutored and unreliable semi-savage.

The *Badia* owned camels and lived in black tents woven of the wool of sheep and hair of goats. When the forage in one part of their *dirah* (tribal range) was exhausted, they moved on. The life was demanding and uncertain for it depended on the quality of pasture. In a year with little rain the growth might be insufficient to nourish the grazing animals. In a short time starvation could ensue, with death for the animals and peril for the herder and his family (*n. 10*). Under such conditions a patriarchal system had evolved millennia before our time. Groups of families shared the range and its vagaries under the leadership of an acknowledged chieftain. The leadership became hereditary in the sense that a family of eminent ancestry and wealthier than most was able to assert its dominance forcefully and to command the respect and allegiance of its dependents. Nevertheless, even these chieftains, called *shaikhs*, had to be recognized and accepted by the group, most of whom were linked by consanguinity.

Even today the shaikhly family and its followers constitute a tribe. If numerous, a tribe may have several subgroups known as Sections, each under a leader who may also be called *shaikh*. To complicate matters, the tribes rank themselves in a hierarchy based on lines of descent. Clans that trace their lineage to Abraham or Qahtan consider themselves *sharif*, or noble. They include many of the tribes whose *dirah* are shown on the accompanying map. These true dwellers of the desert spent nine months of the year breeding and tending their camels, moving from one part of their tribal range to another. They looked down on semi-nomadic tribes who spent part of the time encamped close to towns or villages; those who raised only sheep and goats were also thought to be inferior. The

143

'Anaiza consider themselves the aristocrats of the nomads. The Saud family belongs to the *Masalikh* section of that tribe and the shaikhs of Kuwait and Bahrain are of the *Amarat* section.

The ubiquity of the motor vehicle and the consequent decrease in the value and use of the camel for transport has changed the way of life of the Bedu. But in the days of Ibn Saud great trains of beasts carried dates from Hofuf to Riyadh. In 1940 I saw them in their hundreds, shambling along head to tail at four miles an hour with a huge bale of dates on either flank, their groans of displeasure punctuating their drivers' discordant wails of song. Even then overloaded trucks not adapted for desert travel appeared from time to time in their wake.

The limits of each tribe's grazing rights had been established for hundreds of years before those days of transition, and their *wasm* (tribal mark) was on the thigh, neck, or cheek of each camel, its location depending on the custom of the tribe. If large stones or outcrops of rock lay within the tribal limits, they too would be inscribed with the *wasm*. *Rjims* (heaps of stone) marked prominent geographic features, most commonly high points. Sometimes they too bore the *wasm*.

In times of drought no tribe limited its wandering entirely to its *dirah*, the large area in which lay its permanent wells and its forage. How large it was depended on the quality of the pasturage, that is the number of bushes per acre of *'arfaj* and *hamdh*, and the abundance of *nassi*, a coarse grass, the three together comprising the camels' favorite and most nutritious food. In a region well provided with these plants a *dirah* of some 120 by 180 miles, an irregular oval in most cases, was enough for a tribe or a section of a large tribe. The *dirah* is owned jointly by all the members of the tribe. Its limits are known precisely and passed on from one generation to the next.

There are over a hundred nomadic tribes and sections of tribes in Saudi Arabia and neighboring Yemen, Oman and the United Arab Amirates, with at least thirty more in Iraq and Syria. It is doubtful that the old patriarchal and feudal relationships within and between tribes are maintained to the degree that existed before and during the early decades of the twentieth century. Yet the tribes still claim ownership of their *dirah*, and presumably seek to develop its agricultural possibilities or to exploit any other profitable element of their ownership with the aid of the state and its agencies.

Before cars and trucks replaced the camel for transport, the favorite pursuit of the Bedu was a foray to seize these 'ships of the desert' from other tribes. The raiders sometimes traveled hundreds of miles to surprise their victims. In the adulation paid a successful leader and his followers raiding can be compared to the American passion for team sports like football. Youths awaited eagerly the time that they would be old enough to go along. But in the desert the prize was tangible and valuable: other people's camels and sometimes their sheep.

Success required skill in the desert crafts of fast and secret travel to achieve surprise, a profound knowledge of the terrain and its wells, good mounts, a will and toughness to endure hardship, and, most important in the eyes of the nomad, *Hadh*—luck. The combat involved was fought by the rules. Women were inviolate and were always left enough from the spoils to start over. If you saw defeat, you did not stay to be killed but ran away to fight another day. As a result, deaths were usually few. Only when the *Ikhwan* in the name of religion killed every male and took everything that could be carried away did raiding cease to be a kind of sport that the nomad found necessary for his honor and his well-being. When Ibn Saud discouraged it in his realm, he incurred the resentment, if not the hatred, of many of the desert folk.

Camels were stolen most frequently from members of 'enemy' tribes. The causes of enmity are often lost in the past, and many feuds are now almost traditional, but some are new. The Mutair of northern Nejd, mainstay of the *Ikhwan* in its heyday, were until recently, and perhaps still are, most bitter against their neighbors to the north, the Shammar and the Dhafir of southern Iraq. Since the days of the *Ikhwan* rebellion they have been friends of the 'Ajman who were allied with them against Ibn Saud. The 'Ajman are closely allied with the Murra of the great sand sea. Their hereditary enemies are the Awasim who were formerly subordinate to them. The Awasim are not *sharif*, and intermarry mainly with others of their status like the Rashaida of Kuwait and the Hutaim. The sections of the great 'Anaiza tribe of Syria fight each other, but the hereditary enemy is the Shammar. Individuals can ignore these relationships under certain conditions.

Before the time of Ibn Saud warfare between paramount shaikhs differed from raiding mainly in scale. Instead of tens, hundreds or sometimes several thousand comprised an army made up of cavalry, camelry, and infantry. Nomadic tribes had no cannon, so their strategy was to have a larger force, deployed tactically in surprise when possible. Possession or seizure of wells was crucial to success and the maneuvers to achieve this end required expert skills and intelligence provided by informers and spies. Siege against walled towns succeeded only if the defenders were taken unaware or ran out of food. Early in the nineteenth century Turkish victories against dogged resistance required prolonged investment of towns and forts and bombardment to demolish their walls. Heavy losses among the invaders were made up by continual reinforcement in men and supplies. The Arab townsmen fought to the death when cornered, sometimes aided by nomadic relatives harassing the attackers. Ibn Saud used cannon against Jedda and Medina, but only sporadically. His successes there came from breaking the will to resist.

Over the centuries a code of conduct unique to the desert arose because of the harshness of the environment and the lack of settled communities. One of these unwritten laws was that of *Qasir*, that is the rights of a neighbor encamped close to you. Usually these were family and mutual protection was a matter of course. But anyone of another tribe granted permission to pitch his tent in the vicinity became an *aziz*, a 'dear one', and was shielded by his protector against any threat. This custom involved the honor not only of the individual but also of the tribe. Commonly, the protection concerned only recompense to the *aziz* for loss of property in raids, but included the safeguard of himself and his family from molestation of any kind.

More widely known to westerners was the custom of employing a *rafiq* when undertaking a trip. The word *rafiq* means friend or companion and his duty was to insure that you passed safely through the territory claimed by his tribe. For each new *dirah* traversed another *rafiq* was chosen, but the current 'friend' was obliged to help you obtain one. Custom required payment of a fee for this service which insured your safety, for it involved the honor of the tribe as well as that of the individual. Under Ibn Saud the custom was discouraged, for the safety of travelers became inviolate.

The traveler was protected by other customs—those of hospitality. In the desert if you saw the black tents, whether or not those of your tribe, and wanted shelter or only a drink, you had but to approach them on the open side and stop. Once noticed you would be invited into the portion of the tent reserved for guests and offered the best that your host could muster. This welcome could last for up to three days, but usually only food and lodging for a night was asked. The mere fact of having partaken of food or even just coffee gave you security from molestation for three days. No payment was expected or tendered. Today, with the ubiquity of pickups and trucks such hospitality is not so common nor is it needed in the deserts of Saudi Arabia where a day's journey on wheels easily exceeds a week's travel by camel, even where there are no roads.

Beside the customs governing the reception and guidance of travelers, rules of conduct existed regarding relationships within the family. Both marriage and divorce were easy: marriage of a young, unmarried woman required a gift of money to the bride, a dress or two, and bedding, usually a red quilt. Sometimes a brideprice was exacted from the prospective groom by the father who would lose a daughter. The ceremony could then take place immediately, performed by anyone professing religious leanings, commonly a *mutawa'ah*. The priest asked the man if he was willing to take the girl (never present) and his reply of 'yes' before witnesses was followed by a question regarding the willingness of the bride's family (her father or brother) to the union. The consummation followed at once in a tent pitched by the bridegroom close to that of her father, but by unwritten law the bride's father and her brothers absented themselves from the aftermath of the ceremony. If a woman had been widowed or divorced, the arrangements for the marriage could be made directly with her, because she herself fixed any marriage portion offered. The declaration before witnesses by both parties was still required.

Divorce was even easier. The man had only to say before witnesses, '*Talliq, talliq, talliq.*' The rejected wife bore no disgrace. She kept her dowry and could at once look for a new husband. The system resulted in most women's having been married at least two or three times by the age of thirty, and if desirable to men, even seven or eight. Adultery was rare and usually ended in the death of the woman at the hands of her relatives.

Every child, male or female, on reaching puberty could expect the parents to find a suitable mate. On the other hand, a girl was bound (*bint 'am*) to marry her cousin—the son of her father's brother—unless the son renounced his right to her. Is she refused, her destined consort could forbid her marriage to another or kill her without paying blood money. No man could marry his son's divorced wife or his widow, his brother's or sister's daughters, or his foster sister. The *sharif*, male or female, was forbidden to marry an inferior. If so, the offender could never return to the tribe—the penalty was death on sight.

How strictly these injunctions are observed today is problematic, given the great change made in society by the motor car and industrialization. However, Wahhabite dogma is still in force in Saudi Arabia and its conservatism may have preserved many traditions and rules of conduct. In a pastoral population away from centers of progress old customs are more easily maintained but the number that still follow that mode of life is difficult to estimate given the influx and reflux of foreigners and the difficulty of counting nomads scattered sparsely in their *dirah*. Estimates of the total population of Saudi Arabia in 1996 range from 14 to 19.5 million but of this number only one-fifth is rural and the larger part of this category are farmers. The number of nomads is reportedly decreasing annually, but camels are still prized for food and milk although little used for transport *(Violet Dickson 1971)*. Many Bedu youths have become paid workers in industry and a few are affluent owing to profits from goods and services. The independence of movement and self-reliance characteristic of the nomad is presumably disappearing along with the customs and traditions that made him unique.

The map of tribal *dirah* on the following page is taken from Dickson's classic, *The Arab of the Desert*, published in 1949 but based on information obtained in the two preceding decades. A number of tribes living in Asir do not appear on this map. They are sedentary and their *dirah* occupy only a small tract of predominantly upland terrain, some of which is cultivated.

Everywhere on the peninsula the limits of those *dirah* shown can only be rough approximations, but the effort involved in their delineation was never matched by other authors who have published on this matter. Their maps show only the names of the tribes and sections placed more or less in the area of their wanderings. Considerable diversity in names and locations exists in these works and in the transliteration of the Arabic. The more accessible references are listed in the lower right corner of Map 8.

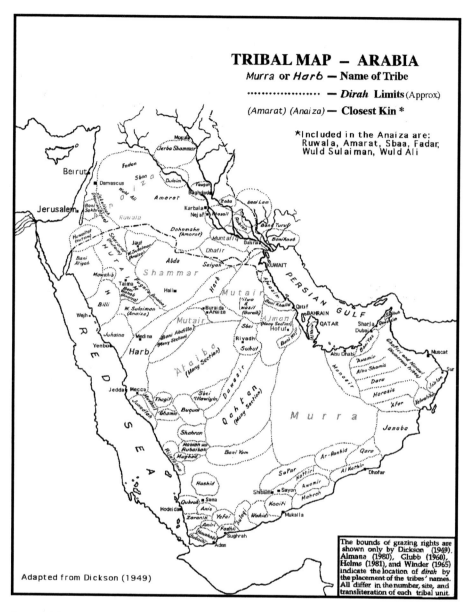

Adapted from Dickson (1949)                                    MAP 8

The map shows clearly the relationship between the area of a *dirah* and the supply of food for man or beast that it can produce. Other factors blur this correlation, but the number of small tribal holdings in Asir, Yemen and Oman reflect the greater productivity of these areas because of the higher rainfall in nountainous terrain near a coast. Too, rugged topography favors fragmentation of ownership. In the marshlands of southern Iraq plentiful food is presumably the reason for the existence of numerous dirah of moderate size. Near Hofuf and in the Qasim cultivation is favored by accessible groundwater and fertile soil. In these choice areas tribal affiliation where all land is held in common is less relevant because of the number of land-owning *hadhari*.

# II. Saud Family History
## (1446–1891)

**Growth:** At about the middle of the fifteenth century the Saud family was invited by a relative to move from al Hasa, the province of Arabia bordering the Persian Gulf, to Nejd, a central inland tract. *(See Maps 1 and 2.)* The family prospered and in 1726 established a flourishing capital, Dhariya. Until the latter half of the eighteenth century the family's hegemony increased but slowly, but in 1744 it espoused the cause of a puritan (God is One and Indivisible, and in prayer only He can be addressed) religious reformer, Mohammed ibn Abdul Wahhab (1703–1787) who had come to the Saudi capital. Because of his advocacy of forcible proselytization along with other tenets appealing to the nomad such as stoning for adultery, Abdul Wahhab, although a learned and widely traveled theologian, had been driven from his home in Awaina by death-threats from a shaikh of the Bani Khalid, a powerful tribe of al Hasa.

Between the years 1765 and 1803 a single Saudi amir (Abdul Aziz ibn Mohammed, see genealogical chart) guided fanatical converts to Wahhab's creed in the conquest of much of Arabia. Riyadh opened its gates to him in 1773, the province of al Hasa was overrun in the years 1793–1796, and much of the shaikhdom of Oman was converted to Wahhabism in 1797.

Rapid aggrandizement began with the occupation of the coastal lands on the Persian Gulf and a large part of Oman. Thereafter, raids terrorized the region to the north. On 20 April 1801 Wahhabi zealots sacked Karbala near Baghdad, revered by the Shia sect as the site of the tomb of its founder Husain, the son of Ali, Mohammed's son-in-law. In the west, Taïf was taken in 1802 with the slaughter of all males. Mecca, the Holy of Holies, was seized in 1802 and annexed in 1806. Medina fell to Saud ibn Abdul Aziz (dubbed 'The Great') in 1804. In 1810, Wahhabis plundered the tomb of Mohammed in Medina, selling and distributing relics and jewels. That same year their forces roamed freely in Iraq, reaching the outskirts of Baghdad and threatening Damascus in Syria. By 1811, the Wahhabi empire extended from Oman to Aleppo, and from the Mediterranean to the Persian Gulf. But the conquerors were hated and feared because of their intolerance, brutal killings, and pillage. In 1803, Abdul Aziz was assassinated by a Shiite in revenge for the sacking of Karbala.

**Downfall:** The titular rulers of the Hejaz, the Turks, sent several strong expeditionary forces and coerced or bribed local tribes to help vanquish the fanatics who had despoiled and desecrated the sacrosanct cities of Medina and Mecca. All of these early efforts failed.

In 1811, in response to the desecration of Mohammed's tomb in Medina, the sultan of the Ottoman Empire in Constantinople ordered the pasha of Egypt, Mohammed Ali, to free the Hejaz and to destroy the abodes of the fanatics. Preliminary action by cavalry units retook the port of Yenbo. A son of the pasha, Tusun, led a well-equipped army provided with cannon and and a siege train from Yenbo to the southern Hejaz. The invaders took Medina in November 1812 and occupied Mecca in February 1813, but met strong resistance and were defeated in battle in an attempt to penetrate into Nejd. Later Tusun was approached by Nejdi tribesmen disillusioned with Wahhabism and with their aid reached ar Rass where he was blockaded. However, the Saudi Amir, Abdullah ibn Saud, fearing that all of his supporters would defect and accept Turkish rule, negotiated a truce which was broken by the Egyptians. In July 1815, another expeditionary force under Mohammed Ali himself returned to Medina and defeated a large Wahhabi army near Taïf. But the ruler of Egypt heard that the Sublime Porte was planning to unseat him and returned to Cairo.

There, he hastened to form another army made up of 2,000 cavalrymen and 3,600 infantry which was sent to Arabia under the command of his adopted son, Ibrahim. This army, even stronger than its predecessor, advanced into the Qasim. *(See Maps 1 and 2.)* Many cannon under the command of a French artilleryman battered down the walls of towns that refused to capitulate. Some of them resisted strongly and thus delayed the advance. Hundreds of Egyptian soldiers died before one of these towns, ar Rass. In October 1817 the siege there was given up after four months of obstinate resistance, but troops were left in the area to keep the town powerless militarily. Buraida and Anaiza were occupied shortly thereafter but by then five months had passed since the army's departure from Medina. In January 1818 Shagra was taken after a month's siege. Although some of the tribes (Harb, 'Ataiba, Mutair, Bani Khalid) aided the invaders, other Bedu harassed the long march toward the fortified Saudi stronghold and capital, Dhariya. Repeated reinforcements came from the Hejaz to make good the continuous depletion in men and supplies caused by this dogged resistance.

The invaders arrived before Dhariya in March 1818. A host of defenders manned the thick, high walls of the city and the forts near it, all sited along the banks of Wadi Hanifa. The epic and bloody siege was long and brutal with many episodes of courage and sacrifice by the defenders, but the city at last fell on 11 September. In return for a promise of clemency for his relatives the Saudi Amir, Abdullah, agreed to being executed in public. He was sent from Egypt to Constantinople where he was beheaded in December 1818. In June 1819, in accordance with the orders of Mohammed Ali, Dhariya was totally and utterly destroyed. At that time some four hundred of the As Saud were deported to Egypt and many more were rounded up and transported later. The Turkish conquerors made a conscious effort to crush the political, military, and religious structure of the As Saud régime.

The order from Mohammed Ali ordering the destruction of Dhariya also required that Nejd be evacuated by his forces. Before leaving, the soldiers felled the walls of many towns and demolished forts previously untouched. The leader of the retiring force, Ibrahim, was in Medina in July and, after a series of unsuccessful forays into the Asir, left for Cairo in November.

An in-law of the As Saud, Mohammed ibn Mishari al Mu'ammar, became ruler of Nejd, probably installed and supported by Ibrahim. He attempted unsuccessfully to reëstablish himself in Dhariya. In a few months one of the true As Saud, Mishari ibn Abdur Rahman, returned to Nejd from Egypt and assumed the title of amir. At first Ibn Mu'ammar recognized his authority, but shortly thereafter seized power again. Mishari ibn Abdur Rahman was taken away by the Turks and died in captivity in 1821. Other As Saud, among them the Amir Turki ibn Abdullah, escaped ibn Mu'ammar's attempts to capture them, won over the population to their cause and established hegemony in much of Nejd. Mohammed Ali, learning of this resurgence of the As Saud, ordered that Nejd be reoccupied.

Late in the autumn of 1820 the new Turkish leader, Husain Bey, arrived in the Qasim with a large army. His rule was marked by excessive taxation and acts of cruelty. The army invested Riyadh where Turki and his followers, greatly outnumbered, had taken refuge. The fort surrendered on a promise of amnesty. Turki escaped just before the surrender and went into hiding. To keep order in the chief towns the Ottomans installed garrisons of Moroccan and Albanian troops. These vicious conscripts levied oppressive taxes and tortured, robbed, and killed many of their inhabitants. Anarchy began again everywhere in the country, the Bedu attacking each other and the townspeople, already suffering from a prolonged drought and the subsequent shortages of food. During the first days of 1822 Husain Bey was killed and his command almost completely destroyed. Only the garrisoned towns remained in Ottoman hands.

Another Turkish commander arrived in the spring of 1822. He, Hassan Bey Abu Zahir, was less barbarous than his predecessor, but his attempts to restore order were hindered by his efforts to collect taxes. In the end the Turks taxed only six key towns in which they maintained garrisons. In 1823, Turki ibn Abdullah began a revolt against the invaders. He soon had support from several shaikhs of the districts of Sudair, Mahmal, and Munaikh. The outnumbered Ottomans withdrew from all of Nejd except Riyadh and its near neighbor Manfuha. Determined to oust them, Turki began an offensive and took the town of Durma, only a short distance west of the capital. Thereafter, in a series of almost bloodless coups he won over to his standard many of the towns of the Qasim and Sudair. In August 1824 he invested Riyadh. Granted amnesty, the Ottoman garrison departed for Medina. The remaining towns soon came under Turki's jurisdiction.

**Revival:** By the end of 1824 Turki ibn Abdullah had reëstablished the As Saud as rulers of central Nejd and in the following years reasserted his hegemony over the districts of Washm, Aflaj, and Haïl. In 1828 his son Faisal returned from captivity in Egypt. In 1830, aided by his father, Faisal retook al Hasa after bitter and costly battles with tribesmen of the Bani Khalid who were aided by sections of several tribes including the 'Anaiza and Mutair. In 1832 Turki took control of the Buraimi oasis and in 1833 the whole western shore of the Persian Gulf paid tribute to the Wahhabis who in return supported Qawasimi piracy in the Gulf.

In May 1834, Turki was assassinated in Riyadh at the instigation of Mishari ibn Abdur Rahman, a relative who had been made governor of Manfuha. His son, Faisal ibn Turki, became amir and imam of the Saudis. As amir, he appointed Abdullah ibn Ali ar Rashid governor of Haïl, a move his sons would regret. *(See Rasheed [1991, p. 43] for another version of Abdullah ibn Ali's accession to the amirate of Haïl.)*

Another invasion by the Turks in 1836 commanded by Isma'il Bey Pasha and a Saudi puppet governor, Khalid ibn Abdul Aziz as Saud,[*] regained much territory in the Qasim apparently because of a lack of will in the Wahhabi forces for battle against a relative of the late head of the family. Faisal fled to Hofuf where he remained until July 1837. During his absence more determined supporters in the Hauta area of southern Nejd defeated the Egyptian forces in several battles. Faisal returned to Nejd posthaste and besieged Isma'il in Riyadh. Because of Bedu attacks he was forced to lift the siege, and thereafter was unsuccessful in an attempt to come to an arrangement with Khalid. From al Hasa he continued to resist the invaders.

In 1838, Khurshid Pasha, a new Turkish leader, arrived in Tharmida and prepared for battle. Accompanied by Khalid he advanced eastward to the Gulf. Faisal fought hard, but in the end retreated to Dilam south of Riyadh where he strengthened the fortifications and attracted supporters. After some months Khurshid took his army south to Dilam, and, after a series of battles and a siege during which he bombarded the town, succeeded in breaking the will of the defenders. Faisal was captured on 19 December 1838 and sent to Egypt for the second time. He remained a prisoner there for nearly four years.

Under Khurshid's aegis Khalid ibn Saud continued to govern. Mistakenly, he relied on Turkish support to maintain himself in power, rather than attempting to win the favor of the people. Because of his attempts to seize power on the littoral of the Persian Gulf, British diplomatic pressure forced Mohammed Ali to order Khurshid home in March 1840. Khalid ruled for only one more year, still a vassal of the Ottomans. Deposed by a kinsman Abdullah ibn Thunaian as Saud, he ended as a pensioner of Mohammed Ali in the Hejaz.

Ibn Thunaian had governed for only ten months when Abdullah ibn Rashid, governor of Haïl since 1834, advised Faisal that the time was ripe for his return. Late in 1843 the As Saud *détenu* escaped from prison in Egypt by making a perilous descent from a fortress prison on a rope. He arrived safely in Haïl and sent messages to his partisans that he had come back. Various factions in the Qasim agreed to support him and ibn Rashid gave him men, arms, and money. All of his old supporters joined him and on 23 May 1843 his army entered Riyadh. Ibn Thunaian was killed. Thereafter, Faisal succeeded in reëstablishing dominion over the territory held by his family in 1800 with the exception of the peripheral regions of Oman, Yemen, and the Hejaz. Bahrain came under British protection after 1861 but Buraimi remained under tenuous Wahhabi jurisdiction. Although Saudi relations with the Rashids remained cordial (Abdullah ibn Rashid died and was replaced by Talal ibn Abdullah [1848–1868]) the Shammari chieftains began to exhibit a degree of independence, in particular in their relations with the towns of Anaiza and Buraida in the Qasim which strained against Saudi overlordship. Intermittently the Bedouin tribes, particularly the Ajman, rebelled against

---

[*]    A brother of Abdullah ibn Saud, beheaded after the fall of Dhariya in 1818. Khalid was held prisoner in Cairo until he agreed to rule under Turkish domination.

Nejdi authority and were severely punished. Faisal died 2 December 1865, aged and blind. (Some Arab sources say 10 December.)

Faisal had four sons. As he aged, he named three of them to be heads of the provinces of his state: Abdullah, governor of centrally located Aridh and coastal al Hasa; Saud, head of Asir on the Red Sea and land-locked Nejran; Mohammed, ruler of the fertile Qasim and Washm in the north. The youngest, Abdur Rahman, who would beget Abdul Aziz the king, lived with Faisal until his demise. He was then fifteen years old.

**Decline:** Six months before his death Faisal chose Abdullah as his successor. Undoubtedly this irked Saud who had a long-enduring rivalry with his brothers, particularly with Abdullah, whom he came to hate. Within the year Saud had fomented unrest in certain tribes in Nejran and Asir but an army led by Mohammed defeated him in battle at Ma'tala, a small settlement fifty miles west of Sulaiyil. Saud was wounded and fled east to shelter with the Murra and later went on to Buraimi.

Five years later, on 21 December 1870, Saud, aided mainly by Ajman and Subai tribesmen of al Hasa, fought again and won, seizing all of eastern Arabia after defeating a loyalist army, mainly townsmen from Nejd, at Ain Judah about sixty miles northwest of Hofuf. Mohammed, who once again had led the Nejdi army, was imprisoned and held in Dammam on the shores of the Gulf. Abdullah, inexplicably losing his nerve, left Riyadh and journeyed northward. He was refused help at Anaiza, and from a camp in the desert north of Buraida he sent a call for help to Midhat Pasha, the governor of Baghdad. But after finding allies among the Qahtan, in mid-February 1871 Abdullah returned to his capital which was not then in danger of assault.

His return was short-lived, for early in April 1871 when Saud's army approached Riyadh he left once again with an escort of artillery, much of his army and his personal possessions. He was planning to go south to the *dirah* of the Qahtan tribe where he hoped to set up a government in exile. The caravan was intercepted and taken intact by Saud's forces a few miles from Riyadh. Abdullah escaped capture but late in July was again beaten in battle by Saud at the town of Barrah some fifty miles northwest of Riyadh. Midhat Pasha's messenger offering shelter reached him shortly afterward, but Abdullah managed to reach the Turkish lines in al Hasa only in September.

Turkish forces commanded by Nafidh Pasha had arrived in al Hasa on 26 May 1871 by sea and by land. The makeshift navy of seven small warships with cannon and three hundred boats carrying four thousand men, mainly infantry, offloaded on the sandy beach at Ras Tanura. A thousand Muntafiq horsemen arrived overland. Qatif was taken after a three-hour bombardment of the fort from the sea. Led by Saud's son Abdul Aziz, the defenders of Dammam fled although in possession of eleven cannon. Mohammed, imprisoned since December 1870, was released from captivity in the Portuguese fort there.

In July the Turks left their temporary headquarters at Qatif and after a fifteen-day march in the summer heat the army reached Hofuf and occupied it without resistance. In their original proclamation after the landing the Ottomans had designated Abdullah a *Qaimaqam*. He soon found that he was to be deported to Baghdad, for the Turks planned to take direct control of Nejd. A virtual prisoner, only weeks after he had joined the Turks he used a ruse to escape. Free, he headed for Riyadh. When Midhat Pasha arrived at Hofuf in November to inspect his conquest and found his quisling gone, he issued a decree stripping him of the title of district governor. But the Ottoman army was in a bad way. Of the more than 3,000 Turks in the force, less than 2,000 were fit for duty, and the Arabs, including a contingent from Kuwait, were drifting away. Nevertheless, they were fit enough to beat off attacks by Murra, Ajman and Subai tribesmen led by Saud's son. Abdullah saw at least one of these encounters during his short stay with his 'protectors'.

Abdullah returned to his capital only after the townspeople, led by his uncle, Abdullah ibn Turki, the dead Faisal's brother, had chased Saud from Riyadh. The populace had become enraged by the insolence and rapacity of his army.

For a time Saud lay low in Qatar. Later, in al Kharj, he attempted to come to terms with Abdullah. He also tried to obtain recognition of his claim to the amirate from a new Turkish governor of Baghdad. His young brother, Abdur Rahman (Ibn Saud's father), accompanied the negotiator who was to present Saud's case in Baghdad. Once there, this Benjamin of the four brothers was detained as a hostage.

In December 1872 Saud collected another army of Ajman who flocked to him because one of their shaikhs had been imprisoned by the Turks. He headed for southern Nejd to reinforce his Bedu with townsmen, for he had not given up hope of regaining primacy. Abdullah learned of his presence and sent his brother Mohammed and his uncle ibn Turki with men from Riyadh and Durma to occupy Dilam (fifty miles south of Riyadh), and thus to guard against attack from the south. When Saud did attack Dilam the townspeople opened the gates to him. Mohammed escaped on a fast horse, but the old uncle was imprisoned and died a few days later.

This seizure of Dilam by the usurper took place early in 1873. Thereafter, Saud lost no time in turning his army against the two towns near Riyadh supporting Abdullah—Durma and Huraimilah. Late in March Abdullah marched out of Riyadh to stop him. At the town of Jiz'ah he lost the battle once more and fled south to sojourn with the Qahtan tribe. Saud occupied Riyadh again. For nearly two years he raided and punished towns and tribes alike. Nevertheless, as Abdullah was nominally supported by the Turks, Saud tried unsuccessfully to get aid from the British.

Released from custody in Baghdad, Abdur Rahman came back to al Hasa in October 1874. His arrival seems to have been the signal for a general uprising against the Ottomans. The outbreak achieved an initial success because in March 1874 for reasons of economy the Turkish regular army had been withdrawn, replaced by constabulary whose mission was to support the rule of Bazi' ibn Urai'rir, a shaikh of the Bani Khalid traditionally paramount in southern al Hasa. Only the main fort at Hofuf held out against the assaults of the Murra and Ajman tribesmen. But in a few weeks 2,400 regulars of the Turkish army with four field pieces landed at Oqair. In a battle near the port the undisciplined Bedu were soon overmatched. Abdur Rahman fled to Riyadh. There he found Saud very ill with smallpox. He had been a recluse since May 1873, probably as the result of wounds suffered in a battle between his nomads and the 'Ataiba now allied with Abdullah. Saud ibn Faisal died 26 January 1875 and Abdul Aziz ibn Abdur Rahman (Ibn Saud) was born late in the fall of 1876, his father and his uncle Abdullah both claimants of the remaining As Saud heritage.

*Saud's lust for power had resulted in the loss of al Hasa and a general decline in As Saud authority over the tribes and towns of the provinces of Qasim, Washm, Sudair and Aridh. This weakening was already being exploited by the ar Rashid, a rising power in the north under Mohammed ibn Abdullah.*

After Saud's death Abdullah, still in the desert, but with his new friends, the 'Ataiba, sent his brother Mohammed to restore As Saud authority in Washm. Mohammed went to the town of Tharmida, an important center in Washm where he reconfirmed Saudi authority. But Abdur Rahman planned to claim the amirate for himself, for in July he wrote the British Resident in Bushire that he was now ruler, and Abdullah a fugitive. To confirm his claim he left Riyadh with Saud's sons and all available men to besiege Tharmida.

Abdur Rahman's considerable army was defeated in the field by Abdullah's 'Ataiba partisans, and he returned to Riyadh for reinforcements. There, Saud's sons murdered his close friend and aide and threatened to take over the amirate. To forestall them he went to his brother Abdullah, still living with the 'Ataiba. In the face of a threat of usurpation the three brothers patched up their differences, probably because Mohammed disavowed any ambition to rule. Their united forces returned to Riyadh on 31 March 1876. Saud's four living sons fled to Dilam, fifty miles south of the capital, where their father had been welcomed.

Relieved of the menace of an immediate coup by his nephews, Abdullah tried to restore his authority in the Qasim where rival houses feuded over leadership. He backed the faction holding Anaiza. Mohammed ibn Rashid, ruler of Haïl and the Shammar tribes but owing fealty to the As Saud, supported Hassan ibn Muhanna al Khayl, then ruling in Buraida. The two amirs met near Buraida, and attempted to come to an arrangement. Abdullah, faced down, agreed to leave the Qasim. His family's long-recognized hegemony over the area ended in 1879.

For five years after Abdullah's return to Riyadh ibn Rashid and his allies defeated the Saudi amir's every attempt to restore his authority in his former domain, but ibn Rashid's clever usurpation of the governing elements in the towns of Washm and Sudair led Abdullah to declare open war in April 1884. During the resulting battle at Hamadah his fickle Bedouin allies deserted. Yet, yielding to a plea by Mohammed, ibn Rashid returned Washm and Sudair to the As Saud in October 1884. His motives for this restoration are unknown.

In October 1887 Saud's sons, who had roused the southern towns and tribes to their cause, imprisoned their uncle in Riyadh and took the reins of government. Ibn Rashid posted to Riyadh with an overwhelming army to free his brother-in-law and to take over what remained of the As Saud holdings. The nephews, granted amnesty, fled to Dilam. Ibn Rashid took Abdullah to Haïl, 'for his protection' leaving Abdur Rahman only the authority of a figurehead.

Ibn Rashid's new military governor of Aridh had been in Riyadh for a year when in August 1888 he learned of a plot by the sons of Saud to overthrow him. In secret, with thirty-five men he went to Dilam and murdered three of them. The fourth, Abdul Aziz, escaped for he was on a mission to the Ajman. Ibn Rashid professed to be shocked at the killings and swore to Abdullah, still in house arrest at Haïl, that he had not ordered their death.

In November 1889, seriously ill with dropsy, Abdullah was allowed to return to Riyadh with Abdur Rahman who had come to stay with him several months before. The 'true heir,' named governor of Riyadh by ibn Rashid, died 24 November 1889 only three days after his arrival in the Saudi capital.

**Debacle:** Ibn Rashid confirmed Abdur Rahman as Abdullah's successor and for a time the Saudi amir appeared to support his new overlord. He was monitored by a Shammari military governor, Salim ibn Subhan. This lieutenant of Ibn Rashid made known his desire to visit the Saud family on the *Id al Adah* (the three-day holiday coinciding with the sacrifice of an animal during the Pilgrimage rites) to present his respects. Abdur Rahman had been warned of treachery, and found it confirmed by the emissary's request that all the male members of the Saud family be present to hear a message from ibn Rashid. The envoy and his staff were set upon as they entered the audience chamber. Ibn Subhan and several of his followers were bound and imprisoned. Others were killed in the encounter. Ibn Subhan was left alive because several of the As Saud were still in Haïl and his life would assure theirs.

Ibn Rashid did not delay in reaching Riyadh with a large army. After a siege of forty days during which the palms and gardens were devastated, the townspeople urged negotiation. Abdur Rahman's older brother, Mohammed, headed the deputation to ibn Rashid. The thirteen-year-old Abdul Aziz went along, possibly as surety for his father. Agreement was reached: ibn Rashid would raise the siege; Abdur Rahman would continue as amir, but only of the province of Aridh; he would not permit actions contrary to ibn Rashid's interests but a Rashidi garrison would not be stationed in Riyadh; the As Saud in Haïl would be released and ibn Subhan and those of his followers still alive were to be freed. Ibn Rashid's leniency in dealing with Abdur Rahman was taken as weakness by the many opponents of his rule.

Before the siege Abdur Rahman had secretly made a pact with 'Anaiza tribesmen, promising them assistance in their struggle against ibn Rashid. That autocrat continued his exactions in the Qasim, installing new amirs and demanding more tribute. Late in 1890 the people of the towns of the Qasim began to mobilize. By January 1891 impositions had become so onerous that the 'Anaiza tribe and the amir of Buraida took the field. For a time the confederation of tribesmen and townsmen held the upper hand in the skirmishing, but on 21 January at a site called Mulaida (near Buraida) ibn Rashid used a classic tactic to lure the enemy into a trap. He feigned a retreat and the insurgents followed. The Rashidi countermove was novel. In the center of the new line were a thousand camels with bundles of brushwood on their backs. Stampeded with the brushwood alight, the suffering beasts broke and scattered the duped attackers who were then assailed by cavalry and camelry swooping from the flank and by infantry following up the stampede. More than six hundred of the townsmen were killed, including many of their leaders. The revolt was ended.

Abdur Rahman was on the way to help his allies in the Qasim, but was at Juraifa, only half-way there, when news of the defeat reached him. He returned to Riyadh in haste and at once quit the town with his family. His brother Mohammed stayed to receive the new Rashidi governor, Ajlan. It is said that for a time he served nominally as amir. At this point the story of Abdul Aziz ibn Abdur Rahman ibn Faisal ibn Turki as Saud, 'Ibn Saud,' becomes discrete. It begins on page 1.

The chart names the successive rulers of the As Saud from the time that it began its century-and-a-half of rapid expansion and swifter decline, followed by ninety-nine years of success in maintaining its authority after Ibn Saud took Riyadh in 1902. Fahd ibn Abdul Aziz, the fourth king since the death of Ibn Saud, temporarily relinquished power to a brother early in 1996, but later reclaimed it. (See Pl. X.)

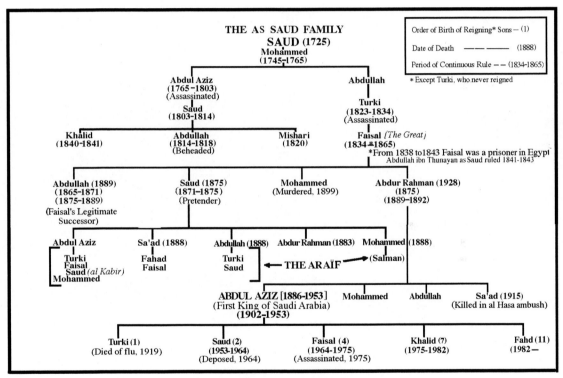

## Saud Genealogy   (Main Branch)

# III. Mubarak ibn Subah as Sabah
## (1837–1915)

**Mubarak ibn Subah as Sabah
(Ruler 1893–1915)**

From the mid-point of the eighteenth century the Sabah family has ruled in Kuwait. Late in 1893 when the Saud family in exile arrived, the amir was Mohammed ibn Subah, the second of Mubarak's three brothers. He had taken power officially only in the previous year when the first-born of four siblings, Abdullah, had died after a long chieftaincy. Mohammed and the youngest brother, Jarrah, had been as one in their disinterest in the affairs of the shaikhdom and neither could or would rule competently. To aid them they employed a man from Basra, Yusuf ibn Ibrahim, shaikh of Dora, who was in the pay of the Turks *(Dickson 1948, but see Alghanim 1998 for a completely different appraisal.)* He, as *Wasir* (minister), in effect controlled government policy and abettted their *laissez faire* ways. As a result, the tribes nominally under Kuwaiti jurisdiction, and others, the Shammar of northern Arabia and the Dhafir of southern Iraq, raided in Kuwait territory with relative impunity.

Mubarak was outraged at the state of affairs and berated his brothers in public almost daily. To rid themselves of his taunts the pair sent him to the desert to restore order with the title, *Amir al Badiya* (Ruler of the Bedouin). Denied funds, Mubarak found great difficulty in accomplishing the task, but after a time by sharing the rigorous life of the nomads he made friends and created an élite corps of vigilantes from the Rashaida and Ajman tribes. Their exploits in punishing raiders and turning their forays into routs were equaled only by their lust for loot, usually meager when taken from fleeing raiding parties. His success astonished his brothers who had thought that he would soon be killed in an attack.

Mubarak's share of the booty taken from raiders was small, and the lack of funds from this source hindered his efforts to strengthen his desert forces. More important the Wasir Yusuf refused him the monies, which, as a member of the ruling family, he had a right to share in—the revenue from taxes and trade. The last straw was Yusuf's refusal to give him ten thousand rupees, ostensibly to buy another wife and a house to put her in, but actually to buy ammunition and supplies for his force.

His patience exhausted, Mubarak decided that he himself had to take the reins of power. To do so he must remove his brothers and their corrupt adviser whom he knew to be in Turkish pay. He returned to the desert to mature his plan of action. As a member of the seignioral family, he occupied a mansion next to the two-storied, mud-brick palace in which his brothers, Mohammed and Jarrah, lived. The harem (women's quarters) of the two residences were connected by a covered bridge above a narrow street. The only other entrances to the palace were the main portal, guarded night and day, and a postern to the street from the harem.

On 17 May 1896 Mubarak rode to the main gate of Kuwait town at eleven in the evening and demanded entrance for him and his escort—seven tribesmen and his two sons, Jabir and Salim. The barred gates opened for a member of the ruling family and the party rode silently through the sleeping city to the family stables and thence went on foot to Mubarak's home. With the arrival of hot weather everyone was sleeping in the open on the flat roofs, so seven men could enter the house, climb the stairs, and cross the bridge to the palace without raising an alarm. Mubarak shot the bolt on the door barring the palace entrance to the bridge and all stole through the harem to an upper reception room. In accordance with the plan, the younger son, Salim, took four men down to the main portal to silence any men or slaves who might give the alarm and to guard against intrusion. This was done noiselessly and the postern gate too was sealed.

While this clandestine entry was in progress, Mubarak's elder son Jabir and two men of the Rashaida tribe had been sent to find Jarrah on his private roof with orders to kill him with sword or dagger when they heard a rifle shot. His wife was to be taken aside and kept quiet. Mubarak himself went to the roof of the palace where Mohammed slept alone. He approached the bed, raised his rifle and fired a single shot point-blank into Mohammed's side. The wounded man groaned, 'My brother, my brother, how could you?' was shot again, this time in the head, and died.

On another terrace, Jabir heard the first shot and raised his sword to slash Jarrah, but the stroke was not completed because the victim's wife threw herself on him as a shield and had to be dragged off before he could be murdered as planned.

No alarm was raised because shots were not uncommon in Kuwait at night, so Mubarak continued his plan of attack. Yusuf, the Turkish agent, who had nurtured the brothers' enmity was the only one of the three whom Mubarak could kill in good heart. But he did not find his quarry. Yusuf had left Kuwait by boat, sailed north across the bay, and taken a swift horse for Basra. (A well-to-do shaikh of a prominent family, he later aided the three sons of the slain amir, Mohammed, in their claim to the Turkish government for a reprisal.)

Salim had kept the gates of the palace closed and the servants cowed so no word of the events of the night reached the citizenry. At the morning *majlis* (council meeting) in the Great Hall of the palace, members of the family and men of importance who habitually attended found three poorly dressed but well-armed Bedouin standing at the entrance, and inside a silent Mubarak seated on the throne-like chair of the ruler. As the visitors entered they gave the usual salutation: *Salaam alaikum ya mafudh* (Peace be upon you, O Protector), but Mubarak remained silent until the room was full. He then drew his sword, laid the bared blade across his knee, and said, 'O ye people of Kuwait, and my blood relatives, be it known to you that Mohammed and Jarrah, my brothers, died last night and I rule in their stead. If any man has something to say, let him stand forth and say it.'

Silence reigned for a good ten minutes and then Mubarak summoned Mohammed's sixteen-year-old son and told him, 'Go wash your father and uncle and arrange for their burial, my son: God decreed that they should die last night and that I should rule in their stead— their time had come—Thanks be to Allah.' The boy did not move, staring as if dumbfounded. Mubarak gazed at him impassively and then as two tears coursed down his cheeks, he said softly, 'My brothers, my brothers, would that this had not come to pass!'

The people of Kuwait found the new shaikh's policies very forceful, in marked contrast to the indifference of the past. He conducted a series of lightning campaigns in the desert that confounded his enemies and revived the respect of the Arab world for the As Sabah. The Turks gave him the title of *Qaimaqam* (district governor) and attempted to install a quarantine officer in Kuwait town. Mubarak, fearing Turkish intentions, in both 1897 and 1898 requested help from the British political resident in the Persian Gulf. The resident, following instructions from Whitehall and the India Office, refused to grant him safeguard. But in 1899 after another Turkish attempt to take jurisdiction in Kuwait, a treaty guaranteed British protection for the amirate

In December 1901, a Turkish sloop, the *Zuhaf*, conveyed a message that Shaikh Mubarak must receive a Turkish military detachment or be sent to Constantinople. Mubarak refused to do either, and the sloop withdrew. In December 1902, a Turkish-led expeditionary force of several hundred riflemen approached Kuwait in small craft. H.M.S. *Lapwing*, a British sloop, pursued the would-be invaders and captured or destroyed all of their boats.

In June 1904, a British political agent was appointed for Kuwait, and in 1907 a plot of land was leased for the construction of a Political Agency.

Shaikh Mubarak was shrewd and ambitious. Protected by the British, he planned alliances with tribes that would make him the eventual victor over his rival ibn Rashid, the amir of Haïl, shaikh of the Shammar, and ally of the Turks. But triumphs in politics were not his only concern. Although his taxation policies were erratic, he fostered the pearl industry, and by easing duty and taxes on imports helped make Kuwait the principal entrepôt for transshipments to the interior. His long friendship with Ibn Saud began when the family was a pensioner of the Turks, living in reduced circumstances in Kuwait town. Mubarak served as mentor in the youth's study of the affairs of government, as well as being a comrade in arms. It is said that he provided instructors in mathematics, history, English, and geography, but later evidence that Ibn Saud did not know that the world was round belies this. As Ibn Saud began to regain his patrimony the friendship was imperiled by Mubarak's intrigues with the tribes of the Qasim. Apparently in old age (in 1907 he was 70) he grew jealous of his young, friendly rival.

In 1901, however, Mubarak showed his friendship concretely, while manifesting his longing for more power. He provided a large force of Bedouin who, along with allies in the Qasim and a number of former Saudi retainers, marched west to engage Abdul Aziz ibn Mitab ar Rashid, successor of Mohammed ibn Abdullah. If the battle had been won, Abdur Rahman might have begun the recovery of his domain. Unfortunately defeat was total—a rout. Only a British warship that threatened bombardment of the invaders saved Kuwait town from the sack. After 1902, as Ibn Saud strengthened his forces Mubarak asked his help against the Ar Rashid on several occasions.

At the outbreak of the World War, Mubarak seized the Ottoman frontier posts of Safwan and Umm Qasr, and another on Bubiyan island. His large mobile force on the flank of the Turkish army not only denied it access to his territory but also offered a threat to its lines of communication. This in spite of British acquiescence to Turkish demands for token sovereignty over Kuwait in the Anglo–Ottoman Treaty of 1913, a clear violation of the protection guaranteed the amirate in the Treaty of 1899.

During his long reign, Mubarak showed his skill as ruler, general, and diplomat, bringing prosperity to his people through judicious application of the law, calming or punishing rebellious tribes, and maintaining good relations with other countries and their representatives. His diplomacy was often devious but more often than not successful in that it kept Kuwait free of foreign domination. He was interested in the pleasures of the table and couch, but by Moslem standards never to excess. He died from a heart attack 28 November 1915, succeeded by his elder son, Jabir. Jabir died only eighteen months later after meeting Ibn Saud at the Durbar. Salim, who then took over the shaikhdom was his avowed enemy.

# IV. PERCY ZACHARIAH COX
## (1864–1937)

**Sir Percy Cox**

Sir Percy was praised highly by all, Christian and Moslem, who worked with or had dealings with him in his 39-year career as soldier, administrator and diplomat. He was the epitome of probity, honor, and dignity. But to these sterling qualities add imperturbability, resolute courage, and a keen and methodical mind housed in a tough and resilient body. Together they comprise an admirable man. He was more: tolerant and kind, courteous and friendly, with a respect for humanity that recognized neither profession, creed nor color. He was sometimes described as silent and secretive. Certainly he was reticent and reserved by nature, and sought always to safeguard matters that public knowledge would jeopardize.

His methodical approach to problems sometimes earned him the epithet 'over-cautious.' But he was unwilling to recommend an action or remedy before all of the relevant facts were to hand. Too, his high standards of accuracy in all things required that investigations and analyses be painstaking and thorough. Consequently, his signature stood inviolably, his word—assertion or denial—was completely sincere and gave an impression of rightness and inevitability.

Percy Cox was born 20 November 1864 at Herongate in the county of Essex, England, to Julienne Emily Cox (née Saunders) and Arthur Zachariah Cox (né Button: Arthur adopted the family name of his cousin in return for an inheritance). Percy was the youngest male of seven children who lived beyond infancy—three older sisters, two older brothers, and a favorite younger sister. As a child he was interested in nature, collecting bird's eggs, butterflies, and shells along with stamps. An avid reader, he spent hours with books of geography, travel, and natural history. He developed an interest in birds that lasted all his life. Naturally unsociable he shunned groups, and as a child had to be urged to participate in sports. But at Harrow he played football and cricket, becoming captain of the Headmaster's House side. Even as a youth he was interested in languages, for he spent at least one summer in France to perfect his abilities in the tongue.

As he was the cadet of the family he entered Sandhurst in 1882, was commissioned in February 1884, and posted to the 2nd battalion of the Cameronians. In March he sailed for India and in April joined his regiment at Shajehanpur in the United Provinces. He played polo and took every opportunity to hunt both game birds and animals as the regiment moved from post to post.

On leave he shot ibex and markhor in the Himalayan foothills. While stationed at Lucknow he met his future wife, Louisa Belle Hamilton, daughter of the Surgeon-General. The two arrived at an understanding. Percy realized that in the army his prospects were mediocre, so he applied for entry into the political department of the Indian government. Once accepted, he had to serve six months in an Indian regiment, and was posted to Peshawar. Before taking up the post he searched for his intended, found her on vacation sleeping in a railway carriage in Delhi, and carried her back to Lucknow. He married her there in the garrison church 14 November 1889.

For a month the young couple found themselves in Fort Jamrud at the entrance to the Khyber Pass where night raids were not unknown. In March 1890 they were in Jhelum and in August Mrs. Cox lost at birth her first child, a girl. In December, Cox was appointed adjutant of the Kolhapur Infantry and in September of the following year was ranked captain and ex-officio assistant to the political superintendent in the small state of Savantwadi.

In the winter of 1892 Cox was told that he would be posted as 'temporary assistant political resident' to Zeila, on the Red Sea coast of Somaliland where Britain had set up a Protectorate after an Egyptian withdrawal. The couple arrived there 4 May 1893. Conditions were primitive, but the Coxes made do. Cox improved his Arabic and Persian and learned Somali. On the side he collected a wide variety of exotic sea shells and added to his income by selling them to conchologists. In March 1894 on an expedition into the interior he and a colleague met some of the local chiefs and bagged big game. But he also worked at his new job. He made a genealogical table showing the relationships between the tribes of the area and had it published at his own expense.

That summer Cox was transferred as 'assistant political resident' to Berbera in northern Somaliland, the capital of the protectorate. In 1895 the depredations of one of the tribes prompted a military expedition into the interior. Cox led the small force and solicited the aid of friendly tribes. Adroitly he managed to locate and visit a number of the enemy's villages where herds of stolen cattle were recovered and returned to their owners. Some of the offenders were shot. The raids between tribes ceased as soon as punishment for wrongdoing seemed inevitable. It was a major feat, and demanded great physical endurance by Cox and his second in command, as well as an ability to impress the tribes with the strength and fairness of the white man's justice. The campaign was roundly applauded by his superiors.

In August 1895 the Coxes, seven years abroad, left Berbera for England. Their second child, a boy, was born in October. In November the family returned to India where Cox was made 'assistant to the governor general's agent at Baroda' assuming his chief's duties for three months during the late summer and autumn of 1896. In October of the following year an outbreak of plague, at first confined to outlying districts, struck Baroda. Cox prescribed sanitary measures and inspected the infected areas. The disease waned in the early months of 1898.

In April he went on leave for a shooting trip to Bastar state in central India where he met again an American sportsman whom he had helped in Somaliland. Together they schemed to gather enough money to back an expedition to Somaliland for the purpose of collecting trophies and specimens of the fauna. They obtained help from the Baroda Council (Durbar), and on 19 December left Aden for Berbera. On 6 April they returned to the coast after a succession of successful hunts during which many skins were collected. For two months thereafter Cox was in northern India. Impressed by his work in Somaliland, the viceroy of India, Lord Curzon, suggested that he be sent to Muscat where British dominance had been undermined by a representative of France.

Cox accepted the appointment, for it meant a permanent place in the political department of the government of India. He feared that he would be separated from his wife and son, realizing that the only means of communication with his superiors was by boat to Bushire in Persia, and that the climate was among the worst in the region. But he was ambitious for his future, and his wife concurred in his decision. After a short home leave, the Cox family returned to India where Percy was coached in his new duties by Lord Curzon himself.

On 1 October 1899 Cox arrived in Muscat. It is not certain that his family accompanied him in this first posting, but Mrs. Cox later served tea to his friends there. His first duty was to establish relations with the sultan of Oman, who had already to some degree succumbed to the blandishments of the representative of France. He had also to safeguard the interests of a colony of British Indians and other foreigners dependent on the British Raj for protection. Of Europeans there were only two—American and Dutch missionaries, one a medical doctor. Two cultured Indians were attached to the British consulate, one a student of Arabic dialects, the other a naturalist. These four became his friends. One missionary, Doctor Cantine, was destined to help him later.

The sultan was uneducated and illiterate, but his apparent dislike of the British was largely ignorance of procedure and the protocol of international relationships. Cox realized this and restored the subsidy that had been withdrawn when the French were granted permission to establish a coaling station. The French representative, now a full consul, had suborned slave traders at Sur by granting them flags and papers designed to protect them from seizure of their ships and human cargo by British gunboats. With the sultan's approval, Cox took the gunboat, H.M.S. *Sphinx*, to Sur in southern Oman, a port used mainly for importing slaves from Africa, and collected some of the flags and papers. Dhows en route to Muscat to turn in their flags were intercepted by the French armed transport *Drome*. Their captains were forced to accept a new French registration and to return to Sur.

With the *Drome* in port, the French consul tried to force the sultan to accept the services of one Abdul Aziz as his accredited agent. Two years before Abdul Aziz had worked for the Court as clerk and confidential agent, but at British insistence had been dismissed. Cox wrote a stiff letter of protest to the consul, referring to the joint French–English Declaration of 1862 guaranteeing the sultan's independence. When the *Drome* left, the question of placing a French consular agent on the sultan's staff was never broached again and the use of the French flag as cover for slavers almost ceased. This was Cox's first important diplomatic fight, and the first victory of many. It was nullified in June 1901 by an order of the Foreign Office that overrode the viceroy of India's (Lord Curzon's) ruling that British warships would not honor a French flag flown by slavers, but would seize the vessel and its cargo.

Shortly thereafter the fleet of slavers' dhows was intercepted by the Portuguese in Mozambique and destroyed, regardless of French flags and papers. Nevertheless, the question of the French flag's protection and its distribution by the French consul in Oman remained an issue until May 1903.

After 1901 Cox helped the sultan to establish order in the interior and in the south by increasing the frequency of visits by British warships. In furtherance of a plan to determine the limits of the sultan's sway he made a trip overland from Abu Dhabi to Muscat by way of Buraimi. Cox and the sultan's son attended the Durbar of 1903 in India celebrating the coronation of Edward VII. Lord Curzon's 'Progress' in the Persian Gulf in November–December 1903 gave that imperious servant of His Majesty the opportunity to thank Cox for his services in changing the sultan's attitude so as to 'confirm him in reliance on our friendship and in an attitude of deference to our wishes.'

On 2 May 1904 Cox arrived in Bushire as 'acting political resident in the Persian Gulf.' After a short leave in England, he had spent much time in seeking advice concerning how best to fill the post. As political resident he was responsible to the government of India, and as consul-general he reported to the Foreign Office through the British minister in Teheran. Persia had conceded extraterritorial jurisdiction to foreign governments, so in this second capacity he was a judge of civil disputes in the southern provinces and in the nearby islands. As the representative of the Indian government he directed foreign affairs for the rulers of Bahrain, Kuwait, Oman, and the Trucial shaikhdoms. All of them had agreed not to alienate any part of their territory without the approval of the British government. He had to keep peace between them—difficult because all were poor and quarrelsome.

Persia claimed Bahrain again, a perennial revendication. Three of the Trucial states began a war that included the capture and imprisonment of a shaikh. Cox's prompt action, including his visit in a warship to a port controlled by the errant ruler, ended the matter peaceably and demonstrated the new Resident's concern for the well-being of all the protectorates. He posted a gunboat on the pearling banks during the season to stop poaching by foreign nationals.

French citizens and Persians in Bahrain were beaten up by toughs led by one of the shaikh's sons. The shaikh refused to punish his offspring and to pay compensation for the injury. Settlement required a visit by a squadron of three warships, a shore party, and threat of bombardment, but the matter was settled without bloodshed. Thereafter the shaikh maintained the peace himself.

The French in Oman and Bahrain were not the only foreigners to trouble the peace of the Gulf. In 1906 a German company obtained rights to mine red ocher (hematite) on the island of Abu Musa off the Trucial Coast, some fifty miles northwest of Sharjah. Operations began, but in May 1907 the shaikh of Sharjah withdrew the concession and ordered the workmen to leave. The work continued without let. In mid-October, H.M.S. *Lapwing* appeared, towing lighters with three hundred armed followers of the shaikh. The workmen left. On that same day the English agent of the German firm appeared off the island in a launch flying the German flag, but was prevented from landing. The German government demanded explanations and the press ranted. But Cox had prepared a meticulous case to prove that the island belonged to Sharjah, and the furor died down.

In mainland Arabia the problem was very different. Cox refused officially Ibn Saud's repeated importunities for an alliance only after Whitehall found his own recommendations for some kind of relationship unacceptable. But when the resident learned of Ibn Saud's plan to visit the Trucial states, he warned him through Mubarak not to go into their territories or to threaten the rulers.

In Persia he had a much graver problem, because of the great number of bandits and robbers who attacked representatives of the British government. Trade and commerce were brought almost to a standstill and Persian merchants defaulted on their debts. In 1907–1908 the revolution against the shah, begun by moderates in 1905, strengthened. The already perilous situation was exacerbated. Cox himself was threatened on his travels in the interior and once was robbed. He reported, '... there is no security for the gathering of the crop and the country generally is at the mercy of the most lawless element of the peasant population.'

The Russians meddled in the affair on the side of the shah who was favorable to the expansion of their interests as long as they helped him stay in power. In August 1907 the Muscovites were forced by international pressures to conclude a treaty with the English regarding spheres of influence. Theirs was in northern Persia, an area contiguous to Russia. The treaty did not stop Muscovite interference in the course of the revolution, nor attempts to play a leading rôle in the development of railroads and other aspects of the modernization of Persia.

On 26 May 1908 the d'Arcy syndicate struck oil in Persia at Maidan-i-Naftan (the Naphtha Plain) some 130 miles north of the Gulf. The oil men had been guarded by Indian soldiers because of raids by Bakhtiari tribesmen. Lieutenant A. T. Wilson in command of a detachment of the 32nd Sikh Pioneers earned the praise of his superiors because of carefully drawn maps and accurate reports on the Bakhtiari hills and their hinterland. In 1910 Cox appointed him political agent at Muhammera and they became friends and close collaborators.

Cox helped the syndicate to obtain rights to the tract on Abadan island which its engineers had chosen as a site suitable for a refinery and site for transshipment to tankers on the Shatt-el-Arab. The land was held by the Shaikh Khaaz'al of Muhammera whom his strong army made completely independent. Negotiation directed by Cox led to a lease of the necessary terrain for annual rent of £650, ten years to be paid in advance, along with a loan of £10,000. The lease was signed 16 July 1909. The European parties thanked Cox for his, 'loyal and efficient defense of the interests of the Company during the whole course of these negotiations to which their success is in great measure to be attributed.'

At the conclusion of the bargaining Cox discussed other matters with Shaikh Khaaz'al, at that time nominally a subject of Persia. Khaaz'al had aided Bakhtiari shaikhs who planned to help the Nationalist revolution, and then to take an important place in the new government. But he had second thoughts about this alliance and asked the British to guarantee that his descendants would inherit. The resident replied that Britain had guaranteed the maintenance of the existing régime in Persia, so that his autonomy too was protected.

Disturbances were rife throughout Persia in 1909 and those in Bandar Abbas and Bushire threatened the personnel of the consulates. Cox called H.M.S. *Fox* which landed sailors to take over the customs house and to restore order. Before their arrival the ringleader, a Shia cleric from Karbala, had a lively correspondence with the resident who, after order was restored, returned him to his chapter house from which he was later exiled.

After a leave begun in August Cox returned to Persia, but was called to London in January 1910 and was again in Bushire only in April. During his absence the Nationalist revolution continued. The shah was at last overthrown and sent to exile. The Nationalists began to quarrel among themselves. Brigandage continued unchecked. Indian troops sent inland late in 1910 to protect the consulates and foreign communities and to keep the roads open did nothing because the government would not authorize their use in combat.

In Turkey the change in government that brought the reforming 'Unionists' to power in 1908 was reflected in attempts to bring Kuwait more firmly under Ottoman control. The British 1899 treaty with Mubarak guaranteed him protection, but Whitehall's desire to maintain the *status quo* with the Ottomans caused Whitehall to disregard Mubarak's fulminations and in 1913 to agree to nominal Turkish sovereignty over Kuwait. Cox was put in difficulty because of this broken pledge and his agent in Kuwait, Captain Shakespear, suffered virtual ostracism for a year.

As a Persian subject the shaikh of Muhammera was in a different position. The new Turkish Wali (governor of a Vilayet) of Basra bombarded one of his villages from the sea. He was recalled at once, but the shaikh was embittered. Cox was relieved when the incident ended, for he was not sure that he could persuade his government to aid Shaikh Khaaz'al in the event of all-out war.

Attempts to halt the traffic in arms supplied clandestinely to Afghanistan and the northwest frontier of India failed until 1911, when, after a bloody encounter in Dubai between sailors hunting concealed arms and Arabs, a large British blockading fleet took station off Mekran in southern Persia and in the coastal waters of Oman. It was supplemented by a military expedition from India that debarked in Mekran. This large force soundly defeated the Afghans and their allies in April, and for a time ended the traffic.

All of these matters, and others too numerous to mention required Cox's continued supervision and, often, his personal intervention. Time at home with his family was frequently interrupted by a new obligation or duty. To these required tasks Cox added those of voluntarily acting as vice consul for French and Dutch interests in Bushire, forwarding the necessary documents to the embassies in Teheran. His own consular service took much of his time. Recreation, besides tennis at home, consisted of infrequent hunting trips and the collection of bird and animal skins. On one three-week excursion in the Musandam peninsula he accompanied a British naval officer who used chronometer and theodolite to determine the geographic coördinates of Buraimi and other points.

After 1911 the Foreign Office was engaged with the Turks in negotiations to regularize the spheres of influence of both nations in the Middle East. The

Foreign Office and Cox were continually in consultation on the matter, but all decisions were made in London. As mentioned, Whitehall's decisions were contrary to the treaty of 1899 and not satisfactory to Cox, for Kuwait was recognized as being under Turkish sovereignty, although only to the extent of stationing an official in the town. Mubarak was outraged.

Cox was forced to visit him and Shaikh Khaaz'al to mollify them for what they considered grave infringements of their rights. The shaikh of Muhammera was deprived of control of traffic in the Shatt-el-Arab. Henceforth it was in the hands of an Anglo–Turkish commission whereas previously the boundary of Muhammera had been the center line of the Shatt and its traffic had been subject to Khazaa'al's dicta. As usual, Cox managed to calm the resentment and fears of these Arab rulers.

In 1912 Cox in Persia visited: Bandar Abbas, Lingah, Henjam and Basidu islands, Ahwaz and Muhammera; in Arabia: Kuwait, Dubai, Ajman, Abu Musa, and Muscat (twice). In Muscat the sultan finally passed a law regulating the traffic in arms. After much public protest and private negotiation the French accepted the law, and in 1914 recalled their agents from Muscat. But the Omanis rebelled at the loss in revenue and Cox had to send a half-battalion of soldiers to keep the shaikh's successor, his son, in power.

While both nations awaited the conclusion of other bilateral agreement between France and Turkey and France and Germany regarding railroads, the Anglo–Ottoman treaty of 1913, which changed the hegemonies of Kuwait and Muhammera, was signed but never ratified. During that year Cox ordered the chastisement of a tribe that, having had a cargo of arms confiscated by the shaikh of Dubai, captured a pearling dhow and killed most of its crew. Three gunboats and Indian soldiers took part in the successful expedition that burned dhows and killed a number of the pirates.

In 1912 and 1913 the new Persian government was still ineffective. The crowning of a new shah, in July 1914, did nothing to curb the almost universal unrest. Depredations by the tribes continued and several British citizens died, one of them a vice consul. Some of the Indian troops stationed in Persia to safeguard British interests were withdrawn when the Swedes established and trained a gendarmerie. With the connivance of its instructors that gendarmerie would serve the interests of the Dreibund during the Great War.

Cox wanted a change of employment. He was 49 and the volume of work increased annually while his staff and his pay remained the same. He had been given a K.C.I.E. (Knight Commander of the Indian Empire) at the Durbar of 1911, but with thirteen summers in the Gulf ports he had had enough. His complaint was heard, for 8 December 1913 Cox went on leave knowing that on his return to India he would be named secretary of the foreign department of the government of India. On 6 April 1914 his ship reached Bombay and he assumed his new duties, but performed them for less than seven months.

As 'chief political officer' Cox accompanied Indian Expeditionary Force D, which on 16 October 1914 left Bombay for Basra. Cox thought its departure provocative, for war with Turkey had not yet begun. On 5 November when war *was* declared, he issued a carefully worded proclamation to the Arabs of the delta region. It informed them that neither person nor property would be harmed by the armed forces, but that if they carried arms they would be shot.

The army found some difficulty in reaching Basra because of Turkish resistance in the Shatt-el-Arab that ended in a battle. Cox's assistant, Captain Birdwood, was shot dead at his side on 17 November. His reply to comments concerning his calm under fire was a grunted remark that he was made so and took no credit for it. On 22 November an advance party entered Basra, just abandoned by the Turks. Cox prepared another proclamation (the original was written in Arabic, as was his usual practice) for publication by the commanding general. It was intended to reassure the population about the army's presence and its mission. The proclamation promised fair treatment, if in return army personnel were treated fairly.

He had hoped to get some help in military operations from the Arabs, but the Foreign Office refused to promise a permanent occupation of Basra. The tribes remained uncommitted, fearing Turkish reprisals when the army left. Some proved actively hostile, and all scavenged the battlefields, killing the wounded and collecting items of value.

Cox found himself with a variety of tasks that would have daunted most men. He was tireless in gleaning information from all and sundry and at the same time in reassuring his shaikhly friends of Kuwait and Muhammera whose intelligence services were excellent and helpful to the British cause. Gathering intelligence about the foe and the strength and state of mind of its potential allies among the tribes was essential. Counter-intelligence against the activities of Turkish and German spies and *agents provocateurs* was an urgent requirement. What in World War II was called 'psychological warfare' was also necessary—both to assure that an advance into enemy-held territory would not be hindered by partisan activities, and to assure the coöperation, or at least the neutrality or passivity, of the fixed and nomadic populations on the flanks of and behind the army. His long experience in dealing with the problems of the British protectorates and his appreciation of the Arab mind helped greatly in formulating policies and plans to reach this objective.

The occupation of Basra presented another set of problems. The Turkish civil administration had to be replaced without delay. Provision for police, transport, food, civilian labor, billets and other requirements had to be made at once, and lines of communication protected from civilian interference. Even the methodical, patient, even-tempered Cox could not do all this without help, and his original staff was enlarged as needed. He worked it and himself to the point of exhaustion. His chief of staff was Captain Arnold T. Wilson, whose books covering this period are listed in the bibliography.

The army advanced only a small part of the way to Baghdad before being ordered to halt. Many tribal chiefs took this as a sign of weakness and some joined the Turks. All but one of the tribes under Khaaz'al revolted. The Turks and their Arab allies began an attack in March 1915, aided by at least one tribe nominally under Persian jurisdiction. The right flank of the expeditionary force was threatened and the oil fields were in danger of capture. A new general and reinforcements retrieved the situation.

After some hesitation it was decided that an advance on Baghdad was practical. Cox accompanied the force, which after an initial success found itself in difficulties when assaulted by Turkish regulars. Short of supplies, and confronted by a much larger army, it was put under siege at Kut, half-way to Baghdad. Cox was ordered to return to Basra and shortly thereafter journeyed to the village of Darin on Tarut Island where on 26 December 1915 he gave Ibn Saud the long-sought treaty that promised British protection and recognized him as the amir of al Hasa and Nejd.

From Basra Cox journeyed up the river and thereafter spent half his time with the force attempting to relieve the beleaguered troops at Kut. All efforts were unsuccessful and 11,600 officers and men surrendered 29 April 1916. Before that date the civil administration of the occupied area was functioning well in the hands of the capable staff that Cox had assembled, and discussions were already in progress concerning what kind of government should be set up in Iraq at war's end.

Before the surrender took place a scheme to offer the Turkish leaders £1,000,000 to release the trapped men brought T. E. Lawrence from Cairo. Cox was vehemently opposed, but could only caution against it. The Turks gained propaganda points from their well-publicized refusal of the offer while British prestige fell sharply.

Shortly before Lawrence's visit Gertrude Bell arrived from India on her way back to Cairo where she had been working for a short time in what was to become the Arab Bureau, the intelligence agency that conducted negotiations with Sharif Husain, and later directed his war effort through Lawrence. She found that she could be more useful working for Cox than for General Clayton in Cairo. The chief political officer in Iraq agreed. There followed nearly eight years of collaboration in molding Arab opinion through the press and in observing the leading elements of the political spectrum.

With the army's position stabilized south of Kut and action reduced to patrols, Cox opposed further withdrawal, pointing out that he had been able to recruit tribes to guard the oil fields and pipeline. They would melt away if withdrawal took place, for it would be viewed as retreat.

Complying with several requests by Ibn Saud, Cox met him on 11 November 1916 at Oqair, and calmed his fears regarding British preference for and support of Sharif Husain. The amir expressed a desire to meet Shaikh Jabir of Kuwait who had replaced his dead father, Mubarak. Perhaps this request hastened Cox's arrangements for the Durbar that took place nine days later in Kuwait. It was a success, for a consensus of the eminent shaikhs that attended urged coöperation with the British. Ibn Saud in concert with the shaikh of Muhammera set an example for the waverers.

At this same time the new commanding general in Iraq was planning an offensive which began 17 January 1917. Kut was occupied again on 25 February. Cox spent most of his time at army headquarters and was with the troops that entered Baghdad on 11 March. His first job was to set up a civil administration for the province. In spite of ill-advised proposals from Whitehall for dividing up the country, and a disastrous proclamation written by Sir Mark Sykes, Cox began to assemble a staff to guide civil administration. He counseled delay in deciding future policy.

The general was opposed in principle to any action which would limit his total untrammeled authority and for a time Cox considered resigning. In the end, after months of correspondence, he was given permission to report directly to the British and Indian governments. Henceforth the military would not supervise the civil administration. These decisions stemmed in part from a long letter by Gertrude Bell to the assistant under-secretary of state, an old friend of Cox's, who passed it to Lord Curzon in August. That august personage, then secretary of state for foreign affairs, acted to free Cox from administrative imbroglios.

The uncoöperative general conveniently died of cholera contracted from contaminated milk in coffee. His successor was more amenable, and equally successful in the field. Reconstruction of destroyed villages began, and only pockets of sedition, including the Shia shrines of Nejef and Karbala, continued active or subversive resistance behind the lines. As the Turks retreated, more tribes joined the British effort.

In October 1917 Cox's son who had married and joined the Royal Air Force was shot down in France. This heavy blow coincided with the dispatch of the British mission to Riyadh headed by Philby. Shortly thereafter Cox was ordered to Cairo for consultation. The civil administration of the liberated territory of Iraq now functioned well. Captain A. T. Wilson was named deputy civil administrator and moved from Basra to Baghdad when Philby was selected for the mission to Ibn Saud. This move marked the beginning of a difference of opinion between Wilson and Gertrude Bell. Miss Bell took it upon herself unofficially to keep the Arab Bureau in Cairo abreast of events in Iraq. She was a fervent supporter of Faisal for king of Iraq, thus an opponent of Philby in this regard.

The journey to Cairo took nearly a month. On 23 March Cox met with the group directing military and civil affairs in Egypt. On the agenda was the British position vis-à-vis the leaders of Middle Eastern countries and what should it be under various contingencies. Cox continued discussions with individuals after the conference ended. It was only on 3 April that he left Egypt for England. The journey was made under rigorous wartime conditions. Two ships of the convoy were torpedoed before it reached Marseilles. Cox arrived in London on 15 April and started a round of visits to government offices, ending with a meeting of the War Council where nearly all of his proposals were accepted. He spent a weekend with the royal family, a few days with political and economic experts, and saw his relatives briefly.

The return to Baghdad was uneventful except for an air raid in Paris. En route, in Cairo a conference was held concerning relations between Sharif Husain and Ibn Saud. Cox arrived in Bombay on 8 July and went to Simla where on 22 July the viceroy named him minister to Persia.

The new minister and his wife reached Teheran 15 September 1918. Although the war was ending with the Allies victorious, many Persians did not recognize the signs, and some still favored entering the war at the side of Turkey. But by October the true situation became obvious to all. The government, pusillanimous and divided as it had been for a decade, made no effort to improve relations with the victors or to foster economic and political reform. Consequently, British policy makers as a whole favored complete withdrawal from Persia, but Lord Curzon wanted to keep the country allied to England as one of a chain of states and alliances together providing a land route to India from Egypt and a bulwark against nascent Communism.

Cox worked hard and long. The Anglo–Persian treaty was signed by the Persian prime minister 9 August 1919. Britain promised to respect the integrity and independence of Persia, to loan two million pounds at 7 per cent, to provide a corps of advisers among whom would be military experts equipped with munitions and equipment sufficient to develop a national army under the supervision of an Anglo–Persian military commission. Other experts would study and recommend procedures for the development of railroads and other transport and would revise the Customs schedule.

But the Persian Assembly refused to ratify the treaty and Bolshevik propaganda turned the people against Britain. When Red forces seized Baku from the White Russians and drove the British garrison from Anzali and other cities on the Caspian, the Persians lost confidence in their government and despaired of Britain's ability to help them. Cox attempted to restore British prestige, but the deteriorating situation in Iraq demanded that he go back.

The Anglo–French declaration promulgated in Baghdad on 8 November 1918 stated that the aim of the two nations was the complete liberation of the peoples oppressed by the Turks and the establishment of national governments chosen by the people. The enthusiasm with which it was received led Wilson to order a plebiscite. The ballot posed three questions: What should be the territorial limits of Iraq? Should an Arab head the state? If so, who? Everyone wanted Mosul, in the French sphere of influence according to the Sykes–Picot memorandum, to be part of Iraq, but opinions regarding the head of state were so diverse that no further action was taken in this regard.

Independence and self-government appealed to all, and these concepts spread quickly, spurred by the example of Syria where on 11 March 1920 Faisal ibn Husain had taken power as king, supported by Britain. But in April at San Remo, France was given a mandate over Syria and Britain was granted mandates over Palestine and Iraq. The people of Iraq thought that this meant permanent foreign rule. By July of 1920 the tribes of Iraq were in revolt and a number of British soldiers were killed. Wilson had foreseen the problems that would stem from this apparent abrogation of the Anglo–French Declaration of 1918.

After the plebiscite he urged that Cox come back to Iraq. The Foreign Office agreed, and in May 1920 ordered Cox to London, Curzon having decided to appoint him high commissioner. The ex-minister handed over to his successor in Persia, and reached England in July. He met with the Cabinet and individual ministers to choose a form of government for Iraq. Cox found the widely held view that the British should pull out of Iraq 'the complete violation of the promises we had made the Arabs during the war, and their inevitable resubjection to chaos and the hated yoke of the Turk....' He felt that the alternative of attempting to set up an Arab government was worth a try, in spite of the risks. After further discussion he agreed to head the attempt provided that he report to a single entity, the Foreign Office. He recruited Philby and Cheeseman to serve him, the latter as his personal secretary. On his way to Baghdad he stopped at Oqair to meet Ibn Saud, and gave him a high decoration of the Indian government.

On 11 October 1920 he arrived in Baghdad to an official reception which included a band playing the national anthem, and an address of welcome in Arabic to which he replied in the same language, calling on the people to help him establish peace and order in preparation for an Arab government under British supervision. The military administration that had governed the country before his arrival was still fighting insurgents, but its rule was ending. Many of the officers dismissed had served with distinction and had hoped for a career in their posts. But rebellion was still alive, so a week after his arrival Cox issued a proclamation stating that he had been sent to assist the leaders of the people to create a national government and was at a loss to know why the tribesmen were still fighting.

To prove his sincerity he persuaded the Naqib, an old patriot named Seyyid Abdur Rahman, to head the government as president of the Council. The appointment was made on 23 October. Wilson selected able men to staff it, all of irreproachable repute with the exception of Seyyid Talib Pasha. Talib was a devious politician but an influential patriot who had lived in India under house arrest at British expense during most of the war because of his anti-British leanings. He accepted with alacrity the post of minister of the interior, offered him by Wilson with misgivings, and only because of the fear that he would disrupt the government if not given a post in it. Abdul Latif Pasha al Mandil, Ibn Saud's representative in Basra and a leading merchant, was named minister of commerce. All the other posts were filled competently. A British adviser was attached to each ministry. Philby was assigned Talib, whom he supported in his aspirations for Iraqi democracy.

On 11 November 1920 the high commissioner issued a proclamation: Under his supervision and direction the Council of State would be the provisional national government pending convocation of a General Assembly to formulate an 'Organic Law.' Until the 'Organic Law' came into effect the Council would be responsible for government, with the exception of foreign and military affairs.

'Military affairs' was for the moment the suppression of rebellion. The Shia communities of Karbala and Nejef were still in revolt, and their offer to send representatives to serve in government was refused on the grounds that religion and politics do not mix—that the *Ulema's* concerns should be only the hereafter. In two years opposition to the new government from this source had ceased, aided by the death of the leader of the faction and the appointment of a *Shia* as minister of education.

The army was another problem. The nucleus of a General Staff was in place early in 1921, but conscription was forbidden, and a long-service army would be too expensive. The Arab ex-officers of the Turkish army were hungry and could have been an element dangerous to stability. Too, the 'Levies' (some 2,000 tribesmen) had protected the railway and pipeline after the departure of some of the British troops and would have to be incorporated into the army where their lack of training would hinder development of the force. They were placed under the jurisdiction of the minister of the interior, Seyyid Talib.

Winston Churchill, named minister for the colonies on 14 February 1921, conceived and organized a new unit of the Colonial Office to replace the confusion arising in the Levant from the overlapping responsibilities of the India and Foreign Offices. This 'Middle East office' would administer the mandated territories. Churchill called a conference of the chief military and political officers of the mandates to meet in Cairo on 12 March 1921. On the agenda was the selection of a ruler for Iraq, the future of the Kurdish minority, the reduction of expenditures and the nature of the forces to defend Iraq after the departure of the British garrison.

Cox arrived in Cairo early in March with no preconceived idea as to the nominee for king of Iraq, although he favored any one of the sons of Husain ibn Ali except Abdullah, for none of the local candidates could win a majority of the vote. Churchill and his fifteen advisers represented all branches of government even remotely concerned with Middle Eastern affairs. Among them was Colonel T. E. Lawrence, who strongly favored his companion-in-arms of the war, Faisal, for king. Faisal, sounded out in London after his expulsion from Syria by the French on 26 July 1920 after 21 months as head of the government under British patronage and at the last named king, refused the post at first. He considered his brother Abdullah to have prior rights. Lawrence convinced him otherwise, and by the first days of March the die was cast in his favor among Churchill's advisers.

When Cox agreed that he was acceptable, a plan for Faisal's step-by-step introduction as the candidate for king was devised. The other two items on the agenda, the Kurdish problem and financial matters in Iraq, took up the remainder of the fortnight of meetings. On 12 April Cox was back in Baghdad where a serious and pressing problem demanded his attention.

This was the activities and propaganda of Seyyid Talib, the minister of the interior, a known blackmailer and suspected murderer, who campaigned openly for himself and supported the Naqib in the expectation that the old man would name him his successor. He had some success among the tribes and with the police under his control. At a dinner party he openly threatened rebellion, citing the 30,000 rifles of one shaikh and the support of another. He vowed that if His Majesty's government took sides in naming a ruler for Iraq, he would appeal to the Islamic world for aid. Cox entrusted his capture to the military. After having had tea with Mrs. Cox and Gertrude Bell at the Cox home on 15 April, Talib was taken prisoner en route to the ministry. Shortly thereafter he was sent under guard to Ceylon. At Cox's request Philby ran the Ministry of the Interior for six weeks.

A period of calm followed during which Faisal's supporters gained some ground. A revision of the schedule for the arrival of Faisal in Iraq was due in part to a delay in the Foreign Office's authorization of amnesty for all persons involved in the revolt of 1920. Cox insisted that it be announced before Faisal's appearance in Iraq. The delay was caused by consultation with the Department of State, the Quai d'Orsay, and the government of India regarding the 'Open Door' policy they advocated. The proclamation of amnesty was made 30 May. Faisal arrived at Basra on 23 June and was taken by special train to Baghdad, escorted by Philby, an avowed nationalist. Philby did not hesitate to inform Faisal of his feelings regarding the future government in Iraq, and the crowds at the several stops en route were slim and glum. Baghdad made up for the slights by a vast concourse and an enthusiastic welcome.

Faisal must have complained to Cox about Philby's reception, for on 7 July 1921 Cox dismissed Philby citing in a note to Philby's associates that, 'Unfortunately, his past experiences have given him a somewhat pronounced anti-Sharifian bias … unable to accommodate his personal view and attitude to the now declared "Sharifian" policy of his Majesty's government.'

Resistance to Faisal's candidature would come from the Kurds, the Muntafiq and from the *Shia Ulema* although Faisal made a point of performing *Shia* rites of prayer in public. Nevertheless support for him grew apace, and both Cox and Faisal had to restrain extremists who would have made him king by a *coup d'état*. The pressure for an immediate election became so strong that the normal processes of registration of voters was seen to be too slow, for a Constituent Assembly, under the law responsible for the election of a ruler, could not meet for three months.

On 11 July the Council passed a resolution declaring Amir Faisal 'King of Iraq, provided that his Highness's Government shall be constitutional, representative and liberal, and limited by law.' Cox vetoed the Council's resolution, for both he and Faisal found that proof of support by the public was required before accession could take place. A referendum began late in July. The forms distributed in the Baghdad region included phrases requiring freedom from foreign control and a meeting of the Constituent Assembly within three months. In other areas other conditions were appended. Cox added a question concerning the continuance of the mandate.

The official figure that 96.5 per cent of the electorate were in favor of Faisal as king was certainly rigged, but it seems probable that a majority approved him, and independent observers granted him two-thirds of the vote. Just before the coronation the Colonial Office cabled Cox that Churchill wanted Faisal to declare in his speech of acceptance that he favored continuation of the mandate. Faisal refused. He said that he had accepted candidature only on the understanding that a treaty of alliance would replace the mandate. Cox agreed with Faisal, and Churchill dropped his demand.

The coronation was held 23 August at six in the morning. The square in front of the palace was filled with notables from all parts of Iraq except Kirkuk and Sulaimaniya. An impressive outdoor ceremony included hoisting the national flag, a twenty-one gun salute, and a dignified speech by Faisal thanking the people for their freely given allegiance and the British for receiving him as king of the Independent State of Iraq. He called on Cox for coöperation and advice.

A seeming unity of views ended as the terms of a treaty of alliance between Britain and Iraq were propounded and discussed. The Foreign Office wanted the mandate to continue with British officers on the staff of the mandate to be independent of local pressures, and those working for the Iraqi government bound to report activity deleterious to British interests. The draft of the treaty contained a clause that allowed the mandate to continue indefinitely. It was approved by the Council of Ministers, but with a proviso added that it must also be approved by the Constituent Assembly.

The *Shia* community argued hard against acceptance of the treaty and Faisal made many backdoor moves to effect its rejection. One was a letter to Cox disclaiming any responsibility for the disorders that might arise, and asking Cox either to accept full responsibility for the control of any outbreaks, or to give him, Faisal, a free hand. Cox considered this a bluff, and replied that the king could not divest himself of his duty of working with the high commissioner in maintaining order. But Faisal hobnobbed with extremists who misrepresented the temper of the people. He allowed one of them to make an anti-British speech at the rear of the palace. On 14 August 1922 the Council resigned.

Fortunately, the king came down with acute appendicitis. Cox took over. He deported seven agitators and closed down two newspapers. The *Shia* religious leaders responsible for the trouble in Karbala and Nejef were told to get out or he would take action. They left for Persia. Bombed from the air, Muntafiq rebels surrendered. Faisal recovered slowly but opposition to the Treaty could not be allowed to continue its course. Under pressure, Faisal was prompted to dismiss the agitators and to support the British position, provided that his *sharaf* (prestige) was maintained.

The cause for dispute ended when Britain decided to join the League of Nations, for members were obligated to assist other states to become members, thus offering a way to negate the mandate. Before Cox left Iraq a revolt of the Kurds, supported by a Turkish contingent, killed two English officers. This was put down by force, using air power to the full.

On 10 October, Cox and the Naqib signed the treaty. Faisal swore unswerving loyalty to his undertakings as prescribed in the text, and announced his great satisfaction at the existence of an alliance. But the election of a Constituent Assembly lay in the future. It alone could approve the treaty and the Organic Law that would lay down the constitution. The Turks were going to claim Mosul at the peace conference, and its inhabitants saw no reason to vote for a chimera.

On 19 November Cox left Baghdad to meet Ibn Saud at Oqair (A. IX). On his return early in December he was able to take some leisure. Relations with Faisal had improved, and he had a new aide who would eventually succeed him. He and Cheesman exercised their hawks in the hunt, and continued their ornithological studies. But he was summoned home to meet a Cabinet Committee formed to investigate the situation of the British government in Iraq and to decide whether the treaty with Iraq should be ratified. He saw King George V and his own relatives. He was in England more than six weeks before returning to Iraq. His last official act as high commissioner was to sign the Protocol of the Treaty of Alliance, reduced in length from twenty to four years.

His announcement of retirement was the signal for a number of demonstrations of the respect and affection which he and his wife had engendered. On 3 May 1923 the Protocol was signed. This triggered more tributes to Cox in Parliament. But retirement (he left Basra 4 May 1923, replaced by Sir Henry Dobbs) was not the end of service to his country.

In May 1924 he went to Constantinople as British plenipotentiary to conduct negotiations for the delineation of the Iraqi–Turkish frontier. Because his instructions were unalterable, no agreement was reached. The boundary was finally drawn 5 June 1926 by direct negotiation. In May 1925 Cox went to Geneva to represent the Indian government at the International Arms Traffic Conference and defended among other statutes the declaration of the Persian Gulf as a prohibited zone.

For four years the Coxes and their orphaned grandson lived in the country where Cox rode to hounds and shot regularly. In 1928 he returned to London, although maintaining his membership in the hunt and his shooting. He had become a fellow of the Royal Geographical Society in 1895 and was elected president in 1933. He took his duties very conscientiously, devoting time almost daily to the affairs of the society.

His accomplishments were rewarded by the academic world: in June 1925 an Honorary D.C.L. from Oxford; in 1929 an LL.D. from the University of Manchester. Occasionally he lectured on the Middle East to learned or patriotic societies and contributed to the *Encyclopædia Britannica* with articles on Persian and Mesopotamian cities and on the zoö-geography of these regions.

The retention of physical fitness and enjoyment of riding to the hounds led to his death from a fall on 20 February 1937 in his seventy-third year. His body was cremated. A tablet in the Anglican church in Baghdad lists his positions in government service and his honors: G.C.M.G., G.C.I.E., K.C.S.I.

# V. HUSAIN IBN ALI, SHARIF OF MECCA (1853–1931)

Husain ibn Ali was appointed sharif of Mecca 1 November 1908 by the sultan of Turkey after a failed rebellion by the previous holder of the title. He was then fifty-five years old. A direct descendant of the Prophet Mohammed's daughter and son-in-law, he was eminently qualified by birth to guard and to govern the two Holy Cities of Islam, the *Haramain*. His family had long held the position: the first Hashemite sharif took power in 1037. The junior branch to which Husain belonged had held the position almost continuously since 1857, relinquishing it only in 1905.

**Husain ibn Ali, Sharif of Mecca (1916)**

He was five years old when his father died in Constantinople. His father's older brother, chosen to be the new sharif, took him and his mother to Mecca. There he learned much about the Bedu character—tribal relationships and feuds, family mores and traditions—and became a student of the flora and fauna of the desert. Adult, he became involved in intrigue directed against Turkish authority, and in 1893 was forced to return to Constantinople. There he lived a life of extreme respectability to avoid the fate that had overtaken some of his fellow conspirators. He became a scholar of religion, and knowledgeable on a wide variety of world affairs. His first wife died, and a second one bore him his fourth son. Because of the elaborate rituals, intrigues and subleties of the court, suspicion and jealousy became inherent in his character, supplementing native cupidity and sadistic cruelty. He was quick to violent anger and was stubbornly opinionated. But his desire, suppressed during his fifteen years in Constantinople, was to become the leader of all Arabs in throwing off the Turkish yoke.

He was a little man, but had much dignity and presence. His usual dress was a black, ankle-length gown and a skull-cap of colored straw with a white turban wrapped around it, the end hanging out to the left. Befitting his origins, his skin was fair, his features regular and fine. Although his manners were correct and he was courteous, at least to foreigners of rank, his smile was rare, and the coldness of his large brown eyes betrayed its insincerity. He charmed Storrs by a 'captivating sincerity of utterance, enhanced by a benignant, a noble simplicity of demeanour.' But he was then (1916) in the initial stages of the revolt which he believed would end in his leadership of a pan-Arab state. The British minister to the Hejaz, Grafftey-Smith, who saw him in the twenties when his hopes were already dimmed, saw a different man. He could still be a charming host, but had the annoying habit of feeding his guests tidbits with his own hand, stuffing them beyond repletion. The minister suggests *(1970, p. 157)* that he took pleasure in their discomfort. In that diplomat's view, this was a mild manifestation of the sadism reported by Rihani *(1930, pp. 25–26)* and that Grafftey-Smith himself saw expressed more overtly on one occasion: After a dinner on the roof of the army barracks a Negro slave brought in a large ape on a chain. Husain ordered the slave to set the ape at a man, a minor official, who fled screaming from the animal in paroxysms of fear. Husain's eyes were lustrous and a trickle of saliva flowed from one corner of his mouth during this chase, which he halted only when the victim was about to throw himself from the roof.

Other victims held in the dungeon below the sharif's palace in Mecca told of repeated beatings with a club wielded late at night by their oppressor. Most of these prisoners were officials of his government, businessmen, or notables whom he feared or disliked. On occasion his rage was directed against his own sons.

But pleasure in inflicting pain was a minor vice when compared to the hardships, suffering, and even the death of pilgrims caused by his neglect of the most elementary measures for their protection and security while in the Hejaz. Those making the *Hajj* by caravan from the north and east were set upon by greedy tribesmen who either demanded payment for safe passage through their territory, or robbed them of their possessions under menace of death, a threat which on occasion was carried out. Husain at first made an attempt to halt these depredations, but later desisted. It was said at the time that he exacted a share of the loot in payment for his inaction.

Pilgrims coming by sea from India and Africa, crowded in slow boats with inadequate sanitation, sometimes arrived ill. They were met by an official guide who collected the exorbitant fees demanded by the Hejazi government for its services. After quarantine proceedings were completed, these guides, each of whom was familiar with the needs and customs of the postulants from a country or district, were responsible for the proper supervision, control, and welfare of their charges. The abuses of authority almost inherent in this system have been detailed by several authors. Husain's share of the take was reportedly elastic, but always inordinate.

Husain had only four legitimate sons. In order of birth they were: Ali, Abdullah, Faisal and Zaid. After a vain effort to hold Jedda against Ibn Saud, Ali ended in exile in Iraq with his brother Faisal. Abdullah escaped the *Ikhwan* at Turaba and was made amir of Transjordan by Churchill's fiat. Faisal, who had been the leader in Lawrence's campaign against the Turks, sought to be king of Syria, was driven out by the French, and then was nominated to be king of Iraq by

Churchill, prodded by Lawrence. After the death of his father, Zaid too went to Iraq and became Iraqi ambassador to London. British policy made two of the Hashemites rulers, and the decendant of one is still king in Jordan. But in spite of Lawrence's efforts on behalf of his sons, Husain in exile ended his friendship with the Englishman.

The enmity between Husain and Ibn Saud, if it had not existed before, began in 1910 when Husain held Ibn Saud's brother Sa'ad for ransom. It was exacerbated by the series of insults and slanders listed in n. 16, which culminated in the series of strikes against Khurma. Many of the acrimonious exchanges were initiated by Husain who considered Ibn Saud an uncouth and unlettered savage. Some of his letters professed friendship, others were insulting. Under British pressure, Husain asked Ibn Saud to help him fight the Turks. Ibn Saud replied that he would enter into an alliance provided that his sovereignty was not threatened. The insulting riposte: the writer of such a letter was bereft of reason. The bad press instigated by Husain that ridiculed and vilified Ibn Saud must have been more than annoying, for to Rihani the sultan said that he had accepted attendance at the Oqair conference mainly to persuade Cox to stop Husain's propaganda.

Husain's interpretation of the McMahon letter of 24 October 1915 promising aid in the revolt led him to assume that after the war he would be supported in his aspirations to lead all the Arabs. Thus his declaration of 5 November 1916 in which he named himself, 'King of the Arab Lands.' The declaration was made four months to the day after the revolt began. It caused consternation among those of the British who recognized the capabilities of Ibn Saud and the resentment it would arouse in him and his subjects. But the exigencies of war stifled their protests.

It was the continuation and exaggeration of this megalomania that led to Husain's assumption of the mantle of Caliph on 5 March, 1924. Eight months later he signed his abdication in favor of his eldest son, Ali. The tale of his trip from Mecca to Jedda in a caravan of five cars laden with his family and sealed kerosene tins containing £800,000 in gold sovereigns and his embarcation at Jedda on his ramshackle steam yacht the 'Two Mercies,' for exile in Aqaba, has been told and retold. His forced departure from Aqaba because of Ibn Saud's threat to take the town if he remained was hastened by a British ultimatum demanding that he leave before the end of June.

On 16 June he was taken to Cyprus on H.M.S. *Delhi*. Storrs, governor of Cyprus (1926–1932), and Baker describe his life in internment and the travesty of his investment by Storrs himself with the Grand Cross and Ribbon of the Order of the Bath. When down from Oxford his youngest son Zaid attended him in his 'small' villa, albeit with marble steps from the garden and a reception room. Storrs suggests that the original hoard of gold sovereigns was less than the rumored amount, and that a portion of it had been given, perhaps reluctantly, to Palestinian petitioners. Any such gift would have been out of character for Husain, although the withdrawal of British support that allowed Ibn Saud to act was in part caused by his incessant protests over the implementation of the Balfour declaration that opened Palestine to the Jews. The other and more weighty factor in the British decision was his intransigence in demanding that Britain keep its promise to help him become leader of the Arabs.

Husain was not entirely unlikeable, once his dream of leading all the Arabs was dead. While in exile he kept Arab mares, one of whom, Zahra, on occasion entered the house to be greeted affectionately by the old king who hand-fed her dates. She left the pits on a plate. Not long before his death all the mares were killed by a disgruntled groom, leaving him disconsolate for the remaining months of his life. Although often visited by his other three sons, Husain had no contact with the Greek and Turkish population of the island whom he accused of cheating in their accounts for goods and services. He died 4 June 1931 in Amman where he had been taken after a stroke late in 1930.

He was buried at the Dome of the Rock in Jerusalem, his funeral dignified by an honor guard of British soldiers. That was a government's belated gesture in recognition of the value of his contribution to the Allied cause. Perhaps the courage he showed in the face of adversity and his persistence in demanding what he believed due him aroused sympathy. The number of commentaries attempting to justify and to explain British actions suggest as much.

# VI. W. H. I. Shakespear
## (1878–1913)

William Henry Irvine Shakespear was born at Multan in the Punjab 29 October 1878 from parents whose families made a career of serving the Crown in India. He was educated in England, the eldest of three sons. Although not at the top of his classes he did well. Athletically inclined, he played on his school teams and went to Sandhurst where he was gazetted as a second lieutenant in January 1898. He left immediately for India. After a year of normal military duties including supervision of cholera camps, the great plague of 1899 gave him the opportunity to distinguish himself which he did by organizing raids on rats when he was appointed assistant district officer in Bombay on 6 March, 1901. In April 1902 he rejoined his regiment and continued language studies that he had begun while in Bombay.

In 1904, then twenty-five and tired of military life although he had done well in the service, he transferred to the viceroy's political department and became the youngest consul in the Indian administration. He was posted to Bandar Abbas in Persia where Major Cox, the political resident for the Gulf, found, after Shakespear had a violent dispute with his Russian counterpart, that he worked best alone, and sent him to Muscat. He had mastered Persian, Pushtu, Urdu, and Arabic while in India.

In 1907 he transferred to Hyderabad in India where he bought a one-cylinder, 8 horse-power Rover with a recommended top speed of 24 miles per hour. After months of practice and participation in cross-country races he returned to Bushire with the motor. In April he left his post on leave and drove through Persia, Turkey, Macedonia, Thessaly, down to Athens, then through Montenegro and Dalmatia to Italy—Venice, Padua, Ferrara, Bologna, Pesaro and south to Rome. Then he motored north to Switzerland and across France to

England, in all a journey of nearly three thousand miles, a good part of them in places where no automobile had been before.

In late summer he was again in India and, returning to his work, was posted by Cox to Kuwait early in 1909 as political agent. Late in the year he began short trips by camel into the desert, learning the routine that he would perfect in later desert journeys. He met Ibn Saud in Kuwait in the first days of the following March and persuaded him and his retinue to be photographed. Shakespear had a fine camera. He developed the plates in improvised dark rooms, often a tent. The amir and he found themselves congenial, but did not meet again for a year—7 March 1911, in a desert camp near Thaj. They talked for three days. Ibn Saud mentioned the meetings of the leaders of the Arab states, Yemen, Asir, Muscat, and himself, attempting to forge an alliance against the Turks. Shakespear was obliged to tell him not to expect British support for he knew Whitehall's opinion that Turkey was the only legitimate power in Arabia, and its view that Britain had no interest in the interior.

After leave, Shakespear came back to Kuwait in the last days of January 1912. He had decided to stop seeing the one woman who interested him and to return to the desert. In Kuwait the whole year passed in soothing Mubarak who had taken offense at the British acceptance of Turkish demands for the posting of an Ottoman representative in Kuwait. After a partial success in calming the ruler, he escaped into the Gulf for a sailing vacation with a friend. In March 1913, he made a long journey of exploration into the hinterland, ending his penetration inland at Majma'a. There he heard that Ibn Saud was at Khafs. He met his friend on 30 March after a three-day march. During their four days together Ibn Saud told him that he was going to attack the Turks at Hofuf. Possibly Shakespear feared for his friend because during his return trip to Kuwait entire days were left unnoted in the journal where events were usually recorded meticulously. (Ibn Saud's attack on Hofuf took place during the night of 4–5 May.)

The errant consul was fiercely reprimanded for having seen Ibn Saud when Britain was engaged in delicate negotiations with Turkey regarding spheres of interest in the Middle East. He apologized only because otherwise he feared that he would not be allowed to make the journey across Arabia that he had planned for the start of his long leave. The idea of such a trip came when he enthusiastically accepted an invitation from the amir to visit him in Riyadh. The political resident supported him in the negotiations for permission to make such a trek and the viceroy of India was persuaded to sanction it. The Foreign Office at last gave its permission.

After Ibn Saud's conquest of al Hasa, Cox, on the eve of leave and a return to India as secretary of the foreign department, was heedful of the amir's adverse reaction to Britain's insistence that Turkey was the sovereign power in Nejd. He sent Shakepear and Major Trevor (political agent in Bahrain) to meet Ibn Saud at Oqair. They assured the amir that his independence was recognized by Britain, and that he should delay for at least three months signing a treaty of alliance with Turkey while Britain attempted a solution through diplomatic channels. Ibn Saud did his best to follow the plan. *(See pp. 83–84.)*

When Shakespear reached England in May 1914 after his 111-day trip across Arabia he spent weeks arranging his collection of plants and animals and collating notes and maps. Late in June he prepared a report summarizing his relations with Ibn Saud who had shown him his correspondence with the rulers of Asir and Yemen, the Turks, and the paramount shaikh of the 'Anaiza tribe. Shakespear repeated his recommendations that Ibn Saud be recognized as the sovereign power in Nejd, and warned that the Turks were planning to retake al Hasa. The war put an end to these efforts to influence government policy.

Shakespear's self-imposed task as an instructor at Aldershot and his return to Arabia at government behest he describes in a letter to Gertrude Bell dated 15 January 1915, written in Ibn Saud's camp at Majma'a, 'just as that [Aldershot] got going nice and smoothly the India Office wired for me and fired me out here, "to get in personal touch" with Bin Saud.... I had got as far as Karachi when war with Turkey was announced ... not a trace of any fanaticism or feeling against the British.... I trust you had a better Christmas and New Year than I ... a 22 mile march and New Year's Day my second bath in 20 days....' Ten days later he was dead, killed by allies of the Rashids while directing the fire of a small caliber cannon.

The friendship between Ibn Saud and Shakespear was genuine. In 1927 Clayton asked the king who was the greatest European he had met. He replied without hesitation: 'Captain Shakespear.' It is not difficult to see why. Both were big men, strong and fit. In the spring of 1913, Shakespear was 34, Ibn Saud 36. Both enjoyed hunting with salukis and hawks. Both were quick-tempered, self-confident, intolerant of interference, As friends both were forthright and frank, but the Englishman was incapable of deviousness or subtlety.

Shakespear had been reared at the end of the Victorian era. He was intelligent, but not intellectual. In general, he was a poor judge of character, and his assessments of men were often inaccurate. In his writings there are no descriptions of men, no judgments as to their appearance, or their oddities in speech or conduct. On the other hand he was most solicitous to map his itineraries accurately, to gather plant and animal specimens, to record the *wasms* of the tribes he dealt with, and to note their customs with regard to circumcision and tattooing.

Stiff and unbending regarding principles, he refused to adopt Arab garb and wore the khaki of his regiment in spite of Ibn Saud's warnings. In the desert, although he observed Arab etiquette with his companions, he nevertheless carried a supply of European food, wine, and whiskey. When alone he dined in style, and used a hip bath when water was available. His refusal to change his standards of conduct killed him.

He endured, albeit not without complaint, the hardships of desert travel. His perseverance was remarkable, his achievements considerable. He loved adventure, and sought out danger for its own sake. His desire to witness the battle of Jarrab cost him his life. If he had lived, Ibn Saud would have been persuaded to give more help to the British in World War I. His collaboration with Ibn Saud in writing the draft of the treaty that gave the Nejdi chieftain Britain's protection may have played a part in the monarch's later assessment of his friend as the greatest European he had known.

# VII. HARRY ST. JOHN BRIDGER PHILBY
## (1885–1960)

H. St. J. B. Philby in 1946

A. T. Wilson described Philby as 'one of those men who are apt to assume that everything that they come across from a government to a fountain-pen is constructed on wrong principles and capable of amendment.' In his autobiography Philby replied that he had never had the good fortune to encounter either a perfect government or a perfect fountain pen. He goes on to state that the British government seldom meant its declared policy to be taken literally, and commented that if he had been able or willing to accept without reluctance or misgivings the constant changes in that policy he might have enjoyed an honorable and profitable, perhaps even a distinguished career in government service. He valued his contributions to society highly, writing that if knowledge is of any value, the world owed him more than it was likely to appreciate or to repay. This opinion, freely expressed throughout his adult life, made him many enemies, and his repeated refrain of, 'I told you so!' even more. He was extraordinarily gifted in repartee, and did not spare its barbs. His fault was to see everything in black and white with no intermediate shades; this in a British milieu where policy was based on the 'inevitability of gradualness.' He saw himself acting from the highest motives and free to say what he thought. His fault was not in what he said, but in the extravagant and excessive way that he said it.

His scholastic record shows a superior intelligence and his explorations a persistence of purpose undaunted by difficulty. Together with unmatched opportunity they increased the West's knowledge of large uncharted regions of Arabia. His industry as a writer before the age of word processors is shown by some fifteen published volumes and eight in manuscript, all lengthy, and almost all concerned in one way or another with his journeys of exploration or his studies of Islamic and pre-Islamic culture and history. These, and reports as an official of the British government, along with contributions to journals and encyclopedias constitute an imposing memorial.

Harry came into the world on 3 April 1885 at St. John's tea plantation in Ceylon (Sri Lanka) the second son of Henry and May (Queenie) Philby. Two more sons completed the family of four brothers: Tom (Ralph Montagu), Jack (Harry), Tim (Harold Payne) and Paddy (Dennis Duncan). Tim and Paddy were killed in action at Ypres.

Jack (Harry) was precocious, for he says that he learned to write at the age of four in order to communicate with his mother who had gone to Ireland in 1888 to await the birth of her child. She returned to Ceylon with her last son late in 1889. Because of the failure of the market for tea, the family emigrated to England in 1891 leaving the father to cope with his debts. He never rejoined his wife.

After instruction at home and in local establishments, in 1894 Tom and Jack were taken to Henfield House, a boarding school. For two years they were given a grounding in the classics. In 1897 their maternal grandfather paid their tuition at Streete Courte in Westgate-on-Sea under J. V. Milne, a well-known educator. Jack did well in the entrance examination and found himself in the first class where he acquitted himself with distinction, soon becoming head of the school.

In 1898 because of academic excellence he won admission to Westminster as a Queen's Scholar. He became captain of the school for 1904 with a place on the first eleven cricket team. In 1905 he was at Trinity College, Cambridge, where he spent four years, already engaged in the argumentation, criticism, and controversy that marked his entire life. He remarks in his autobiography: 'It was a long time before I learned—and I rather doubt that I have realized it yet—that truth, however absolute it may be in the philosophical sense, may be entirely relative amid the complications of social and political life. The same with right and wrong, and other things.' Strangely, during most of his stay at the University he defended the existing order. Only in his last year did he begin to doubt orthodoxy.

In 1907 he took a First in the Modern Languages Tripos, after having taken a Second in the first part of the Classical Tripos the year before. During the vacations he had traveled in Europe and acquired a good knowledge of French and German. He found that he had a considerable facility in language, and because he planned to enter government service in India he took Hindustani and elementary Arabic during his last year at Cambridge, and, as a future member of the India Civil Service, a probationary course in oriental languages and Indian law and history.

On 6 November 1908 he sailed for India. His years at Cambridge had eroded the religious and political background of his Victorian upbringing, but he says in his autobiography, 'I faced the world without a trace of cynicism, honestly believing that all men everywhere were honestly seeking to make the world a good place for men to dwell in. But I was still very young.'

On 8 December he arrived in the Jhelum district of northern Punjab. It includes the upper stretches of the great river and much of the Salt Range. Afterward he worked in several provinces of northern India. He managed to scandalize his superiors by admitting the possibility that Indians might one day take over the government of their own country. Philby improved his command of Urdu and other languages in a variety of tasks. In September 1909 he moved to Rawalpindi and in September 1910 married Dora, the eldest daughter of Adrian Johnston, an official of the Rawalpindi Department of Public Works. His eldest son, Kim, was born 1 January 1912.

Philby was named revenue assistant and became responsible for all branches of revenue and excise in the area of his jurisdiction. After Turkey entered the war on the German side he drafted material for publication intended to maintain the loyalty of the Moslem population. He then became head of the Board of Examinations for proficiency in languages because the previous holder of the post had gone to war. Stationed in Calcutta he had a corps of Indian assistants.

Quite unexpectedly he was drafted by the foreign and political department of the India Office for service in Mesopotamia and arrived in Basra 20 November 1915 to work under Sir Percy Cox, head of the political department in the Persian Gulf. Philby was soon appointed financial assistant to Sir Percy. Then began a long imbroglio with A. T. Wilson (deputy chief of the political department, and his immediate superior), who favored an indefinite British mandate in Iraq. He met Gertrude Bell who was working in the intelligence department. An accomplished linguist and explorer, both subjects of interest to Philby, she found him congenial. They shared an interest in the genealogy of Arab families. Although their views regarding the future government of Iraq differed markedly, they became friends.

As his work progressed, Philby was appointed revenue commissioner in the wartime administration of Mesopotamia. Sometime later he met Captain H. R. P. Dickson, political officer at Suq as Shiyukh. The characterization of Dickson in his autobiography is unflattering, and shows an intellectual arrogance that is perhaps one of Philby's least attractive traits. However, the two worked together during the war as friends, sharing a number of trips and experiences.

The quarrels with Wilson resulted in Philby's removal from the post of revenue commissioner and his acceptance of the position of political officer at 'Amara where he remained for four months, until May 1917. Discouraged and embittered by his posting to a backwater he asked Sir Percy for a change of employment, and was offered a job in Baghdad as editor of a new Arab newspaper. However, for five months his main employment was as secretary to Sir Percy who was overwhelmed by paperwork. But he continued his criticisms of Wilson's views about government in the Mandate which at last provoked Cox to action.

Ibn Saud had been awarded a subsidy at the 1916 Durbar in Kuwait. Subsequently, Sir Percy advised Whitehall that the desert chief could provide more aid to the Allies than a mere blockade of supplies to the Turks, and arranged a mission to Riyadh to consult with and advise him about a larger participation in the war effort. As planned, the mission was to include representatives from both Cairo and Baghdad, for the India Office and Whitehall had for long been at odds regarding the disparity between the large resources of money and arms afforded Husain and the modicum offered Ibn Saud. Col. R. E. A. Hamilton, then political agent in Kuwait, was chosen to head that part of the mission going to Riyadh from the Persian Gulf side.

According to his own story *(Arabian Days, p. 143)* Philby ceded to Wilson his position as assistant to Sir Percy in return for the post of Chief of Mission to Ibn Saud. His meddling with Wilson's plans for the development of Iraq had caused friction that Cox would not tolerate and Philby, to his delight, was gently set aside to do what he had dreamed of—to work on his own.

Cox gave him a letter addressed to Hamilton explaining the change in leadership and giving the soldier the choice of working under Philby or returning to Kuwait. Philby set off accompanied by Colonel H. Cunliffe-Owen as military adviser. They reached Riyadh 30 November 1917. Colonel Hamilton (later Lord Belhaven)—authoritative, a friend of Ibn Saud and fourteen years senior to Philby—had been in Riyadh for some time to investigate a sale of Saudi camels to the Turks. He had been told that he would head the mission, and was so perturbed by having been displaced by a man junior in age and service that he began his return to the coast four days later, after having participated in all discussions involving Kuwait.

Abdur Rahman received Philby and his party on the first floor of the amir's palace. He was, 'a little old man, nearing seventy' who performed all the courtesies due an honored guest. As the old man left saying, 'With your permission we shall now retire, and you will meet our son,' Ibn Saud, who had effaced himself in the presence of his father, came forward. The formal meeting that followed was the prelude to a series of work sessions, the first of which took place that day. Ibn Saud pointed out that intercepting blockade runners to the Turks was difficult because Shaikh Salim (of Kuwait) himself directed their operations. The delegation could not soften the amir's hatred for this peer, although one of its three objectives was to improve relations between Kuwait and Nejd.

One of the other two objectives of the mission—improved relations between Sharif Husain of the Hejaz and Ibn Saud—was achieved quickly, but with reservations. Ibn Saud promised to refrain from all aggression against the Hejaz provided that Husain did not act against him, and that the British would continue to protect him against aggression from any source, including Husain.

The third objective—an attack on Haïl, the seat of the Ar Rashid—was agreed on, the campaign to begin in April 1918, provided that the requirements in money and arms for an army were forthcoming.

Philby then undertook the first of the several actions which led some to judge that he was unsuitable as a servant of the crown. This was his unauthorized overland trip from Riyadh to the Hejaz made to demonstrate the falsity of Husain's contention that travel in Nejd was unsafe. Husain had given insecurity as the reason for his refusal to allow Sir Ronald Storrs, chosen to represent Cairo on the mission, to journey by camel from Jedda to Riyadh. Philby too was prevented from returning to Nejd overland. He found Ibn Saud in the desert only on 11 April 1918 after a stay in Egypt and a long sea voyage. By then, the successes of the Allied armies made a campaign against Haïl unnecessary.

Philby's decision to use the moneys left in his care as an encouragement for Ibn Saud to undertake operations against the Rashids was, it seems, his own. The move of the army northward began in August. It succeeded in amassing booty and in turning the *Ikhwan's* attention away from events at Khurma, but inflicted no great harm on the Rashidi hegemony. When the army returned to Riyadh the war was over. While awaiting this campaign, Philby made a long trip south, locating geographic entities like Wadi Dawasir, and visiting towns and villages. He was not allowed to accompany the army past Buraida and after a year in Arabia returned to Baghdad, leaving Ibn Saud bitter against the British for reducing the quantity of arms to be supplied him while still supporting his enemy Husain.

In Baghdad, Philby found that Cox had gone to Persia as ambassador to settle a factional dispute leaving Wilson, his antagonist over policy, in command of civil administration in Mesopotamia. The Anglo–French declaration issued in Baghdad 8 November 1918 concerning the emancipation of the peoples of Arab territories liberated from Turkish rule led Philby, on his way to England, to write a memorandum concerning the steps to be taken to implement the declaration. It was ignored by Wilson, the Arab Bureau, and the India Office, but Philby, showing his belief in his own genius, says, '... if Wilson had acted on my suggestions he might have made a great reputation as one of Britain's outstanding administrators' (*Arabian Days, p. 174*).

Shortly after Philby's return to England, Husain's repeated attacks on Khurma precipitated a conference of Whitehall's Middle East department, chaired by Lord Curzon. Summoned to present his views, Philby was alone in opposing the general opinion that in any clash between the Arab leaders Husain would easily win because of the British training and armaments given his army. Tacitly, the sharif of Mecca was given permission to attack, although cautioned against it.

Abdullah's debacle at Turaba led to another meeting at which Philby was made a messenger to Ibn Saud. His trip by air to Cairo was ordered because of Whitehall's assumption that he could persuade the sultan to withdraw from the Hejaz. The government was sure, in spite of Philby's assurances to the contrary, that the amir was then invading the Hejaz. But Ibn Saud's army had not left Nejd.

Once again in London, Philby escorted Ibn Saud's second surviving son, Faisal, then fourteen, on his tour of Europe. The boy had been sent to London by Ibn Saud in response to an invitation given by the British government to show its gratitude for Saudi aid in the war.

Philby predicted to all and sundry the uprising of May 1920 in Iraq. He blamed it on Wilson's policies directed toward keeping Iraq under British tutelage. When sedition erupted with serious losses to the British troops stationed there, Cox was recalled from Persia to London for consultation and sent back as high commissioner for Iraq. He selected Philby and Cheesman as aides. En route they stopped at Oqair and talked with Ibn Saud who was invested with the insignia of Grand Commander of the Most Eminent Order of the Indian Empire. As one of Cox's staff, Philby became deeply involved in the politics of creating a democratic provisional government that would be acceptable to all Iraqis. The 150 British officers serving as advisory staff were reduced to 40. Philby was one of those retained, becoming adviser to the Ministry of the Interior.

Winston Churchill left his wartime post to become secretary of state for the colonies. To end the long-term discord between Whitehall and the India

Office regarding Arab interests, he established a new 'Middle East department' in the Colonial Office to regulate these matters. He chose to review all the wartime commitments made in the region by the British government. In March 1921 he convened a great conference to that end in Cairo. *(See Klieman 1970.)*

Churchill had Lawrence at his side, a Lawrence who felt that his promises to the Hashemites in return for their wartime services had not been kept, for Husain's son, Faisal, under British auspices king of Syria for five months, had been ousted in July 1920 by the French. Rumors that Faisal was to be made king of Iraq reached Baghdad, creating consternation among people like Philby who in good faith had expected a democratic régime for the country.

Cox had attended the Cairo conference but told his staff only a few of its rulings. To comply with the decisions made in Cairo he kidnapped the provisional minister of the interior, Seyyid Talib Pasha, a devious politician with strong backing as candidate for head of government, but a patriot whom he himself, albeit with misgivings, had selected for the post. In great secrecy Talib was deported to Ceylon under house arrest. Philby, already named adviser, replaced him.

On 12 June 1921 Faisal arrived at Basra and was met by Philby, whom Cox had selected to greet the candidate for king in the name of the provisional government. On the way to Baghdad by special train Churchill's candidate was given lessons on the virtues of democracy by his host, then coming down with a malarial attack. Greeted very coolly by the people en route, especially the *Shias*, Faisal had a better reception in Baghdad. He was crowned king of Iraq on 23 August 1921. According to the official tally, a plebiscite substituted for an election gave him 96.5 per cent of the popular vote. Owing to Philby's outspoken conviction that a republic was the right government for Iraq and his having told Faisal so, Cox had dismissed him from his post as acting minister of the interior on 7 July. The dissenter was on holiday in Persia on Coronation Day.

Philby returned to Baghdad in the middle of October. Two days later, Cox who had cast about for another job for him showed him a telegram from the Colonial Office in which it was suggested that Philby replace Lawrence as chief British representative in Transjordan. Created by Churchill, this was a state just then becoming a stable entity under its first amir, Abdullah ibn Husain. Abdullah had arrived in that small would-be kingdom by train from Medina repairing the track as he came and burning telegraph poles for fuel.

Philby accepted the post and flew to Amman where he met Lawrence. They got along well together and after a month the transfer of authority was made without incident. The British staff stationed in posts other than Amman was withdrawn. Relations with Amir Abdullah and his cabinet eventually became cordial. A few months later Bertram Thomas replaced Philby's previous assistant.

In May 1922 Philby committed a diplomatic *faux pas*. The British government had French agreement to the construction of a railway from Aqaba or Haifa across Arabia to Baghdad. As the route passed near Jauf, Cox, still high commissioner for Iraq, tacitly acknowledged Saudi jurisdiction in the Wadi Sirhan region by requesting Ibn Saud's help and protection for the surveyors. Sir Herbert Samuel, the first high commissioner for Palestine, was Philby's superior as representative of the mandatory power, but not in his position as head of the administration of Palestine. Nevertheless, he favored including Jauf in Transjordan. He claimed that Nuri as Sha'lan, the paramount shaikh of the Ruwala, still controlled the area. Cox told Samuel that Sha'lan had accepted Saudi overlordship there.

To test this matter, Sir Herbert sent Philby to Jauf in company with the surveyor for the rail line. His orders were, 'to proceed to Jauf and to establish a basis for friendly relations after satisfying himself that no risk of extending Imperial commitment in Transjordan was involved therein.' Philby went to Jauf but disobeyed his orders by concluding with one of the Sha'lan shaikhs a formal offensive and defensive treaty annexing Jauf to Transjordan, with the British government promising funds for military operations: 'If the common interests of the parties require an attack on their neighbours, or if any of their neighbours attack them.' The Colonial Office repudiated the treaty immediately. Philby accompanied the surveyor to Iraq but an irate Cox refused him entry to Baghdad, possibly in part because he feared Ibn Saud's reaction to the treaty, but also, perhaps, because of Philby's stance on democracy and his anti-monarchist articles in the Persian press derogatory of Cox's stand.

In October Philby accompanied Amir Abdullah to London. In November and December they visited government officials and persons of importance, including the king. Abdullah got a promise of independence and funds. On 25 May 1923 Transjordan became independent and Philby's attempts to curb Abdullah's extravagance met with even less success than before.

In December 1923 Husain in Mecca announced an intention to visit his son in Transjordan and arrived at Aqaba on his decrepit Greek steam yacht *al Rahmatain* (the Two Mercies) early in February. Philby met him at Ma'an after the 75-year-old's arduous two-day journey there on the back of a donkey brought with him on the yacht. Philby, who had been honored previously by a high Hejazi decoration, was summoned to the presence. Ibn Saud was one of the subjects discussed. The old, self-styled 'King of the Arab Lands' said, 'Are we not all Arabs together? Why, I cannot but regard him as my son. And you, his friend and mine, you shall be my agent with him. I accept any settlement you agree to.'

A special train took the party to Amman where Abdullah arranged a tremendous demonstration of welcome. Faisal flew from Baghdad to greet his father. On 3 March 1924 Mustafa Kemal, head of the Young Turks in Istanbul, (the new name for Constantinople) deposed the Caliph, Abdul Majid, and abolished the Caliphate. Two days later Husain announced his assumption of the Caliph's title, *Amir al mu'minin* (Commander of the Faithful). Vehicles of propaganda went into action, not the least of them Husain's own newspaper *al Qibla*. Except in the three Hashemite-ruled lands the Islamic world paid little attention to the proclamation, although in India committees were formed and funds collected. The Wahhabis of Nejd were scandalized at the haste and impiety of the gesture by a *mushrikin*, all the more one as venal as Husain. Philby admired the gesture of the indomitable old man, but realized that it would incense the Wahhabis.

Early in 1924 airplanes and armored cars under Philby's orders broke up a threatened rebellion by a paramount shaikh of Transjordan. These same forces, which became the 'Arab Legion,' severely punished the *Ikhwan* involved in the

August raid described in n. 17, which is an excerpt from a letter written by Bertram Thomas, then Philby's assistant.

Throughout his three years as adviser to Amir Abdullah, Philby was frequently engaged in a polemic or worse with Sir Herbert regarding some infringement of the rights or property of Transjordan by Palestinian forces. According to Philby's version, this reactionary interference included advice to Abdullah to disregard the instructions of his adviser and to accept orders from Sir Samuel. As this was contrary to the policy outlined to him by Churchill and the duke of Devonshire, he felt compelled to resign.

On 18 April 1924 he left Amman with his family. They took ship to England while Philby made a tour of Turkey by train. His retirement from government service after sixteen years netted him an annual income of £700, but debts forced him to search for other sources of income.

In September, Philby approached Naji al Asil, London representative of the Hejaz government, with an offer to go to Jedda to help Husain's son Ali, now king, in negotiations with Ibn Saud. War had begun on 29 August. Queried by cable, Ali agreed at once to his coming, although warned by the British that Philby had no official standing. Philby took ship to Suez and the S.S. *Registan* dropped him off in the Red Sea opposite Jedda. King Ali's launch brought him ashore. There, conditions under the new king were less than satisfactory. Both Amin Rihani and Seyyid Talib (the Iraqi nationalist freed after Faisal's enthronement) were there, offering their services as mediators. Philby was told by Reader Bullard, the British agent and consul, that if he went into the interior he would forfeit his pension rights, for his resignation had not yet been accepted. Ibn Saud told him and the two other would-be mediators that they had no part in a purely Arab conflict. Philby left for Aden after developing blood poisoning as a result of an anti-dysentery shot given him by Ali's personal physician, and returned to England with another warning about his pension, and an urgent need for funds.

Within months he arranged support from investors for the establishment of a small importing agency in Jedda to be called 'Sharqiyeh Limited'. To earn a living before hostilities ended he wrote articles for newspapers about events in the Hejaz. On 29 June 1925 he sent the *Times* a letter pointing out the falsehood of a spokesman addressing the House regarding the legal ownership of Aqaba. His comments are typical of his attitude toward the British government and his vitriolic pen:

> Such a statement made by a responsible Minister of the Crown cannot be allowed to pass unchallenged. It is a quibble entirely unworthy of Great Britain and, as one who for two and a half years occupied the post of Chief British Representative in Transjordan, I have no hesitation in stating as a fact that not only the town of Aqaba but the surrounding district (the Hejaz Province of Ma'an) have never ... regarded as falling within any other country than the Hejaz ... the recent extension of the area of mandated Palestine at the expense of the Hejaz, without the sanction of the League of Nations, and in spite of our declaration of neutrality in the conflict between the Wahhabis and the Hejaz is an unpardonable act of aggression against a weak state. And, so far as it is the truth to say that the occupation of Aqaba by the Hejaz has never

had the formal consent of H.M.G., it may not be without point to remind H.M.G., whose memory is remarkably short, that Aqaba was actually occupied by the Hejaz Army with the active cooperation of the H.M. forces. But that, if I remember right, was before the 'Balfour declaration' which has made it so difficult to keep our promises to the Arabs.

In the autumn of 1925 Philby returned to Jedda, still in Ali's hands, with an official Persian mission investigating the alleged damage to historic tombs by Saudi shells. He sent a message to Ibn Saud asking permission to visit him. It was granted only in November when Sir Gilbert Clayton had left Jedda after signing the Hadda-Bahra agreements. Philby quit Jedda secretly after a warning by the British consul against travel in the interior. He went north to Rabigh, sailing in a small boat for three days. From there he rode to Shumaisi where he had a long talk with Ibn Saud during which he reviewed for him the situation in Jedda. Ibn Saud refused discussion of post-war plans, so from Rabigh Philby made an adventure-filled voyage to Port Sudan and from there returned home.

On 1 January 1926 he was again in Jedda, a week after its surrender. Abdullah Damluji was installed as governor and acting minister of foreign affairs, and on 8 January Ibn Saud was proclaimed king of the Hejaz, an item of news that Philby reported to the world's press. He had some difficulty in obtaining Ibn Saud's permission to set up his business, and then returned to England, where he lectured on Middle East problems and inveighed in public against attempts by the government to break the general strike. At that time Faisal and Damluji came to England for discussions and Philby returned to Jedda with them.

He became involved in Clayton's negotiations with Ibn Saud concerning the Treaty of Jedda for which he claims to have offered constructive criticism. While running his business, he reported for the English press the events of the *Ikhwan* revolt and Ibn Saud's meeting with King Faisal as it ended. At the same time he wrote two full-length books about Arabia, a biography of Leachman (unpublished) and a critique of British policy in India. His business probably suffered, for on occasion he was forced to seek help to remain solvent.

Philby sold perambulators and fans and in 1934 was named sole distributor for Ford just at the moment that production of the Model 'T' ceased. He provided the coal for the Jedda condenser. He obtained the Standard Oil marketing contract for kerosene and oil. In the years from 1926 to 1930 his profits were at best marginal, and thereafter the worldwide depression put him in desperate straits financially. He and his wife played a part in the social life of Jedda which boasted a gallery of more or less interesting figures, and occasional oddballs. At this time Philby was highly critical of the lower echelon of British government officials, and his acerbity in their regard is documented by others. When Sir Andrew Ryan, the first British envoy and minister plenipotentiary arrived in Jedda, the Chargé d'Affaires, a certain Bond, attempted to limit the size and make-up of the party allowed aboard the sloop *Clematis* to welcome him. Philby wrote the minister a note of protest that resulted in a reception on the ship for the entire British population of Jedda. Philby composed an ode for the occasion in which every line rhymed with Ryan, and a poem in which the release from Bonds was welcomed.

In *Arabian Days*, his autobiography, Philby characterized his outlook at this period as that of an iconoclast with strong leftward leanings, and said that he was generally regarded in Jidda society as something of a Bolshevik. From the accounts of others it seems that Philby was always ready to criticize the established order. Van der Meulen writes:

> I gladly took every opportunity to talk with this provocative person who seemed to go out of his way to oppose everything British and indeed, wherever Arab interests were concerned, openly scorned everything Western.... The men who represented England in Jedda were no match for him.... Philby fought against prejudice but was a most prejudiced man himself. He was a born controversialist who loved contradiction and opposition. Not understanding himself, he lacked the gift of understanding others and that may be the reason that he was always in conflict: with the Arabs of his caravan, with the Government, with its policy, with his own personnel, and, I think most of all with himself *(1957, pp. 22–24)*.

On 7 August 1930 Philby became a Moslem. With Ibn Saud's consent and under the guidance of Fuad Hamza and Abdullah Suleiman he signed an official document and in Mecca performed the rites of the Lesser Pilgrimage, the 'Umra. His motive for this step was certainly not a religious conversion. A British consul in Jedda stated that, 'He made no pretense whatever that his conversion was spiritual. He had been deliberating the step for four years....'

He himself wrote in a letter to a friend that he had sacrificed neither his sanity nor his sincerity in so doing. In his autobiography he quotes Ryan who reportedly said, 'Mecca and Islam will give Philby the background which he has needed so badly ever since he quarreled with the Government.' Philby himself wrote: 'The Wahhabi creed seemed to me, as the result of deep study, to be the ideal form of religion, and the fanaticism of its followers did not displease me' *(1948, p. 278)*. He discusses at some length the purely pragmatic reasons for his decision, seemingly for the most part practical expedients:'It seemed a pity not to stay on and complete the work (*to learn and then to teach the world about Arabia*), to which I had put my hand long since and for which I had such special qualifications' *(p. 279)*.

Philby did not take a paid position in the Saudi court but after 1945 became financially independent because of his association with Ibn Saud, whom he lectured, and on occasion exasperated to the point of temporary banishment. In the thirties he had no more success than anyone else in being paid for his sales of goods to the government and both he and his company remained in a parlous state until 1933 when in return for his services as intermediary to the Saudi government he was offered a salary and other emoluments by Lloyd Hamilton, lawyer and negotiator for Standard of California. Before that date he himself was never in actual want, for when he was with the king his food and lodging were provided, but his wife and family when in England were often in straitened circumstances which he endeavored to ameliorate, often with little success. His attendance at the king's *majlis* was fairly regular, and 1932–1933 when the Saudi state was most in debt he habitually attended the meetings of the king's counselors where his argumentative posture led Ibn Saud to comment, in comparing his Council with the British Parliament: 'Why, we discuss everything here in complete democratic freedom, and we even have our official opposition. Philby is that!'

Ibn Saud finally allowed him to make his way to al Hasa where he started his attempt to traverse the Rub' al Khali on 7 January 1932, shortly after Bertram Thomas had completed the first crossing. At Wahbar he discovered the meteorite craters, legendary castles. Because of difficulties with his escort he did not complete the journey across the sands into the Hadhramaut, instead turning west to Sulaiyil. He returned to Mecca three months after he had left it.

After the pilgrimage of 1932 he went to London where he gave lectures about his recent experiences and wrote a book about them called *The Empty Quarter*. An executive of the Standard Oil Company of California, Francis Loomis, asked him to lunch and discussed Ibn Saud's requirements for granting a concession. After having traveled by car across Europe to Istanbul, he and his wife returned to Jedda. There he found a telegram from Loomis, confirming Standard's interest in a concession. His part in the subsequent negotiations is outlined on pp. 71–72.

In *Arabian Days* and in *Arabian Oil Ventures* Philby tells a story concerning the reaction of the British minister to Saudi Arabia, Ryan, to news of the granting of the concession to an American company. It suggests that Ryan's opinion of oil prospects in Arabia was not so negative as that recounted elsewhere in this screed. In Philby's story, Ryan was confident that owing to Ibn Saud's long-standing regard for the British Longrigg would obtain the rights. When told that the Americans had triumphed, he was speechless with rage and disappointment (*cf. p. 73*).

Philby indulged to the full his desire for adventure and exploration, making an overland trip with his wife across Asia Minor and Europe to London, and returning to Jedda by car across North Africa. Starting in May 1936 he made a long journey southward on the Arabian peninsula, exploring some 200,000 square miles of the mountains of the Southwest, mapping for the king the Saudi Arabia–Yemen frontier, and visiting the Hadhramaut and the Aden protectorate where he was not welcomed by the British authorities. In London his lectures about the trip included condemnation of the British use of bombs and intimidation to enforce peace in the area. For this opinion he was subjected to editorial and governmental criticism but he made money. He returned to Arabia.

It was then that Ibn Saud asked him to take charge of the royal transportation, which resulted, after Philby's attempt to reduce waste and graft, in a quarrel with the king and in consequence a short disappearance from the court.

In January 1939 he accompanied Faisal to London, but played no official part in the conference on the future of Palestine. His own plan for settlement of the problem he discussed with Chaim Weizmann and David Ben Gurion at a meeting in his London residence. Later he proposed it to both public and private interests in England. Rumors of war brought him actively to support the organizations urging peace. He found the Labor party not sufficiently pacifist, and others were too small and too new to be effective. He stood for a by-election for a seat in Parliament and was defeated so handily that he lost his election deposit. Shortly after the declaration of war Ibn Saud summoned him to return.

In January 1940 he was again in Riyadh after a leisurely trip of more than two months, spent mainly in North Africa, and on 9 April was encamped in the desert with the royal entourage. He elaborated on the German invasion of Denmark and Norway to Ibn Saud, explaining its significance as an end to the 'phony war.' He reported each reverse of the Allies to the king, and, of course, interpreted the import of all of them. His view was always on the dark side. For example, he predicted that submarine warfare would force England to sue for peace.

At this same period he offered to the king his solution to the Jewish problem in Palestine: the one that he had given both public and private entities in England a year earlier. It involved a payment of £20 million to the Saudi state. In return Ibn Saud would facilitate the displacement of Arabs from western portion of Palestine that would then be opened to unlimited Jewish immigration. The king told him that he would give his answer at an appropriate time, but to discuss the matter with no one. Philby promptly made his plan known to Yusuf Yassin and on several occasions during the months that followed urged the king to consider it. The king was non-committal to Philby, but in August 1943 when approached by an American envoy concerning the matter, he erupted in a tirade against proponents of the plan.

Philby's decision to go to America was made, according to his autobiography, in order to be in contact with his family in wartime England, but he planned a series of anti-war lectures. Ibn Saud suggested that his views on the world situation would be unpalatable abroad; that he should remain in Arabia. To the British legation in Jedda he reported that Philby's virulent denunciations suggested mental derangement. The crown prince repeated his father's argument, but Philby motored to Dhahran and took ship for Karachi. On 11 August he arrived in India and was arrested and sent by boat to Liverpool where he was jailed for five months. Freed, he spent the next four years writing, and prepared three books for publication. One appeared in 1945. Other interests included a study of 'Himyaritic inscriptions,' some of which he had collected, and a support of the Pakistani effort for recognition as a discrete entity. His main activity was involvement in the activities of Socialist organizations seeking to change the direction of government.

Philby returned to Arabia in July 1945 and resumed his attendance at the sessions of the Council of State. Besides the usual topics—current events, women, genealogy, hunting—new subjects introduced by the ruler included the debilities of aging and the use of restoratives. But the main preoccupation for the king was the Palestine problem. The rebellion there against the British mandate, the intervention of the United Nations and full-scale war, saddened and embittered the monarch who was annoyed by Philby's repeated strictures on his handling of the matter.

Philby benefited from the post-war demand for goods and his company began to be profitable. In addition, the king at last ordered payment in full for purchases by the state over the years. Philby was able to visit England annually and indulge his children and grandchildren. In 1945 he had a gift from the monarch whom he had now known for almost thirty years. This was a concubine whom he called Rozy Firuba. Young, petite, and biddable, he gave her many presents, including a son who died in 1947 shortly after birth. In 1948 she bore another son. He too died in infancy. Dora, his wife, accepted without reproach the new acquisition, as she had Philby's frequent liaisons in the thirties with an earlier concubine and with European women to whom he dedicated his books, but she did not know of the offspring. Rozy had two more sons, Khalid and Faris. Philby was 65 years old when Khalid was born.

In the fifties he allowed neither his amours nor his flourishing business to interfere with exploration: in 1950 north to the pre-Islamic land of Midian in the region east of Taima and Tabuk; late in 1951 south to Nejran with Professor Ryckmans in search of Himyaritic inscriptions, an investigation this time sponsored by the state. In 1952 and 1953 Philby accompanied geologists to Midian in search of iron, sulfur, and gold reported by Burton nearly a century earlier.

The king was failing, but Philby made an effort to warn him about the excesses of his children and grandchildren. Possibly as a result, his last coherent words to Philby were, 'A man's possessions and his children are his enemies.' Philby wondered whether he should stay in Arabia after the king died. He published two more books, one, *Arabian Jubilee*, the king's biography; the other, his revised history, *Saudi Arabia*. In both, he criticized the extravagant western habits of the princes, even mentioning their use of alcohol. In February 1955 he went to Dhahran to lecture to the staff and apparently repeated his strictures. Shortly thereafter he was ordered to quit the kingdom. Although offered a reprieve if he apologized, Philby left Jedda on 15 April via the Trans-Arabian pipeline road and drove to Lebanon. Rozi and the children arrived in Beirut on 7 September, but the books were held in customs pending censorship.

Banishment lasted only until the end of May 1956 when he signed a letter of contrition and returned alone to Riyadh for a short stay. In October he and his Arab family drove overland from Beirut to Riyadh, settling in on 9 November. He left for England late in June 1957. On the 28th in Beirut, he got a telegram announcing Dora's death (his wife for forty-seven years and mother of four children—Kim, Diana, Pat and Helena).

In spite of his derelictions he loved Dora. She was the only one who was privy to all of his secrets, and had accepted Rozi and her children. Every week he sent Dora a long single-spaced typewritten letter. Back in England in July, he made arrangements to settle her affairs and to have his books and papers sent to Riyadh where he would settle down permanently. He accepted a position on the faculty of the American University in Beirut and during the winter of 1957–58 taught classes and gave two public lectures before returning to Riyadh.

For the next two years in Riyadh, he wrote steadily for publication and kept up a vast correspondence with friends and fellow orientalists as well as taking care of his Arab family. In the summer of 1960 he attended the XXVth Orientalists' Congress in Moscow, staying in London for a time both going and coming. In Beirut on his way home he was with his son Kim, partying every night. After the last one he awoke complaining of breathing problems and was rushed to a hospital where he died in the afternoon of 30 September 1960, in his 76th year.

Kim arranged a Mohammedan funeral service and Philby was buried in the Moslem cemetery in Beirut under a stone engraved, 'Greatest of Arabian Explorers.' Because protection by Ibn Saud facilitated his work he had covered twice as much territory with more precision than any one else. His maps and journals are accurate and detailed, his observations precise. Yet his books are read largely by specialists, for they are too bombastic, too digressive and stylistically too convoluted for the general reader.

But this candid judgment about the many volumes on diverse subjects which flowed from this man's pen must not be taken as denigration of their value as a contribution to our knowledge of the geography and pre-Islamic history of the Arabian peninsula before the era of satellite mapping and computer-aided compilations to help in the decipherment and comparison of ancient inscriptions and their historical and ethnological significance. The accuracy of his geographic and topographic observations has been amply confirmed. But to the historian his accounts of the Saudi State and the man who founded it are more valuable than his collections of the artifacts of pre-Islamic cultures.

No other non-Arab had the opportunity to associate for thirty-five years with the Saudi monarch and as a trusted member of his Council to observe the inner workings of the government as well as the character and personal attributes of its head. Yet, aside from infrequent comments in his reports, he is reticent about the king's person. His biography of the monarch, *Arabian Jubilee*, written to celebrate fifty years of rule, is less than candid in some respects. But Philby, although acerbic in his criticisms, admired Ibn Saud and held him in great esteem. This may account for his reticence.

# VIII. FAISAL IBN ABDUL AZIZ
# (1904–1975)

Faisal ibn Abdul Aziz ibn Abdur Rahman ibn Faisal as Saud was the third son of the future king of Saudi Arabia who lived beyond infancy. He was born in 1904, probably the first child of Tarfa bint Abdullah, Ibn Saud's third wife. Little is known about his early childhood, but the family's move to Riyadh took place well before his birth. Like all the children of the ruling family he was cosseted when a baby, but at age seven was sent to a sage of the *Ulema* to learn the Koran, and instructed in riding and the martial arts by one of his father's warriors.

Amir Faisal ibn Abdul Aziz as Saud, King of Saudi Arabia (1964–1975)

We see him first on the world stage in the year 1919, aged fourteen. After transferring from the R.I.M.S. *Lawrence* to H.M.S. *Kigoma* he and his party landed at Plymouth. He was accompanied by his adult cousin, Ahmed ibn Thunaian, and his father's trusted commercial agent in Bahrain, Abdullah Algosaibi. He was escorted from Plymouth to London by Philby, delegated the task of cicerone by Whitehall that had invited the father of the young prince to London to show its appreciation of Ibn Saud's services during the war. It was the first of many trips abroad for the prince, entrusted by his father with diplomatic and fund-seeking missions throughout that monarch's lifetime.

It was 13 October in London, rainy and cold. After one night in a second-rate hotel in Upper Norwood from which they were summarily ejected because the call to prayer rang down the hotel corridors at 5:15 AM, the boy, slight, small, pale, large-eyed, was forced with his entourage into the street to seek lodging elsewhere. Philby, dapper in uniform with Sam Browne belt and boots, found rooms for the party only at a hostel for Indian Army orderly officers. After King George learned that the party had to go to another hotel to eat, the hospitality of the government improved. The prince visited Wales and walked in snow on Mt. Snowden. In Ireland he rode in a donkey car, and at the end of his stay abroad toured western Europe, including the battlefields of Flanders, still grim with the stench of death. In Paris the group, but not Faisal himself, met the friend of Lawrence and son of the sharif of Mecca, another Faisal, who boasted to them of his wartime exploits and denigrated the valor of the *Ikhwan*. The Saudis walked out.

In England Ibn Saud's son was given the gamut of entertainment appropriate to royalty. He gave a sword of honor to the old sailor, King George V, and received autographed photographs of the monarch and his wife in return. Probably he was shocked by the unveiled faces of women of quality like Queen Mary and her sister. He visited the imperious Lord Curzon at the Foreign Office who treated the Saudi party as inferiors. He was taken to see the *Mikado* and *Chu Chin Chow* whose scantily dressed girls may have puzzled rather than titillated him although he was soon to be married. He saw a captured German submarine and an aeroplane, looked through large telescopes at Greenwich, and listened to incomprehensible speeches by a galaxy of dignitaries. Probably he was amused at the zoo and at Crabbet where he inspected a stud of Arabian horses. He visited the mosque at Woking and Philby's eldest son, Kim, at his school in Eastbourne. On ceremonial occasions he wore the usual finery of a prince including a jeweled dagger, huge on his small frame. In the photo taken with Kim and his schoolmates he displays a sword in its scabbard, the pommel of elaborately enchased gold grasped in a small hand. But the most enjoyable of his experiences was the escalator at Selfridges which he rode for hours.

His adult companions managed to set up a conference with representatives of the Foreign and India Offices. Carrying out his instructions from Ibn Saud, Ahmed ibn Thunaian asked the British: to delimit the as yet undefined boundaries of his domain to include Khurma and Turaba which in any case he would keep; to guarantee the independence of his realm without interference in its internal affairs; to lift the ban on pilgrimage; to grant Ibn Saud a permanent subsidy and to appoint Philby political agent in Nejd. The last two requests were never met, but the others came to pass with or without British compliance.

When Faisal returned to Arabia his father welcomed him at Dammam, probably relieved at his safe return and anxious about the health of this scion for he had just lost his firstborn and two other sons in the great influenza epidemic of 1918–19. We know that Faisal married young. His son, Abdullah, was born in 1921 to the first of his three wives, Sultana bint Ahmed ibn Mohammed as Sudairi. We next see him in February 1923 again being greeted by his father in a triumphant welcoming sword dance in Riyadh when he returned from the subjugation of rebels in Asir. At age 18 he had been put in command of the second force sent to restore order there.

His father placed great confidence in this son. During the invasion of the Hejaz in September–October 1924 he must have been given an important rôle although the *Ikhwan* of the attacking forces were led by their chiefs, ibn Luwai, ibn Bijad and ad Duwish. In 1926 Ibn Saud himself organized administration for the newly conquered province. Faisal was named viceroy of the Hejaz in August, replaced the provisional governor, Abdullah ibn Damluji. This was a post for which he was supposedly fit because of his contacts with foreigners. His staff and six counselors made up a 'Legislative Assembly' which was later reduced to a 'Consultative Assembly.' Few details of his ministry are known, although 'Administrative Councils' were voted for in Mecca and Medina, but later disbanded. Semi-democratic rule lasted for only two years. The worldwide economic crisis that began in 1929 greatly reduced the number of pilgrims at the *Hajj*, although improvements in the arrangements for their reception had been made at considerable expense. Revenue from their taxation dropped to the point that the income of the Saudi state dropped by one-third, and its debt rose alarmingly.

In 1930 Faisal was named minister of foreign affairs and nominally took much of the responsibility for contacts with diplomats, but Ibn Saud still made all the decisions and hence was courted by the representatives of other powers. Faisal and Philby were both members of the Council of State, and so free to offer their opinions. The financial crisis became so acute that Fuad Hamza accompanied Faisal on a loan-seeking mission to Europe in the summer of 1932. In one of the protocol visits of a person of rank to Whitehall, Faisal presented a written offer of a concession in Arabia, which was refused shortly thereafter. Fuad talked to the investment bankers and the Bank of England without success. After purchasing Polish rifles in Warsaw (never paid for?) the two visited Russia where Faisal met all the Russian leaders while being given the fanfare and fêtes reserved for heads of state. The party visited all of European Russia from Leningrad to the Caucasus where Faisal saw the oil fields of Baku.

Far different from the cold shoulder of the British, Molotov promised to forgive a large debt owed for a shipment of petroleum products seized in Jedda by Abdullah Suleiman and to lend the Saudis a million pounds if they would sign a treaty of friendship and lift an embargo on Russian goods. Nothing was signed and the financial crisis did not ease. In 1938 the Russian ambassador who had arrived in 1927 left Jedda to disappear in Stalin's purge.

But the trip, although unrewarding as a source of funds, gained Faisal a wife. On the way home from Russia he stopped in Constantinople to investigate a claim to land near Taïf made by Thunaian cousins of the Sauds. There he met Iffat, who became the dueña of his other two wives.

In the war with Yemen in March 1934 Faisal led the column which advanced along the coastal plain, the Tihama, from Asir southward. In three weeks he captured the port of Hodeida on the road to the Yemeni capital, Sana'a. The victory against poorly armed foes appears to have been easy, but his brother Saud fighting in the inland mountains was held up and suffered losses because his men knew only the desert while the enemy knew the upland terrain and had the will to fight to keep it.

In 1939 Ibn Saud sent Faisal to represent him at a conference in London convened to study new proposals for negotiation on the Jewish position in Palestine, two years after a British commission had proposed partition of the country. The negotiators reached no solution and were so far apart that Arab and Jew refused to sit at the same table. The impasse did not displease the king. Faisal became increasingly cognizant of world leaders and their stance on matters important to the Arabs.

In September 1943, Faisal and his younger brother Khalid went to Washington to meet the president. Their trip was part of the American endeavor to insure that Saudi oil would be available to the West after the war and that lend-lease funds already committed to Arabia would insure consideration for future American enterprise. The princes were put up at Blair House across the street from the presidential mansion and given the full treatment including a private railroad car across the country to San Francisco. In 1946 Faisal got nowhere when he went to Washington to get an affirmation from Truman of Roosevelt's promise that the United States would do nothing to aid the Jews against the Arabs without consultation.

Late in 1947 Britain renounced its mandate and turned the Palestine problem over to the United Nations. Faisal went to New York to plead the Arab cause before the General Assembly. He was jostled, vilified and spat upon by Jewish demonstrators as he entered the building. When the Assembly met, the American vote was in favor of a partition that would set up a Jewish state in the better part of Palestine and an Arab state in the rest. It was not only a political insult, but an affront to Faisal himself who, based on conversations with officials, had been so sure of American support that he had assured his colleagues that an unfavorable outcome was not possible.

The State Department, knowing the need for Saudi oil and afraid of an oil embargo, had been in the Arab camp from the start. But it did nothing that might have influenced the decision of the Assembly in favor of the Arabs. Faisal went home disillusioned with America.

When the Buraimi dispute came to the fore in 1949, Faisal supported the king in every respect possible. He stretched the truth by saying that Sunni tribesmen of Oman wanted to pay fealty to Ibn Saud because of the unorthodoxy of the sultan of Oman, and supported ARAMCO efforts to obtain information and tribal support for the Saudi claims. The increasing debility of the king made Faisal's part in the dispute more significant.

Faisal accompanied the monarch, when, weak and ill, he was transported by air to Taïf. Ibn Saud rallied in the cool mountain air. On 8 November the heir-apparent, Saud, went to Jedda as a part of his pre-arranged tour of the country. When the ruler had a relapse Saud hastened to return but was too late. Faisal closed his father's eyes.

Faisal showed that he recognized Saud as heir to the throne by taking a ring from the little finger of the dead man's right hand and offering it to the new king. Saud reciprocated by naming Faisal crown prince. For some years Faisal made no public remonstrance about the king's extravagant expenditures and his concupiscence. He backed Saud's foreign policy, including support for Nasser in Egypt and the embargo on shipments of oil to the United States. Behind the scene Faisal himself was primarily responsible for foreign policy, although Yusuf Yassin was involved in some of the dirty work.

By 1957 Faisal was thoroughly disillusioned about his half-brother's proclivities in matters of sexual satisfaction and his profligacy, but the ineptness of his handling of foreign affairs was the last straw. Faisal was ill for almost the whole year and had two operations to remove a tumor of the stomach. After seven months away, six of them in the United States, he returned to Riyadh. The stability of the house of Saud had been threatened by Saud's meddling in Syrian affairs. Faisal with two brothers and his uncle Abdullah, Abdur Rahman's youngest son, sat down with Saud and persuaded him to relinquish power. Faisal was given executive authority in April 1958, was forced to relinquish it for a time in 1961, regained it in October 1962 and in November 1964 was named king. He restored stability to finances, salaries to servants of the state, and fostered reform with some success—he maintained the As Saud in control of the government in spite of wars and social unrest—until his assassination on 25 March 1975 by a nephew, Faisal ibn Musaid.

When fully adult Faisal was austere and something of an ascetic as compared to his father and to his brother, Saud. As a young man he had been asked to leave Kuwait after a carouse and searchers had once found him in a bordello when due to represent his country at a meeting of the United Nations. Yet he had only three wives and seventeen children—eight boys and nine girls. His first wife bore only one male child, his second, two (he divorced her in 1940). The third, Iffat bint Ahmed ibn Abdullah as Saud, whom he had married for love in 1932 or 1933, gave him five sons. After he became king she was called queen.

He was much shorter than his father and slight of build. His vulpine visage with prominent nose and deep-set eyes shrank as he aged, becoming gnarled and creased. The almost sinister downward twist of the lips suggests a deep cynicism, belied by a kind smile full of charm. His actions revealed a stern integrity and a persistence in pursuit of objectives (e.g., the Buraimi problem) like that of his father. He was like him too in his refusal to delegate authority, the long hours of work and adherence to an unvarying daily routine.

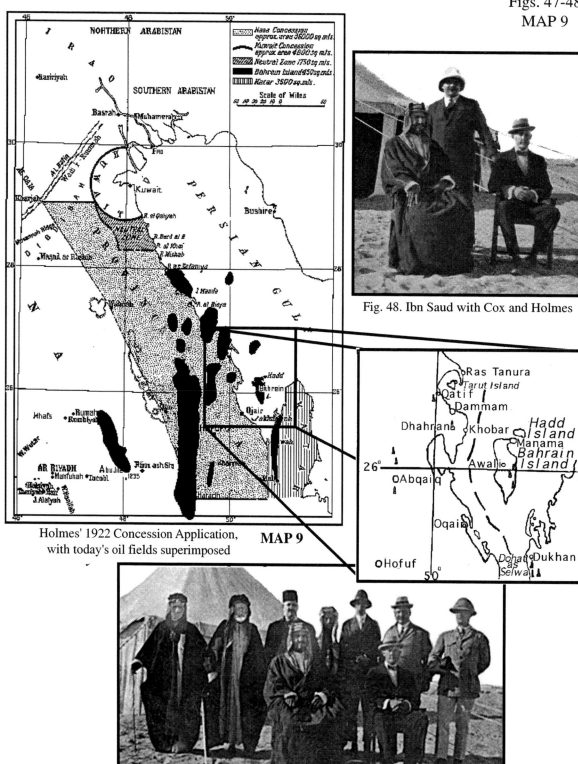

Fig. 48. Ibn Saud with Cox and Holmes

Holmes' 1922 Concession Application,
with today's oil fields superimposed **MAP 9**

Fig. 47. The Oqair Conference, November-December, 1922
*Seated:* Abdul Aziz Ibn Saud and Sir Percy Cox, High Commissioner of Iraq
*Standing, L-R:* Fahd'ul-Hazzal, Chief of the Aneza Tribes; Sabih Bey, representing the government
of Iraq; King Faisal's delegate to Ibn Saud, Abdullah ibn Misfer; Sir Percy Cox's private secretary;
Major Moore, Political Agent at Kuwait; Colonel Dickson, Liaison Officer at Bahrain

# IX. THE OQAIR CONFERENCE
## (1922–1923)

Two who were present at the conference at Oqair in December 1922 published accounts of the proceedings. One was Major H. R. P. Dickson, then on the staff of Sir Percy Cox, high commissioner for Iraq of His Britannic Majesty. The other was a young American of Lebanese stock, Amin Rihani, whom Ibn Saud had invited to visit him. This Arabophile, a Christian, had badgered the English authorities controlling access to the Persian Gulf for months until he obtained Sir Percy's permission for the journey to al Hasa.

Sir Percy had ordered Dickson, a member of his staff, to arrange a meeting with Ibn Saud. As high commissioner of Iraq, he wanted to settle the question of boundaries between three states: the newly created Kingdom of Iraq (a British mandate), Kuwait (a British protectorate) and Nejd and its Dependencies ruled by Ibn Saud. A conference at Muhammera in southwestern Iraq on these boundaries and other matters had ended late in May with the initialing of an acceptance by all parties. The agreement was then negated because Ibn Saud did not approve what his representatives at the conference had acceded to: the premise that two tribes, the Dhafir and 'Amarat, passed most of the year in Iraq and therefore were not his subjects.

Dickson's messages went by boat from Bahrain to the mainland and then by camel-mounted courier to the sultan. After a long delay, on 10 November he received word of Ibn Saud's agreement to attend a conference on the 21st at Oqair, a mainland port in the bay west of the Qatar peninsula. Sir Percy accepted that date by telegraph.

The site of the conference was the open desert a half-mile west of the cluster of buildings at the port. When the sultan and his guests arrived an elaborate encampment was already in place, put up by his commercial agent in Bahrain and Hofuf, Abdul Aziz Algosaibi. Rihani describes the great square of white canvas for the conference, the two magnificent tents of the sultan, one for receptions, the other for sleeping, and the smaller ones for the guests, all wet with the morning fog of late November. Those for Europeans were provided with beds, chairs, and tables stocked with cigars, whiskey, and bottled water. Set well apart were those of the sultan and his entourage, furnished with quilts, cushions, rugs, and camel saddles.

Rihani was at Oqair five days before the delegates' scheduled arrival. Impatient, he started inland toward Hofuf to meet the ruler of Nejd and its Dependencies. He found him somewhere in the 60 miles of desert between Oqair and Hofuf. He was at once enthralled by the bearing and presence of the monarch with whom he established immediate rapport. He returned to Oqair with him. For four days after the date set for the conference Ibn Saud and his guests awaited the arrival of Sir Percy and the envoys of Iraq and Kuwait. His conversations with Rihani during this time were filled with denunciation of the perfidy of the British who had made the sons of Husain rulers of Iraq and Transjordan, and were even now plotting some new scheme to limit his hegemony. He vilified the sharif of Mecca even more strongly, for Husain had denounced him as unprincipled in his newspaper but cajoled him in private correspondence. The sultan told his guest, 'I will strike when I can. Not in betrayal, Allah be my witness, but in self-defense. What I cede of my rights under force, I will get back when I have sufficient force, Insh'allah. No words can be more plain and clear.' He and his retinue had been away from Riyadh for four months and the delay was irksome for all.

Rihani brought up Pan-Arabism as a way of increasing harmony among the chiefs and reducing British influence over them. At that moment Ibn Saud found it impractical.

In the evening of the fifth day of waiting Sir Percy and the delegates to the conference arrived in a motor-driven dhow from Bahrain and were greeted at the landing by Ibn Saud guarded by many of his red-robed slave-soldiers and the curious among his other followers, more than three hundred armed men. The welcoming ceremony took place in the main tent lit by an arc lamp. Sir Percy was accompanied by his personal secretary, an ex-officer of the Royal Navy, and Major J. C. More, the political agent in Kuwait, representing the ruler of that amirate, Shaikh Ahmed ibn Jabir as Sabah. The king of Iraq, Faisal ibn Husain, sent as his personal representative Abdullah ibn Misfer, a soldier. The official agent of the government of Iraq was Sabih Beg, the minister of communications and works. Also in the party was the paramount shaikh of the 'Amarat section of the 'Anaiza, Fahad Beg Al Hadhal (*Pl. XII*). The conferees were accompanied by various staff and clerical officers.

In Ibn Saud's retinue were his secretary and chief of staff, Dr. Abdullah Damluji, and Abdul Latif Pasha al Mandil, a Nejdi merchant and banker who looked after the sultan's interests in Baghdad and had been named minister of commerce in the government of Iraq. Also with him was the ex-amir of Haïl the young Abdullah ibn Mitab, now fifteen, who had fled to Ibn Saud when deposed by his uncle Mohammed ibn Tallal. Saud 'al Kabir,' husband of Nura (Ibn Saud's sister) and reformed leader of the *Araïf*, was one of the sultan's entourage.

Rihani describes Fahad Beg, like Ibn Saud a pensioner of the Crown, as, 'an old Arab, hook-nosed and blear-eyed ... every time I spoke he lifted his head from his breast, peeped out of his *koufiyah* folds surreptitiously and ducked again as quickly as he had turned.' It was this representative of a great tribe who participated with Sabih Beg and others of the Iraqi government's delegation in the discussions of boundaries.

For five days each side made impossible territorial claims. At the outset, Sabih Beg said, 'Since God created the world and history began to be written,

Iraq's boundary extends south to within twelve miles of Ibn Saud's capital Riyadh. It extends west to the Red Sea, so as to include Haïl, Medina, and Yenbo, and east to include Hofuf and Qatif on the Persian Gulf. As God is my witness, this and only this is the true boundary and cannot be disputed.

Ibn Saud replied, 'I know nothing about the creation, but I do know that from the days of Abraham, my great-grandparent, the territories of Nejd and the Bedouin world have extended as far north as Aleppo and the river Orontes in north Syria, and included the whole country on the right bank of the Euphrates from there down to Basra on the Persian Gulf.'

This sort of argument was interrupted by private meetings between Ibn Saud and Sir Percy and by discussions regarding Kuwait between Major More, Sir Percy and Ibn Saud. After five days of wrangling and bombast Cox lost patience with the Arab disputants. Although Ibn Saud had given up his claims to the Dhafir and 'Amarat tribes, he still maintained that a frontier based on *dirah* was the only reasonable way to delineate a boundary between Iraq and Nejd. In his published description of the conference, Dickson (1956) agrees with the monarch's contention, but did not then voice his opinion. Sir Percy maintained from the beginning his stand that linear limits must be established.

First he castigated Ibn Saud in a private audience at which only Dickson was present, telling the sultan that his idea of tribal boundaries was childish. He, Sir Percy Cox, alone would decide on the type of frontier to be drawn and its general position. Ibn Saud almost broke down, saying that Sir Percy was his father and mother who had made him and raised him from nothing to the position he held, and that he would surrender half his kingdom, even the whole, if Sir Percy so ordered. The sight must have been extraordinary: the slight and slim Englishman in dark trousers and tight coat admonishing the tall and broad-shouldered monarch in his robe. What part, if any, did the monthly pension of £5,000 play? Rihani suggests that it was significant.

At a general meeting on the sixth day of the conference Sir Percy took a red pencil and on a map of Arabia drew a boundary line from the Turkish-defined arcuate frontier of Kuwait to the junction of Wadi al Aujah with Wadi ar Rumah near the presumed eastern limit of Transjordan. The diagonal line across Arabia gave Iraq a large part of the territory claimed by the sultan. To appease him, Sir Percy drew the boundary between Kuwait and al Hasa north of a new, roughly quadrilateral 'Neutral Zone' so close to Kuwait town that nearly two-thirds of the territory that the Turks had regarded as Kuwait's was now part of Ibn Saud's realm. The 'Neutral Zone' was a sop to Ibn Saud's contentions regarding the importance of *dirah*. Another 'Neutral Zone,' a rhomboid, was established between Iraq and Nejd, to be shared equally by the two sides and their tribes. (*See Maps 1 and 2.*) Later, Sir Percy further mollified Ibn Saud by allowing him to see a cable sent to Mr. Churchill suggesting that the boundary between Nejd and Transjordan should be drawn so that the Qariyat al Milh (villages and salt mines) would be in Nejdi territory.

The two protocols allowed free movement of nomads across the frontiers, and the use of wells near the boundary by residents of either country. Article 3 of the Iraq-Nejd agreement forbade the construction of forts near the frontier. In less than seven years this provision was to cost many lives, and help to foment insurrection.

Dickson describes an event that seems out of character for both of the players. The evening of the day that Cox drew the frontiers Ibn Saud asked Sir Percy to see him alone. Standing in the center of his great reception tent the sultan of Nejd, clearly distraught, said, 'My friend, you have deprived me of half my kingdom. Better take it all and let me go into retirement.' He then began sobbing, great gasps of anguish shaking him. Sir Percy, perturbed by the display of emotion, began to weep too, then said: 'My friend, I know exactly how you feel and for this reason I gave you two-thirds of Kuwait's territory. I don't know how Al Sabah will take the blow.' Having praised Sir Percy, Dickson remarks, 'Abdul Aziz Al Saud was a very great man too—and a very great actor besides. Both are dead now. *Allah yirhamhum,* which is to say, may God have mercy on their souls.'

One other matter of interest to the sultan was a letter of friendship from King Faisal of Iraq carried to the conference by his personal representative, Abdullah ibn Misfer. A cordial reply was sent, probably in deference to Sir Percy, high commissioner of the new kingdom.

Rihani arrived in Oqair five days before the date set for the conference. Before his sally into the desert to meet Ibn Saud he had an unexpected encounter. Major Holmes came by dhow from Bahrain and appeared at the *Qasr* (fort) where Rihani was staying. Holmes left almost at once for Hofuf on a poor spavined horse followed by three of the white donkeys of al Hasa burdened respectively by his interpreter (Dr. Mann), a Somali servant, and the baggage. But Holmes was not making his first contact with the sultan for when Rihani landed at Oqair Ibn Saud's representative handed him a twenty-page document sent from Hofuf. Every page of this draft of a concession agreement had been signed by Holmes. That night Rihani spent four hours examining the document and its translation into execrable Arabic, made several suggestions in writing, and sent it off by courier to Ibn Saud.

From other sources we know that Ibn Saud had sent Alex Mann, one of his doctors previously on Sir Percy's staff, to be his commercial representative in London. Eastern and General requested permission from Mann to present a proposal to the sultan. As Eastern and General was a syndicate whose business was to obtain mining rights and then to sell them, the fact that Ibn Saud authorized a visit shows understanding that his country might have mineral resources, probably oil, as in Persia and Mesopotamia. Holmes had seen Ibn Saud three months before the Oqair conference convened. Perhaps, as Dickson suggests, the sultan delayed his acceptance of the date of the conference to give Holmes time to examine the terrain.

Holmes, a New Zealander with long experience in the mining industry, was a seasoned negotiator. He was the driving force behind Eastern and General, and was a thorn in the side of the British because of his persistence in attempting to obtain concessions from the amirs of Kuwait and Bahrain, both under their tutelage. A corpulent man, rather short, he spoke but little Arabic, and in the desert his dress was odd. Dickson mentions a green veil (not unwise, given the plague of flies in al Hasa), and Rihani describes his unusual appearance with an *agal* and *gotra* draped over a large pith helmet. But eccentricities in dress and a chronic illness did not affect his abilities in negotiation. His manner was open and friendly with all. Philby described him as, 'a man of considerable personal charm, with a bluff, breezy, blustering, bucaneering way about him.' Although he kept the purpose of his visit from Rihani (they were on the same ship from Basra to Bahrain) he revealed it indirectly to Dickson.

A secret Turkish report described an oil seepage near an artesian pond some six miles northeast of Qatif town. Dickson had seen a copy of it in the village of Darin on Tarut Island and with Ibn Saud's permission had made several visits to the area and also to Jebel Dhahran, a prominent hill fifteen miles south of Qatif, in search of this indication of buried wealth. Obviously, Holmes had heard of it too, and his trip from Bahrain to Qatif by dhow to look for it was probably made at the sultan's request.

Holmes got back to Oqair before the sultan and Rihani arrived. He pitched his tent in an open space near the Arab camp but lived in European style, visiting both groups freely. After the protocols had been signed on 2 December, he discussed with Ibn Saud and Cox his proposal for a concession. Sir Percy was unfriendly, for he thought that negotiations directly with an oil-producing company would be more advantageous to Ibn Saud and to Great Britain. He knew that Anglo–Persian had expressed an interest in taking a concession in al Hasa, and Dickson had briefed him about Holmes' visit to al Hasa before the meeting.

Ibn Saud pursued his talks with Major Holmes in spite of three hand-written notes from Sir Percy urging delay in negotiations. In the end Cox persuaded the sultan to present a formal letter to the negotiator refusing further discussion on the matter. Holmes left the conference without a promise that his application would be considered. In February when Rihani in Riyadh advised Ibn Saud to give the concession to a company not owned mainly by the British government, Holmes was in Baghdad.

The concession was granted Eastern and General in July 1923 at Jedda. It included most of the dotted area of the map on Pl. XII. In the hopes of a favorable report, Holmes sent a renowned Swiss geologist to the desert of al Hasa, where presumably he worked during the winters of two consecutive years, but the scientist, a specialist in Alpine geology, decried the prospects of eastern Arabia. His opinion leaked to the public. That the geologist was wrong is made clear by the overlay showing the location of the nine oil fields producing from the 'Arab Zone' in al Hasa (Pl. XII, Map 9). Fields producing oil or gas from younger and older horizons (not shown) would add at least three more fields.

# X. Finance Minister Suleiman

Abdullah Suleiman al Hamdan from Anaiza in the Qasim was sent by his merchant parents to Bombay to learn trade and bookkeeping. He lived in Bombay as a servant in the house of a rich Nejdi trader. Returning to Nejd after this apprenticeship, he consulted his father and decided to set up on his own in Bahrain. The venture was not successful and he soon looked for a more secure position. His uncle was employed by the Amir Saud as a clerk in the finance section of the 'Domestic Court,' the overseer of most aspects of the government of Nejd and al Hasa. Suleiman accepted a job as assistant to his uncle, and when he died took over. His capabilities then became known to the king.

In 1921 it was he who suggested to Ibn Saud that an attempt be made to divert trade from Kuwait to ports in al Hasa—Jubail, Qatif, Dammam, Oqair. The tribes were ordered not to go to Kuwait for supplies. Although not completely successful, this economic blockade increased the revenue of the Saudi state and decreased that of Kuwait by up to seventy per cent (Shaikh Ahmad of Kuwait in a letter to Col. Biscoe, Political Resident, 1929).

When Ibn Saud took control of the Hejaz, Suleiman accompanied him. After a time he mastered the much more intricate financial structure there and monitored the receipts from customs, the post, and the pilgrimage. Presumably it was he who finally legalized the importation of tobacco, to the ire of the *Ikhwan*.

He was named minister of finance in 1932 and held the post until three years after the king's death. He became responsible for public projects including the expansion of water resources and the construction of port facilities. He promoted the 'farm' near Kharj, which provided the king with fruits and vegetables, as well as serving as an experimental agricultural station.

The king's confidence in him was absolute, and although he was sometimes unable to satisfy the monarch's demands for funds, he was never faulted. The king was seldom entirely without money for Suleiman resorted to twisting the arms of the rich merchants when other sources of revenue failed, as was the case in 1931 with the onset of the slump. His authority was second only to that of his master. Although ostensibly he did nothing without permission, he frequently planned and executed projects without reference to *as Shiyukh*. However, he was never able to establish a stable fiscal policy because of Ibn Saud's disregard of budgetary considerations. Consequently, the history of his dealings with banks, merchants, and loans from foreign governments is complex, as are his several attempts to stabilize the currency, in the end successful with the aid of foreign advisers in the Saudi Arabian Monetary Agency, and the massive influx of payments from the oil industry.

In dealing with this flood of money (until 1950 from royalties and there-after a half share in ARAMCO profits) Suleiman had neither the ability nor the will to stem the ever-increasing demands from the royal household. The king's appetite for money was insatiable, and much was spent on projects with little or no potential for profit, such as the fifty million dollar railroad from Dammam, a port on the Gulf, to Riyadh.

Loans made by banks with both capital and interest to be repaid from future oil revenues were not uncommon. One for $6 million guaranteed by ARAMCO was obtained ostensibly to be allocated to the Syrian government where a faction favorable to the Sauds was in a struggle for power. Too, Syria's permission was required for the right-of-way for the projected Trans-Arabian pipeline. Two million dollars was immediately siphoned off to reimburse unpaid creditors of the Saudi court. Syria obtained the remainder only years later.

A further complication arose from the practice of farming out the collec-tion of taxes to individuals for a cash payment to the treasury in advance. This of course led to corruption which increased when unpaid government debts were sold at a discount to those in favor with the minister of finance, who, it is said, became richer than the king.

Although shunning the limelight, Suleiman wielded great personal power, for after an initial setback because of a concerted attempt to discredit him, he was permitted to choose his staff. Although he recognized incompetence and punished it, he was reluctant to reward talent for fear that advancement would jeopardize his own position. Like his master, he avoided delegating responsibility. He proposed and supported many decrees helpful to the king or to his exchequer. He established tax-collecting offices and set the rates of internal taxes and customs duties. He presumably had much to do with the decision to establish a hospital in Riyadh and certainly forced the oil company to increase its workers' benefits.

As he aged, Suleiman became more and more of a toper, and thus less able to cope with his duties. On some days in the forties and fifties he functioned for an hour or less, whereas in the twenties and thirties he had worked fifteen to eighteen hours because of his desire to do everything himself. After Ibn Saud died he attempted to curb the profligacy of the new monarch, Saud, and was sacked with obloquy after a row with Faisal. Philby described him as, 'a frail little man of "uncertain" age but with something of the inspiration of the prophets in his soul' (*Arabian Jubilee, p. 230*). In photographs he is seen to be slight, his face narrow with regular features except for a straight but prominent nose. In middle age his dark beard was clipped and a small mustache closely trimmed. Later his features thick-ened and the beard grayed.

# GLOSSARY

| | | | |
|---|---|---|---|
| Abba | Cloak, also called *bisht* | Dhalul | Riding camel. Plural: *dhulul* |
| Abd | Slave | | |
| Abu | Father | Dirah | Tribal range |
| Agal | Headdress, usually black cord | | |
| Allah, Ullah, Illah God | | Fajar | Dawn |
| Allah akhbar God is Great | | Fi aman Illah Go in the peace of the Lord | |
| 'Ain | Well or spring | | |
| Al hamdu l'Illa Praise be to God | | Ghazzu | Raid, or party of raiders |
| Amir | Prince, governor, leader | Girba | Goatskin water bag; also *jirba* |
| Araïf | The Recognized. Camels stolen and recovered in raids | | |
| | | Hadh | Favorable luck |
| Ardh | War or victory dance | Hadhar | Town dwellers |
| Arfaj | A desert shrub; camel fodder | Hajj | Pilgrimage to Mecca |
| | | Hamdh | A kind of desert bush, camel food |
| Ar Rimal | 'The sands' Ajman and Murra name for the Rub' al Khali | | |
| | | Hijra | Plural: *Hujar*. Departure, new start for the better. Ikhwan settlement |
| Aziz | One in favor, 'a dear one' | | |
| Bab | Door or gate | Ibn | Son of |
| Bedu | Used here as both singular and plural for the Arab of the desert. True plural is *Badawi* or *Badiya* | Imam | Religious leader |
| | | Jihad | Holy war |
| Bahr | Sea (*Bahrain* = 'two seas') | Ka'aba | *Bait Allah*; House of God |
| Bani | Plural of *ibn* = 'sons of'. Used in tribal names | Kiswa | Clothing gift; cover for Ka'aba |
| Bint | Girl or daughter of. Plural: *banat* | Kut | Fort or keep |
| | | Kuwait | Small fort; diminutive of *Kut* |
| Bisht | Cloak = *abba* | | |
| B'ism Illa | In the name of God. Said before a meal or blooding game | Labbaik | 'Here am I at thy service'. Pilgrim cry during the pilgrimage |
| Dahana | Belts of sand separating Nejd from al Hasa. | Leben | Buttermilk |
| Dallu | Small leather bucket | Mafudh | Protector |
| Dauha(t) | Enclosed bay | Mahmal | Litter for the Kiswa |
| Dhabi | Gazelle (Abu Dhabi shaikhdom) | Majlis | Council session or room |
| | | Malik | King |
| | | Mullah | Teacher |

215

| | |
|---|---|
| Mutawwa'in | Deacons; missionaries |
| Nassi | A desert grass |
| Nefud | Large area of crescent dunes |
| Qadi | Judge; interpreter of the law |
| Qahwa | Coffee or coffee place |
| Qaimaqam | Turkish governor |
| Qariyat | Villages |
| Rafiq | Tribal escort |
| Ras | Cape; headland |
| Raudha(t) | Depression in which rain water collects |
| Rijm | Man-made heap of stones |
| Rub' al Khali | The Empty Quarter; '*ar Ramla*' |
| Sabkha | Salt flat |
| Salaam alaikum | Peace be upon you |
| Shaib | Water course or ravine |
| Shari'a | Religious law |
| Sharif | Honorable; noble |
| Sirhan | Lion |
| Sufi | A Moslem mystic sect to reach Oneness with God. Creates saints. |
| Surah | A chapter of the Koran |
| Thobe | Also *thaub*. Long shirt-like smock |
| Ulema | Religious leaders; priests |
| Umm | Mother |
| Wa alaikum as salaam | And upon you be peace |
| Wadi | Stream bed; in Arabia 90% dry |
| Wali | Regent; governor of a province |
| Wasm | Tribal camel brand-marks |
| Ya | O! Used before a name |
| Zakat | Tax; basically a religious duty |

# Annotated Bibliography

The author is responsible for the observations in italics concerning each reference. For general reading and broader or different interpretations of some of the events related herein, see Armstrong and Howarth for amusing and generally fluent discussions of Ibn Saud alone. Mcloughlin is more scholarly but equally enjoyable. Holden & Johns and Lacey include the rôles of Ibn Saud's sons to date of publication. Both of these references have good photographic coverage, but almost certainly include a few factual inaccuracies. Troeller and Leatherdale focus on Britain's relations with Ibn Saud using official documents. Helms provides a reasoned and valuable but arguably biased treatment of his career slanted toward showing him the beneficiary of historical trends in his favor. Although scholarly, Goldberg is original and readable, as is Winder. Philby wrote more than anyone else on Arabia, but much of his work is so densely written that much effort is required to extract information pertinent to any given topic. Nevertheless, any serious investigator must plow through his sometimes turgid comment. A fairly recent (1979) and reasonably exhaustive annotated bibliography of works in English on Saudi Arabia by Clements is listed below. In it a number of earlier bibliographies are noted. (The 1988 revision was not available.) Alangari's 1998 publication includes the most nearly complete bibliography yet published of government reports, books and articles in English and Arabic regarding the social, political, religious and economic factors involved in Ibn Saud's assumption of authority and his relationships with other governments. Its French and German references to these matters are meager. Brown's 1999 book provided a comprehensive review of the development of the oil industry in Arabia, the personalities involved, and the play of international politics.

## BOOKS

ALANGARI, Haifa 1998
> **The Struggle for Power in Arabia:** Ibn Saud, Hussein and Great Britain, 1914–1924. pp. i–xiv, 1–289, 26 photos (*a number poorly reproduced*), 1 small map, appendix, bibliography, index. An analysis of the factors that resulted in Ibn Saud's hegemony and eventual consolidation of power. *A notable contribution in that it assembles nearly all of the information ever written concerning the mechanisms involved and codifies them. Mainly for specialists.*
> Garnett Publishing Ltd, Reading UK (Ithaca Press)

Ibn Saud: King by Conquest

ALMANA, Mohammed 1980
**Arabia Unified:** A Portrait of ibn Saud. pp. 1–328, 34 photos, 3 maps. *Interesting characterizations from an Arab point of view. Sidelights on and details of events not found elsewhere.*
Hutchinson Benham, London

ALGHANIM, Salwa (Muhammad Ahmad) 1998
**The Reign of Mubarak al Sabah:** Sheikh of Kuwait 1896–1915. pp. i–xiv, 1–242 contents, acknowledgments, introduction, genealogic table, notes, bibliography, index. Focused on the reign of Mubarak, the study includes many subjects that are peripheral to the career of the man, but of more interest to the general reader than the specialist. Relations with Ibn Saud are discussed only broadly. *A doctoral thesis, the notes are meticulous and thorough. She suggests that Dickson's account is inaccurate as regards the character and actions of the victims and Yusuf ibn Ibrahim.*
I. B. Tauris, London, New York

ANTONIUS, George 1938 (1939)
**The Arab Awakening:** The Story of the Arab National Movement. pp. i–xi, 13– 471; 4 maps; 8 appendices: McMahon correspondence with Husain, Sykes–Picot agreement, King–Crane report, Anglo–French Declaration (7 Nov. 1918) Declaration of the Seven, Faisal–Weiszmann Agreement and Resolution of the Syrian Congress. History of Arab movements for liberty from Turkey and of the mandates. Includes Husain's and Faisal's activities before, during, and after WWI. *A viewpoint favoring Arab aspirations. Much detail.*
Hamish Hamilton, London / Putnam, New York

ARMSTRONG, Harold C. 1924 /1938
**Lord of Arabia.** Ibn Saud: An Intimate Study of a King. pp. 1–247. *Dramatic treatment, but factually accurate, easy reading.*
Arthur Barker / Penguin Books

ASAD, Mohammed 1954
**The Road to Mecca.** pp. 1–380, index, 10 photos. The story of an Austrian Jew convert to Islam who spent six years in Saudi Arabia. *Comments on Ibn Saud's appearance and his failings as ruler. Mentions the king's favorite wife and the despondency of his last years.*
Max Reinhardt, London

BAKER, P. Randall 1979
**King Husain and the Kingdom of the Hejaz.** pp. i–xiv: Contents; Illustrations; Foreword by General Sir John Glubb. pp. 1–243, 30 illustrations, mostly small photos, 8 maps. An account of the Hejaz under Husain as sharif and king and his dealings with the English, his sons, and the Arab nationalist movements in Turkey. *Husain's relations with Ibn Saud are not recounted with complete accuracy, but the story of the downfall of the sharif-king is well presented.*
Oleander Press, Cambridge / Oleander Press, New York

BARGER, Thomas C. 2000

**Out in the Blue.** pp. iv–xv. Contents, Notes, Preface, Acknowledgments, Prologue. pp. 1–284, index. 116 photos, several of Ibn Saud, other Arabs, Aramco personnel and Arabian topography. Mainly letters to his wife and her replies. Barger met the king several times and comments on his charisma, his person and his retinue. He was one of the few Americans who could talk to him directly. *More interesting to those who were there, but a good read for anyone.*
Selwa Press, Vista California

BELHAVEN and STENTON, Lord (R. A. B. Hamilton) 1955

**The Uneven Road.** pp. i–ix, 1–335, index. 15 photos, 2 maps. Abbreviated account of the author's life. Detailed only about his activities as commander of levies and political officer in southwest Arabia. *Of interest concerning Ibn Saud only in the author's explanation for his father's decision not to work under Philby.*
John Murray, London

BELL, Lady F. (Mrs. Hugh) 1927

**The Letters of Gertrude Bell. Vol. II.** pp. i–vii, 405–791. 23 photographs, 1 drawing by Sargent (reduced), 1 map (Persia and the Levant), index. Includes summaries by Sir Percy Cox and Sir Henry Dobbs of events in Mesopotamia during WWI and the foundation and early history of the nation of Iraq. Bell's work was the study of tribal relations and attitudes, later archaeology. *View of Anglo–Saudi relations from Baghdad standpoint. Insights into Bell's special status with the British and Iraqi governments.*
Benn, London

BENOIST-MÉCHIN, Jacques 1955

**Ibn Séoud ou la Naissance d'un Royaume.** pp. 1–348, bibliography, Saudi genealogy, 5 maps. A history of the origin and spread of the Moslem faith, followed by a romanticized and dramatized version of Ibn Saud's life and accomplishments in which fact is often not strictly respected. *Many errors in interpretation, and lapses like 'the 'Red-Tape Agreement.' Discussion of World War II events and complex post-war relations between Arab countries appears correct.*
Albin Michel, Paris

————————————— 1957

**Le Roi Saud, ou l'Orient à l'heure des relèves.** pp. 1–575, maps I–VI. Annotated Table of Contents. A study of the events leading to the partition of Palestine. Includes a review of post-World War II events in the Middle East, detailed for Egypt, less complete for Syria, Iraq, Iran, Jordan, Saudi Arabia. Incomplete sketch of Buraimi claim and other activities of King Saud. *Supposedly unbiased review of developments showing complex interrelations between policies and events. Some conclusions are slanted.*
Albin Michel, Paris.

BESSON, Yves 1980

**Ibn Sa'ud: Roi Bédouin.** La Naissance du Royaume d'Arabie Saoudite. pp. 1–284. Notes, four anexes, (abbreviated Saud genealogy, 1915 and 1927 treaties) index, two geographic maps, one tribal map, 17 unnumbered photos.

Extracted from a doctoral thesis. *An interesting analysis of the strategic and tactical reasoning behind Ibn Saud's actions until 1932. Some of the writer's conclusions on these matters are debatable, and some 'facts' are probably not true.*
Editions des Trois Continents, Lausanne

BINDAGJI, Hussein Hamza 1978
**Atlas of Saudi Arabia**. Acknowledgments, Introduction, 6 photos, kings and princes, table of rulers, 60 maps [9–7/8"x11"]: administrative divisions, population, geographical regions, geology, relief, land forms, temperatures, rainfall, wadis, tribes, vegetation, agriculture, minerals, roads, air traffic, detail of 15 administrative regions, 10 town plans. *Inaccurate in many details and out of date concerning others.*
Oxford University Press

BROWN, Anthony G. 1999
**Oil, God, and Gold: The Story of Aramco and the Saudi Kings.**
Dedication, Contents pp. i–x; text pp. 1–370; Acknowledgments pp. 370–373; Notes pp. 374–402; Index pp. 403–420. A comprehensive study of the development of Aramco, its relations with its employees and the several governments. Remarkable for its many sketches of the individuals involved. *A thoroughly researched and well-presented study based on exhaustive research using material not exploited previously Minor errors in interpretation and fact, e.g. Ibn Saud's date of birth given as 1888!*

BULLARD, Sir Reader 1961
**The Camels Must Go**: An Autobiography. pp. 9–300. 11 photos, one drawing, index. Life of a Levant Consular Service representative, later diplomat, working mainly in the Middle East before and during both World Wars. In Jedda during the last years of the reign of Husain, and the early stages of the siege. British Minister in Jedda 1936–1939. *Discussion of Husain's reign and contacts with Ibn Saud in some detail. Engagingly written.*
Faber and Faber, Ltd. London

BUSCH, Briton Cooper 1967
**Britain and the Persian Gulf, 1894–1916**. pp. vii–xix, 1–432, 8 appendices, maps, bibliography, index. Study of British relations with the shaikdoms of the Gulf region and reaction to Turkish, Russian and German interest in the region. *Detailed and scholarly.*
University of California Press

——————————— 1971
**Britain, India, and the Arabs, 1914–1921.** Preface pp. iii–ix, pp. 1–522. 5 maps. Summary of Mesopotamian campaign, Arab revolt 1914–1916, War in Iraq 1914–1916, Asir, Yemen, Nejd 1914–1918, Peace negotiations to 1921. *Good discussion of the long-lasting row over Middle East policies between Whitehall and the India Office.*
University of California Press

CHAPMAN, M. K. 1948

**Great Britain and the Bagdad Railway, 1888–1914**. Preface ix–x, pp. 1–248. 2 maps, Appendix: Convention and Cahier des Charges; bibliographic notes, index. Doctoral thesis. *Densely written and exhaustive account of pre-war negotiations with France, Germany, and Russia involving ownership, financing, siting and construction of the railway.*
George Banta, Menasha

CHEESMAN, R.E. 1926

**In Unknown Arabia**. pp. 1–433, 66 photos, one colored map, scale: 1:950,000, Appendices, index. *Trip to al Hasa in 1923. Sketches of Ibn Saud and ibn Jiluwi. The Ikhwan at Jabrin.*
Macmillan, London

CHILDS, J. Rives 1969

**Foreign Service Farewell**: My Years in the Near East. pp. 1–191, 14 unnumbered illustrations. Frontispiece: photo of Ibn Saud reversed. Notes, Index. *Interesting account of newspaperman-diplomat's career. Minister to Saudi Arabia, 1946–1950. Sidelights on Ibn Saud, held in great esteem.*
University of Virginia Press, Charlottesville.

CLAYTON, Sir Gilbert F. 1969

**An Arabian Diary**. Edited by Robert O. Collins. pp. vii–xiv, 1–379, index. Nine appendices: Text of Hadda-Bahra agreements, drafts of treaties with Yemen, extensive biographical sketches of prominent personalities. Intoduction by Collins, pp. 1–81, summarizes Ibn Saud's career and Clayton's life. *The diary sheds light on Ibn Saud's views regarding Jordan's boundaries and raids by both sides across the Iraqi-Saudi frontier. Denigrates abilities of Yusuf Yassin and Hafiz Wahba.*
University of California Press

CLEMENTS, Frank A. 1979 (1988 revised edition not available)

**Saudi Arabia**. World Bibliographical Series, vol. 5. pp. i–xiv Contents and Introduction, pp. 1–197 Bibliographies in 26 categories which requires repetition of titles, each of which has a number (1–789). Small inaccurate map of Arabian peninsula, index. *The author makes no claim to completeness, and rightly so, particularly as regards the technical aspects of oil exploration and production. The works dealing with Ibn Saud are as listed here with some additions.*
Clio Press. Oxford and Santa Barbara

CORNWALLIS, Sir Kinahan 1916 (1976)

**Asir Before World War I**: A Handbook. pp. 1–155. Map of Asir scale 1:2,000,000. Prefatory Note. Discussion of geography, population, agriculture, trade, currency, taxes, recent history, military organizations, notes on tribes and personalities, roads and communications. Prepared for the Arab Bureau, Cairo as a service to Dominion troops occupying coastal Asir. Issued 1 June 1916. *Of historical interest. Many tribes in Asir were not nomadic.*
Oleander / Falcon Press Reprint, London, New York

DICKSON, Harold R. P. 1949

**The Arab of the Desert**. A glimpse into Badawin life in Kuwait and Sa'udi Arabia. pp. 1–647, 80 text figures, 56 photos, 9 maps, 6 genealogical trees. *Bedouin life and customs in Kuwait and al Hasa. Details of climate, flora and fauna. Life in Kuwait town. Sidelights on 1902 exploit. His wife tells of visit to Ibn Saud in Riyadh.*
George Allen and Unwin Ltd., London

DICKSON, Harold R. P. 1956

**Kuwait and Her Neighbours.** pp. 7–627, photos, genealogical tables, 6 maps, line drawings. *Potpourri of the author's experiences as a political agent in the Gulf. Much detail on the Ikhwan rising and extensive reports on his contacts with Ibn Saud.*
George Allen and Unwin, Ltd., London and Winchester

DICKSON, Violet P. 1971

**Forty years in Kuwait.** pp. 7–20. Dedication, Author's Note, Contents. pp. 21–335, five appendices, index, 17 photos, 5 maps, two line drawings. An auto-biography by Colonel Dickson's wife, equestrienne, good shot, naturalist, friend of the Arabs. Ibn Saud is not in the index, although she visited Riyadh twice during his lifetime. *An interesting story, paricularly as it recounts dealings with Arabs and the changes in their way of life caused by the discovery and development of oil and the use of the motor car.*
George Allen and Unwin, Ltd. London

DONKAN, Rupert 1935

**Die Auferstehung Arabiens:** Ibn Sauds Weg und Ziel. pp. 1–260, 15 unnum-bered photos, 1 map 1:14,000,000. Uncritical bibliography and chapter head-ings at end. *An elaborate treatment of Ibn Saud's career up to the Yemen War, along with brief discussions of the Prophet Mohammed and Wahhabism. Sees possibilities of further enlargement of his realm.*
Wilhelm Goldmann, Leipzig

DOUGHTY, Charles M. 1923 (1888, 1921)

**Travels in Arabia Deserta.** Vol. 1, pp. i–xxvi, 1–623, geographic and geologic map, plates, sketches. Vol. 2. pp. v–xiv, pp. 1–690, sketches, index and glos-sary of Arabic words. *Fundamental to any study in depth of late 19th century mores in Arabia and the situation in Shammar territory.*
Jonathan Cape and the Medici Society, London

EDDY, William A. 1954

**FDR Meets Ibn Saud.** pp. 1–45, 2 photos. Pamphlet describing Ibn Saud's meeting with FDR. *Interesting comment by the interpreter at the meeting.*
American Friends of the Middle East

FACEY William 1994

**The Story of the Eastern Province of Saudi Arabia.** Folio: pp. 1–160, 200› photographs, maps, historical bibliography, index, glossary. A lavish treat-ment sketching the geology, archaeology, history, anthropology, ethnology, oil industry, agriculture, climate, transport, etc., of eastern Arabia. Ibn Saud is treated mainly in the brief discussion of his conquest, but also in the story of oil development. *The vast changes that have taken place in all ways since Ibn Saud's time are well-presented here.*
Stacey International London

GAURY, Gerald de 1946

**Arabia Phoenix.** pp. 1–169, Appendices I–III, bibliography, index, 64 half-tone plates. *A good, somewhat idyllic description of the king and his court in 1935, along with sketches of life and customs in Saudi Arabia. Postscript discusses the effects of modern-ization after 1935, not all bad in the author's opinion.*
Harrap & Co. Ltd., London

GAURY, Gerald de 1951 (1954)

**Rulers of Mecca**. pp. 7–16, Preface and Table of Contents which lists: Illustrations, Chronological Tables, Pedigrees. pp. 17–317, text, glossary, appendices I–IV, bibliography, index. 24 half-tone plates. Illustrations in the text include three maps, two chronological tables and nine family pedigrees (genealogies). *An exhaustive history focused principally on those ruling Mecca from 1200 A.D. on. Treatment of Husain and his sons is sympathetic. Mohammed Ali's invasion of the Hejaz is discussed at length, but ends abruptly before the final march to Dhariya when he himself had returned to Egypt. Nothing of importance concerning Ibn Saud.*
Harrap & Co. Ltd., London / Roy Publishers, New York

GLUBB, Sir John Bagot 1959

**Britain and the Arabs**; a study of fifty years, 1908–1959. 496 pp., 33 maps, index, two appendices. *A British general recounts the major events and the political and economic situations that led to the wars in the Middle East, examines the military campaigns and their results, and attempts to explain Arab aversion to British policy.*
Hodder and Stoughten, London

———————————— 1960 (1970: American Edition)

**War in the Desert**. An R.A.F. Frontier Campaign. Unnumbered Preface, Contents, List of Maps. pp. 21–352, 19 sketch maps. Summary of Ikhwan raids in Iraq and Kuwait. Counter forces led by the author. *An admirer of the Arab recounts his experiences. Summary of Wahhabi history. Describes Bedu character and way of life.*
Hodder & Stoughton London / W. W. Norton & Co., New York

GOLDBERG, Jacob 1986

**The Foreign Policy of Saudi Arabia**: the Formative Years 1902–1918. pp. i–viii, 1–231. App. A–C: Texts of 1914 Turkish treaty and draft and final versions of the 1915 Qatif treaty. Bibliography, notes, index. *Scholarly work showing relationships between Ibn Saud's education, experience, his innate ability, and his foreign policy. Emphasis on political acumen.*
Harvard University Press

GOLDRUP, Laurence P. 1936 [published in 1971]

**Saudi Arabia, 1902–1932**. The Development of a Wahhabi Society. Only Microfilm available. *Very detailed. Appears exact.*
University of California. Published Thesis

GRAFFTEY-SMITH, Laurence 1970

**Bright Levant**. pp. i–xii, 1–295. Index, 22 photos. Career of a British diplomat in the Middle East, posted to Arabia twice. *Entertaining descriptions of life in Jedda and of Sharif Husain in 1920–1924. Description of Jedda and of Ibn Saud in 1945–47.*
John Murray, London

GRAVES, P. 1940

**The Life of Sir Percy Cox**. pp. 1–350, index, 16 photos. Foreword by Sir Arnold Wilson. *A detailed study of the life of a servant of the crown, friend to Ibn Saud. Many particulars of dealings with Ibn Saud and events and intrigues in Oman, Persia and Mesopotamia. Some inconsistencies.*
Hutchison, London

HABIB, John S. 1978
**Ibn Sa'ud's Warriors of Islam**: The Ikhwan of Nejd and Their Role in the Creation of the Saudi Kingdom, 1910–1930. Table of Contents vii–ix, Preface xi–xiii, Note on transliteration, xv–xvi, pp. 1–196, appendix, lists of *Hujar*, bibliography, index. 9 tables, 7 photos. *Detailed; some questionable conclusions. Many printing errors.*
E. J. Brill, Leiden

HELMS, Christine Moss 1981
**The Cohesion of Saudi Arabia**; Evolution of Political Identity. pp. 9–313, 15 text figs. (10 maps), Appendix. Doctoral dissertation: *Extensive quotes of Ibn Saud's speeches and letters. Review of Ibn Saud's tax and revenue problems. Suggests that Ibn Saud is overrated, having benefited from historical trends in his favor.*
Croom Helm, London

HOLDEN, David 1966
**Farewell to Arabia**. pp. 7–268. Appendices I–III British treaties with Aden. Appendix IV tranliteration, 'Books' (recommended reading, 1 p.), index. 17 unnumbered photos, 3 maps. *Developments in the governments and economies of the Arabian peninsula, detailed only after WWII. Summarizes and decries changes. Insights on the Buraimi dispute to that date.*
Faber, London / Walker, New York

HOLDEN, David & JOHNS, Richard, 1981
**The House of Saud**. pp. i–x, pp. 1–569. 32 photos, maps, bibliography, list of Ibn Saud's male descendants. *Good overall treatment of the Sauds. Some detail not available in other studies. Minor errors in fact.*
Sidgewick & Jackson, London

HOWARD, Harry N. 1963
**The King–Crane Commission**. An American Inquiry in the Middle East. pp. vii–xv, Contents, Preface, Acknowledgements. pp. 1–369, Bibliography, Appendix: Text of King–Crane Report, Index. *A very thorough investigation of the events leading to the naming of a commission, its route and people consulted, and its recommendations.*
Khayat's Book Store, Beirut

HOWARTH, David 1965 (1980)
**The Desert King**: The Life of Ibn Saud, pp. 1–213. Sources and Acknowledgements: two pages, unnumbered. *Perceptive, readable; access to documents not seen by others? Chronology is weak.*
William Collins & Son, Ltd. London / McGraw-Hill, New York / Quartette Books, Ltd. (1980)

IQBAL, Shaikh Mohammad 1977
**Emergence of Saudi Arabia**: A Political Study of King Abd-al-Aziz ibn Saud 1901–1953. Contents and Introduction, pp. i–xix, text pp. 1–276; bibliography, index, 'Bio-Data' pp. i–xxxiii, 12 unlisted photos, 1 sketch map. Details of some events such as the 1926 Moslem Congress in Mecca and the judicial sys-

tem are not discussed elsewhere in the works listed here. *The motives ascribed some of Ibn Saud's actions seem most unlikely and rebuttals of criticisms of his rule are contrived.*
Saudiyah Publishers, Kashmir

KELLY, J. B. 1964

**Eastern Arabian Frontiers**. pp. 1–319, index, two maps: Buraimi Oasis, 1/1.000.000; sketch) and Eastern Arabia, 1/28.5 million showing six boundary claims. Careful review of Buraimi dispute to date of publication. Justifies British claims. *Painstaking.*
Faber, London

———— 1968

**Britain and the Persian Gulf**, 1798–1880. pp. vii–xiv: Preface, Acknowledgments, Contents. pp. 1–866, 3 appendices, bibliography, index, two maps. *A definitive detailed and scholarly study which sheds much light on the relations of the Wahhabis with Britain and the shaikhdoms of the Gulf. Excellent discussions of the slave trade, geography, tribes and their history, and British negotiations with Persia and rulers in the Gulf area.*
Oxford University Press

KHATIB, Abdul Hamid el 1952

**The Harbinger of Justice**. pp. i–iv, g–h, Contents, Dedication, Foreword; Vol. I pp. 1–364, vol. II, pp. 1–200. Innumerable errors in syntax, spelling, etc. 102 unnumbered photographs of the king, his brothers, princes, and Saudi government staff, all poorly reproduced in reddish sepia. *An account by the Saudi Minister to Pakistan of Wahhabi history and the life and works of Ibn Saud, larded with encomia of the king and of his speeches, along with those of sons. Some of the data concerning dates and relationships are probably accurate, but confirmation is not available.*
Al Arab Printing Press, Karachi

KHEIRALLAH, George 1952

**Arabia Reborn**. pp. i–ix, Preface, Contents; pp. 1–307, 29 unnumbered photos of the Saud family and people and places in Saudi Arabia. Many decorative woodcuts. *Widely ranging but superficial discussion of Arab history including that of the Sauds and the Rashids. Sketches of Personalities, mainly those associated with the Sauds and Saudi Arabia. Lengthy encomium of Ibn Saud and his régime. Review of his exploits military, diplomatic, and economic.*
University of New Mexico Press

KLIEMAN, Aaron S. 1970

**Foundations of British Policy in the Arab World:** The Cairo Conference of 1921. pp. vii–xiv Preface, Contents, Notes on Transliteration; pp. 1–322 (Text 1–253; Appendices A–G, various maps, letters and speeches regarding disposition of former Turkish territory, pp. 255–288; Bibliography, Biographical Sketches, Index, pp. 289–322.) One photo: Conferees at Cairo Conference. *A complete study of the reasons for, events during, and the consequences of the Cairo conference.*
Johns Hopkins Press, Baltimore

LACEY, Robert 1981 (1982*)

**The Kingdom**. pp. i–xvi, pp. 1–631, 106 photos, maps, genealogical charts, Appendices A–D, Genealogies. E, Islamic Calendar. F, Oil Statistics. G, Notes on Arabic words. Extensive bibliography, Index. *Intensively researched, lavish and fairly complete treatment of the development of Saudi Arabia. Many photos not available in other general publications, description of and anecdotes about Ibn Saud. Minimal politics. Probable minor inaccuracies.*
Hutchinson & Co. London / *Harcourt Brace Jovanich, New York–London

LANDAU, Rom 1938

**Search for Tomorrow**. The Things which are and the Things which shall be Hereafter. pp. xi–xix, Contents, Acknowledgments, Preface, Illustrations. pp. 1–404, bibliography, index. 15 photos. *A tour in 1934?–1936 of the Near and Middle East visiting leaders. One short interview with Ibn Saud using interpreter. Completely outdated by events.*
Nicholson and Watson, London

LAWRENCE, T. E. 1926 (1935, 1991*)

**Seven Pillars of Wisdom**: A Triumph. pp. 1–669 Prefaces, Contents, Synopses pp. 1–23; text, pp. 24–660; Appendices, pp. 662–666; Indices: Place Names, People's Names, pp. 667–669. 54 illustrations (mostly drawings of participants), 4 maps. Paperback edition. *A narrative masterpiece of the Arab Revolt, seasoned by the author's sensitivity and feelings of guilt concerning promises of Arab liberty.*
George Doran 1926 Cape London; 1935 Doubleday, Doran New York, 1935
*Anchor Books, 1991

LEATHERDALE, Clive 1983

**Britain and Saudi Arabia 1925–1939**: The Imperial Oasis. pp. v–x, Contents, Acknowledgments, pp. 1–403, text, Sources and Bibliography, Appendices 1–3, Chronology, Dramatis Personae, 15 Treaties and Agreements with states of the Arabian peninsula. *An exhaustive discussion of Britain's relations with Saudi Arabia and other Arab peninsular states, more wide-ranging than Troeller's coverage to 1925.*
FrankCass, London / Totowa, New Jersey

LEBKICHER, R., RENTZ, G., STEINEKE, M., 1952

**The Arabia of Ibn Saud**. pp. iii–ix, 1–179. Many photographs, maps and illustrations. *An attempt to relate the Arabian peninsula and its peoples to the history of the Middle East with emphasis on the achievements of Ibn Saud. Included are summaries of many discrete fields of study: geology, topography, climate, language, terrain, literature, numismatics, agriculture, government, etc.*
Russell F. Moore, New York

LONG, David E. 1997

**The Kingdom of Saudi Arabia.** pp. i–xiii. Dedication, Contents, Preface, List of Maps. Tables. Figs; pp. 1–154 Text, Appendix (genealogical charts), Notes, Selected Bibliography, Index, 3 maps, 4 tables, 25 figs. (photographs and charts). A concise history, supplemented by equally succinct reviews of the political system, the oil story, economic development, the Hajj, security policies, and 21st century projections. *This slender book is to all appearances the publica-*

*tion of a thesis. It appears accurate in nearly all respects, but gives the life span of Ibn Saud as 1880–1951. Error in both dates makes the remainder of the book suspect as to its accuracy.*
University Press of Florida, Gainesville

LONGRIGG, S. H. 1968 (1954, 1961)
**Oil in the Middle East**. Its Discovery and Development. pp. i–xii, 1–519 App. I–IV, index, 9 maps (oil fields). *Thorough coverage to date of publication.*
Oxford University Press

LORIMER, J. G. 1908 (1970)
**Gazetteer of the Persian Gulf, Oman, and Central Arabia**. Vol. II. Geographical and Statistical (2 books, A & B). Book A: pp. i–iv, Intoduction, pp. 1–1030 Book B: pp. 1031–1952. Alphabetical treatment of known geographical entities: location, size, population, crops, statistics on trade, etc. *A monumental summary of what was known of these areas in the early years of the twentieth century. The lack of exact data on Nejd shows why Philby's work was an important contribution to knowledge.*
Government Printing Office, Calcutta, 1970: Gregg International, Westmead /Irish Univ., Shannon

McLOUGHLIN, Leslie 1993
**Ibn Saud: Founder of a Kingdom**. pp. i–xvi Preface, Introduction. pp. 1–240, Appendices A–F, Notes, Bibliography, Index, 2 photos, 3 maps. Many data on offspring. *Well-balanced and well-written discussion of the country, and the man and his policies, supplemented by direct quotations and new data on his campaigns.*
Oxford University Press; St. Martins Press, New York

MONROE, Elizabeth 1973
**Philby of Arabia**. pp. 1–332. References, bibliography, index, 3 maps, 14 photos. *A comprehensive, sympathetic study of the life of an opinionated man of widely diverse interests, all related to some form of exploration or scientific investigation. A politically naive liberal, with lifelong loyalty to his principles.*
Faber and Faber, London

MUSIL, Alois 1928
**Northern Negd**. A Topographical Itinerary. pp. i–xiii: contents, list of illustrations, preface. pp. 1–368: appendices I–X, bibliography, index. Appendix VIII: History of the House of Eben Rasid. Appendix IX: History of the House of Eben Sa'ud. (48 pp.) 67 small photos, 2 maps, *The itinerary is of little interest, except for descriptions of Arabs and towns. The histories of the Rashids and Sauds are in the main accurate, or at least similar to others.*
American Geographical Society, New York.

NAWWAB, I., SPEERS, P. C. and HOYE, P. F. 1995
**Saudi Aramco and Its World**: Arabia and the Middle East. pp. i–xi, 1–291. (A revision of Aramco and Its World, 1981) 22 maps, 5 charts, 200 plus photos, large and small. 14 select bibliographies: "Further Reading," index. An overview of Arab culture and history. Detail on the House of Saud and the

rule of King Abdul Aziz and his sons. A discussion of Saudi oil, its develop‑
ment and related topics: geology, climate, company concerns for employees,
etc. *A must for the Arabophile.*
Aramco Services Company, Houston

PHILBY, H. St. J. B. 1922 (*1923)
The Heart of Arabia: A Record of Travel and Exploration Vol. I, pp. 1–386, 39
photos. Vol. II, pp. 1–320, 8 photos, 2 maps, 2 appendices: I. Fossils, II. Glos‑
sary. Vol. I, Across Arabia, meeting with Ibn Saud. *Many highlights on Ibn Saud.*
Vol. II, Riyadh to Wadi Dawasir. *Much detail, of interest mainly to geographers and
ethnologists.*
Constable and Company Ltd., London / *G. P. Putnam's Sons, New York–
London

————————— 1928 (1977)
Arabia of the Wahhabis, pp. i–xv, 1–422. 32 photos, 3 genealogical appendi‑
ces, 12 sketches, map, town plan, index. *Continuation of* The Heart of Arabia
*describing preparations for the expedition to Haïl in 1918. Glosses over failure at Haïl.*
Frank Cass

————————— 1930
Arabia. Preface, pp. vii–xi, Introduction, pp. xv–xix. pp. 1–387. *History of Nejd;
densely factual. See Rentz's strictures on accuracy.*
Ernest Benn, Ltd.

————————— 1948
Arabian Days: An Autobiography. pp. i–xvi, 1–336. 54 illustrations, mainly
photographs. *Details of his life to age fifty. Opiniated versions of historical incidents.*
Robert Hale, London

————————— 1952
Arabian Jubilee pp. i–xiv Preface, pp. 1–280, index, Appendices I–III, geneal‑
ogies, 48 photos. *Life of Ibn Saud with much personal opinion.*
Robert Hale, Ltd.

————————— 1955 (1968)
Sa'udi Arabia. Foreword, pp. xi–xix, pp. 1–393. *History of Nejd to date; densely
factual. Revision of 1930 book..*
Ernest Benn, Limited

————————— 1957
Forty Years in the Wilderness pp. v–xvi, Contents, List of Illustrations,
Map. pp. 1–272, Text, Index. 38 photos, map of Philby's itineraries in the Mid‑
dle East. Ten almost independent chapters, reminiscences, regarding Philby's
participation in and opinion of events ranging from a defense of T. E.
Lawrence to the criticisms of the monarchy leading up to his temporary exile
from Saudi Arabia and a report on the last years of Ibn Saud. *Interesting to the
specialist in historical detail. Less turgid than some of his works.*
Robert Hale, London

PHILBY, H. St. J. B. 1964

**Arabian oil ventures.** Frontispiece: Ibn Saud 1924. pp. v–xiii. Preface, Contents, Foreword, pp. 1–134, Text and Notes. 12 full page photos, back cover: map oil installations. Posthumus publication of history of oil ventures. Philby reports his own rôle in detail. *One certain error regarding existence of seeps at Dhahran. Details of correspondence suggest his involvement was as reported herein.* Middle East Institute, Washington

RASHEED, Madawi al 1991

**Politics in an Arabian Oasis:** The Rashidi Tribal Dynasty. pp. vii–ix. Contents, List of Maps, etc. Acknowledgements. pp. 1–300 Text, Glossary, Notes, Biblio-graphy, Index. 4 Maps, 7 Tables, 4 Diagrams. A detailed history of the Rashids based on a doctoral thesis written by an anthropologist, one of the Rashid clan. *An exhaustive study of all facets of the Rashids: history, customs, poetry. Gives the sequence of Rashidi amirs and their relationships. Some anomalies in dates.* I. B. Tauris & Co, London, New York

RAUNKIAER, Barkley 1969 (1913)

**Through Wahhabiland on Camelback.** pp. 1–155, 1 map, 33 illustrations in half-tone. *Short account of trip to Riyadh from east coast in 1912. Meets Abdur Rahman. Describes Wahhabi movement.* Routledge and Kegan Paul London; Praeger, New York

RENDAL, Sir George 1957

**The Sword and the Olive:** Recollections of Diplomacy and the Foreign Service 1913–1954. Contents, List of Illustrations, Acknowledgements, 7 unnumbered pages pp. 1–347 text and index. 12 photos. Memoirs of a high-ranking diplomat. Includes discussion of two visits to the Middle East, one of them across Arabia with his wife in 1937, a year before Princess Alice's trip. *Interesting and well-written. A brief chapter on his favorable impressions of Ibn Saud, whom he praises as open and frank.* John Murray, London

RIHANI, Amin 1928 (1983)

**Ibn Sa'oud of Arabia**; His People and his Land. pp. i–xvii, 1–370, 71 illustrations: 63 photos, 8 line drawings. Map of Middle East, genealogical table. *Probably the most revealing and complete study of Ibn Saud as an adult, age 47.* Constable, London

————— 1930

**Around the Coasts of Arabia.** pp. v–xi, Contents, List of Illustrations; pp. 1–364, text, index. 32 photos. Florid descriptions of visits to and the status of and rulers in the early twenties of the Hejaz, Asir, Kuwait, Bahrain, and Aden and the Protectorates, all except Aden ruled by autocrats. *Descriptions of Sharif Husain that contradict mannerisms ascribed him elsewhere. Sketches of the rulers of all six regions.* Constable, London

RYAN, Sir Andrew. 1951

**The Last of the Dragomans**. pp. 1–351, 7 photos, 2 cartoons, 2 half-tone caricatures in text, index. *A British diplomat's career, interestingly recounted. Little concerning Ibn Saud's character. First Minister to Saudi Arabia. Some highlights on the Saudi court, 1930.*
Geoffrey Bles, London

STEGNER, Wallace 1971

**Discovery**: The Search for Arabian Oil. pp. 1–190. *The men and the events of the early years of the al Hasa concession told in detail in an intimate and gee-whizz style.*
Middle East Export Press, Beirut

STEVENS, J. H. and KING, R. 1973

**A Bibliography of Saudi Arabia**. Ocasional Papers, Series 3. Durham University of Durham, Centre for Middle Eastern and Islamic Studies. *A number of omissions.*

STORRS, Ronald 1937

**Orientations**. pp. i–xvii, contents and preface; pp. 1–624, index, 17 photographs of people and things, 4 maps. *A well-written autobiography of the life of a British diplomat who played a part in persuading Husain to revolt, and later, as military governor of Jerusalem, attempted to keep the peace between Arab and Jew. Much name-dropping, perhaps unavoidable. Attempt to see Ibn Saud aborted by sunstroke.*
Ivor Nicholson & Watson, London

THESIGER, Wilfred 1959

**Arabian Sands**. pp. iv–xii, Contents; lists of plates and maps; xiii–xvii, Introduction, Prologue. pp. 1–326, text, Arabic and botanical plant names, List of characters, index. 69 photos, 10 maps, including route map insert at 1: 3,295,000 app. *Only mentions Wahhabi mores and Ibn Saud, but includes a cogent analysis of Bedu character in an outstanding account of journeys in the Hadhramaut, Oman and the Rub' al Khali. Restricts Murra dirah to northern reaches thereof.*
E. P. Dutton & Co., New York

THOMAS, Bertram 1932

**Arabia Felix**: Across the Empty Quarter of Arabia. pp. vii–xxix, Foreword, Preface, Introduction. pp. 1–397. 60 photos, index. Six Apendices: I Anthropological, pp. 301–333 with 22 photos of heads, 15 figs., 2 charts. II. Zoology and Geology, pp. 334–369 III. Location of 'Uruq and water wells, topographical terminology, pp. 370–376 IV. Flora pp. 377–378. V. Camel brands (*Wasm*), p. 379 VI. Musical notation of Arab chants, pp. 381–384. *A most interesting discussion of the peoples of Dhofar and the problems of crossing the Rub' al Khali using several tribes as guides. One mention of Ibn Saud as guarantor of peace, of no use for study of Ibn Saud.*
Jonathan Cape, London / Charles Scribner, New York

——————— 1937

**The Arabs**: The life-story of a People who have left their deep impress on the world. pp. 1–12 Contents, Illustrations, Foreword; Text pp. 13–372: Appendices, pp. 351–360; Bibliography, pp. 361–362; Index, pp. 363–372. 24 unnumbered illustrations—photos, halftones. 4 maps. An outline of Arab history

and culture. Chapter on Ibn Saud. *Owing to the magnitude of the subject, the treatment in one volume of history, arts and sciences is of necessity sketchy and incomplete. For the general public a fair overview of a people.*
Thornton Butterworth, Ltd., London

TROELLER, Gary 1976

**The Birth of Saudi Arabia**: Britain and the Rise of the House of Saud. pp. i–xxii, 1–287. Appendices I–III, 2 maps, index *Detailed documentation of Whitehall and India Office correspondence concerning relations with Ibn Saud and his activities to 1925. Exhaustively researched. Useful. A few inconsistencies.*
Frank Cass, London / Frank Cass, Oregon

TWITCHELL, K.S. 1947

**Saudi Arabia**: With an Account of the Development of Its Natural Resources. pp. i–xiii, 3–192, index. 24 small photos, glossary of place names, half-tone map, scale 1/8 million. *Summary of many aspects of Saudi Arabia: geography, agricultural and mineral resources, history and policies, including administration. All obsolete, except history, geography, geology and climate.*
Princeton University Press

VAN DER MEULEN, D. 1957

**The Wells of Ibn Sa'ud**. pp. 1–270. Glossary, Index. 19 photographs. *Perceptive and gloomy study of the changes in the land and in Saudi mores with the coming of oil and the Americans. Good sketches of the king, young and aged. Well written.*
Murray, London / Frederick Praeger, New York

WAHBA, Hafiz 1964

**Arabian Days**. pp. 1–184, Index, 29 photographs. Index. *Accounts of customs, government, education, medecine etc. in Arab lands; history of the Saud family and Ibn Saud. All from an Arab standpoint. Mainly generalities.*
Arthur Barker, London

WILLIAMS, Kenneth 1933

**Ibn Sa'ud**: The Puritan King of Arabia. pp. 1–299, one map, one photo, frontispiece, genealogical table, index. *A highly colored, in many details inaccurate review of Ibn Saud's career until 1930. Much rhetorical display.*
Jonathan Cape, London

WILSON, Lt. Col. Sir Arthur T. 1930 (1931, 1936)

**Loyalties: Mesopotamia 1914–1917**; A Personal and Historical Record. pp. i–x, prefaces to three editions, notes, contents, list of illustrations, bibliography; pp. 1–338, Appendices I–III, index, 28 photos, mainly British officers, 4 maps. *A review of military operations in Iraq with asides on the civil administration under army control. Mentions Cox's 1915 and 1916 visits to Ibn Saud. Well done.*
Oxford University Press

———————————————— 1931

**A Clash of Loyalties: Mesopotamia 1917–1920**: A Personal and Historical Record. pp. i–xix, Preface, Contents. pp. 1–420, 4 appendices: lists of personnel in Iraq post-war civil administration, Miss Bell's memorandum, 'Civil Administration in Mesopotamia,' index, 32 photos, 2 maps. *Recounts events the*

last year of the war and post-war efforts to set up civil administration in Iraq; includes details of arrival of Sir Percy Cox as high commissioner; and efforts to install Faisal ibn Husain as king.
Oxford University Press

WINDER, R. Bayly 1965 (1980)
**Saudi Arabia in the Nineteenth Century**. pp. i–xi, 1–312. Extensive bibliography, index, 13 illustrations, 7 maps. *A detailed study of the history of Arabia and the Al Saud, thoroughly researched and documented. A doctoral thesis, eminently readable. Troeller says use with caution.*
St. Martins Press, New York / Macmillan, London

WINSTONE, H. V. F. 1976 1978*
**Captain Shakespear**: A portrait. pp. 1–236. Bibliography, glossary, index, 28 photographs, 3 half-tones: letters and a Himyaritic insciption. *Thoroughly researched but uncritical biography. Illustrations poorly reproduced in New York edition.*
Jonathan Cape, London / *Quartette Books, New York

———————— 1978
**Gertrude Bell**. pp. ix–xiii: Intoduction, Acknowledgments; pp. 1–322, notes, bibliography, index. 36 photos, 1 drawing photographed; 3 facsimile letters; 3 maps. *Sympathetic and thorough study of a rich woman, mountain-climber, writer, linguist, Arabophile, who from 1900–1926 was active in the Middle East, from 1914–1923 as an adviser to British military and civil government, mainly in Iraq.*
Jonathan Cape, London / Quartette Books Inc., New York

YERGIN, Daniel 1991
**The Prize**: The Epic Quest for Oil, Money, and Power. pp. 1–877. Notes, bibliography, 97 photos, 8 unnumbered maps, chronology, index, pp. i–xxxii. *An exhaustive yet entertaining study of the development of the oil industry worldwide. The section dealing with Middle East oil during Ibn Saud's lifetime is necessarily condensed. The importance of Philby's rôle in Saudi concession negotiations may be overstated.*
Simon and Schuster, New York

YOUNG, Arthur N. 1983
**Saudi Arabia**: The Making of a Financial Giant. pp. vii–xvi, Contents, Illustrations, Preface; pp. 1–162, text, Appendixes: Tables 1–9, II Report of Establishment of Saudi Arabian Monetary Agency, III Royal Decree Sanctioning the Charter of the SAMA. Notes, Index. Map, 14 photos, 3 charts. *Includes summary of financial problems of Ibn Saud before and after the discovery and development of oil and a detailed review of the work of the SAMA and its effects on foreign and domestic economies Brief sketches of Ibn Saud confirming other observations concerning his bearing, but revealing also his interest in modernization, not reported by others.*
New York University Press

ZEINE, Zeine N. 1960
**The Struggle for Arab Independence**. Western Diplomacy and the Rise and Fall of Faisal's Kingdom in Syria. pp. i–xiii, Contents, Preface; pp. 1–297, appendices A–I, bibliography, index, 6 plates including originals in Arabic of

letters between Sir Henry MacMahon and Sharif Husain and Sykes–Picot map. *Review of all factors involved in Hashemite efforts to achieve independence. Includes a study of Peace Conference decisions and their effects in the Levant.*
Khayat's Book Store, Beirut

ZIRIKLI, Khair al Din 1970
**The Peninsula in the Time of King Abdul Aziz** (in Arabic: *Shibh al-jazira fi ahd al-malik Abd al-Aziz*) 4 vols. Quoted extensively in McLoughlin (1993)
Khayat's Bookstore, Beirut

# ARTICLES

Of the hundreds of articles on widely diverse topics concerning Saudi Arabia, only a few have been selected as samples of onlookers' views of developments in several fields. In general, they credit Ibn Saud as the wise originator of policies conducive to the continuity of the Saudi state.

BUSCH, Noel F. 1943 (31 May)
**Life visits Arabia.** *Life*, Vol. 14, No. 22, pp. 69–88. 33 photos, 1 map, 1 photocopy of Ibn Saud's statement about Jews in Palestine. *A journalistic review of a visit to Riyadh and Dhahran with a summary of Ibn Saud's career and his habits, along with a sketch of the country, its government, and its people. Although loose as regards dates and the sequence of events, the information is reasonably accurate.*

DAME, Louis P. 1933
**From Bahrain to Taif:** A Missionary Journey Across Arabia. *Moslem World*, Vol. 28, No. 2, pp. 164–178. Summary of a missionary doctor's trip across Arabia in the year that the concession in al Hasa was granted. *Almost nothing said about Ibn Saud himself, but of interest concerning the state of the country and some of its people at that time.*

DAWISHA. Adeed I. 1979
**Internal Values and External Threats:** The Making of Saudi Foreign Policy. *Orbis*, Vol. 23, No. 1, pp. 129–143. *A review of the then current posture of Saudi Arabia with regard to foreign loans and contributions intended to foster Islamic principles and investments in armament and other projects at home and abroad to safeguard the nation. Emphasizes the continuity of implementation of the Wahhabi code of justice and morals from the time of Ibn Saud.*

GOLDBERG, Jacob 1984
**The 1914 Saudi–Ottoman Treaty—Myth or Reality?** *Journal of Contemporary History*, Vol. 19, pp. 289–314. Notes, Appendix: Translation in English of the 1914 Saudi–Ottoman Treaty. *A review of the events leading to Ibn Saud's acceptance of a treaty with the Porte. It refutes G. Rentz's thesis that Ibn Saud would not have signed a treaty in Turkish, and that since no treaty was signed at Subayhiya he did not sign the document found later.*

HUDSON, Michael C. et al. 1999
**Saudi Arabia: 100 Years Later.** *CCAS Occasional Papers and Reports,* pp. 1–25, April conference. Three main topics dicussed by nine speakers—State Building Process; Oil and Economic Development; Foreign Policy. *Generally optimistic forecasts. Many temporal inaccuracies and over-generalizations in reviews of history.*

RENTZ, George 1950
**Literature on the Kingdom of Saudi Arabia.** *The Middle East Journal,* Vol. 4, No. 2, pp. 244–249. *Dr. Rentz comments on selected publications in English, French, German and Arabic concerning Saudi Arabia, praising some, condemning others. Many of those that appeared before the date of publication of this 1950 article are listed in the book section of this bibliography. The lacunae in knowledge of events and discussion of topics that Rentz decries have been filled to some extent by more recent books in several languages.*

——————— 1972
**Wahhabism and Saudi Arabia.** In *The Arabian Peninsula: Society and Politics,* pp. 54–66. *A review of Saudi history, stressing that Wahhabism was integral to the functioning of the Saudi state from 1744. Includes then current Islamic attitude to Wahhabism.* Allen and Undwin, London / Rowman and Littlefield, New Jersey

——————— 1979
**Philby as a Historian of Saudi Arabia.** In *Studies in the History of Arabia,* Vol. 1, Part 2. Sources for the History of Arabia, pp. 25–35. *Rentz is critical of Philby's methods as a historian and cites numerous errors in his writings concerning events and dates.* Riyadh University

SANGER, Richard H. 1947
**Ibn Saud's Program for Arabia.** *The Middle East Journal,* Vol. 1, No. 2, pp. 180–190. *An optimistic sketch of conditions in Saudi Arabia in the first years after World War II. Credits Ibn Saud with worthy objectives.*

# INDEX

# Index

Bullard, Sir Reader (Br. minister to S.A., late 1930s) 102, 135, 194

Buraida (town in the Qasim) 7, 9, 17–18, 21–24, 36, 41, 56, 58, 82, 105, 110, 150, 152–153, 155–156, 191

Buraimi 73, 134–135, 138, 151–153, 166, 168, 204

The Buraimi Dispute 134, 138, 204–205

Busaiya (site of Iraqi police post) 56–58, 87

Bushire (Iranian port) 18, 81–82, 85, 137, 155, 165–166, 168, 183

## C

cable (India to Bushire to Europe, 1865) 112, 137, 176, 194, 209

California Arabian Standard Oil Co. (CASOC) 79

Caliph of Islam (abolished in 1924) 20, 45–46, 128, 181, 193

Cheesman, R. E. 102–103, 110, 136–137, 177, 191

Childs, J. Rives (U.S. ambassador to S.A., 1946–1950) 93, 102, 105

Christians 100, 115

Churchill, Winston Leonard Spencer 41, 92, 111, 129, 174–176, 180, 191–192, 194, 209

Clayton, Sir Gilbert (negotiated Hadda–Bahra and Jedda treaties) 52, 54, 57, 75, 87, 97–98, 105, 107, 111, 115, 126, 137, 171, 185, 195

code (of conduct and law. Bedu, Wahhabi, Ikhwan) 9, 27–28, 47, 53, 117, 145

Cornflower (British warship) 51

Cox, Sir Percy (political resident, Persian Gulf) 18, 29–31, 33–35, 43–44, 46, 52, 69–70, 81–83, 85, 94, 98, 100, 103, 109, 129, 136, 163–178, 181, 183–184, 189–193, 207, 209–211

Crane, Charles R. (Arabophile) 71

Crewe, Lord 31

Cunliffe-Owen, Colonel (political agent, Kuwait, 1917) 35, 190

Curzon, Lord (viceroy of India, foreign secretary) 127, 165–166, 172–173, 191, 202

## D

d'Arcy syndicate 167

Dabha (town in northern Hejaz, Billi revolt) 63

Dahana (broad belts of sand between al Hasa and Nejd) 9, 73

Dame, Dr. (Dutch Reformed Mission, Bahrain) 109, 137

Damluji, Abdullah Said (Ibn Saud's first foreign minister) 75, 195, 203, 208

Dammam (port on Persian Gulf) 29, 91, 110, 135, 153, 202, 213–214

Dammam Dome (Jebel Dhahran) 74, 135

Dammam Wells 135

Dhafir (tribe of southern Iraq) 43, 130, 145, 159, 207, 209

Dhahran (oil town built by concessionaire) 1, 72, 93, 101, 103, 110, 198–199

Dhaidan ibn Khalid al Hithlain (paramount shaikh of the Ajlan) 55, 60, 71, 131

Dhariya (old Saudi capital) 37, 149–151

*dhulul* (riding camels, usually female. Singular *'dhalul'*) 10, 132

Dickson, H. R. P. (political agent under Cox) 23, 43, 61–62, 69–70, 80, 92, 98, 103, 108, 112, 116, 127, 147, 189, 207, 209–211

Dilam (town 60 miles SE of Riyadh) 16, 152, 154–155

dirah (grazing area of a tribe) 26, 33, 41–44, 53, 60, 115, 136, 143–145, 147–148, 153, 209

Dohat Balbul (coastal bay 100 miles south of Kuwait) 39

Dreibund (Germany, Austria–Hungary, Italy at the onset of WWI) 30

*Durbar* (a levee, reception. Here a governmental function) 34–35, 86, 98, 104, 109–110, 125, 137, 162, 165–166, 169, 171, 189

Duwadimi (town in Nejd) 61

Duwish, Faisal ibn Sultan ad (paramount shaikh of the Mutair) 22, 24, 27, 39, 41, 43–45, 50, 54–56, 59–63, 116, 125, 131, 133, 202